Fodor's 96
The Carolinas & the Georgia Coast

D0874383

Reprinted from Fodor's The South '96
Fodor's Travel Publications, Inc.
New York • Toronto • London • Sydney • Auckland

Fodor's Carolinas & the Georgia Coast

Editor: Melissa Rivers

Editorial Contributors: Steven K. Amsterdam, Mark Beffart, Melissa Bigner, Edgar and Patricia Cheatham, Suzanne DeGalan, Bevin McLaughlin, Honey Naylor, Jane Schneider, Mary Ellen Schultz, Eileen Robinson Smith, Carol L. Timblin

Creative Director: Fabrizio La Rocca

Cartographer: David Lindroth

Cover Photograph: Erik Horan/Nawrocki Stock Photo

Text Design: Between the Covers

Copyright

Special Sales

Fodor's Travel Publications are available at special discounts for bulk purchases for sales promotions or premiums. Special editions, including personalized covers, excerpts of existing guides, and corporate imprints, can be created in large quantities for special needs. For more information, contact your local bookseller or write to Special Markets, Fodor's Travel Publications, 201 East 50th Street, New York, NY 10022. Inquiries from Canada should be directed to your local Canadian bookseller or sent to Random House of Canada, Ltd., Marketing Department, 1265 Aerowood Drive, Mississauga, Ontario L4W 1B9. Inquiries from the United Kingdom should be sent to Fodor's Travel Publications, 20 Vauxhall Bridge Road, London SW1V 2SA, England.

PRINTED IN THE UNITED STATES OF AMERICA

10 9 8 7 6 5 4 3 2 1

CONTENTS

Maps

ON THE ROAD WITH FODOR'S

A GOOD TRAVEL GUIDE is like a wonderful traveling companion. It's charming, it's brimming with sound recommendations and solid ideas, it pulls no punches in describing lodging and dining establishments, and it's consistently full of fascinating facts that make you view what you've traveled to see in a new light. In the creation of *The Carolinas & the Georgia Coast '96*, we at Fodor's have gone to great lengths to provide you with the very best of all possible traveling companions—and, by extension, to make your trip the best of all possible vacations.

About Our Writers

The information in these pages is a collaboration of a roster of extraordinary writers.

Mark Beffart has experienced the enormous growth of Atlanta firsthand, having moved here from Alabama in February 1978. Self-employed as a writer since 1979, he is the author of *France on the TGV, Paris for Free (Or Extremely Cheap), Walking Tours of France, Citypack Atlanta,* and over 200 feature magazine articles about art, business, health, and travel topics.

Since 1992, **Jane Schneider** has been chasing the ideal food-and-wine match for readers of the *Atlanta Journal-Constitution,* for whom she writes a column on the subject. She has coauthored a residents' guide to Atlanta, a city in which she has nibbled and sipped for more than 25 years. A former magazine editor and college professor, she now enjoys travel, reading, and writing about Georgia history, hiking, white-water rafting, and a host of other salubrious pursuits.

South Carolina is the bailiwick of **Patricia Cheatham,** who also contributes to Fodor's USA guide. In her fantasy of fantasies, she tells us, she reclines on a Pawleys Island hammock on the veranda of her 14,000-acre Georgetown County rice plantation, proving her theory that re-introduction of indigo cultivation bodes well for the cure of the common cold.

Susan Ladd, a lifetime resident of North Carolina, covers travel for the *News & Record* in Greensboro, North Carolina, and has updated the North Carolina chapters of this and other Fodor's guides. She travels regularly to far-flung locales like Micronesia, but like Dorothy, believes that there's no place like home.

Editing this book brought back fond memories of all the glorious food **Melissa Rivers** indulged in as a teenager growing up in the South (specifically Memphis, Tennessee). She fine-toothed the dining sections, expanding and defining as needed, working with local critics to bring you the latest "in" places . . . just reading the reviews should make you salivate.

What's New

A New Design

If this is not the first Fodor's guide you've purchased, you'll immediately notice our new look. More readable and easier to use than ever? We think so—and we hope you do, too.

Let Us Do Your Booking

Our writers have scoured the Carolinas and the Georgia Coast to come up with an extensive and well-balanced list of the best B&Bs, inns, and hotels, both small and large, new and old. But you don't have to beat the bushes to come up with a reservation. Now we've teamed up with an established hotel-booking service to make it easy for you to secure a room at the property of your choice. It's fast, it's free, and confirmation is guaranteed. If your first choice is booked, the operators can line up your second right away. Just call 800/FODORS–1 (800/363–6771; 0800/89–1030 when in Great Britain; 800/55–9101 when in Ireland; and 0014/800–12–8271 when in Australia).

Travel Updates

In addition, just before your trip, you may want to order a Fodor's Worldview Travel Update. From local publications all over the Carolinas and the Georgia Coast, the lively, cosmopolitan editors at Worldview gather information on concerts, plays, opera, dance performances, gallery and museum shows, sports competitions, and other special events that coincide with your visit. See the order blank at the back of this book or, for up-to-date information about where to find Worldview in cyberspace, call 800/799–9609 or fax 800/799–9619.

And In the Carolinas and the Georgia Coast

Atlanta, Georgia, hosts the **1996 Olympic Games** and, after spending several hundred million dollars, the city is fully geared up to be inundated by visitors this year. Around 11 million tickets went on sale for the various events, so things should really be jumping in Atlanta. Many of the new facilities built for the games—the 85,000 seat Olympic Stadium, the Velodrome, and Oympic Village on the Georgia Tech campus—will become venues for sports and other entertainment options following the games.

In Winston-Salem, North Carolina, the **Museum of Early Southern Decorative Arts** plans to open a new discovery center this year. Big things are also expected at the **North Carolina Zoological Park** in Asheboro, which should complete its large North American exhibit this year; polar bears, grizzly bears, and a large stream-side exhibit are just a few of the new attractions planned. With a new convention center, two pro sports teams, and new attractions underway, Charlotte's reputation is soaring. The Carolina Panthers, the state's new NFL team, should move into their new stadium in downtown Charlotte in 1996, while the Charlotte Hornets, one of the newest NBA franchises, continue to create a buzz throughout the state.

The 350-acre, $250 million **Broadway at the Beach,** South Carolina's newest entertainment complex at Myrtle Beach, got underway in the summer of 1995 with the opening of the Carolina Place Theater. Other theaters, restaurants, shops, and entertainment options—a nightclub district, an amusement area, a miniature golf course, and the Coastal Aquarium of the Carolinas—are planned.

How To Use This Book

Organization

Up front is the **Gold Guide,** comprising two sections on gold paper that are chockfull of information about traveling within your destination and traveling in general. Both are in alphabetical order by topic. **Important Contacts A to Z** gives addresses and telephone numbers of organizations and companies that offer destination-related services and detailed information or publications. Here's where you'll find information about how to get to the Carolinas and the Georgia Coast from wherever you are. **Smart Travel Tips A to Z,** the Gold Guide's second section, gives specific tips on how to get the most out of your travels, as well as information on how to accomplish what you need to in the Carolinas and the Georgia Coast.

Chapters in *The Carolinas and the Georgia Coast* are arranged alphabetically. Each chapter covers exploring, shopping, sports, dining, lodging, and arts and nightlife, and ends with a section called Essentials, which tells you how to get there and get around and gives you important local addresses and telephone numbers.

Stars

Stars in the margin are used to denote highly recommended sights, attractions, hotels, and restaurants.

Restaurant and Hotel Criteria and Price Categories

Restaurants and lodging places are chosen with a view to giving you the cream of the crop in each location and in each price range.

In all restaurant price charts, costs are per person, excluding drinks, tip, and tax. In hotel price charts, rates are for standard double rooms, excluding city and state sales taxes.

Hotel Facilities

Note that in general you incur charges when you use many hotel facilities. We wanted to let you know what facilities a hotel has to offer, but we don't always specify whether or not there's a charge, so when planning a vacation that entails a stay of several days, it's wise to ask what's included in the rate.

Dress Code in Restaurants

In general, we note a dress code only when men are required to wear a jacket or a jacket and tie.

Credit Cards

The following abreviations are used: **AE,** American Express; **D,** Discover; **DC,** Diners Club; **MC,** MasterCard; and **V,** Visa.

Please Write to Us

Everyone who has contributed to *The Carolinas & the Georgia Coast '96* has worked hard to make the text accurate. All prices and opening times are based on information supplied to us at press time, and the publisher cannot accept responsibility for any errors that may have occurred. The passage of time will bring changes, so it's always a good idea to call ahead and confirm information when it matters—particularly if you're making a detour to visit specific sights or attractions. When making reservations at a hotel or inn, be sure to speak up if you have a disability or are traveling with children, if you prefer a private bath or a certain type of bed, or if you have specific dietary needs or any other concerns.

Were the restaurants we recommended as described? Did our hotel picks exceed your expectations? Did you find a museum we recommended a waste of time? We would love your feedback, positive and negative. If you have complaints, we'll look into them and revise our entries when the facts warrant it. If you've happened upon a special place that we haven't included, we'll pass the information along to the writers so they can check it out. So please send us a letter or postcard (we're at 201 East 50th Street, New York, New York 10022). We'll look forward to hearing from you. And in the meantime, have a wonderful trip!

Karen Cure

Editorial Director

Gulf of Mexico

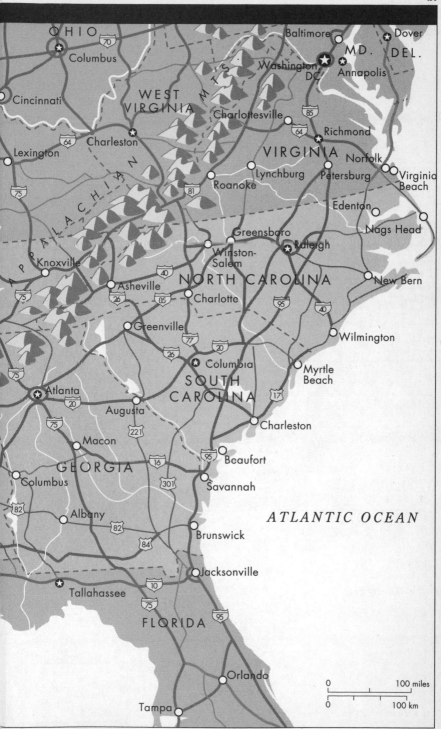

The United States

THE GOLD GUIDE / IMPORTANT CONTACTS

IMPORTANT CONTACTS A TO Z

*An Alphabetical Listing of Publications,
Organizations, and Companies That Will Help You
Before, During, and After Your Trip*

No single travel resource can give you every detail about every topic that might interest or concern you at the various stages of your journey—when you're planning your trip, while you're on the road, and after you get back home. The following organizations, books, and brochures will supplement the information in *The Carolinas & the Georgia Coast.* For related information, including both basic tips on visiting the area and background information on many of the topics below, study Smart Travel Tips A to Z, the section that follows Important Contacts A to Z.

A
AIR TRAVEL
CARRIERS

For information on airports and major airlines serving the Carolinas and the Georgia Coast, *see* individual state chapters.

For inexpensive, no-frills flights, contact **Branson Airlines** (☎ 800/422–4247), **Southwest Airlines** (☎ 800/444–5660), and **ValuJet** (☎ 404/994–8258 or 800/825–8538).

FROM THE U.K.

Major airlines fly from the United Kingdom to most Southern cities, including **American Airlines** (☎ 1345/789789), **British Airways** (☎ 0181/897–4000), **Continental Airlines** (☎ 1293/776464), **Delta Airlines** (☎ 0800/414767), and **TWA** (☎ 0800/222–222).

COMPLAINTS

To register complaints about charter and scheduled airlines, contact the U.S. Department of Transportation's **Aviation Consumer Protection Division** (400 7th St. NW, Washington, DC 20590, ☎ 202/366–2220 or 800/322–7873).

CONSOLIDATORS

Established consolidators selling to the public include **Euram Flight Center** (1522 K St. NW, Suite 430, Washington, DC 20005, ☎ 800/848–6789) and **TFI Tours International** (34 W. 32nd St., New York, NY 10001, ☎ 212/736–1140 or 800/745–8000).

PUBLICATIONS

For general information about charter carriers, ask for the Office of Consumer Affairs' brochure **"Plane Talk:** **Public Charter Flights."** The Department of Transportation also publishes a 58-page booklet, **"Fly Rights"** ($1.75; Consumer Information Center, Dept. 133B, Pueblo, CO 81009).

For other tips and hints, consult the Consumers Union's monthly **"Consumer Reports Travel Letter"** ($39 for the first year; Box 53629, Boulder, CO 80322, ☎ 800/234–1970) and the newsletter **"Travel Smart"** ($37 a year; 40 Beechdale Rd., Dobbs Ferry, NY 10522, ☎ 800/327–3633); *The Official Frequent Flyer Guidebook,* by Randy Petersen ($14.99 plus $3 shipping; 4715-C Town Center Dr., Colorado Springs, CO 80916, ☎ 719/597–8899 or 800/487–8893); *Airfare Secrets Exposed,* by Sharon Tyler and Matthew Wonder (Universal Information Publishing; $16.95 plus $3.75 shipping from Sandcastle Publishing, Box 3070-A, South Pasadena, CA 91031, ☎ 213/255–3616 or 800/655–0053); and *202 Tips Even the Best Business Travelers May Not Know,* by Christopher McGinnis ($11 plus $3.25 shipping; Irwin Professional Publishing, 1333 Burr

Ridge Pkwy., Burr Ridge, IL 60521, ☎ 708/589–4000 or 800/634–3966).

B
BETTER BUSINESS BUREAU

For local contacts, consult the **Council of Better Business Bureaus** (4200 Wilson Blvd. Ste. 800, Arlington, VA 22203, ☎ 703/276–0100).

C
CAR RENTAL

Major car-rental companies represented in the Carolinas and the Georgia Coast include **Alamo** (☎ 800/327–9633, 0800/272–2000 in the U.K.), **Avis** (☎ 800/331–1212, 800/331–1084 in Canada), **Budget** (☎ 800/527–0700, 181/759–2216 in the U.K.), **Hertz** (☎ 800/654–3131, 416/620–9620 in Canada, 181/679–1799 in the U.K.), and **National** (☎ 800/227–7368, 181/897–0811 in the U.K., where it is known as Europcar).

CHILDREN AND TRAVEL

FLYING

Look into **"Flying with Baby"** ($4.95; Third Street Press, Box 261250, Littleton, CO 80163, ☎ 303/595–5959), cowritten by a flight attendant. **"Kids and Teens in Flight,"** free from the U.S. Department of Transportation's Office of Consumer Affairs, offers tips for children flying alone. Every two years the February issue

of **Family Travel Times** (*see* Know-How, *below*) details children's services on three dozen airlines.

KNOW-HOW

Family Travel Times, published 10 times a year by Travel with Your Children (TWYCH, 45 W. 18th St., New York, NY 10011, ☎ 212/206–0688; annual subscription $55), covers destinations, types of vacations, and modes of travel.

The **Family Travel Guides** catalogue ($1 postage; Carousel Press, Box 6061, Albany, CA 94706, ☎ 510/527–5849) lists about 200 books and articles on family travel. Also check **Take Your Baby and Go! A Guide for Traveling with Babies, Toddlers and Young Children,** by Sheri Andrews, Judy Bordeaux, and Vivian Vasquez ($5.95 plus $1.50 shipping; Bear Creek Publications, 2507 Minor Ave., Seattle, WA 98102, ☎ 206/322–7604 or 800/326–6566). **The 100 Best Family Resorts in North America,** by Jane Wilson with Janet Tice ($14.95), and the two-volume **50 Great Family Vacations in North America** ($17.95–$18.95 per volume), both from The Globe Pequot Press (plus $3 shipping; Box 833, 6 Business Park Rd., Old Saybrook, CT 06475, ☎ 203/395–0440 or 800/243–0495) help plan your trip with children, from toddlers to teens.

LOCAL INFORMATION

Atlanta Parent (4330 Georgetown Sq., Suite 506, Atlanta, GA 30338, ☎ 404/454–7599) regularly features a calendar of events that's especially for visiting families. It's available free at area libraries, supermarkets, and museums, or by mail for a small fee.

CUSTOMS

CANADIANS

Contact **Revenue Canada** (2265 St. Laurent Blvd. S, Ottawa, Ontario K1G 4K3, ☎ 613/993–0534) for a copy of the free brochure **"I Declare/Je Déclare"** and for details on duty-free exemptions.

U.K. CITIZENS

HM Customs and Excise (Dorset House, Stamford St., London SE1 9NG, ☎ 0171/202–4227) can answer questions about U.K. customs regulations and publishes **"A Guide for Travellers,"** detailing standard procedures and import rules.

D
FOR TRAVELERS WITH DISABILITIES

COMPLAINTS

To register complaints under the provisions of the Americans with Disabilities Act, contact the U.S. Department of Justice's **Disability Rights Section** (Box 66738, Washington, DC 20035-6738, ☎ 202/514–0301 or 800/514–0301, FAX 202/307–1198, TDD 202/514–0383).

THE GOLD GUIDE / IMPORTANT CONTACTS

ORGANIZATIONS

FOR TRAVELERS WITH HEARING IMPAIRMENTS➣ Contact the **American Academy of Otolaryngology** (1 Prince St., Alexandria, VA 22314, ☎ 703/836–4444, FAX 703/683–5100, TTY 703/519–1585).

FOR TRAVELERS WITH MOBILITY PROBLEMS➣ Contact the **Information Center for Individuals with Disabilities** (29 Stanhope St., Boston, MA 02116, ☎ 617/450–9888, 800/462–5015 in MA); **Mobility International USA** (Box 10767, Eugene, OR 97440, ☎ and TTY 503/343–1284, FAX 503/343–6812), the U.S. branch of an international organization headquartered in Belgium (*see below*) that has affiliates in 30 countries; **MossRehab Hospital Travel Information Service** (☎ 215/456–9603, TTY 215/456–9602); the **Society for the Advancement of Travel for the Handicapped** (347 5th Ave., Suite 610, New York, NY 10016, ☎ 212/447–7284, FAX 212/725–8253); the **Travel Industry and Disabled Exchange** (TIDE, 5435 Donna Ave., Tarzana, CA 91356, ☎ 818/788–8747, FAX 818/344–0078); and **Travelin' Talk** (Box 3534, Clarksville, TN 37043, ☎ 615/552–6670, FAX 615/552–1182).

FOR TRAVELERS WITH VISION IMPAIRMENTS➣ Contact the **American Council of the Blind** (1155 15th St. NW, Suite 720, Washington, DC 20005, ☎ 202/467–5081, FAX 202/467–5085) or the **American Foundation for the Blind** (11 Penn Plaza, Ste. 300, New York, NY 10001, ☎ 212/502–7600, TTD 212/502–7662).

IN THE U.K.

Contact the **Royal Association for Disability and Rehabilitation** (RADAR, 12 City Forum, 250 City Rd., London EC1V 8AF, ☎ 171/250–3222) or **Mobility International** (Rue de Manchester 25, B–1070 Brussels, Belgium, ☎ 00–322–410–6297), an international clearinghouse of travel information for people with disabilities.

PUBLICATIONS

Several free publications are available from the U.S. Information Center (Box 100, Pueblo, CO 81009, ☎ 719/948–3334): **"New Horizons for the Air Traveler with a Disability"** (address to Dept. 389B), describing legally mandated changes; the pocket-size **"Fly Smart"** (Dept. 575B), good on flight safety; and the Airport Operators Council's worldwide **"Access Travel: Airports"** (Dept. 575A).

Fodor's **Great American Vacations for Travelers with Disabilities** ($18; available in bookstores, or call 800/533–6478) details accessible attractions, restaurants, and hotels in U.S. destinations. The 500-page **Travelin' Talk Directory** ($35; Box 3534, Clarksville, TN 37043, ☎ 615/552–6670) lists people and organizations who help travelers with disabilities. For specialist travel agents worldwide, consult the **Directory of Travel Agencies for the Disabled** ($19.95 plus $2 shipping; Twin Peaks Press, Box 129, Vancouver, WA 98666, ☎ 206/694–2462 or 800/637–2256). The Sierra Club publishes **Easy Access to National Parks** ($16 plus $3 shipping; 730 Polk St., San Francisco, CA 94109, ☎ 415/776–2211 or 800/935–1056).

TRAVEL AGENCIES AND TOUR OPERATORS

The Americans with Disabilities Act requires that travel firms serve the needs of all travelers. However, some agencies and operators specialize in making group and individual arrangements for travelers with disabilities, among them **Access Adventures** (206 Chestnut Ridge Rd., Rochester, NY 14624, ☎ 716/889–9096), run by a former physical-rehab counselor. In addition, many general-interest operators and agencies (*see* Tours Operators, *below*) can also arrange vacations for travelers with disabilities.

FOR TRAVELERS WITH MOBILITY PROBLEMS➣ A number of operators specialize in working with travelers with mobility impairments: **Hinsdale Travel Service** (201 E. Ogden Ave., Suite 100, Hinsdale, IL 60521, ☎ 708/325–1335), a travel agency that will give you access to the services of wheelchair traveler Janice Perkins, and **Wheelchair Journeys** (16979 Redmond Way, Redmond, WA 98052, ☎ 206/885–2210), which can handle arrangements world-wide.

FOR TRAVELERS WITH DEVELOPMENTAL DIS-ABILITIES➤ Contact the nonprofit **New Directions** (5276 Hollister Ave., Suite 207, Santa Barbara, CA 93111, ☎ 805/967–2841).

DISCOUNTS

Options include **Entertainment Travel Editions** (fee $28–$53, depending on destination; 300 W. Shrock Rd. Columbus, OH 43081, ☎ 800/445–4137), **Great American Traveler** ($49.95 annually; Box 27965, Salt Lake City, UT 84127, ☎ 800/548–2812), **Moment's Notice Discount Travel Club** ($25 annually, single or family; 7301 New Utrecht Ave. Brooklyn, NY 11204, ☎ 718/234–6295), **Privilege Card** ($74.95 annually; 3391 Peachtree Rd. NE, Suite 110, Atlanta, GA 30326, ☎ 404/262–0222 or 800/236-9732), **Travelers Advantage** ($49 annually, single or family; CUC Travel Service, Box 1015 Trumbull, CT 06611-9938, ☎ 800/548–1116 or 800/648-4037), and **Worldwide Discount Travel Club** ($50 annually for family, $40 single; 1674 Meridian Ave., Miami Beach, FL 33139, ☎ 305/534–2082).

G
GAY AND
LESBIAN TRAVEL

ORGANIZATION

The **International Gay Travel Association** (Box 4974, Key West, FL 33041, ☎ 800/448–8550), a consortium of 800 businesses, can supply names of travel agents and tour opera-tors.

PUBLICATIONS

The premier international travel magazine for gays and lesbians is **Our World** ($35 for 10 issues; 1104 N. Nova Rd., Suite 251, Daytona Beach, FL 32117, ☎ 904/441–5367). The 16-page monthly **"Out & About"** ($49 for 10 issues and quarterly calendar; ☎ 212/645–6922 or 800/929–2268), covers gay-friendly resorts, hotels, cruise lines, destinations and airlines.

TOUR OPERATORS

Toto Tours (1326 W. Albion Ave., Suite 3W, Chicago, IL 60626, ☎ 312/274–8686 or 800/565–1241) has group tours worldwide.

TRAVEL AGENCIES

The largest agencies serving gay travelers are **Advance Travel** (10700 Northwest Freeway, Suite 160, Houston, TX 77092, ☎ 713/682–2002 or 800/695-0880), **Islanders/Kennedy Travel** (183 W. 10th St., New York, NY 10014, ☎ 212/242–3222 or 800/988–1181), **Now, Voyager** (4406 18th St., San Francisco, CA 94114, ☎ 415/626–

1169 or 800/255–6951, FAX 415/626–8626), and **Yellowbrick Road** (1500 W. Balmoral Ave., Chicago, IL 60640, ☎ 312/561–1800 or 800/642–2488). **Skylink Women's Travel** (2953 Lincoln Blvd., Santa Monica, CA 90405, ☎ 310/452–0506 or 800/225–5759) works with lesbians.

I
INSURANCE

Travel insurance covering baggage, health, and trip cancellation or interruptions is available from **Access America** (Box 90315, Richmond, VA 23286, ☎ 804/285–3300 or 800/284–8300), **Carefree Travel Insurance** (Box 9366, 100 Garden City Plaza, Garden City, NY 11530, ☎ 516/294–0220 or 800/323-3149), **Near Travel Services** (Box 1339, Calumet City, IL 60409, ☎ 708/868–6700 or 800/654–6700), **Tele-Trip** (Mutual of Omaha Plaza, Omaha, NE 68175, ☎ 402/342-7600 or 800/228–9792), **Travel Insured International** (Box 280568, East Hartford, CT 06128-0568, ☎ 203/528–7663 or 800/243–3174), **Travel Guard International** (1145 Clark St., Stevens Point, WI 54481, ☎ 715/345–0505 or 800/826–1300), and **Wallach & Company** (107 W. Federal St., Box 480, Middleburg, VA 22117, ☎ 703/687–3166 or 800/237–6615).

IN THE U.K.

The **Association of British Insurers** (51 Gresham St., London EC2V 7HQ, ☎ 0171/600–3333; 30 Gordon St., Glasgow G1 3PU, ☎ 0141/226–3905; Scottish Provident Bldg., Donegall Sq. W., Belfast BT1 6JE, ☎ 01232/249176; call for other locations) gives advice by phone and publishes the free **"Holiday Insurance,"** which sets out typical policy provisions and costs.

L
LODGING

APARTMENT AND VILLA RENTAL

Members of the travel club **Hideaways International** ($99 annually; 767 Islington St., Portsmouth, NH 03801, ☎ 603/430–4433 or 800/843–4433) receive two annual guides plus quarterly newsletters, and arrange rentals among themselves.

HOME EXCHANGE

Principal clearinghouses include **Intervac International** ($65 annually; Box 590504, San Francisco, CA 94159, ☎ 415/435–3497), which has three annual directories; and **Loan-a-Home** ($40–$50 annually; 2 Park La., Apt. 6E, Mount Vernon, NY 10552-3443, ☎ 914/664–7640), which specializes in long-term exchanges.

M
MONEY MATTERS

ATMS

For specific **Cirrus** locations in the United States and Canada, call 800/424–7787. For U.S. **Plus** locations, call 800/843–7587 and enter the area code and first three digits of the number you're calling from (or of the calling area where you want an ATM).

WIRING FUNDS

Funds can be wired via **American Express MoneyGram**^{SM} (☎ 800/926–9400 from the U.S. and Canada for locations and information) or **Western Union** (☎ 800/325–6000 for agent locations or to send using MasterCard or Visa, 800/321–2923 in Canada).

O
THE OLYMPIC GAMES

The Olympic Games will be held in Atlanta, Georgia, July 19–August 4, 1996. Tickets for Olympic events went on sale by mail order in spring 1995. They range in price from $6 to $250 for sporting events, but about 95% of them will sell for less than $75; tickets for opening and closing ceremonies will run between $200–$600. All tickets include local transit on bus and rapid rail. Phone orders will be accepted starting February 1, 1996; however, the telephone numbers had not been released at press time. For further information, dial 404/744–1996 for automated ticket information or contact the **Atlanta Committee for the Olympic Games** (ACOG, Box 1996, Atlanta, GA 30301, ☎ 404/224–1996, FAX 404/224–1993).

P
PASSPORTS AND VISAS

U.K. CITIZENS

For fees, documentation requirements, and to get an emergency passport, call the **London Passport Office** (☎ 0171/271–3000). For visa information, call the **U.S. Embassy Visa Information Line** (☎ 171/499–9000; calls cost 49p per minute or 39p per minute cheap rate) or write the **U.S. Embassy Visa Branch** (5 Upper Grosvenor St., London W1A 2JB). If you live in Northern Ireland, write the **U.S. Consulate General** (Queen's House, Queen St., Belfast BTI 6EQ). In Scotland, apply to the consulate at 3 Regent Terrace, Edinburgh EH7 5BW.

PHOTO HELP

The **Kodak Information Center** (☎ 800/242–2424) answers consumer questions about film and photography.

S
SENIOR CITIZENS

EDUCATIONAL TRAVEL

The nonprofit **Elderhostel** (75 Federal St., 3rd Floor, Boston, MA 02110, ☎ 617/426–7788), for people 60 and older, has offered inexpensive study programs since 1975. The nearly 2,000 courses cover everything from marine science to Greek myths and cowboy poetry. Fees for programs in the

United States and Canada, which usually last one week, run about $300, not including transportation.

ORGANIZATIONS

Contact the **American Association of Retired Persons** (AARP, 601 E St. NW, Washington, DC 20049, ☎ 202/434–2277; $8 per person or couple annually). Its Purchase Privilege Program gets members discounts on lodging, car rentals, and sightseeing, and the AARP Motoring Plan furnishes domestic trip-routing information and emergency road-service aid for an annual fee of $39.95 per person or couple.

For other discounts on lodgings, car rentals, and other travel products, along with magazines and newsletters, contact the **National Council of Senior Citizens** (membership $12 annually; 1331 F St. NW, Washington, DC 20004, ☎ 202/347–8800) and **Mature Outlook** (subscription $9.95 annually; Box 10448, Des Moines, IA 50306-0448, ☎ 800/336–6330).

PUBLICATIONS

The 50+ Traveler's Guidebook: Where to Go, Where to Stay, What to Do, by Anita Williams and Merrimac Dillon ($12.95; St. Martin's Press, 175 5th Ave., New York, NY 10010, ☎ 212/674–5151 or 800/288–2131), offers many useful tips. **"The Mature Traveler"** ($29.95; Box 50400, Reno, NV 89513, ☎ 702/786-

7419), a monthly newsletter, covers travel deals.

STUDENTS

GROUPS

Major tour operators include **Contiki Holidays** (300 Plaza Alicante, Suite 900, Garden Grove, CA 92640, ☎ 714/740–0808 or 800/466–0610).

HOSTELING

Contact **Hostelling International–American Youth Hostels** (Box 37613, Washington, DC 20013-7613, ☎ 202/783–6161) in the United States, **Hostelling International–Canada** (205 Catherine St., Suite 400, Ottawa, Ontario K2P 1C3, ☎ 613/237–7884) in Canada, and the **Youth Hostel Association of England and Wales** (Trevelyan House, 8 St. Stephen's Hill, St. Albans, Hertfordshire AL1 2DY, ☎ 01727/855215 and 01727/845047) in the United Kingdom. Membership ($25 in the U.S., $26.75 in Canada, and £9 in the U.K.) gets you access to 5,000 hostels worldwide that charge $7–$20 nightly per person.

I.D. CARDS

To be eligible for discounts on transportation and admissions, get the **International Student Identity Card** (ISIC), if you're a bona fide student, or the **International Youth Card** (IYC) if you're under 26. In the United States, the ISIC and IYC cards cost $16 each and include basic travel-accident and illness

coverage, plus a toll-free travel hot line. Apply through the Council on International Educational Exchange (*see* Organizations, *below*). Cards are available for $15 each in Canada from **Travel Cuts** (187 College St., Toronto, Ontario M5T 1P7, ☎ 416/979–2406 or 800/667–2887) and in the United Kingdom for £5 each at student unions and student travel companies.

ORGANIZATIONS

A major contact is the **Council on International Educational Exchange** (CIEE, 205 E. 42nd St., 16th Floor, New York, NY 10017, ☎ 212/661–1450) with locations in Boston (729 Boylston St., 02116, ☎ 617/266–1926), Miami (9100 S. Dadeland Blvd. Miami, ☎ 305/670–9261), Los Angeles (10904 Lindbrook Dr., 90024, ☎ 310/208–3551), 43 other college towns nationwide, and the United Kingdom (28A Poland St., London W1V 3DB, ☎ 0171/437–7767). Twice a year, it publishes *Student Travels* magazine. The CIEE's Council Travel Service offers domestic air passes for bargain travel within the United States and is the exclusive U.S. agent for several student-discount cards.

Campus Connections (325 Chestnut St., Suite 1101, Philadelphia, PA 19106, ☎ 215/625–8585 or 800/428–3235) specializes in discounted accommodations and airfares for

THE GOLD GUIDE / IMPORTANT CONTACTS

students. The **Educational Travel Centre** (438 N. Frances St., Madison, WI 53703, ☎ 608/256–5551) offers rail passes and low-cost airline tickets, mostly for flights departing from Chicago.

In Canada, also contact **Travel Cuts** (*see above*).

T

TOUR OPERATORS

Among the companies selling tours and packages to the Carolinas and the Georgia Coast, the following have a proven reputation, are nationally known, and have plenty of options to choose from.

GROUP TOURS

For deluxe escorted tours of the Carolinas and the Georgia Coast, contact **Maupintour** (Box 807, Lawrence, KS 66044, ☎ 800/255–4266 or 913/843–1211) and **Tauck Tours** (276 Post Rd. W, Westport, CT 06880, ☎ 800/468–2825 or 203/226–6911). Another operator falling between deluxe and first class is **Globus** (5301 S. Federal Circle, Littleton, CO 80123, ☎ 800/221–0090 or 303/797–2800). In the first-class and tourist range, try **Collette Tours** (162 Middle St., Pawtucket, RI 02860, ☎ 800/832–4656 or 401/728–3805), and **Mayflower Tours** (1225 Warren Ave., Downers Grove, IL 60515, ☎ 708/960–3430 or 800/323–7604). For budget and tourist-class programs, contact **Cosmos** (*see* Globus, *above*).

PACKAGES

Independent vacation packages are available from major tour operators and airlines. Contact **American Airlines Fly Away Vacations** (☎ 800/321–2121), **Globetrotters** (139 Main St., Cambridge, MA 02142, ☎ 800/999–9696 or 617/621–9911), **Continental Airlines' Grand Destinations** (☎ 800/634–5555), **Delta Dream Vacations** (☎ 800/872–7786), **Certified Vacations** (Box 1525, Fort Lauderdale, FL 33302, ☎ 800/233–7260), **United Vacations** (☎ 800/328–6877), **Kingdom Tours** (300 Market St., Kingston, PA 18704, ☎ 717/283–4241 or 800/872–8857), and **USAir Vacations** (☎ 800/455–0123). **Funjet Vacations,** based in Milwaukee, Wisconsin, and **Gogo Tours** in Ramsey, New Jersey, sell packages to the Carolinas and the Georgia Coast only through travel agents.

FROM THE U.K.➢ Tour operators offering packages to the Carolinas and the Georgia Coast include **Jetsave** (Sussex House, London Rd., East Grinstead, West Sussex RH19 1LD, ☎ 01342/312033), **Key to America** (1–3 Station Rd., Ashford Middlesex, TW15 2UW, ☎ 01784/248777), **Premier Holidays** (Premier Travel Center, Westbrook, Milton Rd., Cambridge CB4 1YG, ☎ 01223/516–688), and **Trailfinders** (42–50 Earl's Court Rd., London W8 6FT, ☎ 0171/937–5400; 58 Deansgate, Manchester M3

2FF, ☎ 0161/839–6969).

ORGANIZATIONS

The **National Tour Association** (546 E. Main St., Lexington, KY 40508, ☎ 606/226–4444 or 800/755–8687) and **United States Tour Operators Association** (USTOA, 211 E. 51st St., Suite 12B, New York, NY 10022, ☎ 212/750–7371) can provide lists of member operators and information on booking tours.

PUBLICATIONS

Consult the brochure **"Worldwide Tour & Vacation Package Finder"** from the United States Tour Operators Association (*see above*) and the Better Business Bureau's **"Tips on Travel Packages"** (publication No. 24-195, $2; 4200 Wilson Blvd., Arlington, VA 22203).

TRAVEL AGENCIES

For names of reputable agencies in your area, contact the **American Society of Travel Agents** (1101 King St., Suite 200, Alexandria, VA 22314, ☎ 703/739–2782).

V

VISITOR INFORMATION

Contact the **Georgia Department of Industry, Trade and Tourism** (Box 1776, Atlanta, GA 30301, ☎ 404/656–3590 or 800/847–4842, FAX 404/651–9063), the **North Carolina Division of Travel and Tourism** (430 N. Salisbury St., Raleigh, NC 27603, ☎ 919/733–4171 or

800/847–4862, FAX 919/733–8582), and **South Carolina Parks, Rescreation, and Tourism** (1205 Pendleton St., Box 71, Columbia, SC 29202, ☎ 803/734–0122, FAX 803/734–0133).

IN THE U.K.

Contact the **United States Travel and** **Tourism Administration** (Box 1EN, London W1A 1EN, ☎ 0171/495–4466). For a free USA pack, write the USTTA at Box 170, Ashford, Kent TN24 0ZX. Enclose stamps worth £1.50.

W
WEATHER

For current conditions and forecasts, plus the local time and helpful travel tips, call the **Weather Channel Connection** (☎ 900/932–8437; 95¢ per minute) from a touch-tone phone.

SMART TRAVEL TIPS A TO Z

Basic Information on Traveling in the Carolinas and the Georgia Coast and Savvy Tips to Make Your Trip a Breeze

The more you travel, the more you know about how to make trips run like clock-work. To help make your travels hassle-free, Fodor's editors have rounded up dozens of tips from our contribu-tors and travel experts all over the world, as well as basic informa-tion on visiting the Carolinas and the Georgia Coast. For names of organizations to contact and publica-tions that can give you more information, *see* Important Contacts A to Z, *above*.

A
AIR TRAVEL

If time is an issue, **always look for nonstop flights,** which require no change of plane. If possible, **avoid connect-ing flights,** which stop at least once and can involve a change of plane, although the flight number remains the same; if the first leg is late, the second waits.

CUTTING COSTS

The Sunday travel section of most newspa-pers is a good source of deals.

MAJOR AIRLINES➤ The least-expensive airfares from the major airlines are priced for round-trip travel and are subject to restrictions.

You must usually **book in advance and buy the ticket within 24 hours** to get cheaper fares, and you may have to **stay over a Saturday night.** The lowest fare is subject to availability, and only a small per-centage of the plane's total seats are sold at that price. It's good to **call a number of air-lines—and when you are quoted a good price, book it on the spot**—the same fare on the same flight may not be available the next day. Airlines generally allow you to change your return date for a $25 to $50 fee, but most low-fare tickets are nonrefundable. However, if you don't use it, you can apply the cost toward the pur-chase price of a new ticket, again for a small charge.

CONSOLIDATORS➤ Consolidators, who buy tickets at reduced rates from scheduled airlines, sell them at prices below the lowest avail-able from the airlines directly—usually with-out advance restric-tions. Sometimes you can even get your money back if you need to return the ticket. Carefully read the fine print detailing penalties for changes and cancel-lations. If you doubt the reliability of a consol-idator, **confirm your reservation with the airline.**

ALOFT

AIRLINE FOOD➤ If you hate airline food, **ask for special meals when booking.** These can be vegetarian, low-choles-terol, or kosher, for example; commonly prepared to order in smaller quantities than standard catered fare, they can be tastier.

SMOKING➤ Smoking is banned on all flights within the United States and on all Canadian flights; the ban also applies to domestic segments of interna-tional flights aboard U.S. and foreign carri-ers. Delta has banned smoking system-wide.

C
CAMERAS, CAMCORDERS, AND COMPUTERS

LAPTOPS

Before you depart, **check your portable computer's battery,** because you may be asked at security to turn on the computer to prove that it is what it appears to be. At the airport, you may prefer to **request a manual inspection,** although security X-rays do not harm hard-disk or floppy-disk storage.

PHOTOGRAPHY

If your camera is new or if you haven't used it for a while, **shoot and develop a few rolls of film** before you leave. Always **store film in a cool, dry place**—never in the car's glove compartment or on the shelf under the rear window.

Every pass of film through an X-ray machine increases the chance of clouding. To protect it, carry it in a clear plastic bag and **ask for hand inspection at security.** Such requests are virtually always honored at U.S. airports. Don't depend on a lead-lined bag to protect film in checked luggage—the airline may increase the radiation to see what's inside.

VIDEO

Before your trip, **test your camcorder, invest in a skylight filter to protect the lens, and charge the batteries.** (Airport security personnel may ask you to turn on the camcorder to prove that it's what it appears to be.)

Videotape is not damaged by X-rays, but it may be harmed by the magnetic field of a walk-through metal detector, so **ask that videotapes be hand-checked.**

CHILDREN
AND TRAVEL

BABY-SITTING

For recommended local sitters, **check with your hotel desk.**

DRIVING

If you are renting a car, **arrange for a car seat**

when you reserve. Sometimes they're free.

FLYING

On domestic flights, children under two not occupying a seat travel free, and older children currently travel on the "lowest applicable" adult fare.

BAGGAGE➤ In general, the adult baggage allowance applies for children paying half or more of the adult fare.

SAFETY SEATS➤ According to the Federal Aviation Administration (FAA), it's a good idea to **use safety seats aloft.** Airline policy varies. U.S. carriers allow FAA-approved models, but airlines usually require that you buy a ticket, even if your child would otherwise ride free, because the seats must be strapped into regular passenger seats.

FACILITIES➤ When making your reservation, **ask for children's meals or a freestanding bassinets** if you need them; the latter are available only to those with seats at the bulkhead, where there's enough legroom. If you don't need the bassinet, **think twice before requesting bulkhead seats**—the only storage for in-flight necessities is in the inconveniently distant overhead bins.

LODGING

Most hotels allow children under a certain age to stay in their parents' room at no extra charge, while others charge them as extra adults; be sure to **ask about the cut-off age.**

CUSTOMS
AND DUTIES

IN THE CAROLINAS AND THE GEORGIA COAST

British visitors ages 21 or over may import the following into the United States: 200 cigarettes or 50 cigars or 2 kilograms of tobacco; 1 U.S. liter of alcohol; gifts to the value of $100. Restricted items include meat products, seeds, plants, and fruits. Never carry illegal drugs.

BACK HOME

IN CANADA➤ Once per calendar year, when you've been out of Canada for at least seven days, you may bring in C$300 worth of goods duty-free. If you've been away less than seven days but more than 48 hours, the duty-free exemption drops to C$100 but can be claimed any number of times (as can a C$20 duty-free exemption for absences of 24 hours or more). You cannot combine the yearly and 48-hour exemptions, use the C$300 exemption only partially (to save the balance for a later trip), or pool exemptions with family members. Goods claimed under the C$300 exemption may follow you by mail; those claimed under the lesser exemptions must accompany you.

Alcohol and tobacco products may be included in the yearly and 48-hour exemptions but not in the 24-hour exemption. If you meet the age requirements of the province through

THE GOLD GUIDE / SMART TRAVEL TIPS

which you reenter Canada, you may bring in, duty-free, 1.14 liters (40 imperial ounces) of wine or liquor *or* 24 12-ounce cans or bottles of beer or ale. If you are 16 or older, you may bring in, duty-free, 200 cigarettes, 50 cigars or cigarillos, and 400 tobacco sticks or 400 grams of manufactured tobacco. Alcohol and tobacco must accompany you on your return.

An unlimited number of gifts valued up to C$60 each may be mailed to Canada duty-free. These do not count as part of your exemption. Label the package "Unsolicited Gift—Value under $60." Alcohol and tobacco are excluded.

IN THE U.K.➤ From countries outside the EU, including the United States, you may import duty-free 200 cigarettes, 100 cigarillos, 50 cigars or 250 grams of tobacco; 1 liter of spirits or 2 liters of fortified or sparkling wine; 2 liters of still table wine; 60 milliliters of perfume; 250 milliliters of toilet water; plus £136 worth of other goods, including gifts and souvenirs.

D

FOR TRAVELERS
WITH DISABILITIES

When discussing accessibility with an operator or reservationist, **ask hard questions.** Are there any stairs, inside *or* out? Are there grab bars next to the toilet *and* in the shower/tub? How wide is the door-

way to the room? To the bathroom? For the most extensive facilities, meeting the latest legal specifications, **opt for newer accommodations,** which more often have been designed with access in mind. Older properties must usually be retrofitted and may offer more limited facilities as a result. Be sure to **discuss your needs before booking.**

DISCOUNT CLUBS

Travel clubs offer members unsold space on airplanes, cruise ships, and package tours at as much as 50% below regular prices. Membership may include a regular bulletin or access to a toll-free hot line giving details of available trips departing from three or four days to several months in the future. Most also offer 50% discounts off hotel rack rates. Before booking with a club, **make sure the hotel or other supplier isn't offering a better deal.**

I

INSURANCE

Travel insurance can protect your investment, replace your luggage and its contents, or provide for medical coverage should you fall ill during your trip. Most tour operators, travel agents, and insurance agents sell specialized health-and-accident, flight, trip-cancellation, and luggage insurance as well as comprehensive policies with some or all of these features. Before you make any purchase, **review your**

existing **health and homeowner's policies** to find out whether they cover expenses incurred while traveling.

BAGGAGE

Airline liability for your baggage is limited to $1,250 per person on domestic flights. On international flights, the airlines' liability is $9.07 per pound or $20 per kilogram for checked baggage (roughly $640 per 70-pound bag). However, this excludes valuable items such as jewelry and cameras that are listed in your ticket's fine print. Insurance for losses exceeding the terms of your airline ticket can be bought directly from the airline at check-in for about $10 per $1,000 of coverage, but first **see if your home-owner's policy covers lost luggage.**

FLIGHT

You should **think twice before buying flight insurance.** Often purchased as a last-minute impulse at the airport, it pays a lump sum when a plane crashes, either to a beneficiary if the insured dies or sometimes to a surviving passenger who loses eyesight or a limb. Supplementing the airlines' coverage described in the limits-of-liability paragraphs on your ticket, it's expensive and basically unnecessary. Charging an airline ticket to a major credit card often automatically entitles you to coverage and may also embrace travel by bus, train, and ship.

For U.K. Travelers➤ According to the Association of British Insurers, a trade association representing 450 insurance companies, it's wise to **buy extra medical coverage when you visit the United States.** You can buy an annual travel-insurance policy valid for most vacations during the year in which it's purchased. If you go this route, make sure it covers you if you have a preexisting medical condition or are pregnant.

TRIP

Without insurance, you will lose all or most of your money if you must cancel your trip due to illness or any other reason. Especially if your airline ticket, cruise, or package tour is nonrefundable and cannot be changed, it's essential that you **buy trip-cancellation-and-interruption insurance.** When considering how much coverage you need, look for a policy that will cover the cost of your trip plus the nondiscounted price of a one-way airline ticket should you need to return home early. Read the fine print carefully, especially sections defining "family member" and "preexisting medical conditions." Also **consider default or bankruptcy insurance,** which protects you against a supplier's failure to deliver. However, such policies often do not cover default by a travel agency, tour operator, airline, or cruise line if you bought your tour and the

coverage directly from the firm in question.

L
LODGING

APARTMENT AND VILLA RENTALS

If you want a home base that's roomy enough for a family and comes with cooking facilities, **consider a furnished rental.** It's generally cost-wise, too, although not always—some rentals are luxury properties (economical only when your party is large). Home-exchange directories do list rentals—often second homes owned by prospective house swappers—and some services search for a house or apartment for you (even a castle if that's your fancy) and handle the paperwork. Some send an illustrated catalogue and others send photographs of specific properties, sometimes at a charge; up-front registration fees may apply.

HOME EXCHANGE

If you would like to find a house, an apartment, or other vacation property to exchange for your own while on vacation, **become a member of a home-exchange organization,** which will send you its annual directories listing available exchanges and will include your own listing in at least one of them. Arrangements for the actual exchange are made by the two parties to it, not by the organization.

M
MONEY AND EXPENSES

ATMS

Chances are that you can **use your bank card at ATMs** to withdraw money from an account and get cash advances on a credit-card account if your card has been programmed with a personal identification number, or PIN. Before leaving home, **check in on frequency limits** for withdrawals and cash advances.

On cash advances you are charged interest from the day you receive the money, whether from a teller or an ATM. Transaction fees for ATM withdrawals outside your home turf may be higher than for withdrawals at home.

TRAVELER'S CHECKS

Whether or not to buy traveler's checks depends on where you are headed; **take cash to rural areas and small towns, traveler's checks to cities.** The most widely recognized are American Express, Citicorp, Thomas Cook, and Visa, which are sold by major commercial banks for 1% to 3% of the checks' face value—it pays to **shop around.** Both American Express and Thomas Cook issue checks that can be countersigned and used by you or your traveling companion. Record the numbers of the checks, cross them off as you spend them, and keep this information separate from your checks.

WIRING MONEY

You don't have to be a cardholder to send or receive funds through MoneyGram℠ from American Express. Just go to a MoneyGram agent, located in retail and convenience stores and in American Express Travel Offices. Pay up to $1,000 with cash or a credit card, anything over that in cash. The money can be picked up within 10 minutes in cash or check at the nearest MoneyGram agent. There's no limit, and the recipient need only present photo identification. The cost, which includes a free long-distance phone call, runs from 3% to 10%, depending on the amount sent, the destination, and how you pay.

You can also send money using Western Union. Money sent from the United States or Canada will be available for pickup at agent locations in 100 countries within 15 minutes. Once the money is in the system, it can be picked up at any one of 25,000 locations. Fees range from 4% to 10%, depending on the amount you send.

P
PACKAGES
AND TOURS

A package or tour to the Carolinas and the Georgia Coast can make your vacation less

expensive and more convenient. Firms that sell tours and packages purchase airline seats, hotel rooms, and rental cars in bulk and pass some of the savings on to you. In addition, the best operators have local representatives to help you out at your destination.

A GOOD DEAL?

The more your package or tour includes, the better you can predict the ultimate cost of your vacation. Make sure you know exactly what is included, and **beware of hidden costs.** Are taxes, tips, and service charges included? Transfers and baggage handling? Entertainment and excursions? These can add up.

Most packages and tours are rated deluxe, first-class superior, first class, tourist, and budget. The key difference is usually accommodations. If the package or tour you are considering is priced lower than in your wildest dreams, **be skeptical.** Also, **make sure your travel agent knows the hotels** and other services. Ask about location, room size, beds, and whether it has a pool, room service, or programs for children, if you care about these. Has your agent been there or sent others you can contact?

BUYER BEWARE

Each year consumers are stranded or lose their money when operators go out of business—even very large ones with excel-

lent reputations. If you can't afford a loss, take the time to **check out the operator**—find out how long the company has been in business, and ask several agents about its reputation. Next, **don't book unless the firm has a consumer-protection program.** Members of the United States Tour Operators Association and the National Tour Association are required to set aside funds exclusively to cover your payments and travel arrangements in case of default. Nonmember operators may instead carry insurance; look for the details in the operator's brochure—and the name of an underwriter with a solid reputation. Note: When it comes to tour operators, **don't trust escrow accounts.** Although there are laws governing those of charter-flight operators, no governmental body prevents tour operators from raiding the till.

Next, **contact your local Better Business Bureau and the attorney general's office** in both your own state and the operator's; have any complaints been filed? Last, **pay with a major credit card.** Then you can cancel payment, provided that you can document your complaint. Always **consider trip-cancellation insurance** (see Insurance, above).

BIG VS. SMALL➤ An operator that handles several hundred thousand travelers annually can use its purchasing power to give you a good price. Its high volume may also indicate financial stability. But some small companies provide more personalized service; because they tend to specialize, they may also be experts on an area.

USING AN AGENT

Travel agents are an excellent resource. In fact, large operators accept bookings only through travel agents. But it's good to **collect brochures from several agencies,** because some agents' suggestions may be skewed by promotional relationships with tour and package firms that reward them for volume sales. If you have a special interest, **find an agent with expertise in that area;** the American Society of Travel Agents can give you leads in the United States. (Don't rely solely on your agent, though; agents may be unaware of small-niche operators, and some special-interest travel companies only sell direct.)

SINGLE TRAVELERS

Prices are usually quoted per person, based on two sharing a room. If traveling solo, you may be required to pay the full double-occupancy rate. Some operators eliminate this surcharge if you agree to be matched up with a roommate of the same sex, even if one is not found by departure time.

PACKING FOR THE CAROLINAS AND THE GEORGIA COAST

Much of the Carolinas and the Georgia Coast has hot, humid summers and sunny, mild winters. For colder months, pack a lightweight coat, slacks, and sweaters; you'll need heavier clothing in the more northern states, where cold, damp weather prevails and snow is not unusual. Keeping summer's humidity in mind, **pack absorbent natural fabrics that breathe;** bring an umbrella, but leave the plastic raincoat at home. You'll want a jacket or sweater for summer evenings and for too-cool air-conditioning. And **don't forget insect repellent.**

Bring an extra pair of eyeglasses or contact lenses in your carry-on luggage, and if you have a health problem, **pack enough medication** to last the trip. **Don't put prescription drugs or valuables in luggage to be checked,** for it could go astray.

LUGGAGE

Free airline baggage allowances depend on the airline, the route, and the class of your ticket; ask in advance. In general, on domestic flights you are entitled to check two bags—neither exceeding 62 inches, or 158 centimeters (length + width + height), or weighing more than 70 pounds (32 kilograms). A third piece may be brought

aboard; its total dimensions are generally limited to less than 45 inches (114 centimeters), so it will fit easily under the seat in front of you or in the overhead compartment. In the United States, the FAA gives airlines broad latitude to limit carry-on allowances and tailor them to different aircraft and operational conditions. Charges for excess, oversize, or overweight pieces vary.

SAFEGUARDING YOUR LUGGAGE➤ Before leaving home, **itemize your bags' contents** and their worth, and label them with your name, address, and phone number. (If you use your home address, cover it so that potential thieves can't see it.) Inside your bag, **pack a copy of your itinerary.** At check-in, **make sure that your bag is correctly tagged** with the airport's three-letter destination code. If your bags arrive damaged or not at all, file a written report with the airline before leaving the airport.

PASSPORTS AND VISAS

U.K. CITIZENS

British citizens need a valid passport. If you are staying fewer than 90 days and traveling on a vacation, with a return or onward ticket, you will not need a visa.

While traveling, **keep one photocopy of the data page** separate from your wallet and leave another copy with someone at home. If

THE GOLD GUIDE / SMART TRAVEL TIPS

you lose your passport, promptly call the nearest embassy or consulate, and the local police; having the data page can speed replacement.

R
RENTING A CAR

CUTTING COSTS

To get the best deal, **book through a travel agent and shop around.** When pricing cars, **ask where the rental lot is located.** Some off-airport locations offer lower rates—even though their lots are only minutes away from the terminal via complimentary shuttle. You may also want to **price local car-rental companies,** whose rates may be lower still, although service and maintenance standards may not be up to those of a national firm. Also **ask your travel agent about a company's customer-service record.** How has it responded to late plane arrivals and vehicle mishaps? Are there often lines at the rental counter, and, if you're traveling during a holiday period, does a confirmed reservation guarantee you a car?

INSURANCE

When you drive a rented car, you are generally responsible for any damage or personal injury that you cause as well as damage to the vehicle. Before you rent, **see what coverage you already have** by means of your personal auto-insurance policy and credit cards. For about $14 a day, rental companies sell

insurance, known as a collision damage waiver (CDW), that eliminates your liability for damage to the car; it's always optional and should never be automatically added to your bill.

SURCHARGES

Before picking up the car in one city and leaving it in another, **ask about drop-off charges or one-way service fees,** which can be substantial. Note, too, that some rental agencies charge extra if you return the car before the time specified on your contract. To avoid a hefty refueling fee, **fill the tank just before you turn in the car.**

FOR U.K. CITIZENS

In the United States you must be 21 to rent a car; rates may be higher for those under 25. Extra costs cover child seats, compulsory for children under five (about $3 per day), and additional drivers (about $1.50 per day). To pick up your reserved car you will need the reservation voucher, a passport, a U.K. driver's license, and a travel policy covering each driver.

S
SENIOR-CITIZEN DISCOUNTS

To qualify for age-related discounts, **mention your senior-citizen status up front** when booking hotel reservations, not when checking out, and before you're seated in restaurants, not when

paying your bill. Note that discounts may be limited to certain menus, days, or hours. When renting a car, **ask about promotional car-rental discounts**—they can net lower costs than your senior-citizen discount.

STUDENTS ON THE ROAD

To save money, **look into deals available through student-oriented travel agencies.** To qualify, you'll need to have a bona fide student I.D. card. Members of international student groups also are eligible. *See* Students *in* Important Contacts A to Z, *above.*

T
TELEPHONES

LONG-DISTANCE

The long-distance services of AT&T, MCI, and Sprint make calling home relatively convenient and let you avoid hotel surcharges; typically, you dial an 800 number in the United States and a local number abroad.

W
WHEN TO GO

Spring is probably the most attractive season in this part of the United States. Cherry blossoms are followed throughout the region by azaleas, dogwood, and camellias from April into May, and by apple blossoms in May. Folk, crafts, art, and music festivals tend to take place in summer, as do sports events. State and local fairs are held mainly in August and

September, though there are a few in early July and into October.

CLIMATE

In winter, temperatures generally average in the low 40s inland, in the 60s by the shore. Summer temperatures, modified by mountains in some areas, by water in others, range from the high 70s to the mid-80s, now and then the low 90s.

The following are average daily maximum and minimum temperatures for key Southern cities.

Climate in the Carolinas and the Georgia Coast

ATLANTA, GEORGIA

	F	C		F	C		F	C
Jan.	52F	11C	May	79F	26C	Sept.	83F	28C
	36	2		61	16		65	18
Feb.	54F	12C	June	86F	30C	Oct.	72F	22C
	38	3		67	19		54	12
Mar.	63F	17C	July	88F	31C	Nov.	61F	16C
	43	6		70	21		43	6
Apr.	72F	22C	Aug.	86F	30C	Dec.	52F	11C
	52	11		70	21		38	5

RALEIGH, NORTH CAROLINA

	F	C		F	C		F	C
Jan.	50F	10C	May	78F	26C	Sept.	81F	27C
	29	− 2		55	13		60	16
Feb.	52F	11C	June	85F	29C	Oct.	71F	22C
	30	− 1		62	17		47	8
Mar.	61F	16C	July	88F	31C	Nov.	61F	16C
	37	3		67	19		38	3
Apr.	72F	22C	Aug.	87F	31C	Dec.	52F	11C
	46	8		66	18	52	11	

CHARLESTON, SOUTH CAROLINA

	F	C		F	C		F	C
Jan.	59F	15C	May	81F	27C	Sept.	84F	29C
	41	6		64	18		69	21
Feb.	60F	16C	June	86F	30C	Oct.	76F	24C
	43	7		71	22		59	15
Mar.	66F	19C	July	88F	31C	Nov.	67F	19C
	49	9		74	23		49	9
Apr.	73F	23C	Aug.	88F	31C	Dec.	59F	11C
	56	13		73	23		42	6

1 Destination: The Carolinas and the Georgia Coast

BLOOM COUNTY

THROW AWAY ALL THE CLICHÉS about the Carolinas and coastal Georgia. Very few of them fit anymore and the others probably never did. It took the world a long time to discover that this area is not Tobacco Road but, rather, energetic, nature-rich, and quietly dignified. It's a thriving area with very little bustle—there is drive without push.

This area has never been "dirt poor." Its agriculture is, by many standards, "soil rich." Things grow here, almost in spite of themselves. Everywhere but on the sandy strip of coastal islands, trees dominate the region's landscape. Pines are the overwhelming favorites of nature here, growing solid and thick over the mountaintops and tall and graceful in the sandy soils of the eastern coastal plain. They camouflage the bare limbs of the hardwoods in winter and add vivid green contrast to the flame of autum just before Thanksgiving.

Closer to sea level, almost everything can—and does—grow in one part or another of the area. Even in tidy suburban backyards, honeysuckle can scent a summer night so powerfully that owners are often tempted to "let it grow" just because it smells so nice. (Few succumb to this notion twice—like its antitheses, poison ivy, kudzu, and spanish moss, it spreads faster than you'd believe.) Jonquils and forsythia begin their yellow show long before the vernal equinox, followed by azaleas and camellias, and finally, magnolias with their lemon fragrance. Daylilies sprout along roadsides, and English ivy climbs trees with alacrity. And these are things theat grow without a farmer's help!

Cotton is no longer agricultural king here, and tobacco is losing its place as crown prince. They are being replaced by peanuts, soybeans, cucumbers, grapes, Christmas trees, and peaches. (You have never *really* tasted a peach until you had one grown in the surrounding Sandhills orchards and bought from a roadside stand.) More and more cornfields are appearing across the Piedmont, as are herds of dairy cows, feeding on the lush grass. Pickle production is up, along with that of peanut butter and a new contender, wine.

There are four seasons here—spring is wet and fall is dry, but they are just about the loveliest spring and fall to be found in the continental United States. The hardwood trees bud in March, and the profusion of flowers, both wild and cultivated, is breathtaking. Everyone comes outdoors to look, and feel, and to wake up. Golfers, tennis players, gardeners, and sunbathers appear with renewed energy. The rains are warm and usually brief. Fall is even prettier, with foliage that rivals the gold of sunlight. Outdoor activity continues until at least the end of November, when the leaves finally fall.

That leaves summer and winter—surely too hot and too cold to enjoy? Definitely not. Air-conditioning is a fact of life in the humid summers, when the sun bakes the air until thunderheads pile up. But the beaches, the myriad lakes, and the local swimming pools beckon even the non-swimmers, and mountains—a cool haven— are less than a day's drive from anywhere. In winter the mountains are often snowy while the rest of the area is just chilly. Skiers scurry to the slopes, but those who remain in the low country probably can't remember where they put boots after last year's one day of snow. If and when that snowfall comes to the low country (as it usually does a couple of times each year) everything comes to a halt—schools close and meetings are cancelled, and local disc jockeys recount their harrowing journey into the station through a couple of inches of serious snow. (Low-country people do not handle driving in the snow at all well, and local governments have no snow removal equipment. If it snows, be content to stay where you are.) It's almost a holiday when winter comes to the southeast. Adults and children alike find the slightest rise in land contour an excuse to go sledding "before it's gone tomorrow." A sprinkle of snow along the coast draws crowds.

Not too long ago the geography books described this area as "agriculture." We've told you what grows here, but what is more important now is what is *made* here—fabrics and pharmaceuticals, bath towels and beer, furniture and film, chemicals, electronic components, lumber, tobacco products, and nuclear power. Most of the current boom is, of course, concentrated in the metropolitan centers. Atlanta and surrounding cities will host the 1996 summer Olympics, and Charlotte is fast becoming one of America's preeminent banking empires. However, commercial success is emerging rapidly in rural areas, too. Tourism is a major industry all over and is widely supported. Officals in charge of such things have already awakened to the need for long range planning to maintain the quality of the environment. Visitors are welcomed warmly, and there are plenty of accommodations available, but development is being programmed to avoid destruction of natural resources and precious beaches. Even in the dense-built Grand Strand at Myrtle Beach in South Carolina one doesn't have to step over recumbent bodies to reach the water. And on most of the beaches, even at the height if the summer season, a lonesome dawn stroll is still possible.

WINSTON CHURCHILL once said that "change is not necessarily progress." It is *here,* with one exception—the people. If there should come a change in the courteous, friendly, and helpful attitudes of these charming inhabitants of North and South Carolina and the Georgia Coast, it will be a shame. The men are courtly—not antifeminist, but apt to address a woman as "young lady" regardless of her age.

And the women, although generally not antifeminist, are nonetheless soft-spoken. The children learn "ma'am" and "sir" when they're toddlers, and all of this politeness is contagious. Service people (the plumber, the shoe clerk, the auto mechanic) go far out of their way to accommodate, and they know you'll understand if things move just a *mite* slower here than in some other places. There are smiling faces everywhere, and "Hey, how are you?" sounds genuine. The pace is steady but relaxed; the ambience is open and friendly;

the geniality is authentic. Once you've been here, you'll be quick to respond to "y'all come back, y'heah."

WHAT'S WHERE

Georgia

Georgia is notable for its contrasting landscapes and varied cities and towns, each reflecting its own special Southern charm. The northern part of the state has the Appalachian Mountains and their waterfalls; Dahlonega, the site of the nation's first gold rush; and Alpine Helen, a recreated Bavarian village in the Blue Ridge Mountains. Also in the north are Atlanta, a fast-growing city that serves as a banking center and is hosting the 1996 Summer Olympics, and Macon, an antebellum town with thousands of cherry trees. If you drive some five hours southeast from Atlanta, you'll reach Savannah, which has the nation's largest historic district, filled with restored Colonial buildings. From Savannah, the state's 100-mile Atlantic coast runs from the Savannah River south to the mouth of St. Mary's near the Florida border. Along this coast is a string of lush, subtropical barrier islands, the Golden Isles, which include the elegant seaside communities of Jekyll, Sea, and St. Simons islands. Further south is Cumberland Island National Seashore, a sanctuary of marshes, beaches, forests, lakes, and ponds. Southern Georgia consists of black, gator-infested swampland, including the mysterious rivers and lakes of Okefenokee Swamp.

North Carolina

Historic sights and natural wonders galore dot North Carolina, from Old Salem, where the 1700s spring to life once again today; to the Great Smoky and Blue Ridge Mountains, where waterfalls cascade over high cliffs into gorges thick with evergreens; to the Cape Hatteras and Cape Lookout national seashores, where tides wash over the wooden skeletons of ancient shipwrecks and lighthouses still stand as they have for 200 years. Here, too, you'll find sophisticated cities like Charlotte, world-class golf in the Pinehurst Sandhills, and fields of tobacco in the rich farmland of the gently rolling Piedmont.

South Carolina

South Carolina's scenic Low Country shoreline is punctuated by the lively port city of Charleston, decked out with fine museums (several in restored antebellum homes), and the recreational resorts of Myrtle Bach and Hilton Head at each end of the coast. The state capital of Columbia is set in the fertile interior of the state that stretches toward the Blue Ridge Mountains, providing the western border of the state. Also to the west are the rolling fields of Thoroughbred country, noted for top race horses and sprawling mansions, and Upcountry South Carolina, at the northwestern tip of the state, with incredible mountain scenery and whitewater rafting.

FODOR'S CHOICE

Special Moments

★ **The King Center, Atlanta, Georgia.** Memories of the civil rights movement in '50s and '60s America come alive as you view the eternal flame burning at Martin Luther King, Jr.'s tomb in front of the downtown center.

★ **The top the Westin Peachtree Plaza Hotel, Atlanta, Georgia.** For the best views of the city, have a relaxing drink or meal in the revolving, multilevel Sun Dial Restaurant and Lounge.

★ **Historic District, Savannah, Georgia.** Architecture buffs will have a field day strolling by the hundreds of Colonial buildings that have been lovingly restored downtown within a ½-square-mile area.

★ **Old Salem, North Carolina.** A 1700s village of brick and wood structures peopled by tradesmen and gentlewomen in period costume provides a slice of living history, a close-up of the life of early immigrants who came to America in search of religious freedom.

★ **Exploring the Cape Hatteras National Seashore, North Carolina.** Stretching from Oregon Inlet to Ocracoke Island, this scenic coastline is dotted with charming beach communities, historic lifesaving stations, wildlife refuges, and undeveloped beaches cluttered only by wild sea oats.

★ **Cypress Gardens, South Carolina.** A boat tour among the spring blossoms reflected in the black waters of the gardens is a visual dazzler.

★ **Shelling on Kiawah Island, South Carolina.** This island is a convergence area, so the beach is one of the best places on the east coast to collect shells and sand dollars. Go early in the morning before others have picked over the finds.

Dining

★ **Dining Room in the Ritz-Carlton Buckhead, Atlanta, Georgia.** Sample the freshest regional products and haute cuisine at its finest at one of the best restaurants not only in town but in the country. $$$$

★ **Ciboulette, Atlanta, Georgia.** Hot smoked salmon, Lyonnaise sausage, and game dishes are inventively prepared at this popular French bistro. $$$

★ **Elizabeth on 37th, Savannah, Georgia.** In an elegant, turn-of-the-century mansion in the city's Victorian district, the emphasis is on seafood enhanced by delicate sauces. $$$

★ **Buckhead Diner, Atlanta, Georgia.** American food with an elegant twist is served in a shimmering faux-diner wrapped in luscious neon hues. $$–$$$

★ **Mrs. Wilkes Dining Room, Savannah, Georgia.** Expect long lines waiting to devour the reasonably priced, well-prepared Southern food, served family-style at big tables. $

★ **Gabrielle's at Richmond Hill, Asheville, North Carolina.** You'll find this Victorian inn under lodging in our reviews, but its fabulous dinners are not to be missed—held by some to be the most imaginative (wild boar sausage and grilled antelope medallions) and delicious food in the state.

★ **Lamplighter, Charlotte, North Carolina.** Fine gourmet cuisine served in the softly lit interior of an old Dilworth home is the hallmark of this favorite. $$$$

★ **Pewter Rose Bistro, Charlotte, North Carolina.** Drawn by the fresh seafood, inventive pasta dishes, and smart setting,

Charlotte's young movers and shakers hang out in this renovated textile mill. $$

★ **Louis's Charleston Grill, Charleston, South Carolina.** Highly personalized service, attention to detail, and an intimate setting make this the choice for that romantic dinner. $$$

★ **82 Queen, Charleston, South Carolina.** Locals and visitors to Charleston flock to this laid-back eatery for the top-quality Low Country cuisine. $$

★ **Sea Captain's House, Myrtle Beach, South Carolina.** The seafood is fresh, simply prepared, and affordable at this casual restaurant—a good choice for a family meal. $$

★ **Magnolias–Uptown/Down South, Charleston, South Carolina.** Lots of Low Country dishes and a magnolia theme infuse this refurbished warehouse with southern charm. $

Lodging

★ **Cloister Hotel, Sea Island, Georgia.** This famed resort with spacious rooms in a Spanish Mediterranean building has a superb spa and outdoor activities galore—golf, tennis, swimming, skeet shooting, sailing, biking, and fishing. $$$$

★ **Gastonian, Savannah, Georgia.** At this superior B&B in a 19th-century mansion, the sumptuous suites have working fireplaces and antiques from the Georgian and Regency periods. $$$$

★ **Ritz-Carlton, Atlanta, Georgia.** Marble writing tables, plump sofas, four-poster beds, and white marble bathrooms create a luxurious ambience in the large guest rooms of this efficiently run, European-flavored hotel. $$$$

★ **Ritz-Carlton, Buckhead, Georgia.** The Ritz's signature 18th- and 19th-century furnishings grace this discreetly elegant gem close to Lenox Mall and Phipps Plaza shopping. $$$$

★ **Mulberry Inn, Savannah, Georgia.** This traditional, dependable lodging features a number of artistic treasures in its public rooms, including valuable Chinese vases and 18th-century oil paintings. $$$

★ **Fearrington House, Chapel Hill, North Carolina.** This French-style country inn was once a working farm and looks like an English country village. Top-notch service in a genteel atmosphere. $$$$

★ **Grove Park Inn, Asheville, North Carolina.** Asheville's premier resort, Grove Park Inn has been the haunt of guests like Thomas Edison, Henry Ford, and F. Scott Fitzgerald since its opening in 1913. $$$$

★ **First Colony Inn, Nags Head, North Carolina.** Four-poster beds, English antiques, and Jacuzzis lend an air of romance to this inn by the ocean, reminiscent of the beach hotels of years past. $$$–$$$$

★ **John Rutledge House Inn, Charleston, South Carolina.** One of the newer inns in Charleston, the elegant John Rutledge House is impeccably furnished and maintained. $$$$

★ **Kingston Plantation: A Radisson Resort, Myrtle Beach, South Carolina.** This self-contained resort, loaded with facilities like a full-service spa and a marina, has a great location on a broad beach well removed from the bustle of the pavilion area. $$$$

★ **Westin Resort, Hilton Head Island, South Carolina.** Top of the line for Hilton Head, the Westin concentrates on luxury and service. $$$

★ **Omni Hotel at Charleston Place, Charleston, South Carolina.** The upscale address for Charleston, the Omni is conveniently located in the historic district. $$$

Scenic Drives

★ **Blue Ridge Parkway, North Carolina.** This 469-mile scenic corridor meanders through breathtaking mountains and meadows, stretching from North Carolina into Virginia.

GREAT ITINERARIES

The following recommended itineraries, arranged by both theme and area, are offered as a guide to planning your own individual tour.

Prominent Sites of African-American History

LOW COUNTRY TOUR➤ Blacks and whites in South Carolina's Low Country have always lived side by side, though as evidenced by the 1739 Stono Plantation Rebellion and the 1822 Denmark Vesey plot to take over Charleston, not always peaceably. This natural distrust also motivated blacks to develop a lilting dialect called Gullah to communicate exclusively with one another. Historic sites in the Low Country recall the culture of slavery.

Duration: One or two days

The Main Route: One day: In Charleston, begin with a walking tour of Catfish Row, home of DuBose Heyward and setting for his novel *Porgy*. Then see the Emmanuel A.M.E. Church—the place of worship for the South's oldest A.M.E. congregation. Also here is the Old Exchange and Provost Dungeon, site of the city's busiest slave market. The Avery Research Center in the historic district has an archive and museum that document the heritage of Low Country blacks.

One day: Travel on to Beaufort, where you'll see the Penn School Historic District and York W. Bailey Cultural Museum on St. Helena Island. This community center consists of 17 buildings on the campus of a school established in 1862 for freed slaves. Also in Beaufort County is self-sufficient Daufuskie Island, until recently inhabited exclusively by descendants of slaves.

Information: *See* Chapter 4.

Prominent Civil War Sites

THE SOUTHEASTERN TOUR➤ South Carolina seceded from the Union on December 20, 1860, and the first shot of the war was fired the following April. The war was fought for the most part on Southern soil, and there are more commemorative plaques in the South than there are black-eyed peas. The following itineraries take in the major sites.

Duration: Seven to 10 days

The Main Route: One day: Begin in Charleston, South Carolina, and visit the Ft. Sumter National Monument. On April 12, 1861, Confederate General P.G.T. Beauregard ordered the first shot fired, and the bloody four-year struggle began.

Two or three days: Drive the 300 miles south to Atlanta. See the Eternal Flame of the Confederacy, and visit the Cyclorama, depicting the 1864 Battle of Atlanta. Explore 3,200-acre Stone Mountain Park, where there's a Confederate Memorial—the world's largest monument, and the Kennesaw Mountain National Battlefield.

Information: *See* Chapters 2 and 4.

FESTIVALS AND SEASONAL EVENTS

The Carolinas and Georgia hold a wide variety of festivals and special events throughout the year.

WINTER

DECEMBER➤ Christmas is celebrated with events in almost every city. One of the highlights is Old Salem's Christmas, which re-creates a Moravian Christmas in Winston-Salem, North Carolina. New Year's events include the Peach Bowl, played in Atlanta, and the First Night festival held on the Town Square in Charlotte, North Carolina.

JANUARY➤ In South Carolina, Orangeburg invites the country's finest coon dogs to compete in the Grand American Coon Hunt. The Savannah Marathon and Half-Marathon in Savannah, Georgia; and the Charlotte Observer Marathon and Runner's Expo in Charlotte, North Carolina, attract the region's runners. Martin Luther King, Jr., Week is celebrated in Atlanta.

FEBRUARY➤ Black History Month is observed throughout the South. In North Carolina, Asheville welcomes visitors to its annual Winterfest Arts and Crafts Show, and Wilmington stages the North Carolina Jazz Festival.

SPRING

MARCH➤ The Old South comes alive: Antebellum mansion and garden tours are given in Charleston and Beaufort, South Carolina. A Revolutionary War battle is reenacted on the anniversary of the Battle of Guilford Courthouse in Greensboro, North Carolina. Spring is celebrated with Springfest on Hilton Head Island, South Carolina.

APRIL➤ Spring festivals abound, including a Dogwood festival in Fayetteville, North Carolina. Music festivals include North Carolina's Merle Watson Memorial Festival in Wilkesboro, featuring Doc Watson's renowned bluegrass picking.

MAY➤ Festivals take to the air this month with the Hang Gliding Spectacular in Nags Head, North Carolina. Spoleto Festival USA in Charleston, South Carolina, is one of the world's biggest arts festivals; Piccolo Spoleto, running concurrently, showcases local and regional talent. Also in South Carolina, Beaufort's Gullah Festival highlights the fine arts, customs, language, and dress of Low Country blacks.

SUMMER

JUNE➤ Summer gets underway at the Sun Fun Festival on Myrtle Beach's Grand Strand on the South Carolina coast.

JULY➤ Independence Day celebrations are especially colorful in Atlanta, Savannah, and Columbus, Georgia, and in Greenville, South Carolina, which hosts Freedom Weekend Aloft, the second-largest balloon rally in the country. In North Carolina, clog and figure dancing are part of the Shindig-on-the-Green in Asheville, and the annual Highland Games & Gathering of the Scottish Clans is held on Grandfather Mountain near Linville.

AUGUST➤ Happenings around the area include North Carolina's Apple Festival in Hendersonville. August music festivals include a Beach Music Festival in Jekyll Island, Georgia, and the annual Mountain Dance and Folk Festival in Asheville, North Carolina.

AUTUMN

SEPTEMBER➤ In Georgia, Atlanta's Fine Arts and Crafts Festival is held in Piedmont Park, and the Hot Air Balloon Festival floats over Helen. The annual Woolly Worm Festival takes place in Banner Elk, North Carolina.

OCTOBER➤ A barbecue and parade of pigs guarantee fun at the Lexington Barbecue Festival in North Carolina. Oktoberfest is celebrated in Savannah, Georgia, and in Myrtle Beach and Walhalla, South Carolina. The "Ghost Capital of the World"—Georgetown, South Carolina—stages a Ghost Tour.

NOVEMBER➤ Thanksgiving celebrations take place all over. The Catfish Festival takes place in Society Hill, South Carolina, and the Chitlin' Strut in Salley, South Carolina.

2 Georgia

Georgia is notable for its contrasting landscapes and varied cities and towns, each reflecting its own special Southern charm. The northern part of the state has the Appalachian Mountains and their waterfalls; Atlanta, a fast-growing banking center and host for the 1996 Summer Olympics; and Macon, an antebellum town with thousands of cherry trees. Five hours southeast of Atlanta is Savannah, which has the nation's largest historic district, filled with restored Colonial buildings. Along the state's 100-mile coast are the lush, subtropical Golden Isles.

Updated by
Mark Beffart

GEORGIA IS LIKE A CLEVERLY MADE PATCHWORK quilt. First, consider its wildly varied landscapes: from the Appalachian mountains in the north to the pristine white beaches of the Atlantic; to the pine barrens dotted with azaleas and the black-water, gator-infested swamps that make up the state's southern portion. Next, observe its towns, each with its own brand of southern charm: from Dahlonega, site of the nation's first gold rush in 1828; to Helen, a re-created Bavarian-style alpine village in the Blue Ridge Mountains; to graceful Savannah, so beautiful that General Sherman spared the city during the Union Army's destructive march to the sea; to Macon, full of flowering Japanese cherry trees and the ghosts of the antebellum South.

Atlanta, a world apart from all of these, catapulted into the international spotlight when it was named the host city for the 1996 Olympic Games. The undisputed boomtown of the southeast, Atlanta is a vibrant city with a gleaming skyline, largely designed by local architect John Portman. Yet despite the progress, Atlanta has retained its reputation as a city of trees; a bird's eye view of the city from one of those skyscrapers will tell you why.

A five-hour car ride away lies another world. Georgia's 100-mile coast runs from the mouth of the Savannah River south to the mouth of the St. Mary's River. Colonial Savannah lures visitors to its 21 cobblestone squares, giant parterre gardens, waterfront gift shops, jazz bars, and parks draped in Spanish moss.

The seaside resort communities blend southern elegance with a casual sensibility. St. Simons Island, about 70 miles south, attracts a laid-back crowd of anglers, beach-goers, golfers, and tennis players. On nearby Jekyll Island, the lavish lifestyle of America's early 19th-century rich and famous is still evident in their stately Victorian "cottages." Cumberland Island's protected forests and miles of sandy coastline and the dark waters of Okefenokee Swamp are favorite haunts of nature lovers.

Other historical riches include thousand-year-old Native American homesites and burial mounds, antebellum mansions, war heroes' memorials, and intriguing monuments built by eccentric folk artists and obsessive gardeners. Georgia's large number of state parks offer superb facilities for white-water rafting, canoeing, fishing, golf, and tennis, plus nature trails through mountain forests delicately laced with wild rhododendron, dogwoods, and azaleas.

ATLANTA

"Her patron saint is Scarlett O'Hara," the writer James Street once said of Atlanta, "and the town is just like her—shrewd, proud and full of gumption—her Confederate slip showing under a Yankee mink coat."

Although no born-and-bred Atlantan would ever claim to have been influenced by a Yankee, transplanted northerners and those from elsewhere, who account for 50% of the population, have undeniably affected the mood and character of the city. The traditional South, which in a romantic version consists of lacy moss dangling from tree limbs, thick sugary Southern drawls, a leisurely pace, and luxurious antebellum mansions, is rarely found here. Still viewed by diehard Southerners as the heart of the Old Confederacy, Atlanta has emerged from a backward and negative past to become the best example of the New South, a fast-paced, modern city proud of its heritage (the daily newspaper still calls its regional news section "Dixie Living," while a top tourist attraction depicts the Battle of Atlanta during the Civil War) yet one forcefully moving into the future.

From its founding in 1837, Atlanta—then called Terminus—was a vital railroad freight center. Today it's called the "Crossroads of the South," as three interstates converge near downtown and Hartsfield Atlanta International Airport is the nation's third busiest airport in daily passenger flights. Atlanta has emerged as a banking center, and the city is the world headquarters for such Fortune 500 companies as CNN, Coca-Cola, Delta Air Lines, Georgia-Pacific, Holiday Inn Worldwide, Home Depot, Scientific-Atlanta, and United Parcel Service.

Part of the city's vibrancy comes from its international community. Direct flights to Europe, South America, and Asia have made Atlanta easily accessible to the 1,200 international businesses that operate here, and the 48 countries that have representation in the city through consulates, trade offices, and foreign chambers of commerce.

For more than three decades, Atlanta has been linked to the civil rights movement. Among the many accomplishments of Atlanta's African-American community is the Nobel Peace Prize that Martin Luther King Jr. won in 1964. Dr. King's widow, Coretta Scott King, continues to operate the King Center, which she founded after her husband's assassination in 1968, and their four children maintain high profiles in the community. In 1972, Andrew Young was elected the first black congressman from the South since Reconstruction. After serving as Ambassador to the United Nations during President Jimmy Carter's administration, Young was elected mayor of Atlanta. Today, he serves on the city's Olympic committee.

The 1996 Summer Olympics have had a great impact on Atlanta as several new facilities have been created and existing buildings from offices to shopping centers have been renovated and spruced up. Atlanta was picked to join the 20 international cities that have hosted the summer games since 1896 in Athens, Greece. Athletes from 200 countries will descend on Atlanta in July, accompanied by an estimated 2 million other visitors.

Exploring

In the past two decades, Atlanta has experienced unprecedented growth. A good measure of that is its ever-changing downtown skyline, along with skyscrapers constructed in the Midtown, Buckhead, and outer Perimeter business districts. Since the late 1970's, dozens of architecturally dazzling skyscrapers have reshaped the city's profile. Architect John Portman, who graduated from Atlanta's Georgia Tech in 1950, has designed numerous projects, including Peachtree Center, notable as a city within the city. Residents, however, are less likely to measure the city's growth by skyscrapers than by increasing traffic jams, crowds, higher prices, and the ever-burgeoning subdivisions that continue to push the city's limits further and further into surrounding rural areas. Although the Chamber of Commerce advertises Atlanta as a 20-county metropolitan area, the core of Atlanta revolves around five counties. The City of Atlanta is primarily in Fulton and DeKalb counties, with the southern part and the airport in Clayton County. Outside of I–285, Cobb and Gwinnett counties on the northwest and northeast corners of the city are experiencing much of Atlanta's population increase.

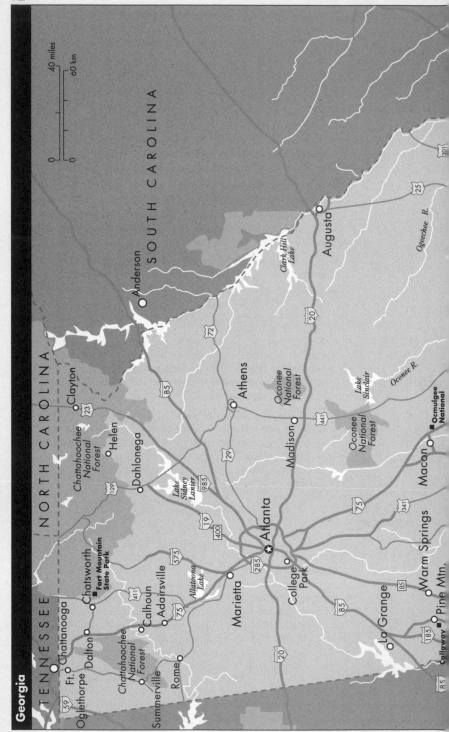

40 miles

60 km

0

0

TENNESSEE

NORTH CAROLINA

SOUTH CAROLINA

Chattanooga

Ft. Oglethorpe

Dalton

Chatsworth

Fort Mountain State Park

Chattahoochee National Forest

Sumnerville

Calhoun

Adairsville

Rome

Helen

Dahlonega

Clayton

Chattahoochee National Forest

Lake Sidney Lanier

Allatoona Lake

Marietta

Atlanta

College Park

La Grange

Warm Springs

Pine Mtn.

Callaway

Anderson

Athens

Madison

Oconee National Forest

Oconee National Forest

Lake Sinclair

Augusta

Clark Hill Lake

Macon

Ocmulgee National

Oconee R.

Ogeechee R.

59

411

75

575

285

400

19

985

129

23

85

72

29

441

20

25

301

75

341

85

85

185

85

20

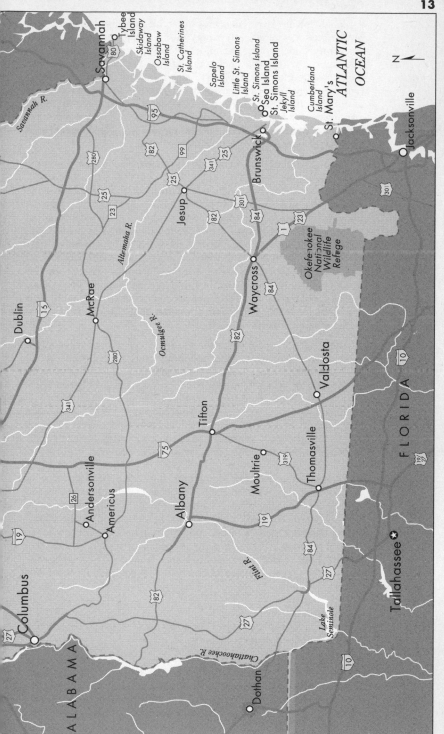

Although downtown offers interesting architecture and some excellent restaurants, it is practically empty during nighttime and weekends (except for Underground Atlanta); for locals, a night on the town usually means a visit to the Buckhead, Virginia-Highland, or Little Five Points neighborhoods. Residents love the area's recreational opportunities—from "shooting the "Hooch" (local talk for riding the rapids of the Chattahoochee River) to waterskiing at Lake Lanier. Atlanta is a young city. At last count, the median age was 28. This youthful face helps account for much of the energy here and has helped Atlanta gain a reputation for nightlife, especially live music.

The main complaint of most residents is traffic—and it may become yours when you visit. With attractions scattered and public transportation limited in some areas, it can be difficult to get to all the sights without your own wheels. Rush-hour traffic runs from about 7 AM (sometimes earlier) to 9 AM and from 4:30 PM to about 7 PM. If you can, avoid interstates and such main streets as Piedmont Road, Peachtree Road, and Ponce de Leon Avenue during these hours. In particular, steer clear of I–285, which encircles the city and is always jam-packed with traffic. Known by locals as "the perimeter," it is filled with trucks who cannot come into Atlanta on the other interstates unless they have a delivery, and commuters who have no other choice but to use it. It is notorious for traffic snarls and delays due to accidents, bad drivers, and continuous road construction.

Atlanta's lack of a grid system in most parts of the city will confuse some drivers. With many hills and meandering streets, locals like to tell visitors that the city's streets follow ancient cow paths and Native American trails, which have since been paved, renamed, and given lights. Whether this is the truth or legend doesn't help you much when you are looking for an address on a winding road and trying to pay attention to the traffic. At the same time, you'll discover some streets changing their name along the same stretch of road, including the city's most famous thoroughfare, Peachtree Street, which follows a mountain ridge from downtown to suburban Norcross outside of north I-285; it becomes Peachtree Road after it crosses I-85 and then Peachtree Industrial Boulevard beyond the Buckhead neighborhood. And to add to the confusion, there are 60 other streets in the metropolitan area with the word Peachtree in their names. Before setting out anywhere, get the complete street address of your destination, including whether it has a NE, NW, SE, or SW suffix at the end of address (which indicates the part of town you need to be in); Peachtree Street is the division line for east and west, and Five Points (downtown) for north and south.

Downtown

Numbers in the margin correspond to points of interest on the Downtown Atlanta and Atlanta Vicinity maps.

The Martin Luther King Jr. National Historic District occupies several blocks on Auburn Avenue, a few blocks east of Peachtree Street. In the black business community of Sweet Auburn, the neighborhood was the birthplace of Martin Luther King Jr., the undisputed leader of the civil rights movement, in 1929. After his assassination in 1968, King's widow, Coretta Scott King, established the **King Center.** It contains a museum with King's Nobel Peace Prize, bible, and typewriter, as well as photos chronicling the Civil Rights Movement, plus a library, souvenir gift shop, and meeting rooms for educational programs. If enough funding is available, a **Civil Rights Museum** will open at the center in

1996. In the courtyard, on a circular brick pad in the middle of a rect-angular "meditation" pool, is King's white marble tomb, where an eter-nal flame burns and the inscription reads, "Free at last!" Tours of Sweet Auburn, given by National Park Service guides, commence from here. *449 Auburn Ave.,* ☎ *404/524–1956.* ☛ *Free.* ☉ *Daily 9–5:30.*

❷ Next door is **Ebenezer Baptist Church** (407 Auburn Ave., ☎ 404/688–7263), a Gothic-Revival style building completed in 1922, which be-came known as the spiritual center for the movement after Dr. King won the Nobel Peace Prize in 1964. Members of the King family have preached at the church for three generations; Dr. King's funeral was here.

❸ **Dr. King's birthplace** (501 Auburn Ave., ☎ 404/331–1590), a Queen Anne–style bungalow, is managed by the National Park Service and is open to the public daily.

❹ **Auburn Avenue** is still the heart of the black community's entrepreneurial district. The landmark **Atlanta Life Insurance Company,** founded by Alonzo Herndon, was located in modest quarters at 148 Auburn Av-enue until the modern complex at No. 100 was opened in 1980.

❺ At 145 Auburn Avenue is the **Atlanta Daily World** building, home of one of the nation's oldest black newspapers. The church with the "Jesus Saves" sign on its steeple is the Big Bethel African Methodist
❻ Episcopal Church. Nearby is the **Royal Peacock** (186 Auburn Ave., ☎ 404/880–0745, ☉ daily 4 PM–2 AM), the club where the king and queen of soul—James Brown and Aretha Franklin—frequently held court in the '60s. Now it's the home of reggae, hip-hop, and international music.

❼ For a history of Sweet Auburn, view the permanent exhibit at the **African American Panoramic Experience(APEX);** there are also changing exhibits on African-American culture. *135 Auburn Ave.,* ☎ *404/521–2739.* ☛ *$2 adults, $1 children.* ☉ *Tues.–Sat. 10–5.*

❽ On Edgewood Avenue is the **Sweet Auburn Curb Market** (209 Edge-wood Ave., ☎ 404/659–1665, ☉ Mon.–Sat. 8 AM–5:45 PM), a thriv-ing food market where you can buy every part of the pig but the oink—as well as vegetables, fish, and meat. At 125 Edgewood Avenue is the site of the first bottling plant for the Coca-Cola Company—today
❾ occupied by the **Baptist Student Center** for the adjoining campus of **Geor-gia State University.** Take a shortcut through the urban GSU campus
❿ toward the glittering gold dome of the **Georgia State Capitol,** a Re-naissance-style building dedicated on July 4, 1889. The capitol's dome was gilded in 1958 with gold leaf mined from Dahlonega, a small town in north Georgia. In addition to housing politicos, it also contains a Georgia history museum, which is open to the public. State historical markers on the grounds commemorate the 1864 Battle of Atlanta, which destroyed 90% of the city. *206 Washington St.,* ☎ *404/656–2844. Free guided tours every ½ hr, weekdays 9:30–11:30, 1–2.*

⓫ Across the street from the capitol's southwest corner is Atlanta's **City Hall** (68 Mitchell St.). When this 14-story, neo-Gothic structure with lavish marble interior was built in 1926, critics dubbed it "The Painted Lady of Mitchell Street."

⓬ The **Five Points MARTA** station (corner of Peachtree and Alabama streets, downtown) services Underground Atlanta and nearby Woodruff Park, Georgia State University, city and county government offices, and numerous businesses. Stand on the corner of Peachtree and Alabama streets, outside the station, and notice the old-fashioned gas street

Downtown Atlanta

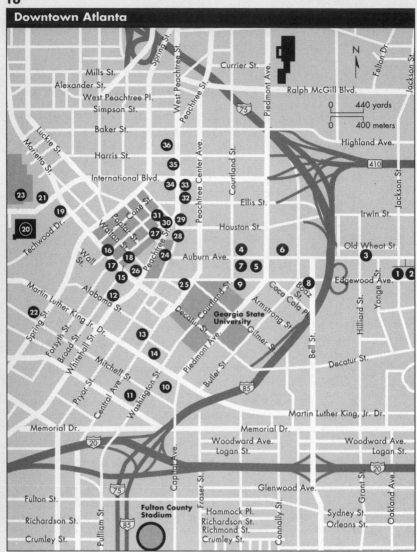

African American Panoramic Experience, **7**

Atlanta Daily World, **5**

Atlanta-Fulton County Public Library, **31**

Atlanta History Center, **46**

Atlanta Life Insurance Company, **4**

Bank of the South Building, **16**

Baptist Student Center, **9**

The Candler Building, **28**

Capital City Club, **36**

City Hall, **11**

CNN Center, **19**

Dr. King's Birthplace, **3**

Ebenezer Baptist Church, **2**

Fay Gold Gallery, **45**

Fernbank Museum of Natural History, **52**

Fernbank Science Center, **53**

Five Points MARTA, **12**

The Flatiron Building, **27**

Fox Theatre, **38**

Georgia Dome, **23**

Georgia Governor's Mansion, **47**

Atlanta Vicinity

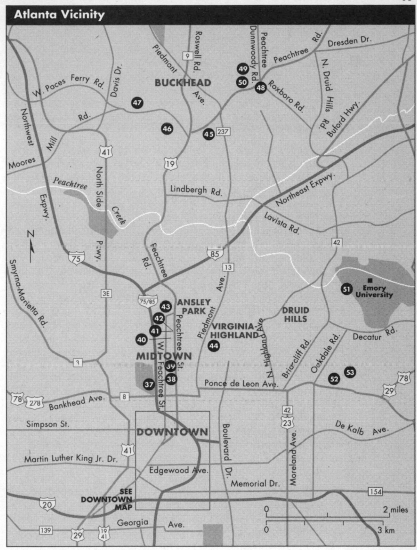

Georgia-Pacific
Building, **29**

Georgia State
Capitol **10**

Healy Building, **18**

High Museum
of Art, **42**

The Hurt Building, **25**

King Center, **1**

Lenox Square, **48**

Margaret Mitchell
Park, **30**

Michael C. Carlos
Museum, **51**

Nation's Bank
Building, **15**

Nation's Bank Plaza
Tower, **37**

Omni, **20**

One Atlantic Center/
IBM Tower, **40**

One Ninety
OnePeachtree
Tower, **33**

Peachtree Center, **35**

Phipps Plaza, **49**

Piedmont Park, **44**

Rhodes Memorial
Hall, **43**

Richard B. Russell
Federal Building, **22**

Ritz-Carlton
Buckhead, **50**

Ritz-Carlton Hotel, **32**

Road to Tara
Museum, **39**

Royal Peacock, **6**

Sweet Auburn Curb
Market, **8**

Statue of Henry
Grady, **17**

Underground
Atlanta, **13**

Westin-Peachtree
Plaza Hotel, **34**

The William Oliver
Building, **26**

Woodruff Arts
Center, **41**

Woodruff Park, **24**

World Congress
Center, **21**

The World of
Coca-Cola, **14**

light, with its historic marker proclaiming it as the **Eternal Flame of the Confederacy.**

⑬ Across from the Five Points MARTA Station and at Plaza. Depot are entrances to **Underground Atlanta** (☎ 404/523–2311). This six-block entertainment and shopping district was created from the web of underground brick streets, ornamental building facades, and tunnels that fell into disuse in 1929, when the city built viaducts over the train tracks. Merchants moved their storefronts to the new viaduct level, leaving the original street level for storage.

Developed as a tourist attraction in the late 1960's, then closed in the late 1970's due to a lack of popularity and crime problems, Underground was resurrected in 1989 by the Rouse Company, the creators of Baltimore's highly successful Harborplace. Given their track record, it was expected to draw scores of residents and visitors back to the downtown area. Unfortunately, most residents, especially suburbanites, avoid downtown due to its reputation for crime (not totally unfounded, so exercise caution, especially at night). Therefore, the result has been disappointing, with conventioneers and tourists a stronger presence than locals, who opt for Midtown, Buckhead, and Virginia-Highland night spots instead. Still, Underground's atmosphere is lively enough—if a bit contrived—on weekend nights. The complex accommodates 50 specialty shops, as well as 22 fast-food vendors and 15 restaurants and nightclubs on three levels. Merchants—45–50—selling their wares from push-carts add to the carnival atmosphere. The entertainment strip, Kenny's Alley—once occupied by saloons and livery stables—styles itself as Atlanta's version of New Orleans's Bourbon Street, with bars and night spots offering comedy acts, a variety of music (rock, country, pop, folk, jazz), and dancing. **Dante's Down the Hatch** stars live alligators, fondue, and jazz and is a favorite of locals and tourists alike. Underground's main entrance is highlighted by the Peachtree Fountains Plaza, with its distinctive 138-foot light tower, a stage where various special events take place, and a series of cascading waterfalls and splashing fountains. Two parking garages are on Martin Luther King Jr. (locally, MLK) Drive.

Look closely for the historic markers that dot Underground Atlanta. Opposite the Plaza Depot entrance is downtown's oldest building, the Georgia Railroad Freight Depot. Built in 1869 with three stories (to replace the one torched by Sherman's troops in 1864), it was once the city's tallest building, but a fire reduced it to a single story in 1935. It is now used by several downtown companies as a meeting hall and for special events.

⑭ Across the plaza from the Depot and the entrance to Kenny's Alley is the **World of Coca-Cola** (55 Martin Luther King Jr. Dr., ☎ 404/676–5151), where you can sip samples of more than 100 Coke products from around the world and marvel over memorabilia from more than a century's worth of corporate archives in this four-story, $10 million facility.

⑮ From Five Points (Peachtree and Marietta Sts.) head down Marietta Street into Atlanta's banking district, stopping at the **NationsBank Building** (35 Broad St.) to see the lavish lobby designed by noted architect Philip Shutze and the 21-story **Bank of the South Building** (55 Marietta St.), Atlanta's tallest building from 1955–64.

⑰ At the corner of Marietta and Forsyth streets is a bronze **statue of Henry Grady,** the post–Civil War editor of the *Atlanta Constitution* and early champion of the so-called "New South." To the right at 57 Forsyth

⑱ Street is the **Healy Building,** an early skyscraper (1913) with Tudor decoration. At 72 Marietta Street are the offices of the *Atlanta Journal-Constitution.* Its lobby features a display of front page news documenting historic events and photographs of famous individuals who have worked for the paper. Next door is the **Federal Reserve Bank.** Tours of its monetary museum can be arranged. *104 Marietta St.,* ☎ *404/521–8747.* ☞ *Free.* ⊙ *Weekdays 9–4.*

⑲ Two blocks away, at the corner of Marietta Street and Techwood Drive, is **CNN Center,** the home of Ted Turner's Cable News Network. The 45-minute CNN studio tour begins with a ride up the world's longest escalator to an eighth-floor exhibit on Turner's global broadcasting empire. This center will serve as the command post to thousands of international journalists during the Olympics. *1 CNN Center,* ☎ *404/827–2300. Tour reservations strongly recommended.* ☞ *$6 adults, $4 senior citizens, $3.50 children under 13. Not recommended for children under 6.* ⊙ *Daily 9–5:30. Closed major holidays.*

⑳ Behind the CNN Center is the **Omni** (100 Techwood Dr.), home to the Atlanta Hawks NBA basketball team and Atlanta Knights minor league hockey team, as well as the site of special events, from rock concerts to the 1988 Democratic National Convention. The Hawks plan to build a new arena in the north suburbs by 1996, leaving the Omni's future
㉑ in doubt. The **World Congress Center** (285 International Blvd.), used primarily for large conventions and trade shows, is across the street.
㉒ A couple of blocks south is the **Richard B. Russell Federal Building** (Spring St. between Mitchell St. and Martin Luther King Jr. Dr.), the largest building in Atlanta owned by the U.S. government; its lobby features magnificent tile mosaics and art.

㉓ The 70,500-seat **Georgia Dome** (1 Georgia Dome Dr.), with a white, plum, and turquoise facade, is the site of Atlanta Falcons football games, major rock concerts, conventions, and trade shows. A design team of local architects crowned the 1-million-square-foot facility with the world's largest cable-supported oval, giving the roof a circus-tent top.

㉔ Returning to Five Points by foot or MARTA Rail, visit **Woodruff Park** (Peachtree St. and Park Pl.), named after the city's great philanthropist, Robert W. Woodruff, the late Coca-Cola magnate; it presents a cross section of Atlanta life. During lunchtime on weekdays, the park is filled with executives, street preachers, politicians, Georgia State University students, and homeless people.

Not much of old Atlanta still exists downtown, although a few turn-of-the-century buildings remain. These elaborately decorated structures stand in sharp contrast to the postmodern skyscrapers of recent years.
㉕ The **Hurt Building** (45 Edgewood Ave.) features intricate grillwork and
㉖ an elaborate marble staircase. The **William–Oliver Building** (32 Peachtree St.) is an Art Deco gem. Walk through its lobby and admire the ceil-
㉗ ing mural, brass grills, and elevator doors. The **Flatiron Building** (84 Peachtree St.) dates from 1897 and is the city's oldest high rise. The
㉘ magnificent mosaic lobby of the **Candler Building** (127 Peachtree St.) shouldn't be missed.

㉙ The towering, 52-story **Georgia-Pacific Building** (133 Peachtree St. at John Wesley Dobbs Ave.) occupies hallowed ground, the site of the old Loew's Grand Theatre, where *Gone with the Wind* premiered in 1939. One of the architectural oddities of this red-marble high rise is that from certain angles the building appears to be two-dimensional, or flat against the sky. The **High Museum of Art Folk Art and Photography**

Galleries is inside the building. *30 John Wesley Dobbs Ave.,* ☎ *404/577–6940.* ☛ *Free.* ☾ *Mon.–Sat. 10–5.*

③⓪ Across from the Georgia-Pacific building is the miniscule **Margaret Mitchell Park,** with its cascading waterfall and columned sculpture. Within sight of the park named for Atlanta's most famous author is
③① the **Atlanta–Fulton County Public Library** (126 Carnegie Way), which houses a large collection of *Gone with the Wind* memorabilia and newspapers from most major cities in the United States and elsewhere on its fourth floor.

③② On the next corner is the downtown **Ritz-Carlton Hotel** (181 Peachtree St.), elegant with the company's trademark 18th- and 19th-century En-
③③ glish antiques. The Ritz-Carlton's neighbor is **One Ninety One Peachtree Tower,** designed by Philip Johnson.

Across the street is **Macy's** department store (180 Peachtree St.), and
③④ next to it is the 73-story **Westin Peachtree Plaza Hotel** (210 Peachtree St.). Designed by Atlanta architect John Portman, the glassy, cylindrical tower with its trademark exterior elevator features a postmodern interior and the Sundial, a revolving bar/restaurant offering the best panoramic view of the city. Until a few years ago, it was the tallest building in the city.

③⑤ In the next block, on both sides of the street, is **Peachtree Center,** also designed by John Portman. This complex, with its connecting skywalks, includes the massive **Atlanta Market Center,** housing the **Merchandise Mart, Apparel Mart, Gift Mart and Inforum** (technological companies); and the twin office towers of Peachtree Center, with an underground shopping and restaurant area. The adjacent **Hyatt Regency Hotel,** a block north on Peachtree Street and connected to the center by a skywalk, is another Portman creation, a model when it was built in 1967 for other American hotels with its bunkerlike exterior, low entrance, soaring atrium, and blue-domed Polaris Lounge.

Behind Peachtree Center in the Marriott Marquis Two Tower is the **Atlanta International Museum of Art and Design,** which exhibits art and crafts from around the globe. *285 Peachtree Center Ave.,* ☎ *404/688–2467.* ☛ *Free.* ☾ *Tues.–Sat. 11–5.*

③⑥ Dwarfed by the skyscrapers around it, the modestly sized Italian Renaissance-style **Capital City Club** (7 Harris St.), built in 1911, continues to attract the city's power brokers.

Midtown
Just north of downtown lies this thriving area, a former hippie hangout in the late '60s and '70s, now populated by a large segment of the city's gay population who reside in the area. Formerly in decline, a massive gentrification program during the past decade has transformed Midtown into one of the city's most interesting neighborhoods. Its gleaming new office towers give it a skyline to rival downtown, and the renovated mansions and bungalows in its residential section have made it a city showcase. As the city's primary art and theater district, complimented by several interesting bars and restaurants, it is a favorite of Atlantans for nighttime entertainment. Our tour takes you north along Peachtree Street and then east to Piedmont Park.

③⑦ Built in 1992, the **NationsBankPlaza Tower** (600 Peachtree St. at North Ave.), its graceful birdcage roof easily visible from the interstate, is the South's tallest building at 1,023 feet. Its elegant and marbled central lobby is worth seeing.

38 The not-to-be-missed **Fox Theatre** is one of only a handful of classic movie palaces in the nation saved from the wrecker's ball. It was built in 1929 in a fabulous Moorish-Egyptian style to be the headquarters for the Shriner's Club. The interior's crowning glory is its "sky" ceiling—complete with clouds and stars above Alhambralike minarets. The Fox is still a prime venue for Broadway shows, rock concerts, dance performances, and film festivals. *660 Peachtree St.,* ☎ *404/881–2100 or 404/876–2040.* ☛ *Tour $5 adults, $4 senior citizens, $3 students. Tours given Mon. and Thurs. at 10 AM, Sat. at 10 AM and 11:30 AM.*

TIME OUT A few blocks from the Fox, in an old drugstore with the original tile floors and pressed-tin ceilings, is a branch of **Mick's** (557 Peachtree St. at Linden St., ☎ 404/875-6425), a popular Atlanta chain featuring great burgers and traditional American food.

39 Across the street from the Fox is the **Road to Tara Museum.** This museum, named for the original title of *Gone with the Wind,* houses an impressive collection of *Gone with the Wind* memorabilia from around the world. Especially peachy are the David O. Selznick Screening Room, where clips on the making of the film classic are shown, and the new costume gallery. *Georgian Terrace Apartments, 659 Peachtree St.,* ☎ *404/897–1939.* ☉ *Mon.–Sat. 10–6, Sun. 1–6.*

At Peachtree and 10th streets once stood a piece of Atlanta history, the dilapidated apartment house where Margaret Mitchell penned *Gone with the Wind.* Fought over for years by historical preservationists who wanted to make it a national landmark and developers who highly desired the land on which it stood, the building was destroyed by arson in September 1994. Daimler-Benz, AG of Stuttgart, Germany, makers of Mercedes-Benz automobiles, have pledged to rebuild it in time for the 1996 Summer Olympics.

40 Down 14th Street is **One Atlantic Center** (1201 W. Peachtree St.), also known as the **IBM Tower.** Visible from many parts of the city, this pyramid-topped office tower with a Gothic motif, built in 1987, was designed by Philip Johnson.

41 The **Woodruff Arts Center** (1280 Peachtree St.) is home to the world-renowned **Atlanta Symphony Orchestra** and the **Alliance Theatre.** The Alliance has a primary stage, where mainstream works are produced for general audiences, and a downstairs studio that offers innovative productions.

42 Next door is the bold white porcelain–paneled **High Museum of Art,** a building that many call far superior to the collection within. This high-tech showplace built in 1983 is the award-winning design of premier architect Richard Meier. In 1991, the American Institute of Architects listed the sleek museum among the 10 best works of American architecture of the 1980s. Best bets among the museum's permanent collection are its American decorative arts collection and its African folk art collection. Several temporary exhibits featuring major artists and art movements are held here each year. *1280 Peachtree St.,* ☎ *404/733–4444 for recorded information.* ☛ *$6 adults, $4 students and senior citizens, $2 children 6–17; free Thurs. after 1. Special exhibits often have an additional charge.* ☉ *Tues.–Thurs. 10–5, Fri. 10–9, Sat. 10–5, Sun. noon–5.*

43 North on Peachtree Street, **Rhodes Memorial Hall,** headquarters of the **Georgia Trust for Historic Preservation,** is one of the finest works of Willis F. Denny II. Built of Stone Mountain granite in 1904 for Amos Giles Rhodes, the wealthy founder of a local furniture chain, the hall now shelters a permanent exhibit on Atlanta architecture of bygone eras. *1516 Peachtree St.,* ☎ *404/881–9980.* ☞ *$2.* ⊙ *Weekdays 11– 4.*

㊹ A few blocks off Peachtree Street is beautiful **Piedmont Park,** the city's outdoor recreation center and the site of most *plein air* festivals and events in Atlanta's calendar (a source of rancor for those who say the numerous mega-events scheduled there each year result in damage to the park and excessive traffic congestion in and around the area during the events). Tennis courts; a swimming pool; and paths for walking, jogging, and rollerblading are part of the attraction, but many retreat to the park's great lawn for picnics with a smashing view of the Midtown skyline. Each April the park hosts the popular Dogwood Festival, and in September is the nine-day Arts Festival of Atlanta. The **Atlanta Botanical Garden** (1345 Piedmont Ave. at the Prado, ☎ 404/876–5859), occupying 60 acres inside the park, has 15 acres of formal gardens; a 15-acre hardwood forest with walking trails; a serene Japanese garden; and the Fuqua Conservatory, featuring unusual and threatened flora from tropical and desert climates. A whimsical dragon topiary guards the entrance. ☞ *$6.50 adults, $4.75 children 6–12 and senior citizens; free Thurs. 1–6.* ⊙ *Tues.–Sun. 9–6.*

Buckhead

Take to the road for the remainder of the tours; Atlanta's sprawl doesn't lend itself to walking. Drive north on Peachtree Road to **Buckhead,** the heart of affluent and trendy Atlanta. Many of Atlanta's see-and-be-seen restaurants, music clubs, chic shops, and hip art galleries are concentrated in this neighborhood. Finding a parking spot on the weekends can be a real headache, and waits of two hours or more are common in the hottest restaurants.

㊺ Start a tour at the **Fay Gold Gallery** (247 Buckhead Ave., ☎ 404/233– 3843; ⊙ Tues.–Fri. 9:30–5:30, Sat. 10–6), noted for its shows of nationally renowned contemporary artists. Fine photography is sold at the **Jackson Fine Art Gallery** (3115 E. Shadowlawn, ☎ 404/233– 3739).

TIME OUT   **Café Tu Tu Tango** (220 Pharr Rd., ☎ 404/841–6222), a small space with local art—and artists—in every nook and cranny, serves tasty tapas throughout the day. At night, the crush of Buckhead's beautiful people often means two-hour waits for tables.

㊻ A short distance west of the Buckhead commercial district is the **Atlanta History Center**. The 28-foot-high atrium in its museum highlights materials native to Georgia, with a floor of heart pine and polished Stone Mountain granite. Displays are provocative, juxtaposing *Gone with the Wind* romanticism with the grim reality of Ku Klux Klan racism. Also on the 32-acre site, but not new to it, are the elegant **Swan House,** a Palladian mansion designed by architect Philip Trammell Shutze in 1926; the **Tullie Smith Plantation,** a two-story plantation house (1845) brought here from another Georgia site; **McElreath Hall,** an exhibition space for artifacts from Atlanta's history, with lectures given in its auditorium; and the **Coach House Restaurant**. *130 W. Paces Ferry Rd.,* ☎ *404/814–4000.* ☞ *$7 adults, $5 senior citizens and students, $3 children 5–17, under 5 free.* ⊙ *Mon.–Sat. 10–5:30, Sun. noon–5.*

㊼ The **Georgia Governor's Mansion** is a few blocks farther on West Paces Ferry Road. Built in the late 1970s in Greek Revival style, the house features Federal-period antiques in its public rooms. *391 W. Paces*

Ferry Rd., ☎ *404/261–1858.* ☛ *Free. Guided tours Tues.–Thurs. 10–11:30 AM.*

Beyond here, look for the green-and-white "Scenic Drive" signs along Tuxedo, Valley, and Habersham roads to get a look at the lawns, gardens, and mansions of Atlanta's well-to-do. Greek Revival, Spanish, Italianate, English Tudor, and French château mansions vie for viewers' attention.

At the intersection of Peachtree Street and Lenox Road are Atlanta's
48 two premier shopping malls: **Lenox Square,** which boasts 268 stores
49 with its new second level, and the newly refurbished and enlarged **Phipps Plaza,** which now has 200 stores. At the latter, catering to well-to-do shoppers, such amenities as valet parking and concierge service are taken in stride. Break up boutique visits with a stop at **Il Centro,** the center's chic coffee bar, or one of several restaurants here.

50 Across the street lies the **Ritz-Carlton Buckhead,** next door to the luxury hotel chain's headquarters. Considered one of the finest hotels in the country, it contains one of the South's most valuable private art collections, primarily 18th- and 19th-century American and European painting, sculpture, and porcelain. It's also home to Atlanta's only five-star restaurant, the **Dining Room** (*see* Dining, *below*).

Virginia-Highland and the Emory Area
Restaurants, bars, and art galleries are the backbone of the eclectic Virginia-Highland/Morningside neighborhood, northeast of Midtown. Emory University, site of the Centers for Disease Control and one of the city's cultural and academic hubs, lies east of here. A number of museums and other attractions are scattered throughout the area.

51 The postmodern **Michael C. Carlos Museum**'s interior was designed by architect Michael Graves. Exhibits range from an Egyptian mummy to contemporary art. *Emory University, 571 Kilgo St.,* ☎ *404/727–4282. Suggested donation: $3.* ☉ *Mon.–Sat. 10–4:30, Fri. 10–9, Sun. noon–5; closed major holidays.*

Drive east on North Decatur Avenue, turn right on Clifton Road, and
52 continue for 1 mile to the **Fernbank Museum of Natural History,** which maintains the largest natural history collection south of the Smithsonian. A permanent exhibit, "A Walk Through Time in Georgia," takes the visitor through 15 galleries to explore the beauty of the state. The museum's IMAX theater shows films on a six-story screen. *767 Clifton Rd.,* ☎ *404/370–0960, 404/370–0019 (IMAX only), or 404/370–0850 (directions hot line).* ☛ *$5.50 adults, $4.50 students and senior citizens, under 2 free; prices vary for IMAX.* ☉ *Tues.–Thurs., Sat. 10–5, Fri. 10–9, Sun. noon–5; closed Dec. 25.*

From the museum, turn left on Ponce de Leon Avenue and left again on Altwood Road. A right onto Heaton Park Drive takes you to the
53 large planetarium at the **Fernbank Science Center,** the only one in the nation owned by a public school system. This small museum focuses on geology, space exploration, and ecology; older children will likely find its displays outdated. *156 Heaton Park Dr.,* ☎ *404/378–4311.* ☛ *Museum free (planetarium shows: $2 adults, $1 students).* ☉ *Mon. 8:30–5 (except for Planetarium), Tues.–Fri. 8:30–10, Sat. 10–5, Sun. 1–5.*

Although you can walk much of the Virginia-Highland area, with most points of interest being along or off North Highland Avenue, you'll often find clusters of shops, restaurants, and galleries separated by longish stretches of residential area. If you plan to do the entire area, a car is your best bet; parking is usually available along the street or in lots behind or next to stores. Virginia-Highland's funky galleries specialize in works by local and regional contemporary artists. The **Modern Primitive Gallery** (1402 N. Highland Ave., ☎ 404/892–0556) features the folk art of Howard Finster, an internationally recognized artist who has done album covers for the rock bands REM and the Talking Heads. For a touch of nostalgia, check out **20th Century Antiques** (1044 N. Highland Ave., ☎ 404/892–2065).

Nearby, about 2 miles south of Virginia Avenue via North Highland Avenue, is the **Carter Presidential Center,** located on the site where General Sherman orchestrated the Battle of Atlanta. The museum and archives focus on Jimmy Carter's political career, while the center sponsors foreign affairs conferences and projects on such issues as world food supply. Outside, its Japanese garden is a serene spot to unwind. *1 Copenhill Ave.,* ☎ *404/420–5100.* ☛ *$4 adults, $3 senior citizens, children under 16 free.* ⊙ *Mon.–Sat. 9–4:45, Sun. noon–4:45 except major holidays. Cafeteria open Mon.–Sat. 11–4, Sun. noon–4:30.*

When you tire of gallery-hopping, some of the city's best restaurants and bars are here (*see* Dining, *below*).

What to See and Do with Children

The "Weekend" tabloid section of Saturday's *Atlanta Journal-Constitution* has a listing called "Kids," which highlights special happenings around the city for youngsters.

American Adventures/White Water Atlanta. The former, with a $1 million tree house, 15 indoor and outdoor rides, miniature golf, a race-car track, and Imagination Station, will keep your children busy for hours. The latter features more than 40 water attractions, including the largest kid's water playground in the country. After you've worked up an appetite, visit one of the attraction's five restaurants. *250 North Cobb Parkway, Marietta,* ☎ *404/424–9283.* ☛ *From $9.99 per child, depending on what park you visit, age, and few other factors; $2 for parking.* ⊙ *Memorial Day–Labor Day, Mon.–Thurs. 11–7, weekends 10–9; Labor Day–Memorial Day, hours vary—call ahead.*

Center for Puppetry Arts. This center, designed to teach visitors about the craft, displays puppets from all over the world. Children who attend a workshop on puppet making take home their creations. Performances by professional puppeteers leave youngsters spellbound. *1404 Spring St. at 18th St.,* ☎ *404/873–3391.* ☛ *$3 adults, $2 children 13 and under. Not recommended for children below age 4.* ⊙ *Mon.–Sat. 9–5.*

Chattahoochee Nature Center. Birds and animals in their natural habitats may be seen from nature trails and a boardwalk winding through 100 acres of woodlands and wetlands. *9135 Willeo Rd., Roswell,* ☎ *404/992–2055.* ☛ *$2 adults, $1 children and senior citizens.* ⊙ *Daily 9–5.*

SciTrek. The Science and Technology Museum of Atlanta covers 96,000 square feet of space and has about 100 hands-on exhibits in four halls: Simple Machines; Light, Color, and Perception; Electricity and Magnetism; and Kidspace, for children ages two to seven. *395 Piedmont Ave.,* ☎ *404/522–5500.* ☛ *$7 adults, $5 children 3–17 and senior citizens, under 3 free.* ⊙ *Mon.–Sat. 10–5, Sun. noon–5.*

Six Flags Over Georgia. This is Atlanta's major theme park, with more than 100 rides, many of them heart-stopping roller coasters and water rides (the latter best saved for last to prevent being damp all day). An especially popular spectacle is the Batman Stunt Show. The park also features well-staged musical revues, diving demonstrations, concerts by top-name artists, and other performances. *I–20W at 7561 Six Flags Rd., Austell,* ☎ *404/739–3400.* ☛ *(all-inclusive 1-day pass) $28 adults, $14 ages 55 and older, $19 children 3–9, under 3 free; $5 parking fee.* ☉ *10 AM–11 PM daily in summer, with weekend-only operations Mar.–May and Sept.–Oct. Closed Nov.–Feb.; closing times vary. Take MARTA's West Line to Hightower Station and then Six Flags bus (No. 201).*

Stone Mountain Park. This park features the largest exposed granite outcropping on earth. The Confederate Memorial on the north face of the 825-foot-high domed mountain is the world's largest sculpture. The 3,200-acre state park has a skylift to the mountaintop, a steam locomotive ride around the mountain's 5-mile-diameter base, an antebellum plantation, two golf courses, a swimming beach, a campground, two hotels, a resort and conference center, an upscale restaurant, a paddle wheel steamboat, and a Civil War museum. Summer nights are capped with a laser light show, and annual events like the Yellow Daisy Festival and the Scottish Highland Games are well attended. *U.S. 78, Stone Mountain Pkwy.,* ☎ *404/498–5600.* ☛ *$5 per car, $20 annual pass; additional fees for attractions and special events.* ☉ *Daily 6 AM–midnight.*

Zoo Atlanta. Recently named by *Good Housekeeping* magazine as one of the top 10 zoos in the United States, Zoo Atlanta has more than 1,000 animals inhabiting its property. An ongoing $35-million renovation program has already produced the Birds of Prey Amphitheater, the Ford African Rain Forest, Flamingo Lagoon, Masai Mara (re-created plains of Kenya), Sumatran Tiger Exhibit, and the new Sea Lion Cove. Longtime resident gorilla, Willie B., and his child, Kudzu, who was conceived a few years ago after a decade of trying, are always hits with zoo visitors. *Grant Park, 800 Cherokee Ave.,* ☎ *404/624–5600.* ☛ *$6 adults and children 12 and older, $4 children 3–11, under 3 free.* ☉ *Daily 10–4:30 (10–5:30 on weekends during daylight savings time); closed major holidays.*

Off the Beaten Path

Just 30 minutes north of Atlanta, **Chateau Elan** (7000 Old Winder Hwy., I–85 to GA 211, exit 48, Braselton, ☎ 404/932–0900 or 800/233–9463, FAX 404/271–6005), a 16th-century–style French chateau and Georgia's premiere winery, sits on 2,400 rolling acres. Winery tours and tastings are free; European luxury blends with southern hospitality at the 144-room inn and newly opened spa. Rounding out the offerings are two golf courses, fishing, tennis, an equestrian center, an art gallery, a restaurant, a wine market, and a gift shop.

Shopping

Atlanta is second only to Chicago in space devoted to shopping areas, and its department stores, specialty shops, large enclosed malls, and antiques markets draw shoppers from across the Southeast. Most stores are open Monday–Saturday 10–9:30, Sunday noon–6. Many downtown stores close Sunday. Sales tax is 6% in the city of Atlanta and Fulton County, and 4%–5% in the suburbs.

Unlike many urban centers, downtown stores—although not abundant—do a steady business. Stores here are anchored on the north by Peachtree Center's **Mall,** with 30 retailers, including **Brooks Brothers** (235 Peachtree St., ☎ 404/577–4040) in its Gaslight Tower, and by **Underground's** 46 retailers on the south end. In between are **Macy's** (180 Peachtree St., ☎ 404/221–7221) and the **Limited** (209 Peachtree St., ☎ 404/523–1728).

At the intersection of Peachtree and Lenox roads, 8 miles north of downtown, are two of Atlanta's oldest and most popular shopping malls (*see* Buckhead, *above*). **Lenox Square Mall,** the largest shopping space (per square foot) in Atlanta, has branches of **Neiman Marcus, Macy's, Rich's;** 265 other specialty stores ; and restaurants and fast food chains in its large food court. Diagonally across the street from Lenox is the upscale **Phipps Plaza,** catering more to the tastes of the affluent with branches of **Saks Fifth Avenue, Lord & Taylor, Parisian, Gucci, Tiffany & Co., Abercrombie & Fitch,** and other small specialty shops. Phipps will more than double its size from 90 to 200 stores by July 1996, with a new wing that includes a branch of **Bloomingdale's.**

Cumberland Mall (Cobb Parkway at I–285) and the more upscale **Galleria Specialty Mall** (One Galleria Parkway) offer prime shopping for residents of Atlanta's northwestern suburbs. The refurbished **Northlake Mall,** east of the I–85/I–285 intersection, is anchored by **Macy's** and a new **Parisian** department store. The newest entry on the mall scene, the vast **North Point Mall** (1000 North Point Circle, Alpharetta), has five department stores. About 15 minutes north of Lenox Square Mall, in the affluent suburb of Dunwoody, is **Perimeter Mall** (4400 Ashford–Dunwoody Rd.), known for upscale family shopping, with shops such as the **High Museum of Art Gift Shop, Gap Kids,** and the **Nature Company.** Also child-friendly are **Town Center** (400 Barrett Parkway, Kennesaw) and **Gwinnett Place Mall** (2100 Pleasant Hill Rd., Duluth), both with on-site child-care facilities.

Outlets

Atlanta and surrounding towns are a bargain-hunter's delight. For new clothes and shoes, **Macy's Close-Out** at **Avondale Mall** (3588 Memorial Dr., Decatur, tel 404/286–0829) and **Rich's Finale** at **Greenbriar Mall** (2841 Greenbriar Parkway, ☎ 404/346–2615) are two of the best discounters here. **Ballard's Backroom Catalog Clearance Center** (1670 Defoor Ave., ☎ 404/352–2776) carries the uniquely designed rugs, lamps, tables, and pillows usually available only through Ballard Design's stylish catalogs.

The **Dalton Factory Stores** (80 mi north of Atlanta; exit 136 off I–75) offer **Jones of New York, West Point Pepperell,** and more. **Outlets Ltd. Mall** (3750 Venture Dr., Duluth) yields good buys in men's, women's, and children's clothing, as well as numerous specialty items. **Outlet Square of Atlanta** (4166 Buford Hwy.) is anchored by the **Burlington Coat Factory, Rack Room Shoes,** and **Marshall's.**

Specialty Shops

ANTIQUES

Buckhead is home to several antiques shops, with most of them along or near Peachtree Road. Expect rare goods and high prices in many stores. More than 25 shops line the cobblestone courtyard of Buckhead's **2300 Peachtree Road** complex. Along **Miami Circle,** off Piedmont Road, is another enclave for antiques and decorative arts lovers.

The **Stalls** (116 Bennett St., ☎ 404/352–4430) is an upscale flea market.

"Junking" addicts find nirvana in **Little Five Points,** at the intersection of Moreland and Euclid avenues. The neighborhood, Atlanta's version of Greenwich Village, is characterized by vintage clothing stores, art galleries, used record and book shops, and some stores that defy description.

Other fertile ground for serious antiques shoppers includes suburban Chamblee's "Antiques Row," a few blocks off Peachtree Industrial Boulevard with some shops near the Chamblee MARTA rail station, and historic Roswell, about a 30-minute drive north of downtown.

BOOKS
Atlanta's largest selection of books and newspapers is at **Oxford Books at Buckhead** (360 Pharr Rd., ☎ 404/262–3333), a local institution where frequent book signings are prominently noted on the store's marquee. Oxford's narrow balcony is a coffee shop, and the store also contains a full-service art gallery that emphasizes local artists' works. New to the neighborhood, the nearby **Barnes & Noble** (2900 Peachtree Rd., ☎ 404/261–7747), adjoined by a **Starbucks** (the famed coffee shop chain that began in Seattle), promises competition.

FOOD
DeKalb Farmers Market (3000 E. Ponce de Leon Ave., Decatur, ☎ 404/377–6400) has 140,000 square feet of exotic fruits, cheeses, seafood, sausages, breads, and delicacies from around the world. Gourmands stock up at **Harry's Farmers Markets** (1180 Upper Hembree Rd., Alpharetta, ☎ 404/664–6300; 2025 Satellite Blvd., Duluth, ☎ 404/416–6900) north of the city, with their dazzling array of prepared foods as well as produce, meats, seafood, and wines.

Participant Sports

In a city where outdoor recreation is possible almost year-round, sports play a major role. At almost any time of the year, in parks, private clubs, and neighborhoods throughout the city, you'll find Atlantans pursuing everything from tennis to soccer to rollerblading. *Atlanta Sports & Fitness Magazine* (☎ 404/842–0359), available for free at many grocery stores and health clubs, is a good link to Atlanta's athletic community.

Bicycling and Rollerblading
Piedmont Park (Piedmont Ave. between 10th and 14th Sts.) is closed to traffic and popular for rollerblading. **Skate Escape** (across from the park at 1086 Piedmont Ave., ☎ 404/892–1292) has rental bikes, Rollerblades, and skates. The **Southern Bicycle League** (☎ 404/594–8350) and **Cycle South** (☎ 404/991–6642) offer regularly scheduled tours.

Golf
Golf is enormously popular here, as the many courses will attest. The only public course within sight of downtown Atlanta is the **Bobby Jones Golf Course** (384 Woodward Way, ☎ 404/355–1009), named after the famed golfer and Atlanta native and located on a portion of the site of the Battle of Peachtree Creek. Despite having some of the city's worst fairways and greens, the immensely popular 18-hole, par 71 course is always crowded. Another club on a Civil War site is the **Alfred Tup Holmes Club** (2300 Wilson Dr., ☎ 404/753–6158), built upon a former Con-

federate breastworks; golf-wise, it's known for numerous doglegs and blind shots. Also within I–285 are the **Browns Mill Golf Course** (480 Cleveland Ave., ☎ 404/366–3573), considered the best operated by the City of Atlanta, and **North Fulton Golf Course** (216 W. Wieuca Rd., ☎ 404/255–0723), offering one of the best layouts, but also some of the smallest greens. The **Sugar Creek Golf Course** (2706 Bouldercrest Rd., ☎ 404/241–7671), straddling I–285 (11 holes on one side, seven on the other) in southeast Atlanta, is a challenging course with several long drives and good Bermuda greens. Outside I–285 in the suburbs, the best public course is the **Southerness Golf Club** (4871 Flat Bridge Rd., Stockbridge, ☎ 404/808–6000), with a great variety of challenging holes—from long par fours to shots over water requiring pinpoint accuracy. Among Stone Mountain Park's (U.S. 78, ☎ 404/498–5715) two 18-hole courses, **Stonemont** is the best, with several challenging and scenic holes; it was voted one of the top 75 public courses by *Golf Digest*. The former private **Lakeside Country Club** (3600 Old Fairburn Rd., ☎ 404/344–3620), just outside I–285 in southwest Atlanta, offers many challenges, with a dogleg on nearly every hole. **Eagle Watch Golf Club** (3055 Eagle Watch Dr., Woodstock, ☎ 404/591–1000), designed by Arnold Palmer, is a huge course that will please long distance drivers.

Health Clubs

SportsLife (3340 Peachtree Rd., ☎ 404/ 262–2120; six other locations) and the **YMCA** (☎ 404/588–9622; 15 locations) are both open to the public. Hotels with health clubs include the **Ritz-Carlton Buckhead, Westin Peachtree Plaza, Hotel Nikko,** the **Swissotel,** and the **Atlanta Marriott Marquis** (*see* Lodging, *below*).

Jogging

This is one of the city's most popular sports. The **Peachtree Road Race 10K,** held annually on July 4, has become so popular that there are no longer enough slots for those wanting to sign up (up to 25,000 runners allowed). Atlanta's hills provide joggers with plenty of challenges. On the plus side, most streets are heavily shaded, offering some respite from the miserable summer humidity. Traffic-free **Piedmont Park** is ideal for running, as is the **Chattahoochee National Recreation Area.** Contact the **Atlanta Track Club** (3097 Shadowlawn Ave., ☎ 404/231–9064) or **Chattahoochee Road Runners** (Box 724745, 31139, ☎ 404/916–2820) for other suggestions.

Rafting and Rowing

The **Chattahoochee River** is a favorite among rafters and rowers alike. The **Atlanta Rowing Club** (☎ 404/993–1879) provides information.

Swimming

White Water Park (*see* What to See and Do with Children, *above*) has a huge wave pool, several water slides, picnic areas, lockers, and showers. **Lake Lanier,** 45 minutes northeast of Atlanta (I–85 to I–985), is frequented by swimmers and boaters during the summer months.

Tennis

Bitsy Grant Tennis Center (2125 Northside Dr., ☎ 404/351–2774; ☉ Weekdays 8:30–7, weekends 8:30–6), with 13 clay courts and 10 hard courts, is the area's best public facility. **Piedmont Park** (☎ 404/872–1507) has 12 hard courts with night lights available, but no locker facilities (☉ Weekdays noon–9, weekends 9–5).

Waterskiing
Lake Lanier and **Callaway Gardens** both offer superior waterskiing, although the former can be extremely crowded on weekends. Contact the **Atlanta Water Ski Club** (☎ 404/425–7166).

Spectator Sports
As much as they play sports, Atlantans love to watch them. Sports fever grew in 1991 and 1992, when the Atlanta Braves won back-to-back National League titles. The Braves currently play home games at **Atlanta–Fulton County Stadium** (521 Capitol Ave., ☎ 404/ 249–6400). In 1997, they will cross the street to occupy Olympic Stadium, which will be converted into baseball stadium dimensions after the 1996 Summer Olympics. The National Basketball Association's Atlanta Hawks play home games at the **Omni Coliseum** (100 Techwood Dr., ☎ 404/827–DUNK). The National Football League's Atlanta Falcons play home games at the **Georgia Dome** (1 Georgia Dome Dr., ☎ 404/223–8000). The International Hockey League's 1994 champions, the Atlanta Knights, play at the **Omni** (☎ 404/525–8900).

Dining
Updated by
Jane Schneider

From a million-dollar Patrick Kuleto–designed diner to a humble meat-and-three establishment, one can find almost anything in the capital of the New South: prestigious kitchens run by world-class chefs; a multitude of ethnic restaurants; and such regional favorites as fried chicken, Brunswick stew, fried catfish, and hush puppies.

As is probably inevitable in a city where enthusiasm and growth has outstripped experience, however, some of the so-called hottest or trendiest Atlanta restaurants can be something of a letdown. Service, too, has a long way to go at many popular establishments. Wine enthusiasts will marvel at some of the wine lists assembled in the city's finer restaurants, and find others exasperating. Visitors would do well to approach each meal here with cautious optimism.

The local taste for things sweet and fried holds true for restaurants serving traditional Southern food. To taste Southern iced tea, order it sweet. (When ordering tea in the South, it is assumed you want iced tea. To get hot tea, specify hot.) Don't pass up desserts in the South; they're legendary. And fried chicken, seafood, collard greens, and okra are the staples of Southern cooking for all Southerners. Catch the flavor of the South at breakfast and lunch in modest establishments that serve only these two meals. Reserve evenings for culinary exploration, including some of the new Southern-style restaurants that present regional dishes and traditional ingredients in fresh and inventive ways

CATEGORY	COST*
$$$$	over $45
$$$	$35–$45
$$	$25–$35
$	under $25

*per person for a three-course meal, excluding drinks, service, and 6% tax.

What to Wear
Dress in Atlanta is casual unless noted otherwise.

Downtown

$$$$ **City Grill.** This posh but breezy restaurant has made the most of its grand
★ location in the elegantly renovated historic Hurt building. The bustle
of success greets you at the door, while bucolic murals and stunning
high ceilings create a feeling of glamour. Chef Roger Kaplan's regional
American menu chiefly explores the specialties of the South and Southwest. The excellent wine list covers the world, offering many unusual
selections. City Grill is a top Atlanta "power lunch" spot. ✕ *50 Hurt
Plaza,* ☎ *404/524–2489. Reservations recommended far in advance
for weekend dining. AE, D, DC, MC, V. No lunch Sat. Closed Sun.*

$$$$ **The Restaurant, Ritz-Carlton, Atlanta.** The elegant, clublike interior of
the Restaurant is an ideal business dining spot. Lunch is a buffet arrangement, serving dishes that change daily. Save this one for dinner.
Chef Daniel Schaffhauser, a native of Alsace, presents an international
menu with regional American touches. Braised Georgia quail partners
with roasted garlic polenta. Venison chops are paired with Napa cabbage and a confit of apples and pecans. The well-selected wine list is
ably administered by a knowledgeable sommelier. ✕ *181 Peachtree St.,*
☎ *404/659–0400, ext. 6450. Reservations advised. Jacket and tie. AE,
D, DC, MC, V. No lunch Sat. Closed Sun.*

$$$ **Savannah Fish Company.** Have a drink in the revolving lounge at the
top of the hotel, but come to the ground floor for a smashingly good
and simple meal of fresh grilled or sautéed fish. Begin with the restau-
rant's famous smoked bluefish spread, a complimentary opener.Enjoy
the house's saffron- and fennel-flavored fish stew. And don't forget to
save room for the simple Savannah hot puffs, fried dough sprinkled
with sugar and cinnamon and served with three sauces. ✕ *Westin
Peachtree Plaza, 210 Peachtree St. at International Blvd.,* ☎ *404/589–
7456. No reservations at dinner. AE, D, DC, MC, V*

$$ **Dailey's.** The downstairs dining room of this enormous converted
warehouse is casual fun. Upstairs there's spectacular decor (merry-go-
round horses and huge shop lamps) and more serious dining: swordfish au poivre, Georgia peach rack of lamb, duck in apple brandy, and
fried yeast rolls. Revved-up versions of pastry classics are paraded before the adoring eyes of the crowd. ✕ *17 International Blvd.,* ☎
*404/681–3303. No reservations; expect a wait. AE, D, DC, MC, V.
Entertainment nightly in downstairs lounge. No lunch Sun.*

$ **Deacon Burton's Soul Food Restaurant.** The deacon who presided over
this temple of Southern cooking is gone, but his affable son stands in,
presiding over some of the best fried chicken in town. Opposite the
Inman Park/Reynoldstown MARTA station, this humble eatery serves
up perfectly prepared down-home collards, hoe cakes, mashed potatoes and gravy, and peach cobbler. No alcohol is served. ✕ *1029 Edgewood Ave.,* ☎ *404/658–9452. No reservations. No credit cards. No
dinner. Closed weekends and Aug.*

$ **Delectables.** One of downtown's best-kept secrets; don't let the loca-
tion (inside the central branch of the Atlanta–Fulton Public Library)
or the format (cafeteria) deter you. This is a sophisticated little operation serving ravishing salads, wholesome soups, yummy cookies, and
freshly baked cakes. Enjoy your meal to the strains of classical music
and sunshine on the patio. ✕ *Atlanta–Fulton Public Library, corner
of Margaret Mitchell Sq. and Carnegie Way (enter through Carnegie
Way),* ☎ *404/681–2909. AE, MC, V. No dinner. Closed weekends.*

$ **Harold's Barbecue.** Legislators, political groupies, and small fry from
the capitol sit side by side, wolfing down delicious sliced pork sandwiches, huge platters of freshly sliced meat, and overflowing bowls of
Brunswick stew. Don't miss the crackling bread. The knotty pine,

Dining
Ciboulette, **3**
City Grill, **17**
Dailey's, **12**
Deacon Burton's
Soul Food
Restaurant, **16**
Delectables, **15**
French Quarter Food
Shop, **4**
Harold's Barbecue, **18**
Indigo Coastal Grill, **6**
Partners Morningside
Cafe, **7**
The Restaurant,
The Ritz-Carlton
Atlanta, **14**
Savannah Fish
Company, **11**
The Varsity, **5**

Lodging
Ansley Inn, **2**
Atlanta Marriott
Marquis, **8**
Barclay Hotel, **10**
Colony Square Hotel, **1**
Atlanta Hyatt
Regency, **9**
Omni Hotel at CNN
Center, **13**
The Ritz-Carlton
Atlanta, **14**
Westin Peachtree
Plaza, **11**

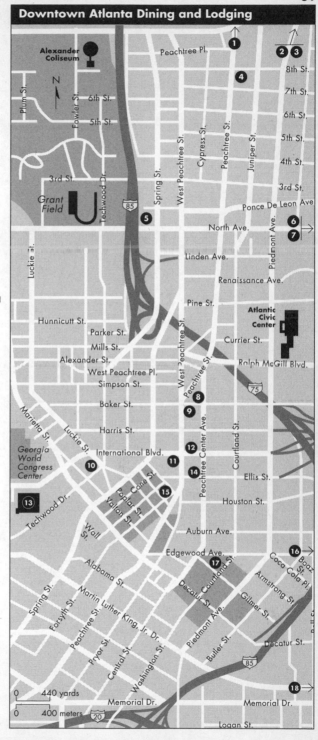

Downtown Atlanta Dining and Lodging

Atlanta Vicinity Dining and Lodging

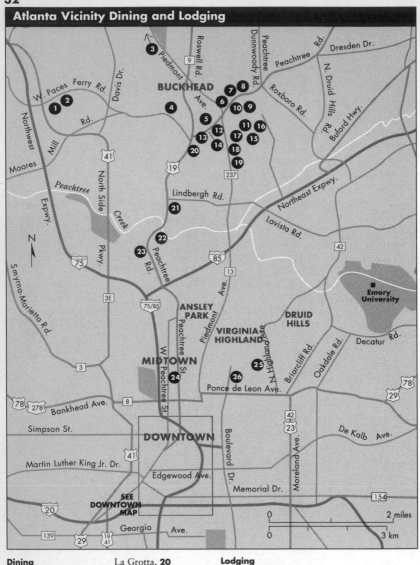

Dining
Abruzzi Ristorante, **21**
Annie's Thai Castle, **5**
Atlanta Fish Market, **11**
Azalea, **12**
Bacchanalia, **18**
Basil's Mediterranean Cafe, **17**
Bone's, **14**
Buckhead Diner, **19**
Dining Room, in the Ritz-Carlton Buckhead, **8**
Horseradish Grill, **3**
Kudzu Cafe, **13**

La Grotta, **20**
Luna Sí, **22**
OK Café, **1**
103 West, **4**
Pano's and Paul's, **2**
Pricci, **15**
Rocky's Brick Oven Pizzeria, **23**
South City Kitchen, **24**
Surin of Thailand, **25**
Tortillas, **26**

Lodging
Embassy Suites, **10**
Hotel Nikko, **6**
JW Marriott, **16**
The Ritz-Carlton, Buckhead, **8**
Swissôtel, **9**
Windham Garden Hotel, **7**

tacky art, and management haven't changed in a half century. It's a short distance from downtown, but worth the ride. ✕ *171 McDonough Blvd.,* ☎ *404/627–9268. No reservations. No credit cards. Closed Sun.*

$ **The Varsity.** Part of Atlanta's collective past, this sprawling diner near the Georgia Tech campus pioneered the drive-in eatery concept. It attracts people from all walks of life who come for the famous chili dogs, hamburgers, and gigantic orders of fresh and delicious—but greasy—onion rings. Line up behind the locals and pay close attention to the lingo: "One naked dog, walkin' and a bag o' rags," will get you a plain hot dog and some potato chips. Connoisseurs drink orange frosties. Folks in a hurry get curb service. ✕ *61 North Ave.,* ☎ *404/881–1706. No reservations. No credit cards.*

Midtown

$$$ **Ciboulette.** French-bistro food and atmosphere from Tom Coohill have Atlantans lining up for hot smoked salmon with wild mushrooms and ginger, Lyonnaise sausage in crust with warm lentil salad, and lamb with garlic mashed potatoes. Game dishes are frequent specials in season. The wine list is well chosen and embraces many good selections by the glass. The dining room is a bit tight, making intimate conversation difficult, but the counter seats, with their kitchen view, provide a true bistro ambience. ✕ *1529 Piedmont Ave. NE,* ☎ *404/874–7600. Reservations accepted weekdays. AE, DC, MC, V. No lunch. Closed Sun.*

$$–$$$ **Indigo Coastal Grill.** Trendy coastal cuisine packs them in at this lively Virginia–Highland eatery. Cuisine is more fun than fabulous, with some dishes suffering from overwrought flavors and mediocre preparation. Popular here are conch fritters, heavy-cream biscuits, lobster corn chowder, and fish and fresh herbs in a twist of parchment. Don't miss the refreshing Key lime pie or the sautéed bananas with rum and lime. Sunday brunch is served. ✕ *1397 N. Highland Ave.,* ☎ *404/876–0676. No reservations; expect a wait. AE, MC, V. No sit-down lunch, but take-out service available.*

$$–$$$ **Partners Morningside Cafe.** This upbeat, noisy, and colorful spot is next door to Indigo Coastal Grill (*see above*), its companion operation. Cuisine blends several influences, particularly Mediterranean and Pacific Rim. Ravioli stuffing and sauce changes daily; there's also grilled portobello mushrooms, pasta specials that change daily, Vietnamese chicken cakes, and nostalgic, old-fashioned desserts. An appealing small wine list is full of good values. ✕ *1399 N. Highland Ave.,* ☎ *404/876–8104. No reservations; expect a wait. AE, MC, V. No lunch.*

$$–$$$ **South City Kitchen.** The food traditions of South Carolina's coastal low country inspire the cooking at this bright, very popular in-town restaurant. The clean, spare, art-filled interior of this former modest residence attracts a frisky crowd of hip in-towners. This is the place for catfish, prepared in a variety of intriguing ways, such as in a unique Reuben sandwich or on a bed of grits. The very good, well-priced wine list focuses on American wines. ✕ *1144 Crescent Ave.,* ☎ *404/873–7358. Reservations accepted for dinner. AE, MC, V.*

$ **French Quarter Food Shop.** Sandwiched between two bars, this ultra-casual eatery has a pleasant sidewalk café. Sit down to some crawfish étouffée, shrimp jambalaya, gumbo, a huge muffaletta that could easily serve two, or a shrimp or oyster po'boy; takeout is also available. ✕ *923 Peachtree Rd.,* ☎ *404/875–2489. No reservations. AE, D, DC, MC, V. Closed Sun.*

$ **Surin of Thailand.** This dining spot opened in 1991 in a renovated drugstore in Virginia-Highland. Big windows let in plenty of light, and the owners' own photographs of Thailand hang on the yellow walls. Try the French basil rolls stuffed with shrimp, cucumber, and pork—one of Chef Surin Techarukpong's best dishes—and save room for the delicately flavored, homemade coconut or mango ice cream for dessert. ✕ *810 N.Highland Ave.,* ☎ *404/892–7789. No reservations. AE, D, MC, V.*

$ **Tortillas.** This funky California–Spanish joint rates raves from the business and student crowd it attracts at lunch. Weekends and evenings find it packed with 20-somethings. The burritos stuffed with pork or shrimp, the cheese-stuffed quesadillas, and freshly prepared extras like green salsa, guacamole, and potatoes taste authentic and satisfying. ✕ *774 Ponce de Leon Ave.,* ☎ *404/892–0193. No reservations. No credit cards.*

Buckhead

$$$$ **Bone's.** In this brash, New York–style steakhouse, sports celebs and fast-track businesspeople rub egos and compare lifestyles over excellent prime beef, chops, Maine lobster, and potatoes baked in a crust of salt. Silky, aromatic lobster bisque warms the heart. The award winning wine list strikes a balance between French and American wines, and includes a fair number of Italian vintages. Good wines are available by the glass. Most patrons wear jackets, but if your idea of fun is spending big bucks in a sport shirt, they won't turn you down. Private dining rooms are available. ✕ *3130 Piedmont Rd.,* ☎ *404/237–2663. Reservations advised. AE, DC, MC, V. No lunch weekends.*

$$$$ **The Dining Room, Ritz-Carlton, Buckhead.** This is the best restaurant in town and among the country's 10 greatest. Under Chef Guenter Seeger, haute cuisine is not flashy or ostentatious. Strictly limiting himself to the freshest regional products, Seeger doesn't like calling attention to the culinary process. The menu, handwritten every day, is likely to involve local sun-dried sweet potatoes (in ravioli), Vidalia onions (with lobster and lobster coral sauce), or persimmons (in a mousse with muscadine sorbet and Georgia golden raspberries). Don't ask for your food to be well-done. Surrender to this imperious genius and the exquisite, discreet service. The wine list and service are extraordinary, worthy of the awards both have won. ✕ *3434 Peachtree Rd.,* ☎ *404/237–2700. Reservations required, several days ahead for weekend dining. Jacket and tie. AE, D, DC, MC, V. No lunch. Closed Sun.*

$$$$ **Horseradish Grill.** One of *Bon Appétit* magazine's 1994 "10 best new restaurants" selections is a must stop for anyone looking for good Southern-style food. Horseradish Grill reflects the expertise of Alabama native Scott Peacock and his mentor, Edna Lewis, of Virginia. Perfect fried chicken and cream gravy is just one example. The juicy hot browns, an open-faced sandwich originating in Kentucky, feature succulent turkey smoked on the premises over all-natural hickory wood that has not been treated with chemicals. The menu changes often, but Southern ingredients hold sway. The wine list is extensive and growing, as many more selections by the glass are being added. ✕ *4320 Powers Ferry Rd.,* ☎ *404/255–7277. No reservations. AE, MC, V. No lunch Sat.*

$$$$ **La Grotta.** Despite its odd location in the basement of a posh Buckhead condominium, this is one of the best-managed dining rooms in town. Magnetic, dynamic Sergio Favalli is a superb host, and waiters are on their toes. The kitchen experiments cautiously with new concepts and trendy ingredients, but old Northern Italian favorites remain at the core of the menu. Don't miss the warm grilled portobello mushrooms, the baby quails over polenta, or the tiramisù. Veal and fresh pasta are outstanding. There's an excellent wine list. ✕ *2637 Peachtree Rd.,* ☎ *404/231–1368. Reservations required well in advance for*

weekend dining. Jacket and tie. AE, D, DC, MC, V. No lunch. Closed Sun.

$$$ **Abruzzi Ristorante.** "Understated elegance" is the buzz phrase for this modern yet traditional restaurant frequented by the city's old guard. If you're not taken with one of the myriad menu offerings, have managing partner Nico Petrucci suggest a specialty. Excellent dishes include salmon carpaccio, green-and-white *gnocchi* in pesto, sautéed sweetbreads, veal chop, baked fish with rosemary, and ricotta cheesecake. ✕ *2355 Peachtree Rd., ☎ 404/261–8186. Reservations advised. AE, DC, MC, V. No lunch Sat., closed Sun.*

$$$ **Bacchanalia.** *Bon Appétit* magazine included Bacchanalia in its annual list of 10 best new restaurants in 1993. Chefs and companions, Anne Quatrano and Clifford Harrison dazzle diners with dishes that the pair labels "new American," but that take inspiration chiefly from country Mediterranean sources, with occasional touches of Asian ingredients. The four-course fixed-price menu ($35 without wine; $55 with three preselected wines) offers plenty of options. The dishes changes weekly, while exhibiting seasonal emphasis, and may include, for starters, a perfect risotto topped with a generous sprinkle of aromatic fresh white truffle or a roasted butternut squash and apple soup made surprising with a slice of pan-seared foie gras. Main courses range from fish through fowl and red meats, but vegetarians will enjoy offerings tailored to their requirements. Turbot encrusted in potato, sautéed and served with braised leeks is perfect with any one of the wine list's many Pinot Noirs. The wine list, while maddeningly short on offerings by the glass, contains a host of unusual selections, including a separate list of Viogniers. À la carte ordering is available upon request. ✕ *3125 Piedmont Rd., ☎ 404/365–0410. Reservations strongly advised. AE, DC, MC, V. No smoking. No lunch. Closed Sun. and Mon.*

$$$ **Pano's and Paul's.** This is an Atlanta classic that's known for stylish pampering. Pano Karatassos and Paul Albrecht hit gold with their single-minded devotion to their customers' needs, from whims to dietary restrictions. Many new ideas percolate through the kitchen; state-of-the-art dishes are introduced as specials and eventually included in the menu. Look for lemon-roasted, farm-raised chicken with a crisp, celery-potato cake, sautéed gulf red snapper fillet, and jumbo cold lobster tail fried in a light batter and served with Chinese honey mustard. ✕ *1232 W. Paces Ferry Rd., ☎ 404/261–3662. Reservations required (days, sometimes weeks ahead for a prime slot). Jacket required. AE, D, DC, MC, V. No lunch. Closed Sun.*

$$–$$$ **Atlanta Fish Market.** An overwhelming selection of fresh seafood is served in this cavernous space, reminiscent of an old train station. Swordfish with roasted cashew and cracked-pepper crust, served with white-corn cheese grits, exemplifies the creatively prepared cuisine on the ever-changing menu. The wine list has many good choices by the glass. The noise level is high, but the more intimate Geechee Porch presents a quieter ambiance adjacent to the main dining room. ✕ *265 Pharr Rd., ☎ 404/262–3165. Reservations limited. AE, D, DC, MC, V. No lunch Sun.*

$$–$$$ **Buckhead Diner.** This million-dollar fantasy by the owners of Pano's and Paul's is still one of the hottest restaurants in town, a shimmering faux-diner wrapped in luscious hues of neon. Inlaid wood, Italian leather, hand-cut marble and mellow lights establish a languorous ambience reminiscent of the Orient Express. The cuisine is anything but diner: salt-and-pepper squid, fresh goat cheese and tomato fondue, veal-and-wild-mushroom meat loaf, and white chocolate banana cream pie are a sampling. Interesting wines are available by the glass. ✕ *3073*

Piedmont Rd., ☎ *404/262–3336. No reservations; expect a long wait.*
AE, D, DC, MC, V.

$$–$$$ **Kudzu Cafe.** Come here for witty, updated southern food that includes
fresh vegetables, such as fried green tomatoes. Savannah crab cakes
with creole sauce are also worth the trip, and don't forget the pecan
pie for dessert. Have someone here tell you the history of kudzu. ✕
3215 Peachtree Rd., ☎ *404/262–0661. No reservations. AE, MC, V.*
No lunch weekends.

$$–$$$ **Pricci.** The stamp of acclaimed designer Patrick Kuleto is apparent in
the chic mirrored and windowed decor of this high-style hot spot. De-
ceptively simple southern Italian fare is accompanied by Pricci's own
freshly baked breads. The homemade spinach-filled tortellini is delicious. ✕ *500 Pharr Rd.,* ☎ *404/237–2941. Reservations advised. AE,*
D, DC, MC, V. No lunch weekends.

$$ **Basil's Mediterranean Café.** Tucked down a side street, in a renovated
bungalow, this restaurant is handsomely decorated with original art.
In good weather you can dine on the front deck. Dishes—mostly
seafood—are well-seasoned, and each plate is an artistic masterpiece.
The Greek-style shrimp with artichoke hearts, sun-dried tomatoes,
olives, and feta cheese is superb. Dishes reflect the influence of Mediter-
ranean cooking, from southern France to the Middle East and Morocco.
Pasta may come topped with tomato and seafood, a spicy tomato
sauce, or steamed vegetables. ✕ *2985 Grandview,* ☎ *404/233–9755.*
Reservations accepted. AE, D, DC, MC, V. Closed Sun.

$ **Annie's Thai Castle.** A family-run delight transplanted from a subur-
ban location into the heart of Buckhead, this small restaurant is lov-
ingly decorated with objets d'art from Annie's native Thailand. Soups
are perfectly flavored with spices and lemon grass, and the seafood salad,
aromatic with garlic and lime, dazzles. *Nam sod,* chicken satay, and
spicy catfish are excellent choices. Traditional curries and noodle dishes
seem to have an extra dash of finesse. ✕ *3195 Roswell Rd.,* ☎ *404/264–*
9546. Reservations advised on weekends. AE, MC, V.

$ **Azalea.** East meets West on the menu at this see-and-be-seen restau-
rant, with its black-on-white contemporary decor. Try the potato-
crusted salmon with a wild mushroom cream sauce. Whole sizzling
catfish with black bean chile sauce has been a hit from the beginning.
Excellent wines by the glass are a specialty. ✕ *3167 Peachtree Rd.,* ☎
404/237–9939. Reservations accepted Sun.–Thurs. AE, D, DC, MC,
V. No lunch.

$ **Luna Sí.** The emphasis is on fun at this New York loft–style restaurant
where Latin music blares, and customers are encouraged to write on
the walls. The menu, which changes weekly, is dominated by seafood—
seared Atlantic salmon with a ginger crust is a favorite. The chef es-
chews cream and butter in the preparations. The entire restaurant is
nonsmoking. ✕ *1931 Peachtree Rd.,* ☎ *404/355–5993. Reservations*
accepted for large parties. AE, D, MC, V. No lunch. Closed Mon.

$ **OK Café.** Go "back to the future" in this witty take-off on small-town
eateries. The cheeky waitresses, whimsical art, and roomy, comfort-
able booths make this a favorite hangout for Atlanta's artsy crowd—
and lots of ordinary folk besides. The fried chicken ginger salad is popular.
Vegetable plates are supremely satisfying. Mammoth breakfasts, old-
fashioned blue-plate specials, and chocolate shakes satisfy that high-
cholesterol craving in all of us. ✕ *1284 W. Paces Ferry Rd.,* ☎
404/233–2888. No reservations. AE, MC, V.

$ **Rocky's Brick Oven Pizzeria.** It's a find in a city where good pizza is
hard to come by. The bustling kitchen turns out thick, square Sicilian
pizzas and thin-crusted Neapolitan pies with the city's most appeal-

ing combination of toppings. Clientele includes well-heeled parents with tots in tow, art school students, and rocker Mick Jagger, who frequented it while filming a movie. ✕ *1770 Peachtree St.,* ☎ *404/876–1111. No reservations. AE, D, DC, MC, V.*

Lodging

One of America's three most popular convention destinations, Atlanta offers a broad range of lodgings. More than 12,000 rooms are in the compact downtown area, close to the Georgia World Congress Center, Atlanta Civic Center, Atlanta Merchandise Mart, and Omni Coliseum. Other clusters are in Buckhead, in the north I–285 perimeter, and around Hartsfield Atlanta International Airport.

CATEGORY	COST*
$$$$	over $160
$$$	$115–$160
$$	$80–$115
$	under $80

All prices are for a standard double room, excluding 11% tax.

Downtown and Midtown

$$$$ **Atlanta Marriott Marquis.** Immense and coolly contemporary, the Marquis seems to go on forever as you stand under the lobby's huge fabric sculpture that appears to float from the sky-lit roof 48 stories above. Each guest room—of average size and with standard-issue hotel decor—opens onto this atrium. ▦ *265 Peachtree Center Ave., 30303,* ☎ *404/521–0000 or 800/328–9290,* FAX *404/586–6299. 1,671 rooms, 71 suites. 5 restaurants, 4 bars and lounges, indoor-outdoor pool, health club. AE, D, DC, MC, V.*

$$$$ **Omni Hotel at CNN Center.** The hotel is adjacent to the CNN Center, home of Ted Turner's Cable News Network. The lobby combines Old World and modern accents, with marble floors, Oriental rugs, exotic floral and plant arrangements, and contemporary furnishings. Rooms are large and decorated in shades of mauve. Guests have access to the Downtown Athletic Club. ▦ *100 CNN Center (MARTA's Omni rail station is adjacent to CNN Center), 30305,* ☎ *404/659–0000 or 800/843–6664,* FAX *404/525–5050. 465 rooms. 2 restaurants, lounge. AE, D, DC, MC, V.*

$$$$ **Ritz-Carlton, Atlanta.** The mood here is set by traditional afternoon tea served in the intimate, sunken lobby beneath an 18th-century chandelier. Notice the 17th-century Flemish tapestry when you enter from Peachtree Street. Spacious guest rooms are luxuriously decorated with marble writing tables, plump sofas, four-poster beds, and white marble bathrooms. The Cafe's Sunday brunch spread is spectacular. In the evenings, live jazz music is performed at the Bar upstairs. Service is very European, cold but efficient. ▦ *181 Peachtree St. (entrance to MARTA's Peachtree Center rail station is across the street), 30303,* ☎ *404/659–0400 or 800/241–3333,* FAX *404/577–8366. 447 rooms. 2 restaurants, bar, exercise room. AE, D, DC, MC, V.*

$$$$ **Westin Peachtree Plaza.** Every photograph of Atlanta's skyline taken in the last 10 years features this cylindrical glass tower, the second tallest hotel in North America. Designed by John Portman, its blockhouse-like entrance at Peachtree Street leads to a five story atrium surrounding the narrow glass elevator attached to the outside of the building. For the best views of Atlanta, have a drink or meal in the revolving, multi-level Sun Dial Restaurant & Lounge atop the hotel. ▦ *210 Peachtree St. at International Blvd., 30303,* ☎ *404/659–1400 or 800/228–*

3000, FAX *404/589–7591. 1,074 rooms. 3 restaurants, 3 bars, indoor-outdoor pool, sauna, health club. AE, D, DC, MC, V.*

$$$ **Ansley Inn.** Above a sloping lawn a block from Piedmont Park and in the heart of Ansley Park, one of Atlanta's most beautiful neighborhoods, stands this handsome three-story brick Tudor mansion. Its oversize guest rooms with private baths and common areas are furnished with Chinese porcelains, antiques, and original art. A Continental breakfast is included in the price. Guests have access to an athletic club ($10 per visit). ☎ *253 15th St., 30309,* ☎ *404/872–9000 or 800/446–5416,* FAX *404/892–2318. 15 rooms. AE, D, DC, MC, V.*

$$$ **Colony Square Hotel.** Theatricality and opulence are epitomized by the dimly lit lobby with overhanging balconies, piano music, and fresh flowers. Rooms are modern and done in muted tones—those on higher floors have nice city views. The hotel is three blocks from MARTA's Art Center station and two blocks from the Woodruff Arts Center and the High Museum of Art; it anchors the Colony Square office/residential/retail complex. Several restaurants are within or near the center. Guests have access (for a fee) to the Colony Club health club, racquetball courts, and pool. ☎ *Peachtree and 14th Sts., 30361,* ☎ *404/892–6000 or 800/422–7895,* FAX *404/872–9192. 428 rooms, 33 suites. Restaurant, lobby lounge. AE, D, DC, MC, V.*

$$$ **Hyatt Regency Atlanta.** The Hyatt's 23-story lobby (built in 1965) launched the chain's "atrium look." Easily identified at night by its brightly lit blue bubble dome over the rooftop Polaris restaurant, it remains one of Atlanta's more unique hotels. ☎ *265 Peachtree St. (connected by skywalk to Peachtree Center), 30303,* ☎ *404/577–1234 or 800/233–1234,* FAX *404/588–4808. 1,278 rooms, 58 suites. 4 restaurants, pool, sauna, health club. AE, D, DC, MC, V.*

$ **Barclay Hotel.** This quiet, older downtown hotel, two blocks off of Peachtree Street, was renovated in 1994. The teal-carpeted lobby dominated by two modern chandeliers features works by black artists. Done in mauve with floral accents, each room has a view of downtown; some rooms have balconies. The Celebrity Cafe is known for its waffles and fried chicken. ☎ *89 Luckie St., 30303,* ☎ *404/524–7991,* FAX *404/525–0672. 73 rooms. 2 restaurants, pool. AE, DC, MC, V.*

Buckhead

$$$$ **Hotel Nikko.** A dual-height lobby facing a courtyard with Japanese garden and cascading 35-foot waterfall is the opening statement of this modern, towering hotel. The understated decor features mainly hues of black, gray, and purple. Rooms are spacious and comfortable, with a style that's more American than Japanese. Japanese and Mediterranean cuisine are featured in the hotel's two restaurants. ☎ *3300 Peachtree Rd., 30305,* ☎ *404/365–8100 or 800/645–5687,* FAX *404/233–5686. 439 rooms, 32 suites. 2 restaurants, bar, lounge, pool, health club, 14 meeting rooms. AE, D, DC, MC, V.*

$$$$ **Ritz-Carlton, Buckhead.** Decorated with the Ritz's signature 18th- and 19th-century antiques, this elegant gem bids a discreet welcome to locals and visitors alike. Shoppers from nearby Lenox Mall and Phipps Plaza often revive here over afternoon tea or cocktails in the richly paneled Lobby Lounge; the Café and the Bar offer other spots to relax within luxurious surroundings. The Dining Room (*see* Dining, *above*) is the city's finest restaurant. The spacious rooms are furnished with traditional reproductions and have luxurious white-marble baths. From the hotel's club floors you get a view of Buckhead and an understanding of why Atlanta is known as a city of trees. ☎ *3434 Peachtree Rd., 30326,*

☎ *404/237–2700 or 800/241–3333,* ☎ *404/239–0078. 524 rooms, 29 suites. Restaurant, 2 bars, lounge, indoor pool, hot tub, health center. AE, D, DC, MC, V.*

$$$$ **Swissôtel.** Sleek and efficient, this stunner boasts a chic contemporary glass-and-white-enamel exterior and sophisticated Biedermeier-style interiors. Comfortable sofas and chairs beckon in common areas. Handy to Lenox Square Mall, a prime location for shopping and dining, the hotel is a favorite with business travelers. ☎ *3391 Peachtree Rd., 30326,* ☎ *404/365–0065 or 800/253–1397,* ☎ *404/365–8787. 362 rooms, 15 suites. Restaurant, lounge, indoor pool, health club, meeting rooms. AE, D, DC, MC, V.*

$$$ **JW Marriott.** This elegant 25-story hotel, connected to Lenox Square Mall, is traditionally decorated with reproduction furniture, hunter green and floral hues, and accents of brass and crystal. Irregularly shaped rooms have spacious baths with separate shower stall and tub. ☎ *3300 Lenox Rd., 30326,* ☎ *404/262–3344 or 800/328–9290,* ☎ *404/262–8689. 371 rooms, 30 suites. Restaurant, 2 lounges, indoor pool, health club, meeting rooms. AE, D, DC, MC, V.*

$$$ **Embassy Suites.** This contemporary high-rise in Buckhead is just blocks from thePhipps Plaza and Lenox Square malls. A variety of suites ranging from deluxe presidential (with wet bars) to more basic sleeping- and sitting-room combinations are available, as are a limited number of double-bed rooms. ☎ *3285 Peachtree Rd., 30305,* ☎ *404/261–7733 or 800/362–2779,* ☎ *404/261–6857. 313 suites, 15 rooms. Restaurant, lounge, indoor-outdoor pool, exercise room. AE, D, DC, MC, V.*

$$ **Wyndham Garden Hotel.** In the shadow of Hotel Nikko, this hotel's neat rooms are spacious and decorated with botanical prints, and rates are reasonable given the excellent location. Service is adequate, but doesn't compare with the luxury establishments in the area. Guests have access to a health club. ☎ *3340 Peachtree Rd., 30326,* ☎ *404/231–1234 or 800/822–4200,* ☎ *404/231–5236. 221 rooms. Restaurant, pool. AE, D, DC, MC, V.*

The Arts

For the most complete schedule of cultural events, check the *Atlanta Journal-Constitution*'s Friday "Weekend Preview" or Saturday "Leisure" sections. Also, check *Creative Loafing,* a lively community weekly distributed free at Atlanta restaurants, bars, and stores. You can also call the 24-hour **Arts Hotline** (☎ 404/853–3ART) or connect with **Access Atlanta,** via computer modem (☎ 800/224–5285, ext. 79 for hookup).

TicketMaster (☎ 404/249–6400 or 800/326–4000) and **Tic-X-Press, Inc.** (☎ 404/231–5888) handle tickets for the Fox Theatre, Atlanta Civic Center, and other locations. However, most companies sell tickets through their own box offices.

Concerts

The world-class **Atlanta Symphony Orchestra (ASO)** (☎ 404/733–5000), under the musical direction of Yoel Levi, recently celebrated its 50th anniversary. It performs its fall–spring subscription series in the 1,800-seat Symphony Hall at Woodruff Arts Center (1280 Peachtree St., tel 404/733–5000). During the summer, the orchestra occasionally accompanies big-name artists in Chastain Park's outdoor amphitheater (4469 Stella Dr.). Despite its international reputation, the ASO fails to sell out most local performances and suffers from financial problems and an acoustically flawed performance space. The acoustically magnificent little **Spivey Hall** (☎ 404/898–1189), located at Clayton State College 15 miles south of Atlanta in Morrow, is widely considered to be one of the finest concert venues in the country. Internationally renowned musicians perform everything from choral works to chamber music to jazz.

Modeled after the Vienna Boys' Choir, the **Atlanta Boys' Choir** (☎ 404/378–0064) performs frequently at Atlanta locations and makes national and international tours. The long-established **Atlanta Chamber Players** (☎ 404/651–1228) perform classical works at various Atlanta locations.

Dance
Atlanta Ballet Company (☎ 404/873–5811), founded in 1929, has received international recognition for its high-quality productions of classical and contemporary works. Performances are at the Fox Theatre and Atlanta Civic Center. Although, it is the nation's oldest continually operating professional ballet company, it is constantly plagued by financial problems, which limits its productions. New artistic director John McFall, only the third in its history after an exceptional 32-year stint by Robert Barnett, brings new ideas and vision to the group.

Opera
Atlanta Opera Association (☎ 404/355–3311), made up of local singers and musicians, is augmented by internationally known artists.

Theater
Consistently one of the region's best, the **Alliance Theatre** performs everything from Shakespeare to the latest Broadway and off-Broadway shows in the Woodruff Arts Center (*see* Exploring, *above*). The **Horizon Theatre Co.** (1083 Austin Ave., ☎ 404/584–7450) in Little Five Points produces new works by contemporary playwrights. **Theatrical Outfit** (1012 Peachtree at 10th St., ☎ 404/872–0665) produces original and nationally known contemporary works.

Actor's Express (887 W. Marietta St., ☎ 404/607–7469) presents an eclectic selection of cutting-edge productions that take place in the 150-seat theater of the King Plow Arts Center, a stylish artist's complex hailed by local critics as a showplace of industrial chic.

Touring Broadway musicals, pop music, and dance concerts are presented in the **Atlanta Civic Center** (395 Piedmont Ave., ☎ 404/523–6275), **Center Stage** (1374 W. Peachtree St., ☎ 404/874–1511), and at the **Fox Theatre** (660 Peachtree St., ☎ 404/881–2100; *see* Exploring, *above*).

Nightlife

The pursuit of entertainment—from Midtown to Buckhead—is known as the "Peachtree Shuffle." Atlanta's vibrant nightlife can mean anything from coffee bars to sports bars, from country line dancing to high-energy dance clubs. Atlanta has long been known for having more bars than churches, and in the South, that's an oddity.

Most bars and clubs are open seven nights, until 2–4 AM. Those with live entertainment usually have a cover charge. Consult *Creative Loafing* and the *Atlanta Journal-Constitution*.

Bars

Limerick Junction (822 N. Highland Ave., ☎ 404/874–7147) is a lively Irish pub.

The antithesis of hip-and-trendy, 33-year-old **Manuel's Tavern** (602 N. Highland Ave., ☎ 404/525–3447)—ancient by Atlanta standards—is a neighborhood saloon in the truest sense. Families, politicians, writers, students, professionals, and blue-collar workers enjoy drinks, bar food (chili dogs, french fries, strip steaks), and conversation.

Prince of Wales (1144 Piedmont Ave, ☎ 404/876–0227) is a cozy, authentic English pub with live music, from alternative rock to jazz.

For great burgers, try the **Vortex** (1041 W. Peachtree St., ☎ 404/875–1667). The atmosphere is friendly and the beer list is long.

Country

Hot spots for boot-scoot and boogie include the **Buckboard Country Music Showcase** (2080 Cobb Parkway in Windy Hill Plaza, ☎ 404/955–7340) and the **Crystal Chandelier** (1750 North Roberts Rd., Kennesaw, ☎ 404/426–5006), both north of the city.

Jazz and Blues

New Orleans–style blues sends jam-packed crowds into a frenzy at **Blind Willie's** (828 N. Highland Ave., ☎ 404/873–2583), a storefront club in Virginia-Highland.

Cafe 290 (290 Hilderbrand Dr., ☎ 404/256–3942) showcases talented local jazz bands in a casual neighborhood restaurant/bar setting.

Dante's Down the Hatch's venues (3380 Peachtree Rd., ☎ 404/266–1600; Underground Atlanta, Lower Pryor St., ☎ 404/577–1800) are two of the city's most popular nightspots. In Buckhead, the Paul Mitchell Trio conjures silky-smooth jazz sounds in the "hold" of a make-believe sailing ship. Downtown, jazz entertainers perform nightly. Swiss fondue and a large wine selection are part of the Dante's experience.

Just Jazz (595 Piedmont Ave., ☎ 404/897–1555; closed Mon.–Tues.) and the upscale **Echelon** (585 Franklin Rd., Marietta, ☎ 404/419–3393) feature jazz musicians from around the country.

Rock

The **Cotton Club** (1021 Peachtree St., ☎ 404/874–9524) is a loud, usually packed, Midtown club that features local and national performers in a variety of musical styles.

The **Masquerade** (695 North Ave., ☎ 404/577–8178), a tri-level grunge hangout, features just about everything in popular music, from disco to techno to industrial rock. Crowds are an odd mix that reflects the club's three separate spaces, dubbed Heaven, Hell, and Purgatory.

The **Point** (420 Moreland Ave., ☎ 404/ 659–3522) in Little Five Points showcases up-and-coming rock and progressive music groups in a small club setting.

Rupert's (3330 Piedmont Rd., ☎ 404/266–9834) attracts the Buckhead after-work crowd with its 10-piece orchestra playing big band and contemporary dance music. The club's multi-tiered balcony overlooks the large dance floor.

More than one generation dances to the beat at **Axys** (1150-B Peachtree St., ☎ 404/607–0922), an upscale, high-tech dance club in Midtown.

Atlanta Essentials

Arriving and Departing

BY BUS

Greyhound Bus Lines (81 International Blvd., ☎ 404/522–6300 or 800/231–2222) provides transport to downtown Atlanta.

BY CAR

Some refer to Atlanta as the Los Angeles of the South, because travel by car is virtually the only way to get to most parts of the city. Although the congestion isn't comparable to L.A.'s yet, Atlantans have grown accustomed to frequent delays at rush hour. Beware, the South as a whole may be laid back, but Atlanta drivers are not; they tend to drive faster than drivers in other southern cities. Visiting drivers should be vigilant.

The city is encircled by I–285. Three interstates—I–85, running northeast–southwest from Virginia to Alabama; I–75, north–south from Michigan to Florida; and I–20, east–west from South Carolina to Texas—also crisscross Atlanta.

BY PLANE

Hartsfield Atlanta International Airport, off I–85 and I–285, 13 miles south of downtown, is served by the following airlines: **Aero Costa Rica, AreoMexico, Air Jamaica, Air South, ALM Antillean, AMC, ASA, America West, American, British Airways, Cayman Airways, Continental, Delta, GP Express, Japan Airlines, Kiwi International, KLM, Korean Air, Leisure Air, Lufthansa, Markair, Midwest Express, National, Northwest, Sabena, Swissair, TWA, United, USAir, ValuJet,** and **VARIG Brazilian.**

Atlanta Airport shuttle vans (☎ 404/766–5312) operate every half hour between 7 AM and 11 PM. The downtown trip ($8 one-way, $14 round-trip) takes about 20 minutes and stops at major hotels. Vans also go to Emory University and Lenox Square ($12 one-way, $20 round-trip).

If your luggage is light, you can take **MARTA**'s (Metropolitan Atlanta Rapid Transit Authority, ☎ 404/848–4711) high-speed trains between the airport and downtown and other locations. Trains operate 4:34 AM– 1:17 AM (weekdays) and 5:30 AM–1:30 AM (weekends). The trip downtown takes about 15 minutes to the Five Points station, and the fare is $1.25.

Taxi fare between the airport and downtown hotels is fixed at $15 for one person; $8 each for two people; $6 each for three people. Taxi drivers, many of whom are recent immigrants and speak poor English, sometimes appear as befuddled as the visitor by Atlanta's notoriously winding and hilly streets, which often complicates the finding of an address if it is off a popular thoroughfare like Peachtree Street. The problem gets worse when big events are in town, because out-of-town operators come into Atlanta to pick up business. These drivers are even less familiar with the roads, so come armed with directions if your destination is something other than a major hotel or popular sight. Supposedly, the city is tightening up its rules on who can get a taxi permit, so the situation may get better in the future..

BY TRAIN

Amtrak's *Crescent* (☎ 404/881–3060 or 800/872–7245) operates daily to New Orleans, Greenville; Charlotte; Washington, DC; Baltimore; Philadelphia; and New York from Atlanta's Brookwood Station (1688 Peachtree St.). Its *Gulf Breeze* travels from Atlanta to Birmingham and Mobile, Alabama.

Getting Around

BY BUS

The **Metropolitan Atlanta Rapid Transit Authority (MARTA)** (☎ 404/848–4711), with a fleet of 700 buses, operates 150 routes covering 1,500 miles. The fare is $1.25, and exact change is required. Weekly and monthly *TransCards,* giving you a slight ride discount, are available, too. Outside the perimeter set by I–285, except for a few important areas of Clayton, DeKalb, and Fulton counties, service is very limited.

BY SUBWAY

MARTA's clean and safe rapid-rail subway trains have somewhat limited routes, but do link downtown with many major landmarks. The rail system's two main lines cross at the **Five Points Station** downtown, where TransCards and information on public transportation are available at the **Ride Store** (weekdays 7–7 and Sat. 8:30–5). Trains run 4:34 AM– 1:17 AM, and large parking (free) lots are at most stations beyond downtown. Tokens, costing $1.25 each, required to enter the station, can be bought from machines outside the station entrance or at the Ride Store. Free transfers, needed for some bus routes, are available by pressing a button on the subway turnstile or requesting one from the bus driver.

BY TAXI

Taxi fares start at $1.50 for the first ⅛ mile and 20¢ for each additional ⅛ mile; 50¢ per extra passenger and $12 per hour waiting time. Each additional person is charged another $1. Within the Downtown Convention Zone a flat rate of $4 for one person or $2 each for more than one will be charged for any destination. **Executive Limousine** (☎ 404/223–2000), **Checker Cab** (☎ 404/351–1111), and **Buckhead Safety Cab** (☎ 404/233–1152) offer 24-hour service.

Guided Tours

ORIENTATION

Gray Line of Atlanta (☎ 404/767–0594; 3½-hour tour $16.50 per person, full-day tour $27.50 per person) gives tours of Downtown, Midtown, and Buckhead, plus a day-long tour that includes Stone Mountain and the King Center. **Historic Air Tours** (1954 Airport Rd., Suite 215, Chamblee 30341, ☎ 404/457–5217; 3 tours lasting 20–55 min; $35–$85 per person) takes visitors high above the city in a private airplane.

WALKING TOURS

The **Atlanta Preservation Center** (156 7th St., Suite 3, ☎ 404/876–2041 or 404/876–2040) offers 10 walking tours of historic areas and neighborhoods ($5 adults, $4 senior citizens, $3 students; children under 19 free; tours conducted primarily on weekends). Especially noteworthy are tours of Sweet Auburn, the neighborhood associated with Martin Luther King Jr. and other leaders in Atlanta's African-American community; Druid Hills, the verdant, genteel neighborhood where *Driving Miss Daisy* was filmed; and the Fox Theatre, the elaborate, Moorish 1920s picture palace.

1996 Summer Olympics

The Atlanta Committee for the Olympic Games has spent over $1.6 billion to ready Atlanta for the event. Built on the former south parking lot of Atlanta–Fulton County Stadium (521 Capitol Ave., ☎ 404/

249–6400)—home of the Atlanta Braves baseball team—Olympic Stadium seats 85,000 people and will be converted into a baseball arena for use by the Braves beginning with the 1997 season. The Velodrome, an indoor bicycle race track, has been constructed at Stone Mountain Park, and the Olympic Village, where athletes and their families will stay, is on the Georgia Institute of Technology campus in the heart of the city. By the opening day ceremony, nearly 11 million tickets are expected to have been sold. For ticket information, contact the ACOG (*see* Visitor Information, *above*).

Important Addresses and Numbers

EMERGENCIES
Dial 911 for assistance. Both **Grady Memorial Hospital** (80 Butler St., ☎ 404/616–4307) and **Georgia Baptist Medical Center** (300 Blvd., ☎ 404/653–4000) have 24-hour emergency rooms. **Big B Drug** (1061 Ponce de Leon Ave., ☎ 404/876–0381) is open 24 hours, seven days a week.

RADIO STATIONS
AM: WPLO 610, country; WGST 640, news/talk; WCNN 680, sports/talk; WSB 750, news/talk; WQXI 790, music/talk; WAEC 860, Christian talk/music. **FM:** WABE 90.1, National Public Radio/classical; WCLK 91.9, jazz/soul; WZGC 92.9, classic rock; WPCH 94.9, light rock; WKLS 96.1, album rock; WFOX 97.1, oldies; WKHX 101.5, country; WVEE 103.3, top 40/soul.

VISITOR INFORMATION
To plan your trip, write to the **Georgia Department of Industry, Trade, and Tourism** (Box 1776, 30301, ☎ 800/847–4842, ℻ 404/656–3567) or, for Atlanta only, contact the **Atlanta Convention & Visitors Bureau** (ACVB; 233 Peachtree St., Suite 2000, 30303, ☎ 404/222–6688 or 800/285–2682). For information on the 1996 Olympic Games (July 19–Aug. 4), contact the **Atlanta Committee for the Olympic Games** (ACOG; Box 1996, Atlanta 30301-1996, ☎ 404/224–1996). Once in Atlanta, the ACVB has five visitor information centers stocked with maps and brochures: **Hartsfield Atlanta International Airport** (north terminal at west crossover), **Peachtree Center Mall** (233 Peachtree St.), **Underground Atlanta** (65 Upper Alabama St.), **Georgia World Congress Center** (285 International Blvd.), and **Lenox Square Mall** (3393 Peachtree Rd.). ACOG also runs **The Olympic Experience,** a public information/gallery/gift shop at Underground Atlanta, plus a booth at Lenox Square and other major malls.

SAVANNAH

By Honey Naylor

The very sound of the word Savannah conjures up misty images of mint juleps, live oaks dripping with Spanish moss, handsome mansions, and a somewhat decadent city moving at a lazy Southern pace. Why, you can hardly say "Savannah" without drawling.

Well, brace yourself. The mint juleps are there all right, along with the moss and the mansions and the easygoing pace, but this Southern belle rings with surprises.

Take, for example, St. Patrick's Day: Why on earth does Savannah, of all places, have a St. Patrick's Day celebration second only to New York's? The greening of Savannah began more than 164 years ago and nobody seems to know why, although everybody in town talks a blue (green) streak about St. Patrick's Day. Everything turns green on March 17, including the faces of startled visitors when green scrambled eggs and green grits are put before them. One year, some well-oiled revelers even tried to dye the Savannah River green.

Savannah's beginning was February 12, 1733, when English General James Edward Oglethorpe and 120 colonists arrived at Yamacraw Bluff on the Savannah River to found the 13th and last colony in the New World. As the port city grew, Englishmen, Scottish Highlanders, French Huguenots, Germans, Austrian Salzburgers, Sephardic Jews from Spain and Portugal, Moravians, Italians, Swiss, Welsh, and the Irish all arrived to create what could be called a rich gumbo.

In 1793, Eli Whitney of Connecticut, who was tutoring on a plantation near Savannah, invented a mechanized means of "ginning" seeds from cotton bolls. Cotton soon became king, and Savannah, already a busy seaport, flourished under its reign. Waterfront warehouses were filled with "white gold," and brokers trading in the Savannah Cotton Exchange set world prices. The white gold brought in solid gold, and fine mansions were built in the prospering city.

In 1864, Savannahians surrendered their city to Union General Sherman rather than see it torched. Following Reconstruction and the collapse of the cotton market, the city itself virtually collapsed, and languished for more than 50 years. Elegant mansions were either razed or allowed to decay, and cobwebs replaced cotton in the dilapidated riverfront warehouses.

But in 1955, Savannah's spirits rose again. News that the exquisite Isaiah Davenport home (324 E. State St.) was to be destroyed prompted seven outraged ladies to raise enough money to buy the house. They saved it the day before the wrecking ball was to swing.

Thus was born the Historic Savannah Foundation, the organization responsible for the restoration of downtown Savannah, where more than 1,000 restored buildings form the 2.5-square-mile Historic District, the nation's largest. Many of these buildings are open to the public during the annual tour of homes, and today Savannah is recognized as one of the top 10 cities in the U.S. for walking tours.

John Berendt's wildly popular *Midnight in the Garden of Good and Evil,* published in 1994, has dispatched many new visitors to Savannah. A nonfiction account of a notorious murder that took place in the city during the 1980s, the book brings to life such Savannah sites as Monterey Square, Mercer House, and Bonaventure Cemetery.

Exploring

Numbers in the margin correspond to points of interest on the Savannah Historic District map.

Georgia's founder, General James Oglethorpe, designed the original town of Savannah and laid it out in a perfect grid. The Historic District is neatly hemmed in by the Savannah River, Gaston Street, East Street, and Martin Luther King Jr. Boulevard. Streets are arrow-straight, public squares of varying sizes are tucked into the grid at precise intervals, and each block is sliced in half by a lane. Bull Street, anchored on the north by City Hall and the south by Forsyth Park, charges down the center of the grid and lunges around the five public squares that stand in its way. (Maneuvering a car around Savannah's squares is a minor art form.)

The Historic District

❶ Make your first stop the **Savannah Visitor's Center** (*see* Important Addresses and Numbers, *below*), to pick up the maps and brochures you'll need for exploring, and to look at the structure that houses the Center. The big redbrick building with its high ceilings and sweeping arches was the old Central of Georgia railway station, completed in 1860.

The Visitor's Center lies just north of the **site of the Siege of Savannah.** In 1779, the Colonial forces, led by Polish Count Casimir Pulaski, laid siege to Savannah in an attempt to retake the city from the Redcoats. They were beaten back, and Pulaski was killed while leading a cavalry charge against the British. On the battle site, adjacent to the
❷ Visitor's Center, the **Savannah History Museum,** in a restored shed of the railway station, offers an excellent introduction to the city. Two theaters present special-effects depictions of Oglethorpe's landing and of the siege. Exhibits range from old locomotives to a tribute to Savannah-born songwriter Johnny Mercer. There are two restored dining cars that aren't going anywhere, but you can climb aboard for a bite to eat. *303 Martin Luther King Jr. Blvd.,* ☎ *912/238–1779.* ☛ *$3 adults, $2.50 senior citizens, $1.75 children 6–12, under 6 free.* ☉ *Weekdays 8:30–5, weekends 9–5.*

❸ Turn left on Broad Street and walk two blocks to the **Scarbrough House** (41 Martin Luther King Jr. Dr.). The exuberant Regency mansion was built during the 1819 cotton boom for Savannah merchant prince William Scarbrough and designed by English architect William Jay. A Doric portico is capped by one of Jay's characteristic half-moon windows. Four massive Greek Doric columns form a peristyle in the atrium entrance hall. Three stories overhead is an arched, sky-blue ceiling with sunshine filtering through a skylight. Visitors can admire its Regency architecture from outside; Scarbrough House is not open to the public.

Continue east across Franklin Square and stroll through City Market, which includes an art center with working studios of 35 area artists, along with sidewalk cafés, jazz joints, and shops. Now head east on
❹ St. Julian Street to **Johnson Square.** Laid out in 1733 and named for South Carolina Governor Robert Johnson, this was the earliest of Oglethorpe's original 24 squares. The square was once a popular gathering place, where Savannahians came to welcome President Monroe in 1819, to greet the Marquis de Lafayette in 1825, and to cheer for Georgia's secession in 1861.

As you stand at the foot of Bull Street, the building to the north with the glittering dome (regilded in 1987) is **City Hall,** dating from 1905. Its lower stories face the spot from which the SS *Savannah* set sail in 1819, the first steamship to cross an ocean. Just west of City Hall, on Yamacraw Bluff, is a marble bench, appropriately called **Oglethorpe's Bench,** marking the site of the general's field tent.

❺ Cobblestone ramps lead from Bay Street down to **Factors Walk** and,
❻ below it, to **River Street.** Cars can enter Factors Walk via the ramps, and so can pedestrians. (These are serious cobblestones, and you will suffer if you wear anything but the most comfortable shoes you own.) There is also a network of iron walkways connecting Bay Street with the multistoried buildings that rise up from the river level, and iron stairways descend from Bay Street down to Factors Walk.

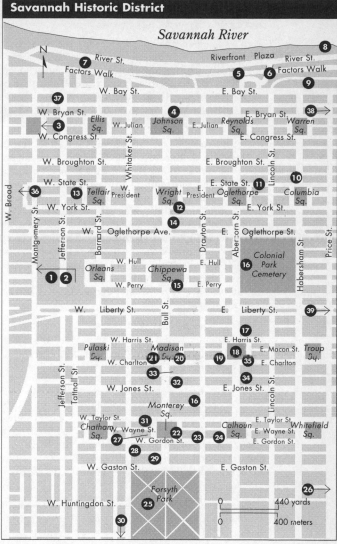

Savannah Historic District

Children enjoy the **River Street Train Museum,** which offers guided tours of antique train displays and railroad memorabilia. *315 W. River St.,* ☎ *912/233–6175.* ☛ *$1.50 adults, 50¢ children 5–12, under 5 free.* ☺ *Mon.–Sat. 11–5:30, Sun. 1–6.*

Foreign vessels still call at the Port of Savannah, the largest port between Baltimore and New Orleans. Paper and other products have replaced the cotton exports, and in 1977 a multimillion-dollar riverfront revitalization transformed the decayed warehouses into a nine-block marketplace housing unique boutiques alongside musty taverns.

Benches line **Riverfront Plaza,** where you can watch a parade of freighters and pug-nosed tugs; youngsters can play in the tugboat-shaped sandboxes here. Each weekday, Dixieland music can be heard from the cabin of the *River Street Rambler,* a brightly painted freight train that rumbles down River Street to the port. River Street is the main venue for many of the city's celebrations, including the First Saturday festivals when flea marketeers, artists, and craftspeople display their wares and musicians entertain the crowds.

Even landlubbers can appreciate the fine craftsmanship of the ship models in the **Ships of the Sea Museum.** The four floors of the museum contain models of steamships, nuclear subs, China clippers with their sails unfurled, Columbus's ships, a showcase filled with ships-in-bottles, and a collection of fine Royal Doulton porcelain seafarers. *503 East River St. and 504 East Bay St.,* ☎ *912/232–1511.* ☛ *$3 adults, $1.50 children 7–12, under 7 free.* ☉ *Daily 10–5.*

If you entered the museum at the River Street entrance and worked your way up all four floors, you'll be topside again on Bay Street. The tree-shaded park along Bay Street is **Emmet Park,** named for Robert Emmet, a late 18th-century Irish patriot and orator. Walk west along Bay Street and turn left onto Abercorn Street. In **Reynolds Square** you'll see the statue of John Wesley, who preached in Savannah and wrote the first English hymnal here in 1736. The monument to the founder of the Methodist Church is shaded by greenery and surrounded by park benches. On the square is the **Olde Pink House** (23 Abercorn St.). Built in 1771, it is one of the oldest buildings in town. The porticoed pink stucco Georgian mansion has been a private home, a bank, and headquarters for a Yankee general during the war. It is now a restaurant (*see* Dining, *below*).

From Reynolds Square walk south on Abercorn Street, turn left onto Broughton Street, and two blocks down turn right onto Habersham Street. Ahead stands the **Isaiah Davenport House.** Semicircular stairs with wrought-iron trim lead to the recessed doorway of the redbrick Federal mansion that master builder Isaiah Davenport built for himself in 1815, using architectural texts available in his day. Three dormer windows poke through the sloping roof of the stately house, and inside there are polished hardwood floors, fine woodwork and plasterwork, and a soaring elliptical staircase. The furnishings are Hepplewhite, Chippendale, and Sheraton, and in the attic there is a collection of antique dolls and a dollhouse with tiny 19th-century furnishings. *324 E. State St.,* ☎ *912/236–8097.* ☛ *$4 adults, $3 children 6–18.* ☉ *Daily 10–4.*

Walk west on State Street two blocks to the **Owens Thomas House & Museum.** This was William Jay's first Regency mansion in Savannah, built in 1816, and it is the city's finest example of that architectural style. The thoroughly English house was built largely with local materials, including tabby—a mixture of oyster shells, sand, and water that resembles concrete. The entry portico is of Doric design with curving stairs leading to a recessed door topped by a fanlight. Of particular note are the curving walls of the house, Greek-inspired ornamental molding, Jay's half-moon arches, stained-glass panels, and Duncan Phyfe furniture. You'll find canopied beds, a pianoforte, and displays of ornate silver. From a wrought-iron balcony, in 1825, the Marquis de Lafayette bade a two-hour au revoir to the crowd below. *124 Abercorn St.,* ☎ *912/233–9743.* ☛ *$5 adults, $3 students, $2 children 6–12, under 6 free.* ☉ *Sun. 2–4:30, Tues.–Sat. 10–4:30.*

Stroll through **Oglethorpe Square,** across State Street, and continue two blocks west to **Wright Square.** The square was named for James Wright, Georgia's last Colonial governor. The centerpiece of the square is an elaborate monument erected in honor of William Washington Gordon, founder of the Central of Georgia Railroad. A slab of granite from Stone

Mountain marks the grave of Tomo-Chi-Chi, the Yamacraw chief who befriended General Oglethorpe and the colonists.

⑬ Continue west on State Street, strolling through **Telfair Square** to reach the **Telfair Mansion and Art Museum.** The South's oldest public art museum is housed in yet another of Jay's Regency creations, this one designed in 1819. Within its marbled halls are American, French, and Dutch Impressionist paintings; German Tonalist paintings; a large collection of works by Kahlil Gibran; plaster casts of the Elgin Marbles, the Venus de Milo, and the Laocoön, among other classical sculptures; and a room that contains some of the Telfair family furnishings, including a Duncan Phyfe sideboard and Savannah-made silver. *121 Barnard St.,* ☎ *912/232–1177.* ☛ *$3 adults, $1 students and senior citizens, 50¢ children 6–12; free on Sun.* ☉ *Tues.–Sat. 10–5, Sun. 2–5.*

⑭ At the next corner, turn left onto Oglethorpe Avenue and cross onto Bull Street to reach the **Juliette Gordon Low Birthplace.** This majestic Regency mansion is attributed to William Jay and in 1965 was designated Savannah's first National Historic Landmark. "Daisy" Low, founder of the Girl Scouts, was born here, and the house is now owned and operated by the Girl Scouts of America. Mrs. Low's paintings and other artworks are on display in the house, restored to the style of 1886, the year of Mrs. Low's marriage. *142 Bull St.,* ☎ *912/233–4501.* ☛ *$5 adults, $4.50 senior citizens, $4 children under 18; discounts for Girl Scouts.* ☉ *Mon.–Tues. and Thurs.–Sat. 10–4, Sun. 12:30–4:30.*

⑮ **Chippewa Square** is a straight shot south on Bull Street. There you can see Daniel Chester French's imposing bronze statue of the general himself, James Edward Oglethorpe. Also note the Savannah Theatre, the longest continuously operated theater site in North America.

⑯ From Chippewa Square, go east on McDonough Street to reach the **Colonial Park Cemetery.** Savannahians were buried here from 1750 to 1853. Shaded pathways lace through the park, and you may want to stroll through and read some of the old inscriptions. There are several historical plaques in the cemetery, one of which marks the grave of Button Gwinnett, a signer of the Declaration of Independence.

⑰ The **Cathedral of St. John the Baptist** soars like a hymn over the corner of Abercorn and Harris streets, two blocks south of the cemetery. The French Gothic cathedral, with the pointed arches and free-flowing traceries characteristic of the style, is the seat of the Diocese of Savannah. It is the oldest Roman Catholic church in Georgia, having been founded in the early 1700s. Fire destroyed the early structures, and the present cathedral dates from 1876. Most of the cathedral's impressive stained-glass windows were made by Austrian glassmakers and imported around the turn of the century. The high altar is of Italian marble, and the Stations of the Cross were imported from Munich.

⑱ Across from the cathedral is **Lafayette Square,** named for the Marquis de Lafayette. The graceful three-tier fountain in the square was donated by the Georgia chapter of the Colonial Dames of America.

⑲ Across the square is the **Andrew Low House.** The house was built for Andrew Low in 1848, and later belonged to his son William, who married Juliette Gordon. After her husband's death, "Daisy" Low founded the Girl Scouts in this house on March 12, 1912. Robert E. Lee and William Thackeray were both entertained in this mansion. In addition to its historical significance, the house boasts some of the finest ornamental ironwork in Savannah. Members and friends of the Colonial

Dames have donated fine 19th-century antiques and stunning silver to the house. *329 Abercorn St.,* ☎ *912/233–6854.* ☛ *$5 adults, $2 students, $1 children and Girl Scouts.* ☼ *Mon.–Wed. and Fri.–Sat. 10:30–4:30, Sun. noon–4:30.*

㉒ Two blocks to the west is **Madison Square,** laid out in 1839 and named for James Madison. The statue depicts Sergeant William Jasper hoisting a flag and is a tribute to his bravery during the Siege of Savannah. Though mortally wounded, he rescued the colors of his regiment in the assault on the British lines.

㉑ On the west side of the square is the **Green-Meldrim House,** designed by New York architect John Norris and built in about 1850 for cotton merchant Charles Green. The house was bought in 1892 by Judge Peter Meldrim, whose heirs sold it to St. John's Episcopal Church, for which it is now the working parish house. It was here that General Sherman lived after taking the city in 1864—in the splendid Gothic Revival mansion, complete with crenellated roof and oriel windows. The gallery that sweeps around three sides of the house is awash with filigreed ironwork. The mantels are Carrara marble, the woodwork is carved black walnut, and the doorknobs and hinges are silver-plated. There is a magnificent skylight above a gracefully curved staircase. The house is furnished with 16th- and 17th-century antiques. *14 West Macon St. on Madison Sq.,* ☎ *912/233–3845.* ☛ *$3.* ☼ *Oct.–Feb., Tues. and Thurs.–Sat. 10–4; Mar.–Sept., Mon. and Wed. 1–4. Closed the first Wed. of each month.*

TIME OUT Students from the Savannah College of Art and Design buy art supplies and books at **Design Works Bookstore.** There is also a soda fountain and tables in this old Victorian drugstore, where you can get short orders, burgers, and deli sandwiches. *Corner of Bull and Charlton Sts.,* ☎ *912/238-2481.* ☼ *Weekdays 9–5, Sat. 10–2.*

The fifth and last of Bull Street's squares is **Monterey Square,** which commemorates the victory of General Zachary Taylor's forces in Monterrey, Mexico, in 1846. The square's monument honors General Casimir Pulaski, the Polish nobleman who lost his life in the Siege of Savannah during the Revolutionary War.

㉒ On the east side of the square stands **Temple Mickve Israel,** home to the third oldest Jewish congregation in America, who settled in town five months after the founding of Savannah in 1733. The original congregation, a group of Spanish and German Jews, brought with them the prized "Sephar Torah" now in the present temple, which was consecrated in 1878. The splendid Gothic Revival synagogue contains a collection of documents and letters (some from George Washington and Thomas Jefferson) pertaining to early Jewish life in Savannah and Georgia. *20 E. Gordon St.,* ☎ *912/233–1547.* ☛ *Free.* ☼ *Weekdays 10–noon and 2–4.*

㉓ A block east of the temple is a Gothic Revival church memorializing the founders of Methodism. The **Wesley Monumental Church,** patterned after Queen's Kirk in Amsterdam, celebrated a century of service in 1968. The church is noted for its magnificent stained-glass windows. In the Wesley Window there are busts of John and Charles Wesley.

㉔ At the **Massie Heritage Interpretation Center,** in addition to a scale model of the city, maps and plans, and architectural displays, is a "Heritage Classroom" that offers schoolchildren hands-on instruction about early Colonial life. *207 E. Gordon St.,* ☎ *912/651–7022.* ☛ *Free, but a donation of $1.50 is appreciated.* ☼ *Weekdays 9–4:30.*

㉕ The southern anchor of Bull Street is **Forsyth Park,** with 20 luxuriant acres. The glorious white fountain, dating from 1858, was restored in 1988. In addition to its Confederate and Spanish-American War memorials, the park contains the Fragrant Garden for the Blind, a project of Savannah garden clubs. There are tennis courts and a tree-shaded jogging path. The park is often the scene of outdoor plays and concerts.

㉖ The **King-Tisdell Cottage,** perched behind a picket fence, is a museum dedicated to the preservation of African-American history and culture. The Negro Heritage Trail Tour (*see* Special-interest Tours in Guided Tours, *below*) visits here, in this little Victorian house. Broad steps lead to a porch that's loaded with gewgaws, and dormer windows pop up through a steep roof. The interior is furnished to resemble an African-American coastal home of the 1890s. *514 E. Huntingdon St., ☎ 912/234–8000. ☞ $2.50. ⊙ Tues.–Fri. 1–4:30.*

Other houses of interest in the Victorian district are at **118 E. Waldburg Street** and **111 W. Gwinnett Street.** A stroll along **Bolton Street** will be especially rewarding for fans of fanciful architecture. Of particular note is the entire 200 block, 114 W. Bolton Street, 109 W. Bolton Street, and 321 E. Bolton Street.

Tour 2: Midnight in the Garden of Good and Evil
A true town gossip can give you the best introduction to a city and, as author John Berendt discovered, Savannah's not short on them. In his 1994 bestseller, *Midnight in the Garden of Good and Evil,* Berendt shares the juiciest of tales imparted to him during the eight years he spent here wining and dining with Savannah's high society and dancing with her Grand Empress drag queen, the Lady Chablis, among others. By the time he left, there had been one scandalous homicide and several follow-up trials, each played out among lavishly drunken party after party.

Before you enter the city limits, first try to grab a copy of the book, pour yourself a cool martini, and enter an eccentric world of killers and backstabbers, voodoo witches and garden-club women, all surrounded by graveyards and inhabiting mansions. After you've read the book, slip on a pair of comfortable shoes and head over to the historic district to follow the characters steps to their homes and haunts. By the end of this walking tour, you'll be hard-pressed to find the line between Berendt's creative nonfiction and Savannah's reality. *Note: Unless otherwise indicated, the sights on this tour are not open to the public.*

㉗ Begin this tour at **Mercer House** at 429 Bull Street. Songwriter and crooner Johnny Mercer's great-grandfather began building the residence in 1860 but dropped the project on the eve of the Civil War. A redbrick Italianate mansion on the southwest corner of Monterey Square, the house became the Taj Mahal of the book's main character Jim Williams; here he ran a world-class antique dealership, held *the* Christmas party of the season, and shot and killed his sometime house partner Danny Hansford. Williams himself died in 1990 in the den near the very spot where Hansford fell. Today, his sister lives there quietly among the remnants of his Fabergé collection, and Joshua Reynolds paintings, in rooms lit by Waterford crystal chandeliers.

㉘ Next, walk south on Bull Street to West Gordon Street and take a right until you come to **Serena Dawes's house** (17 W. Gordon St.). Serena, who in real life went by the name of Helen Driscoll, was a high-profile beauty in the 1930s and '40s who married into the fortunes of a Pennsylvania steel family. After her husband accidentally and fatally shot himself in the head, she retired here, back in her hometown. Dawes, Berendt writes, "spent most of her day in bed, holding court, drinking martinis and pink ladies, playing with her white toy poodle, Lulu." One neighbor remarked to the author that Serena's callers were all gentlemen, and chief among them was Luther Driggers, rumored to possess a poison strong enough to wipe out the entire city.

㉙ Head back to Bull Street and take a right, walking south toward Forsyth Park, until you reach the **Armstrong House** (447 Bull St.), where Jim Williams once lived and worked before purchasing the Mercer House. This unique mansion was on Berendt's jogging path, and he occasionally strolled by during his late afternoon walks. On its surrounding sidewalk, he met Mr. Simon Glover, the 86-year-old singer and porter for the law firm of Bouhan, Williams, and Levy, who occupy the building. Glover's daily jaunts lead him up and down Bull street to earn a weekly $10 for walking one of the firm's former partner's deceased dogs. Baffled? So was the author. Behind the house's cast-iron gates, are the offices of Jim Williams's attorney, who doubles as keeper of Uga, the Georgia Bulldog mascot.

㉚ Continue south on Bull Street until you come to the northwest corner of Forsyth Park. Take a right there, down West Gaston till it crosses Whitaker, and proceed south till you get to the **Forsyth Parkside Apartments** (Whitaker and Gwinnett streets). This complex became Berendt's second home in Savannah, and from his fourth-floor rooms he pieced together the majority of the book. Parking his newly acquired 1973 Pontiac Grand Prix outside these apartments, Berendt first met the Lady Chablis coming out of her nearby doctor's office, freshly feminine from a new round of hormone shots.

Walk through Forsyth Park, heading north back to Monterey Square, to complete the first circle of the walking tour. At the southeast corner of the Square, you'll find **Temple Mickve Israel** (20 E. Gordon St., *see* Tour 1, *above*) near the intersection of Bull and East Gordon streets. The Mercer House (*see above*) is in easy view of the temple, as was the Nazi swastika flag Jim Williams once flew from his windows, supposedly to disrupt the filming of a TV movie. His antics temporarily stopped the shooting, but did deeper damage, offending the temple's congregation and the rest of the neighborhood.

㉛ Cross the square heading west, back toward the Mercer House, and walk north to **Lee Adler's Home** (425 Bull St.). One of Williams's biggest adversaries, Adler lives in half of the double town house facing West Wayne Street, where he runs his business of restoring historic Savannah properties. Adler's howling dogs drove Williams to his pipe organ, where he churned out a deafening version of César Franck's *Pièce Heroique*. Later, Adler stuck reelection signs in his front lawn, showing his support for the District Attorney who prosecuted Williams three time before he was finally found not guilty.

TIME OUT By now, you should have worked up a pretty good appetite, so head over to **Mrs. Wilkes Dining Room** (107 W. Jones St., *see* Dining, *below*) and sample some of the fare that Jim Williams had delivered to him while in jail at Chatham County Courthouse. Go west away from Monterey Square, till you get to Whitaker Street. Then go north until you find West Jones Street.

㉜ Head east on Jones Street to view the **first of Joe Odom's homes** (16 E. Jones St.). Odom, a combination tax lawyer, real-estate broker, and piano player, played host to a 24-hour steady stream of visitors in this stucco town house. The author met Odom through his fourth fiancée-in-waiting, Mandy, a former Miss Big Beautiful Woman, who stopped by to borrow ice for yet another party, when their power had been cut off yet another time.

33 Within earshot of 16 East Street, you'll find **Berendt's first Savannah residence,** one street north on Charlton Lane, on the backside of 22 East Jones Street. Here, from the second story of the redbrick carriage house, Berendt first heard Joe's all-night parties, as the music and laughter filtered into his tiny magnolia-and-banana-tree-stocked garden below.

Next, take the East Jones Street sidewalk east toward Abercorn Street.
34 At the southeast corner of Abercorn and East Jones, look for **Clary's Café** at 402 Abercorn Street. John Berendt came here following his morning jogs to load up on a typical greasy spoon–style breakfast, and to catch the latest gossip. With locals gathered at tables and along the soda fountain counter, Clary's makes for some fine people-watching. Berendt first observed Serena Dawes's tormented boyfriend Luther Driggers at Clary's, while the man sat in front of his usual eggs and bacon and milk of magnesia breakfast, with thread-leashed flies attached to his clothes.

From Clary's, go right on Abercorn Street toward Lafayette Square. At the southeastern corner of the square, you will see the towering hulk
35 of the sturdily elegant **Hamilton-Turner House** (330 Abercorn St.). After one too many of Odom's deals went sour, Mandy left him and took over his third residence, a Second Empire–style mansion from 1873. Mandy (or Nancy Hillis, as her driver's license reads) filled it with 17th- and 18th-century antiques and has since transformed it into a successful museum through which she sometimes leads tour groups. ☎ 912/233–4800. ☛ $5. ☉ For tours mid-Apr.–Sept., daily 10–5; Oct.–mid.-Apr., daily 11–4.

Leave the Hamilton-Turner House and head west on East Charlton Street till you find Bull Street once again. Go right on Bull Street, through Chippewa Square, then turn left onto Oglethorpe Avenue till you come
36 to the **Chatham County Courthouse** at 133 Montgomery Street. Here, Williams was triple-tried for murder over the course of about eight years. An underground tunnel leads from the courthouse to the jail where he was held in a specially modified cell that allowed him to conduct his antiques business.

Three more essential stops from the book are best taken in as they were
37 in the book—at nightfall or later. Don't miss a trip to the gay bar **Club One** (1 Jefferson St.), where the Lady Chablis still bumps and grinds her wild way down the catwalk, lip-syncing disco tunes in a shimmer of sequin and satin gowns. Call 912/232–0200 to find out when Chablis sings. ☛ $5 adults, $10 ages 18–20. Shows at 10:30 PM and 1 AM.

For tunes that are a little more low-key but no less flamboyant, head
38 over to **Hard Hearted Hannah's East** (upstairs in the Pirates' House, 20 E. Broad St.) to find Emma Kelly pouring out her best show tunes and blues bits. Emma moved here after her self-named club went bankrupt under Joe Odom's direction. Nicknamed "The Lady of 6,000 Songs" by Johnny Mercer, who convinced her to start singing, Miss Kelly has got quite a repertoire. Yes, she does take requests, so come prepared to be serenaded by this lovely woman who has entertained countless church groups and Lions clubs, not to mention three presi-

dents and at least 20 governors. ☏ *912/233–2225. Cover: $3 Fri. and Sat. Ms. Kelly performs Tues. and Wed. 6–11 PM, Thurs.–Sat. 6–9 PM.*

㊴ Last of all, end your pilgrimage at the **Bonaventure Cemetery** by following Wheaton Street west out of downtown to Bonaventure Road. (Note: get there before sundown, when it closes). Once the grounds of a magnificent live oak-choked plantation, whose mansion burned to the ground in the midst of a dinner party, Bonaventure is the final resting place for both Jim Williams and Danny Hansford. While you may be able to find their markers, don't look too hard for the haunting female tombstone figure from the book's cover. Apparently, Berendt fans beat too tough a path to her feet, and she was removed to protect surrounding graves. Savannah, no matter how wild the city was portrayed, seems to know how to pay last respects.

Day-Tripping to Tybee Island

Tybee Island, which lies 18 miles east of Savannah on the Atlantic Ocean, offers all manner of water and beach activities. Take Victory Drive (U.S. 80), which sometimes takes the alias of Tybee Road. There are two historic forts to visit on the way.

Fort Pulaski National Monument is 14 miles east of downtown Savannah. You'll see the entrance on your left just before U.S. 80E reaches Tybee Island. A must for Civil War buffs, the fort was built on Cockspur Island between 1829 and 1847 and named for Casimir Pulaski, a Polish count who was a Revolutionary War hero. Robert E. Lee's first assignment after graduating from West Point was as an engineer here. During the Civil War the fort fell on April 12, 1862, after a mere 30 hours of bombardment by newfangled rifled cannons. It was the first time such cannons had been used in warfare—and the last time a masonry fort was thought to be impregnable. The restored fortification, operated by the National Park Service, is complete with moats, drawbridges, massive ramparts, and towering walls. The visitor center includes museum exhibits and an audiovisual program. The park has self-guided trails and ample picnic areas. *U.S. 80,* ☏ *912/786–5787.* ☛ *$2 adults, children 16 and under free.* ☉ *Daily 8:30–5, hours extended during summer.*

Three miles farther along U.S. 80 is **Tybee Island.** "Tybee" is an Indian word meaning salt. The Yamacraw Indians came to the island to hunt and fish, and legend has it that pirates buried their treasure here. The island is about 5 miles long and 2 miles wide, with a plethora of seafood restaurants, chain motels, condos, and shops, most of which sprung up during the 1950s and haven't changed much since. The entire expanse of white sand is divided into a number of public beaches, where visitors go shelling and crabbing, play on waterslides, charter fishing boats, swim, and build sand castles. Contact Tybee Island Beach Visitor Information (Box 1628, Savannah 31402, ☏ 800/868–2322).

The **Tybee Museum and Lighthouse** are at the island's tip. In the museum you'll see Indian artifacts, pirate pistols, powder flasks, old prints tracing the history of Savannah, even some sheet music of Johnny Mercer songs. The Civil War Room has old maps and newspaper articles pertaining to Sherman's occupation of the city. On the second floor there are model antique cars and ship models, and a collection of antique dolls. The lighthouse across the road is Georgia's oldest and tallest, dating from 1773, with an observation deck 145 feet above the sea. Bright red steps—178 of them—lead to the deck and the awesome Tybee

Light. The view of the ocean will take away whatever breath you have left after the climb. *30 Meddin Dr., ☎ 912/786–4077. ☛ To both lighthouse and museum: $2.50 adults, $1.50 senior citizens, 75¢ children 6–12. ☉ Both daily 10–6 in summer; Mon., Wed.–Fri. noon–4, weekends 10–4 in winter.*

TIME OUT Spanky's Pizza Galley & Saloon has fried shrimp, burgers, chicken fingers, and salads. *317 E. River St., ☎ 912/236-3009. AE, MC, V. ☉ Daily 11 AM–midnight.*

Heading west back to Savannah, take the Islands Expressway, which becomes the President Street Extension. About 3½ miles outside the city you'll see a sign for **Fort Jackson,** located on Salter's Island. The Colonial fort was purchased in 1808 by the federal government and is the oldest standing fort in Georgia. It was garrisoned in 1812 and was the Confederate headquarters of the river batteries. The brick fort is surrounded by a tidal moat, and there are 13 exhibit areas. Battle reenactments, blacksmithing demonstrations, and programs of 19th-century music are among the fort's schedule of activities. The Trooping of the Colors and military tattoo take place at regular intervals during summer. *1 Ft. Jackson Rd., ☎ 912/232–3945. ☛ $2.50 adults; $2 students, senior citizens, and military personnel; children 6 and under free. ☉ Daily 9–5.*

What to See and Do with Children

Forts Pulaski and **Jackson** (*see* Day-tripping to Tybee Island, *above*).

Juliette Gordon Low Girl Scout National Center (*see* Exploring, *above*).

Oatland Island Education Center. This 175-acre maritime forest, 5 minutes from downtown, is a natural habitat for coastal wildlife, including timber wolves and panthers. The center also houses the coastal offices of the Georgia Conservancy. *711 Sandtown Rd., tel 912/897–3773. Donation (about $1) requested. ☉ Weekdays 8:30–5; special events and programs take place Oct.–May, on the 2nd Sat. of each month 11–5.*

Exhibits at the **Savannah Science Museum** include a Plexiglas "crawl through" that allows kids to view reptiles and amphibians; a discovery room; a 32-foot, two-deck boat; an 800-gallon aquarium; Indian artifacts; and planetarium shows. *4405 Paulsen St., ☎ 912/355–6705. ☛ $3 adults; $2 senior citizens, students, and children 12 and under. ☉ Tues.–Sat. 10–5, Sun. 2–5; free planetarium shows every second Sun. at 3.*

Skidaway Island Marine Science Complex. On the grounds of the former Modena Plantation, the complex features a 12-panel, 12,000-gallon aquarium with marine and plant life of the Continental Shelf. Other exhibits highlight coastal archaeology and fossils of the Georgia coast. Nature trails overlook marsh and water. *30 Ocean Science Circle, Skidaway Island, ☎ 912/598–2325. ☛ $1, children under 7 free. ☉ Weekdays 9–4, Sat. noon–5.*

Tybee Island Museum and Lighthouse (*see* Day-Tripping to Tybee Island, *above*).

Off the Beaten Path

If your tastebuds crave down-home barbecue, head for **Walls',** place your order at the counter, then wait at an orange plastic booth. Entertainment is provided by a small color TV set. Drinks are serve-yourself from the refrigerator case, and your food comes in Styrofoam cartons. A sign taped above the counter reads, "When I work, I works hard. When I sit, I sits loose—when I think, I falls asleep." Plain? Not really. Barbecued spare ribs, barbecued sandwiches, and deviled crabs—the only items on the menu—are plenty rich. A large carton of ribs costs $8.50. *515 E. York La., between Oglethorpe Ave. and York St.,* ☎ *912/232–9754. No credit cards.* ☉ *Wed. 11–5, Thurs. 11–10, Fri. and Sat. 11–10:30.*

Shopping

Find your own Low Country treasures among a bevy of handcrafted wares—handmade quilts and baskets; wreaths made from Chinese tallow trees and Spanish moss; preserves, jams, and jellies. The favorite Savannah snack, and a popular gift item, is the benne wafer. It's about the size of a quarter and comes in a variety of flavors.

Shopping Districts
Riverfront Plaza/River Street is nine blocks of shops housed in the renovated waterfront warehouses, where you can find everything from popcorn to pottery. **City Market,** located on West St. Julian Street between Ellis and Franklin squares, has sidewalk cafés, jazz haunts, shops, and art galleries. If you're in need of anything from aspirin to anklets, head for **Broughton Street** and wander through its many variety and specialty stores.

Oglethorpe Mall (7804 Abercorn Extension, ☎ 912/354–7038) is an enclosed center with four department stores (Sears, JC Penney, Belks, and Rich's) and more than 140 specialty shops and fast-food and full-service restaurants. The **Savannah Mall** (14045 Abercorn St. and Rio Rd., ☎ 912/927–7467) just off I–95 also has four major anchor stores (JB White's, Belks, Parisians, and Montgomery Ward), along with more than 100 specialty shops and fast-food and full-service restaurants. Kids delight in its old-fashioned carousel. **Savannah Festival Factory Stores** (11 Gateway Blvd. S, ☎ 912/925–3089) has manufacturers' merchandise at 25%–75% off. .

Specialty Shops
ANTIQUES
Arthur Smith (1 W. Jones St., ☎ 912/236–9701) houses four floors of 18th- and 19th-century European furniture, porcelain, rugs, and paintings. At **Claire West Antiques and Fine Linen** (411–413 Whitaker St., ☎ 912/236–8163) you will find two buildings filled with an extensive collection of fine European linens, antiques, prints and engravings, old and new decorative tabletop objects, and a children's boutique with handmade bonnets and pinafores.

ARTWORK
Exhibit A Gallery (340 Bull St., ☎ 912/238–2480), the gallery of the Savannah College of Art and Design, has hand-painted cards, handmade jewelry, and paintings by regional artists. **Gallery 209** (209 E. River St., ☎ 912/236–4583) is a co-op gallery with paintings, watercolors, pottery, jewelry, batik, stained glass, and sculpture by local artists. Original artwork, prints, and books by internationally acclaimed artist Ray Ellis are sold in the **Compass Prints, Inc. Ray Ellis Gallery** (205 W. Congress St., ☎ 912/234–3537).

BENNE WAFERS
You can buy boxed bennes in most gift shops, but the **Byrd Cookie Company, Inc.** (2233 Norwood Ave., ☎ 912/355–1716) is where they

originated in 1924. The popular cookies are sold in 50 gift shops around town or on site at the **Cooky Shanty.**

BOOKS

The 12 rooms of **E. Shaver's, Bookseller** (326 Bull St., ☎ 912/234–7257) are stocked with books on architecture and regional history, among other great finds. The **Book Lady** (17 W. York St., ☎ 912/233–3628) specializes in used, rare, and out-of-print books; it also provides a search service.

COUNTRY CRAFTS

At **Charlotte's Corner** (1 W. Liberty St., ☎ 912/233–8061) browse through regional cookbooks, children's clothes and handmade toys, and potpourris. **Georgia Gifts** (217 W. St. Julian St., ☎ 912/236–1220) has handmade baskets, jams, jellies, preserves, and wreaths.

Participant Sports

Bicycling

Pedaling is a breeze on these flatlands. Rental bikes are available at **Cyclological** (322 W. Broughton St., ☎ 912/233–9401) beginning in March.

Boating

Saltwater Charters (111 Wickersham Dr., ☎ 912/598–1814) operates everything from two-hour sightseeing tours to 13-hour deep-sea fishing expeditions. Pedal boats can be rented for tooling around **Lake Mayer** (Lake Mayer Park, Sallie Mood Dr. and Montgomery Crossroads Dr., ☎ 912/652–6780). There are public boat ramps at **Bell's Landing** on the Forest River (Apache Rd. off Abercorn St.); **Islands Expressway** on the Wilmington River (Islands Expressway adjacent to Frank W. Spencer Park); and **Savannah Marina** on the Wilmington River in the town of Thunderbolt.

Golf

Try the 27-hole course at **Bacon Park** (Shorty Cooper Dr., ☎ 912/354–2625) and the 9-hole course at **Mary Calder** (W. Lathrop Ave., ☎ 912/238–7100).

Health Clubs

Jewish Educational Alliance (5111 Abercorn St., ☎ 912/355–8111) has racquetball courts, a gymnasium, weight room, sauna, whirlpool, outdoor Olympic-size pool, and aerobic dance classes.

Savannah Downtown Athletic Club (7 E. Congress St., ☎ 912/236–4874) has Lifecycles, StairMasters, Nautilus and free-weight equipment, sauna, swimming pool, aerobics, and tae kwon do classes.

YMCA Family Center (6400 Habersham St., ☎ 912/354–6223) offers a gymnasium, aerobics, racquetball, pool, and tennis.

Jogging

Flat-as-a-benne wafer **Forsyth Park** and the beach at **Tybee Island** are favorites with runners. Suburbanites favor the jogging trails in **Lake Mayer Park** (Montgomery Crossroads Rd. at Sallie Mood Dr.) and **Daffin Park** (1500 E. Victory Dr.).

Tennis

There are 14 lighted courts in **Bacon Park** (Skidaway Rd., ☎ 912/351–3850), four lighted courts in **Forsyth Park** (Drayton and Gaston Sts.,

☎ 912/351–3852), and eight lighted courts in **Lake Mayer Park** (Montgomery Crossroads Rd. and Sallie Mood Dr., ☎ 912/652–6780). Five other local parks have courts as well.

Dining

On a river, 18 miles inland from the Atlantic Ocean, Savannah naturally has excellent seafood restaurants. Locals also have a passion for spicy barbecue. The Historic District yields culinary treasures among its architectural diamonds—especially along River Street. Savannahians also like to drive out to eat in Thunderbolt and on Skidaway, Tybee, and Wilmington islands.

CATEGORY	COST*
$$$$	over $30
$$$	$25–$30
$$	$15–$25
$	under $15

per person for a three-course meal, excluding drinks, service, and tax

What to Wear
Dress in Savannah is casual except where noted otherwise.

American

$$$$ **45 South.** This popular southside eatery moved in 1988 to the sprawling Pirates' House complex. It's a small, stylish restaurant with contemporary decor in lush mauve and green (typical of Savannah) colors. The ever-changing menu includes contemporary American dinner entrées such as sliced breast of duck with au gratin potatoes and grilled tuna with black angel-hair pasta and a pomeray mustard butter sauce. ✕ 20 E. Broad St., ☎ 912/233–1881. Reservations advised. AE, MC, V. No lunch. Closed Sun.

$$$ **Olde Pink House.** The brick Georgian mansion was built for James Habersham, one of the wealthiest Americans of his time, in 1771. The elegant tavern, one of Savannah's oldest buildings, has original Georgia pine floors, Venetian chandeliers, and 18th-century English antiques. The new owners have taken great pains to research Colonial cooking style and have introduced it where appropriate. Signature dishes are a colonial version of crisp roast duck with a savory wild-berry compote, and black grouper stuffed with blue crab and finished with Vidalia onion sauce. The restaurant is graced with one of the largest wine cellars in the state of Georgia—fitting, as the Habersham family dominated the Madeira trade for years. Piano jazz (Tues.–Sun. 7:30–midnight) is played downstairs at Planters Tavern, where Martha Washington chairs and a Queen Anne settee are pulled up to the original cooking hearths on cool days. ✕ 23 Abercorn St., ☎ 912/232–4286. Reservations advised. AE, MC, V.

$$ **Bistro Savannah.** This Beaux Arts–style gallery setting featuring new works by rising local artists is the place to see and be seen. Tucked in a historic building and featuring Savannah-gray brick walls, marble tables, and wicker chairs, this bistro has emerged as a favorite meeting and feeding spot among locals who love the Southern coastal cuisine. Items on the changing menu might include sweet onion-crusted North American red snapper with Madeira sauce and a 20-ounce "cowboy steak" with homemade smoked tomato-mustard barbecue sauce. Late-night cappuccino is popular here. ✕ 309 W. Congress St., ☎ 912/233–6266. Reservations accepted. AE, MC, V. No lunch.

Dining

Bistro
Savannah, **2**

Crystal Beer
Parlor, **18**

Elizabeth
on 37th, **23**

45 South, **11**

Garibaldi's
Cafe, **1**

Johnny Harris, **9**

Mrs. Wilkes
Dining
Room, **19**

The Olde Pink
House, **13**

Pirates'
House, **12**

River House, **4**

Sea Shell
House, **24**

Shrimp
Factory, **6**

Lodging

Ballastone Inn &
Townhouse, **14**

Days Inn/Days
Suites, **3**

DeSoto
Hilton, **16**

Foley House
Inn, **15**

Forsyth Park
Inn, **20**

The
Gastonian, **21**

Hyatt, **5**

Jesse Mount
House, **17**

Marriot, **22**

The Mulberry
Inn, **10**

Olde Harbour
Inn, **7**

River Street
Inn, **8**

Savannah River

$$ Garibaldi's Cafe. The 19th-century Savannah Germantown Firehouse houses this fanciful eatery with antique tin ceilings, hand-painted murals depicting the African tropics, and original oil paintings. Here the emphasis is on fresh fish—caught daily by the restaurant's small fleet. Try the crisp local flounder with apricot-shallot glaze or the local lump blue crab fettucine with pepper cream. ✕ *315 W. Congress St.,* ☎ *912/232–7118. Reservations accepted. AE, MC, V. No lunch.*

$ Crystal Beer Parlor. This comfortable family tavern is famed for hamburgers, thick-cut french fries, huge onion rings, and frosted mugs of draft beer. The menu also offers fried oyster sandwiches, gumbo, and shrimp salad. ✕ *301 W. Jones St. at Jefferson St.,* ☎ *912/232–1153. No reservations. MC, V. Closed Sun.*

$ Johnny Harris. What started as a small roadside stand in 1924 has grown into one of the city's mainstays, with a menu that includes steaks, fried chicken, seafood, and a variety of barbecued meats spiced with the restaurant's famous sauce. ✕ *1651 E. Victory Dr.,* ☎ *912/354–7810. Reservations recommended for weekends. AE, DC, MC, V. Closed Sun.*

$ **Mrs. Wilkes Dining Room.** There's no sign out front, but you won't have
★   any trouble finding this famed establishment. At breakfast time and
noon (no dinner is served) there are long lines of folks waiting to get
in for a culinary orgy. Charles Kuralt and David Brinkley are among
the celebrities who have feasted on the fine Southern food, served
family-style at big tables. For breakfast there are eggs, sausage, piping
hot biscuits, and grits. At lunch, bowl after bowl is passed around the
table. Fried or roast chicken, collard greens, okra, mashed potatoes,
cornbread, biscuits—the dishes just keep coming. ✕ *107 W. Jones St.,*
☎ *912/232–5997. No reservations. No credit cards. No dinner.*

Seafood

$$$ **Elizabeth on 37th.** Elizabeth is the chef, and her namesake was recently
★   toasted by *Food & Wine* magazine as one of the top 25 restaurants in
America. Elizabeth and Michael Terry's restaurant is located in the city's
Victorian District, in an elegant turn-of-the-century mansion with
hardwood floors and spacious rooms. Among the chef's seasonal spe-
cialties are shad stuffed with sautéed shad roe and stuffed Vidalia
onions. While the emphasis is on sea creatures served in delicate sauces,
there are other excellent offerings, including beef tenderloin, quail, lamb,
and chicken dishes. ✕ *105 E. 37th St.,* ☎ *912/236–5547. Reserva-
tions advised. AE, MC, V. No lunch. Closed Sun.*

$$$ **Pirates' House.** You'll probably start hearing about the Pirates' House
about 10 minutes after you hit town. There are all sorts of legends about
it involving shanghaied sailors and ghosts. It's a sprawling complex
with nautical and piratical trappings, and 15 rooms with names like
the Jolly Roger and the Buccaneer's Room; children love the place. The
menu is almost as big as the building, with heavy emphasis on sea crit-
ters. For starters, try oysters, crab-stuffed mushrooms, or soft-shell crabs.
The large portions of gumbo and seafood bisque come in iron kettles.
Flounder Belle Franklin is crabmeat, shrimp, and fillet of flounder baked
in butter with herbs and wines and a glaze of cheeses and toasted al-
monds. The Key lime pie is the best choice among the 40 listings on
the dessert menu. Hard Hearted Hannah's Jazz Club is upstairs. ✕ *20
E. Broad St.,* ☎ *912/233–5757. Reservations accepted. AE, DC, MC,
V.*

$$–$$$ **River House.** This stylish restaurant sits over the spot where the SS *Sa-
vannah* set sail for her maiden voyage across the ocean in 1819. A number of mesquite-grilled entrées, including swordfish topped with
raspberry-butter sauce and grouper Florentine, served with creamed
spinach and a fresh dill and lemon-butter sauce, are good. Entrées are
served with freshly baked loaves of sourdough bread, and fish dishes
come with homemade angel-hair pasta. ✕ *125 W. River St.,* ☎ *912/234–
1900. Reservations accepted. AE, DC, MC, V.*

$–$$ **Sea Shell House.** It may not look like much from the outside, but the
★   steamed and fried seafood inside is regarded by many to be the city's
best. Specialties are crab, shrimp, and oysters, as well as a Low Country Boil that includes shrimp, sausage, corn, and whatever else comes
to mind that day. It also features a seafood platter second to none. The
restaurant's pastry chef prepares a beautiful bananas Foster flambé.
French-style coffee is brewed tableside. ✕ *3111 Skidaway Rd.,* ☎
912/352–8116. No reservations. MC, V.

$–$$ **Shrimp Factory.** Like all of Savannah's riverfront restaurants, this was
once an old warehouse. Now it's a light and airy place with exposed
brick, wood paneling, beamed ceilings, and huge windows that let you
gaze at the passing parade of ships. A house specialty is pine bark stew—
five native seafoods simmered with potatoes, onions, and herbs, and
served with blueberry muffins. Blackened dolphinfish fillet is smoth-

ered with herbs and julienned sweet red peppers in butter sauce. Baked deviled crabs are served with chicken-baked rice, and fish entrées come with angel-hair pasta. ✕ *313 E. River St.,* ☎ *912/236–4229. Reservations accepted. AE, DC, MC, V.*

Lodging

While Savannah has its share of chain hotels and motels, the city's most distinctive lodgings are the more than two dozen historic inns, guest houses, and bed-and-breakfasts gracing the Historic District.

If "historic inn" brings to mind images of roughing it in shabbily genteel mansions with slightly antiquated plumbing, you're in for a surprise. Most of the inns are in mansions with the requisite high ceilings, spacious rooms, and ornate carved millwork. Most have canopied, four-poster, or Victorian brass beds that dominate most quarters. And amid antique surroundings, modern luxury: enormous baths, many with whirlpools, hot tubs, or Jacuzzis; film libraries for in-room VCRs; and turn-down service with a chocolate, praline, or even a discreet brandy on your nightstand. Continental breakfast and afternoon refreshments are often included in the rate.

CATEGORY	COST*
$$$$	over $100
$$$	$75–$100
$$	$50–$75
$	under $50

All prices are for a standard double room, excluding TK tax.

Inns and Guest Houses

$$$$ **Ballastone Inn & Townhouse.** This sumptuous inn within a mansion,
★ dating from 1838, once served as a bordello. Notable for the wildly dramatic designs of its Scalamandre wallpaper and fabrics, each of its 17 rooms has a different theme. In Scarborough Fair, a deep China blue and yellow room, the fabric pattern was adapted from a Victorian china serving platter in the Davenport House. This exquisite third-floor room has two queen-size Victorian brass beds, a Queen Anne lowboy and writing desk, and a Victorian slipper chair. On the garden level, rooms are small and cozy, with exposed brick walls, beamed ceilings, and, in some cases, windows at eye level with the lush courtyard. One such room is the Sorghum Cane, trimmed in the bronze color of sugarcane molasses; it has two queen-size brass beds, wicker furniture, and wall fabric patterned after the etched glass window of a restored local house. Rooms have fireplaces and whirlpool baths. The townhouse, four blocks away, houses another five units (one room and four suites). Built in 1830, it's the oldest building south of Liberty Street. ⌧ *14 E. Oglethorpe Ave., 31401,* ☎ *912/236–1484 or 800/822–4553. 17 rooms with bath. In-room VCRs, concierge. AE, MC, V.*

$$$$ **Gastonian.** Hugh and Roberta Lineburger's inn will probably, to put
★ it modestly, knock your socks off. The mansion was built in 1868, and each of its 13 sumptuous suites is distinguished with vivid Scalamandre colors. The Caracalla Suite is named for the marble bath with an eight-foot whirlpool tub. The huge bedroom has a king-size canopy bed, two working fireplaces, and a lounge with a mirrored wet bar. The Layfayette Room, resembling a 19th-century French boudoir, is done in blues and whites, with Oriental rugs and flocked wallpaper. All rooms have working fireplaces and antiques from the Georgian and Regency periods. At bedtime, a turn-down service leaves schnapps by your bedside and Savannah pralines on your pillow. In the morning, a full breakfast is served in the formal dining room—or you can opt

for a Continental breakfast in your room. Each guest receives a fruit basket and split of wine upon arrival. ☎ *220 E. Gaston St., 31401,* ☎ *912/232–2869, fax 912/232–0710. 13 rooms, 6 with oversize hot tubs. Outdoor hot tub, concierge. AE, MC, V.*

$$$–$$$$ **Olde Harbour Inn.** The building dates from 1892, when it was built on the riverfront as an overall factory, but the old inn is actually a thoroughly modern facility that housed condos until 1987. Each suite has a fully equipped kitchen, including dishwasher and detergent. All suites overlook the river and have wall-to-wall carpeting, exposed brick walls painted white, and a four-poster bed. There are studio suites; regular suites with living room, bedroom, kitchen, and bath; and loft suites. (The latter are lofty indeed, with 25-foot ceilings, balconies overlooking the water, huge skylights, and ample room to sleep six.) Each evening a dish of ice cream is brought to your room and placed in the freezer. Cereal, fruit, hot muffins and biscuits, juice, tea, and coffee are served in a cozy breakfast room each morning. ☎ *508 E. Factors Walk, 31401,* ☎ *912/234–4100 or 800/553–6533; FAX 912/233–5979. 24 housekeeping suites with bath. Laundry service, concierge, parking. AE, DC, MC, V.*

$$$ **Forsyth Park Inn.** Rooms in this Victorian mansion across the street
★ from Forsyth Park are outfitted with 19th-century furnishings, including king- and queen-size four-poster beds, and have working fireplaces and large marble baths (some with whirlpools). The carriage house, just off the courtyard, has a suite with bath, a complete kitchen, and a new intimate deck. In the foyer is a grand piano, and afternoon wine is served here. ☎ *102 W. Hall St., 31401,* ☎ *912/233–6800. 9 rooms with bath, 1 private guest cottage. AE, D, MC, V.*

Bed-and-Breakfasts

$$$ **Jesse Mount House.** The Georgian home of Sue Dron has two two-bed-
★ room suites, a garden suite with a kitchen and whirlpool, and a one-bedroom suite. All units have their own fireplace with gas logs. Full breakfast is served in your room or in the formal dining room. ☎ *209 W. Jones St., 31401,* ☎ *912/236–1774. 4 suites with bath. VCRs. AE, D, MC, V.*

Hotels and Motels

$$$–$$$$ **DeSoto Hilton.** Three massive chandeliers glisten over the jardinieres and discreetly placed conversation areas of the spacious, newly redecorated lobby. The chandeliers are from the historic DeSoto Hotel that stood on this site long ago. Guest rooms are on the cushy side, in Savannah peach and green, with wall-to-wall carpeting, traditional furniture, and king-size, queen-size, or two double beds. (The best view is from the corner king-size rooms, which have the added attraction of coffeemakers.) Suites come with refrigerators upon request, and custom-made furnishings fill the bedroom, sitting room, and dining area. Golf, tennis, and athletic club privileges in the area are available to guests. ☎ *15 E. Liberty St., 31401,* ☎ *912/232–9000 or 800/426–8483, fax 912/232–6018. 250 rooms, 6 suites with bath. 2 restaurants, lounge, outdoor heated pool, concierge. AE,D, DC, MC.*

$$$–$$$$ **Hyatt.** When this riverfront hotel was built in 1981, preservationists opposed a seven-story modern structure in the historic district. Although it doesn't blend well with its surroundings, the hotel has some points to recommend it. The main architectural features are the towering atrium and a pleasant central lounge, as well as glass elevators. Rooms have mauve furnishings and balconies overlooking the atrium and the Savannah River. MD's Lounge is the ideal spot to have a drink and watch the river traffic drift by. ☎ *2 W. Bay St.,* ☎ *912/238–1234 or 800/233–*

1234, FAX *912/944–3678. 346 rooms with bath.* Restaurant, lounge, indoor pool. AE, DC, MC, V.

$$$–$$$$ **Marriott.** Located in the Historic District, the eight-story property with rounded balconies facing the river occupies a choice spot on the city's riverfront, adjacent to River Street and Factor's Walk. *100 Gen. McIntosh Blvd., 31401,* ☎ *912/233–7722 or 800/228–9290,* FAX *912/233–3765. 386 rooms, 46 suites with bath. 2 restaurants, lobby lounge, indoor-outdoor pools, hot tub, health club.* AE, D, DC, MC, V.

$$$–$$$$ **Mulberry Inn.** So many objets d'art fill the public rooms that the man-
★ agement has obligingly provided a walking tour brochure. Treasures include 18th-century oil paintings, an English grandfather clock dating from 1803, Chinese vases from the Ch'ing Dynasty, and an ornate Empire game table. The restaurant is a sophisticated affair, with crystal chandeliers and mauve velvet Regency furniture. The spacious courtyard is covered with a mosquito net, which keeps it about 10 degrees cooler in the summer. The guest rooms are in a traditional motif; suites have king-size beds and wet bars. Accommodations are available for nonsmokers and those with disabilities. ☎ *601 E. Bay St., 31401,* ☎ *912/238–1200 or 800/465–4329,* FAX *912/236–2184. 122 rooms, 22 suites with bath. Restaurant, bar, pool, outdoor hot tub.* AE, DC, MC, V.

$$$–$$$$ **River Street Inn.** This elegant hotel offers panoramic views of the Savannah River. Rooms are furnished with antiques and reproductions from the era of King Cotton. Amenities include turn-down service. The interior is so lavish, it's difficult to believe it was only recently a vacant warehouse dating back to 1817. One floor includes charming shops and a New Orleans–style restaurant. ☎ *115 E. River St.,* ☎ *912/234–6400 or 800/253–4229. 44 rooms with bath.* 3 restaurants, 3 bars. AE, MC, V.

$$ **Days Inn/Days Suites.** This downtown hotel is located in the Historic District near the City Market, only a block off River Street. Its compact rooms have modular furnishings and most amenities, including HBO/ESPN on the tube. Interior corridors and an adjacent parking garage minimize its motel qualities. ☎ *201 W. Bay St.,* ☎ *912/236–4440 or 800/325–2525. 253 rooms with bath. Restaurant, pool, health club.* AE, DC, MC, V.

Nightlife

Savannah's nightlife is a reflection of the city's laid-back, easy-going personality. Some clubs feature live reggae, hard rock, and other contemporary music, but most stay with traditional blues, jazz, and piano bar vocalists. After-dark merrymakers usually head for watering holes on Riverfront Plaza or the south side.

Jazz Clubs

Crossroads (219 W. Saint Julian St., ☎ 912/234–5438) is Savannah's sole blues nightclub, featuring live performances by local and national talent Monday through Saturday.

Hard Hearted Hannah's East (20 E. Broad St., ☎ 912/233–2225) features Emma Kelly, the undisputed "Lady of 6,000 Songs," performing Tuesday through Saturday.

Bars and Nightclubs

Axis (121 W. Congress St., ☎ 912/236–6266) is the city's liveliest music hall, featuring a variety of name performers in rock, blues, jazz, reggae, folk, country, and comedy. The age of the crowd on the tiny dance floor depends on who's on the bandstand.

Bottom Line (206 W. Julian St., ☎ 912/232–0812) is the place to swing and sway to big band music.

Kevin Barry's Irish Pub (117 W. River St., ☎ 912/233–9626), a cozy pub with a friendly bar and traditional Irish music, is *the* place to be on St. Patrick's Day. The rest of the year there's a mixed bag of tourists and locals, young and old.

Savannah Essentials

Arriving and Departing

BY BUS

The **Greyhound/Trailways** station (☎ 912/232–2135) is downtown at 610 W. Oglethorpe Avenue.

BY CAR

I–95 slices north–south along the Eastern Seaboard, intersecting 10 miles west of town with east–west I–16, which dead-ends in downtown Savannah. U.S. 17, the Coastal Highway, also runs north–south through town. U.S. 80, which connects the Atlantic to the Pacific, is another east–west route through Savannah.

BY PLANE

Savannah International Airport (☎ 912/964–0514), 8 miles west of downtown, is served by **Delta, Continental, USAir, and ValuJet.** Despite the name, international flights are nonexistent.

Vans operated by **McCall's Limousine Service** (☎ 912/966–5364 or 800/673–9365) leave the airport daily 6 AM–10 PM, after the arrival of each flight, bound for downtown locations. The trip takes 15 minutes, and the one-way fare is $12.

Taxi fare from the airport to downtown is $15 for one person, $3 for each additional person.

By car, drive south on Dean Forest Drive to I–16, then east on I–16 into downtown Savannah.

BY TRAIN

Amtrak (☎ 800/872–7245) has regular service along the Eastern Seaboard, with daily stops in Savannah. The Amtrak station (2611 Seaboard Coastline Dr., ☎ 912/234–2611) is 4 miles southwest of downtown. Cab fare into the city is $5–$10.

Getting Around

Despite its size, the downtown Historic District should be explored on foot. Its grid shape makes getting around a breeze, and you'll find any number of places to stop and rest.

BY BUS

Buses require $1 in exact change, and 5¢ extra for a transfer. **Chatham Area Transit (CAT)** (☎ 912/233–5767) operates buses in Savannah and Chatham County Monday–Saturday from 6 AM to midnight, Sunday 7 AM to 7 PM.

BY TAXI

Taxis start at 60¢ and cost $1.20 for each mile. **Adam Cab Co.**(☎ 912/927–7466) is a reliable, 24-hour taxi service.

Guided Tours

LOWCOUNTRY

The **Associated Guides of the Low Country** (☎ 912/234–4088 or 800/627–5030; closed Mon.), and **Gray Line** (☎ 912/234–8687) make four-hour excursions to the fishing village of Thunderbolt; the Isle of Hope, with stately mansions lining Bluff Drive; the much-photographed Bonaventure Cemetery on the banks of the Wilmington River; and Wormsloe Plantation Site, with its mile-long avenue of arching oaks.

ORIENTATION

Gray Line Tours (☎ 912/234–8687) is the official tour organization for the Historic Savannah Foundation. Knowledgeable and enthusiastic guides whisk you about in 20-passenger, climate-controlled vans. Tours of the Historic District and of the Victorian District take about two hours each. **Old Town Trolley Tours** (☎ 912/233–0083) offers tours providing an old-time view of the Historic District. Trolleys come by nine designated stops every half hour from 9–4:30 (cost: $14).

SPECIAL-INTEREST

In May, the **Garden Club of Savannah** (☎ 912/238–0248) takes you into private gardens tucked behind old-brick walls and wrought-iron gates. For groups of five or more, the **Negro Heritage Trail Tour** (☎ 912/234 8000) provides a knowledgeable guide who traces the city's more than 250 years of Black history. Tours commence at the Savannah Visitor's Center.

Carriage Tours of Savannah (10 Warner St., ☎ 912/236–6756 or 800/442–5933) show you the Historic District by day or by night at a 19th-century clip-clop pace, with coachmen spinning tales and telling ghost stories along the way. A romantic evening champagne tour in a private carriage will set you back $60, plus $16 per bottle of bubbly. Regular tours are a more modest $13 adults, $5 children 11 and under.

WALKING TOURS

A Ghost Talk Ghost Walk Tour (☎ 912/233–3896) will send chills up your spine during a two-hour jaunt through the Old Colonial City. Call for reservations; cost: $10 adults, $5 children.

The **Square Routes** (☎ 912/232–6866 or 800/868–6867) offers customized strolls through the Historic District and along Tybee Beach. In-town tours focus on the city's architecture and gardens, and specialized tours include the *Midnight in the Garden of Good and Evil* walk based on the current bestseller. Tours usually last two hours and cost from $15 to $25.

Important Addresses and Numbers

EMERGENCIES

Dial 911 for **police** and **ambulance** in an emergency.

HOSPITALS

Area hospitals with 24-hour emergency rooms are **Candler Hospital** (5353 Reynolds St., ☎ 912/354–9211) and **Memorial Medical Center** (4700 Waters Ave., ☎ 912/350–8000).

24-HOUR PHARMACY

Revco Drug Center (Medical Arts Shopping Center, 4725 Waters Ave., ☎ 912/355–7111).

VISITOR INFORMATION

For trip planning information, write to the **Savannah Area Convention & Visitor's Bureau** (222 W. Oglethorpe Ave., Savannah 31401, ☎ 912/944–0456 or 800/444–2427). The **Savannah Visitor's Center** (301 Martin Luther King Jr. Blvd., ☎ 912/944–0455) has free maps and brochures, lots of friendly advice, and an audiovisual overview of the city. The center is also the starting point for a number of guided tours. ⊙ *Weekdays 8:30–5, weekends and holidays 9–5.*

THE GOLDEN ISLES AND OKEFENOKEE SWAMP

The Golden Isles are a string of lush, subtropical barrier islands meandering lazily down Georgia's Atlantic coast from Savannah to the Florida border. They have a long history of human habitation; Indian relics have been found on these islands that date to about 2500 BC. According to legend, the Indian nations agreed that no wars would be fought there and that tribal members would visit only in a spirit of friendship. In a latter-day spirit of friendship today, all of Georgia's beaches are in the public domain. Each Golden Isle has a distinctive personality, shaped by its history and ecology. Three of them—Jekyll Island, Sea Island, and St. Simons Island—are connected to the mainland by bridges in the vicinity of Brunswick; these are the only ones accessible by automobile. The Cumberland Island National Seashore is accessible by ferry from St. Mary's. Little St. Simons Island, a privately owned retreat with a guest lodge, is reached by a private launch from St. Simons. About 50 miles inland is the Okefenokee Swamp National Wildlife Refuge, which has a character all its own.

Cumberland Island National Seashore

Numbers in the margin correspond to points of interest on the Golden Isles map.

The largest, most southerly, and most accessible of Georgia's primitive coastal islands is **Cumberland,** a 16-by-3-mile sanctuary of marshes, dunes, beaches, forests, lakes and ponds, estuaries, and inlets. Waterways are home to gators, sea turtles, otters, snowy egrets, great blue herons, ibis, wood storks, and more than 300 other species of birds. In the forests are armadillos, wild horses, deer, raccoons, and an assortment of reptiles.

After the ancient Guale Indians came 16th-century Spanish missionaries, 18th-century English soldiers, and 19th-century planters. During the 1880s, Thomas Carnegie of Pittsburgh built several lavish homes here, but the island remained largely as nature created it. In the early 1970s, the federal government established the Cumberland Island National Seashore and opened this natural treasure to the public.

There is no transportation on the island itself, and the only public access to the island is on the *Cumberland Queen,* a reservations-only, 146-passenger ferry based near the National Park Service Information Center at St. Mary's. Ferry bookings are heavy in summer, but cancellations and no-shows often make last-minute space available. *Cumberland Island National Seashore, Box 806, 31558, ☎ 912/882–4335. Roundtrip fare: $10.07 adults, $7.95 senior citizens, $5.99 children 12 and under. Mid-May–Sept., ferry departure from St. Mary's daily 9 AM and 11:45 AM, from Cumberland 10:15 AM and 4:45 PM. No ferry service Tues.–Wed. Oct.–May 14.*

Exploring

From the Park Service docks at the island's southern end, you can follow wooded nature trails, swim and sun on 18 miles of undeveloped beaches, go fishing and bird-watching, and view the ruins of Carnegie's great estate, **Dungeness.** You can also join history and nature walks led by Park Service rangers. Bear in mind that summers are hot and humid, and that you must bring your own food, soft drinks, sun-

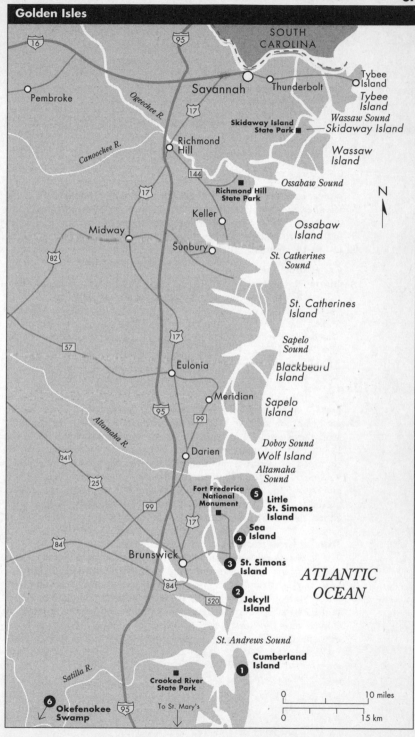

Golden Isles

screen, and a reliable insect repellent. All trash must be transported back to the mainland by campers and picnickers. Nothing can be purchased on the island.

Lodging

ISLAND

$$$$ **Greyfield Inn.** The island's only accommodations are in a turn-of-the-century Carnegie family home. Greyfield's public areas are filled with family mementoes, furnishings, and portraits (you may feel as though you've stepped into one of Agatha Christie's mysterious Cornwall manors). Prices include all meals, transportation, tours led by a naturalist, and bike rentals. ☎ *Box 900 Fernandina Beach, FL 32035,* ☎ *904/261–6408. 11 rooms, 1 suite. MC, V.*

Novice campers usually prefer **Sea Camp,** a five-minute walk from the *Cumberland Queen* dock, with rest rooms and showers adjacent to campsites. The beach is just beyond the dunes. Experienced campers will want to hike 3–10 miles to several areas where cold-water spigots are the only amenities.

MAINLAND

$ **Charter House Inn.** Two miles from the Cumberland ferry dock is a 120-room motel, whose accommodations are spartan but air-conditioned. Rooms have kitchenettes with microwaves for those who like to haul their own grub, and the on-site restaurant serves reasonably priced breakfasts, lunches, and dinners. ☎ *2710 Osborne St., St. Mary's 31558,* ☎ *800/768–6250. 120 rooms. Restaurant, lounge. AE, D, DC, MC, V.*

Jekyll Island

❷ For 56 winters, between 1886 and 1942, America's rich and famous faithfully came south to **Jekyll Island.** Through the Gilded Age, the Great War, the Roaring '20s, and the Great Depression, Vanderbilts and Rockefellers, Morgans and Astors, Macys, Pulitzers, and Goodyears shuttered their Fifth Avenue castles and retreated to the serenity of their wild Georgia island. There they built elegant "cottages," played golf and tennis, and socialized. Early in World War II, the millionaires departed for the last time. In 1947, the state of Georgia purchased the entire island for the bargain price of $675,000.

Tourist Information

The **Jekyll Island Welcome Center,** at the end of the causeway, offers ninety-minute open-air trolley tours of the Jekyll Island Club Historic Landmark District. Tours originate at the Museum Orientation Center on Stable Road and include several restored homes and buildings in the 240-acre historic district. Faith Chapel, illuminated by Tiffany stained-glass windows, is open for meditation Sunday–Friday 2–4. Audiovisual orientations are presented before each tour departs. *Go north on 95 to Exit 6, south on 95 to Exit 8, Box 13186, Jekyll Island Causeway, Jekyll Island 31527,* ☎ *912/635–3636 or 800/841–6586.* ☛ *$8 adults, $6 students 6–18.* ◷ *Daily 9–5, tours daily 10–3.*

Exploring

Jekyll Island is still a 7½-mile playground, but no longer restricted to the rich and famous. The golf, tennis, fishing, biking, jogging, water park, and picnic grounds are open to all. One side of the island is flanked by nearly 10 miles of hard-packed Atlantic beaches; the other, by the Intracoastal Waterway and picturesque salt marshes. Deer and wild turkeys inhabit interior forests of pine, magnolia, and moss-veiled live oaks. Egrets, pelicans, herons, and sandpipers skim the gentle surf.

Jekyll's clean, mostly uncommercialized public beaches are free and open year-round. Bathhouses with rest rooms, changing areas, and showers are open at regular intervals along the beach. Beachwear, suntan lotion, rafts, snacks, and drinks are available at the **Jekyll Shopping Center,** facing the beach at Beachview Drive.

Participant Sports

GOLF

Jekyll's 63 holes of golf include three 18-hole courses with a main clubhouse on Capt. Wylly Road (☎ 912/635–2368) and a 9-hole course on Beachview Drive (☎ 912/635–2170).

TENNIS

Eight courts include J. P. Morgan's indoor court (☎ 912/635–2600, ext. 1060) and the Kelly Gunterman tennis school (☎ 800/426–3930).

WATER PARK

Summer Waves, the 11-acre water park, has an 18,000-square-foot wave pool, eight water slides, a children's activity pool with two slides, and a 1,000-foot river for tubing and rafting. *210 S. Riverview Dr.,* ☎ *912/635–2074.* ☛ *$11.95 adults, $9.95 children under 48".* ⊙ *May 28–Sept. 5, Sun.–Fri. 10–6, Sat. 10–8.*

Dining

$$$ **Grand Dining Room.** In the Jekyll Island Club Hotel the dining room sparkles with silver and crystal. Low Country cuisine by the hotel's young chef includes delicately flavored fresh seafood, beef, veal, and chicken. ✕ *371 Riverview Dr.,* ☎ *912/635–2600, ext. 1002. Reservations advised. Jacket required at dinner. AE, DC, MC, V.*

Lodging

$$$–$$$$ **Jekyll Island Club Hotel.** Built in 1887, the four-story clubhouse with wraparound verandas and Queen Anne–style towers and turrets once served as the winter hunting retreat for wealthy financiers. In 1985, a group of Georgia businessmen spent $17 million restoring it to a splendor that would astonish even the Astors and Vanderbilts. The guest rooms and suites are custom-decorated with mahogany beds, armoires, and plush sofas and chairs. Some have flowery views of the Intracoastal Waterway, Jekyll River, and the hotel's croquet lawn. Several suites have Jacuzzis. The adjacent Sans Souci Apartments, built in 1896 by William Rockefeller, have been converted into spacious guest rooms. The hotel is operated as a Radisson resort; it has 22 miles of bicycle trails and a free shuttle to area beaches. ⌂ *371 Riverview Dr., Jekyll Island 31527,* ☎ *912/635–2600 or 800/333–3333,* ℻ *912/635–2818. 134 units. Restaurant, pool, 8 tennis courts, croquet. AE, DC, MC, V.*

$$–$$$$ **Best Western Jekyll Inn.** Located on a landscaped 15-acre site, these oceanfront units, the largest facility on the island, recently underwent a $2.5 million renovation. Rooms were redecorated with new lighting and carpeting. Units include some villas with kitchenettes. ⌂ *975 N. Beachview Dr., Jekyll Island 31527,* ☎ *912/635–2531 or 800/736–1046. 264 units. Restaurant, pool, bicycles, playground. AE, D,DC, MC, V.*

$–$$$ **Holiday Inn Beach Resort.** Nestled amid natural dunes and oaks in a secluded oceanfront setting, this hotel has a private beach, but its rooms with balconies still don't have an ocean view. ⌂ *200 S. Beachview Dr., Jekyll Island 31527,* ☎ *912/635–3311 or 800/753–5955. 205* *rooms. Restaurant, lounge, pool, golf course, tennis courts, bicycles, playground. AE, D, DC, MC, V.*

RENTALS

Jekyll's more than 200 rental cottages and condos are handled by **Jekyll Realty** (912/635–3301) and **Parker-Kaufman Realty** (912/635–2512).

St. Simons Island

❸ As large as Manhattan, with more than 14,000 year-round residents, **St. Simons** is the Golden Isles' most complete resort destination. Fortunately, the accelerated development in recent years has failed to spoil the natural beauty of the island's regal live oaks, beaches, and salt marshes. Visits are highlighted by swimming and sunning on hard-packed beaches, golf, biking, hiking, fishing, horseback riding, touring historic sites, and feasting on fresh local seafood at more than 50 restaurants.

Tourist Information

St. Simons Island Chamber of Commerce (530 Beachview Dr., St. Simons Island 31522, ☎ 912/638–9014 or 800/525–8678, ᴙ 912/638–2172; closed Sun.) provides helpful information.

Exploring

Many sights and activities are in the **village** area along Mallery Street at the more developed south end of the island, where there are shops, several restaurants, pubs, and a popular public pier. A quaint "trolley" takes visitors on a 1½-hour guided tour of the island, leaving from near the pier, several times a day in high season, less frequently in winter ($10 adults, $6 children).

Also at the island's south end is **Neptune Park,** which includes picnic tables, a children's play park, miniature golf, and beach access. A freshwater swimming pool, with showers and rest rooms, is open each summer in the **Neptune Park Casino** (☎ 912/638–2393), which also has a recreation room and snack bars. Also in the park is **St. Simons Lighthouse,** a beacon since 1872. The **Museum of Coastal History** in the lightkeeper's cottage has a permanent exhibit of coastal history. ☎ 912/638–4666. ☛ *(including the lighthouse): $3 adults, $1 children 6–12. ◔ Tues.–Sat. 10–5, Sun. 1:30–5.*

At the burgeoning north end of the island there's a marina, a golf club, and a housing development, as well as **Fort Frederica National Monument.** Tabby ruins remain of a fort built by English troops in the mid-1730s as a bulwark against a Spanish invasion from Florida. Around the fort are the foundations of homes and shops. Start at the **National Park Service Visitors Center,** which has a film and displays. ☎ *912/638–3639.* ☛ *$4 per car. ◔ Daily 9–5.*

On your way to Fort Frederica, pause at **Christ Episcopal Church** (donations welcome) on Frederica Road. Consecrated in 1886 following an earlier structure's desecration by Union troops, the white frame Gothic structure is surrounded by live oaks, dogwoods, and azaleas. The interior is highlighted by beautiful stained-glass windows.

Dining

$$ **Alfonza's Olde Plantation Supper Club.** Down-home versions of seafood, superb steaks, and plantation fried chicken are served in a gracious and relaxed environment. ✗ *Harrington La.,* ☎ *912/638–9883. Reservations advised. D, DC, MC, V. No lunch. Closed Sun.*

$$ **Blanche's Courtyard.** In the village, this lively restaurant/nightclub is gussied up in "Bayou Victorian" dress, with lots of antiques and nostalgic memorabilia. True to its bayou decor, the menu features Cajun-style seafood as well as basic steak and chicken. A ragtime band plays for dancers on Saturday. ✕ *440 Kings Way,* ☎ *912/638–3030. Reservations accepted. AE, DC, MC, V.*

$ **CJ's.** This tiny village-area restaurant serves the island's best Italian food. Deep-dish and thin-crust pizzas, pastas, and all of the menu's sandwiches draw a faithful local clientele. The limited seating capacity creates lengthy waits, but the cuisine is worth your patience, and take-out is available. ✕ *405 Mallory St.,* ☎ *912/634–1022. No reservations. No credit cards; local checks accepted. Lunch served late Mar.–late Sept.*

$ **Crab Trap.** One of the island's most popular spots, the Crab Trap offers a variety of fried, blackened, and broiled fresh seafood; oysters on the half shell; blue crab soup; heaps of batter fries; and hush puppies. The atmosphere is rustic-casual—there's a hole in the middle of every table to deposit corn cobs and shrimp shells. ✕ *1209 Ocean Blvd.,* ☎ *912/638–3552. No reservations. MC, V.*

Lodging

$$–$$$ **King and Prince Beach and Golf Resort.** This hotel faces the beach. Guest rooms are spacious, and villas offer two or three bedrooms. ⊞ *Box 20798, 201 Arnold Rd., St. Simons Island 31522,* ☎ *912/638–3631 or 800/342–0212. 137 rooms, 47 villas. Restaurant, lounge, indoor pool, 4 pools, bicycles. AE, D, DC, MC, V.*

$$$ **Sea Palms Golf and Tennis Resort.** A contemporary resort complex with fully furnished villas nestles on an 800-acre site. ⊞ *5415 Frederica Rd., St. Simons Island 31522,* ☎ *912/638–3351. 163 rooms. 2 pools, 27-hole golf course, tennis, bicycles, children's programs. AE, DC, MC, V.*

$$ **Days Inn of America.** This facility opened in 1989 on an inland stretch of the island's main thoroughfare. Each room has a built-in microwave and refrigerator. Continental breakfast is included in the rate. ⊞ *1701 Frederica Rd., St. Simons Island 31522,* ☎ *912/634–0660,* FAX *912/638–7115. 101 rooms. Pool. AE, MC, V.*

$$ **Island Inn.** On wooded land just off one of the island's main streets, this newer antebellum-style motel offers convenience and privacy with its efficiency accommodations. Continental breakfast is included, and complimentary wine and cheese are served weekdays from 5:30 to 6:30. *301 Main St.,* ☎ *912/638–7805. 74 rooms. Pool, hot tub, meeting rooms. AE, MC, V.*

$$ **Queen's Court.** This family-oriented complex in the village has clean, modest rooms with shower-baths, some with kitchenettes. The grounds, with their ancient live oaks, are beautiful. *437 Kings Way, St. Simons Island 31522,* ☎ *912/638–8459. 23 rooms. Pool. MC, V.*

RENTALS

For St. Simons condo and cottage rentals, contact **Trupp–Hodnett Enterprises** (☎ 800/627–6850) or **Golden Isles Realty** (☎ 912/638–8623).

Sea Island

❹ **Sea Island** has been the domain of the **Cloister Hotel** since 1928. Separated from St. Simons Island by a narrow waterway and a good many steps up the social ladder, this famed resort lives up to its celebrity status. Guests lodge in spacious, comfortably appointed rooms and suites in the Spanish Mediterranean hotel. The owners of the 500 or so private cottages and villas treat the hotel like a country club, and their tenants may use the hotel's facilities. Contact **Sea Island Cottage Rentals** (☎ 912/638–5112) to arrange to rent one.

For recreation, there's 54 holes of golf; tennis, swimming in pools or at the beach, skeet shooting, horseback riding, sailing, biking, lawn games, and surf and deep-sea fishing. After dinner, guests dance to live music in the lounge. All meals are included in the rate.

Like a person of some years, the Cloister has its eccentricities. Guest rooms were only recently equipped with TVs. Credit cards are not honored, but personal checks are accepted. Gentlemen must cover their arms in the dining rooms, even at breakfast. A complete and superb spa facility opened in 1989 in a beautiful building of its own by the pool and beach and features a fully equipped workout room, daily aerobics classes, personal trainers, facials and massages, and other beauty treatments.

There is no entrance gate, and nonguests are free to admire the beautifully planted grounds and to drive past the mansions lining Sea Island Drive. Space permitting, they may also play at the Sea Island Golf Course (on St. Simons) and dine in the main dining room. *The Cloister, Sea Island 31561, ☎ 912/638–3611 or, for reservations, 800/732–4752. 262 rooms. 4 restaurants, 2 pools, spa, golf, tennis, health club, airport shuttle. No credit cards; personal checks are accepted.* **$$$$** *($288–$552 for 2 in high season).*

Little St. Simons Island

❺ Six miles long, 2 to 3 miles wide, skirted by Atlantic beaches and salt marshes teeming with birds and wildlife, **Little St. Simons** is custommade for Robinson Crusoe–style getaways. The island has been owned by one family since the early 1900s, and the only development is a rustic but comfortable guest compound.

The island's forests and marshes are inhabited by deer, armadillos, horses, raccoons, gators, otters, and over 200 species of birds. Guests are free to walk the 6 miles of undisturbed beaches, swim in the mild surf, fish from the dock, and seine for shrimp and crabs in the marshes. There are also horses to ride, nature walks with experts, and other island explorations via boat or the back of a pickup truck. From June through September, up to 10 nonguests per day may visit the island by reservation; the $60 cost includes the ferry to the island, an island tour by truck, lunch at the lodge, and a beach walk.

Dining and Lodging

$$$$ **River Lodge** and **Cedar House.** Up to 24 guests can be accommodated in the lodge and house. Each has four bedrooms with twin or king-size beds, private baths, sitting rooms, and screened porches. Two other lodges have two bedrooms each; one with private and the other with shared baths. None of the rooms are air-conditioned, but ceiling fans make sleeping comfortable. The rates include all meals and dinner wines (cocktails available at additional cost). Meals, often featuring fresh fish, pecan pie, and home-baked breads, are served family-style in the lodge dining room. The properties also provide transportation from St. Simons Island, transportation on the island, and interpretive guides. ☒ *21078 Little St. Simons Island 31522, ☎ 912/638–7472,* FAX *912/634–1811. Pool, beach, fishing. Minimum 2-night reservations. MC, V.*

Okefenokee Swamp National Wildlife Refuge

Covering more than 700 square miles of southeast Georgia and spilling over into northeast Florida, the mysterious rivers and lakes of the **Okefenokee Swamp** bristle with seen and unseen life. Scientists agree that Okefenokee is not duplicated anywhere else on earth. The swamp is actually a vast peat bog, remarkable in geologic origin and history. Once part of the ocean floor, it now rises more than 100 feet above sea level.

As you travel by canoe or speedboat among the water-lily islands and the great stands of live oaks and cypress, be on the lookout for otters, egrets, muskrats, herons, cranes, and gators cruising the dark channels like iron-clad subs. The Okefenokee Swamp Park, 8 miles south of Waycross, is a major visitor gateway to the refuge. The Swamp Park is a nonprofit development operating under a long-term lease. There are two other gateways to the swamp: an eastern entrance in the Suwanee Canal Recreation Area, near Folkston; and a western entrance at Stephen C. Foster State Park, outside the town of Fargo.

Seminole Indians, in their migrations south toward Florida's Everglades, once took refuge in the Great Okefenokee. Noting the many floating islands, they provided its name—"Land of the Trembling Earth."

Exploring

Okefenokee Swamp Park. South of Waycross, via U.S. 1, the park offers orientation programs, exhibits, observation areas, wilderness walkways, an outdoor museum of pioneer life, and boat tours into the swamp that reveal its ecological uniqueness. A boardwalk and 90-foot tower are excellent places to glimpse cruising gators and a variety of birds. Gate admission includes a guided boat tour and all exhibits and shows. You may also arrange for lengthier explorations with a guide and a boat. *Waycross 31501,* ☎ *912/283–0583.* ☛ *$10 adults, $7 children 4–11.* ☉ *Summer, daily 9–6:30; spring, fall, and winter, 9–5:30.*

Suwanee Canal Recreation Area. This area, 8 miles south of Folkston via GA 121/23, is administered by the U.S. Fish and Wildlife Service. Stop first at the Visitor Information Center, which has an orientation film and exhibits on the Okefenokee's flora and fauna. A boardwalk takes you over the water to a 40-foot observation tower. At the concession building you may purchase snacks and sign up for guided boat tours into an 11-mile waterway, which resulted from efforts to drain the swamp a century ago. Hikers, bicyclists, and private motor vehicles are welcome on the Swamp Island Drive; several interpretive walking trails may be taken along the way. Picnicking is allowed. *Rte. 2, Folkston 31537,* ☎ *912/496–7156.* ☛ *To the park is free (there's a $4 charge per car).* 1*-hr tours: $7.50 adults, $3.75 children 5–11, $2.50 children 1–4;* 2*-hr tours: $15 adults, $7.50 children 5–11, $5 children 1–4. Refuge open Mar.–Sept. 10, daily 7 AM–7:30 PM; Sept. 11–Feb., daily 8–6; tours offered 10–2.*

Stephen C. Foster State Park. Eighteen miles from Fargo, via GA 11, is an 80-acre island park entirely within the Okefenokee Swamp National Wildlife Refuge. The park encompasses a large cypress and black gum forest, a majestic backdrop for one of the thickest growths of vegetation in the southeastern United States. The lush terrain and the mirrorlike black waters of the swamp provide at least a part-time home for more than 225 species of birds, 41 species of mammals, 54 species of reptiles, 32 species of amphibians, and 37 species of fish.

Park naturalists leading boat tours will spill out a wealth of swamp lore as riders observe gators, many bird species, and native trees and plants. You may also take a self-guided excursion in rental canoes and fishing boats. Camping is also available here (*see* Lodging, *below*). *Fargo 31631,* ☎ *912/637–5274.* ☛ *$4 to National Wildlife Refuge.* ☉ *Mar.–Aug., daily 6:30 AM–8:30 PM; Sept.–Feb., 7 AM–7 PM.*

Lodging
CAMPING

$–$$ **Stephen C. Foster State Park.** The park has furnished two-bedroom cottages and campsites with water, electricity, rest rooms, and showers. Because of roaming wildlife and poachers, the park's gates close between sunset and sunrise. If you're staying overnight, stop for groceries in Fargo beforehand. ⌖ *Park Supt., Fargo 31631,* ☎ *912/637–5274.*

$ **Laura S. Walker State Park.** Nine miles from Okefenokee Swamp Park are campsites ($11) with electrical and water hookups. Be sure to pick up food and supplies on the way to the park. ⌖ *Park Supt., Waycross 31503,* ☎ *912/287–4900. Picnic areas, pool, fishing, playground.*

The Golden Isles and Okefenokee Swamp Essentials

Getting There and Getting Around
BY CAR
From Brunswick by car, take the Jekyll Island Causeway ($2 per car) to Jekyll Island, and the Torras Causeway to St. Simons and Sea Island. You can get by without a car on Jekyll Island and Sea Island, but you'll need one on St. Simons. You cannot bring a car to Cumberland Island or Little St. Simons.

BY FERRY
Cumberland Island and Little St. Simons are accessible only by ferry (*see above*).

BY PLANE
The Golden Isles are served by **Glynco Jetport,** 6 miles north of Brunswick, which is served in turn by Delta affiliate **Atlantic Southeast Airlines** (☎ 800/282–3424), with flights from Atlanta.

ELSEWHERE IN THE STATE

Alpine Helen. The idea is an Alpine village in the Georgia mountains; the look is Bavaria; the attractions are mostly of the fun-and-fudge variety. The town's annual Oktoberfest draws crowds. *Rte. 385N from Atlanta to U.S. 129N to Cleveland, then Rte. 75N to Helen.*

Andersonville National Historic Site. Andersonville, which opened in 1864, was the Civil War's most notorious prisoner-of-war site: 13,000 prisoners died here, and at war's end the commandant was tried, convicted, and hanged. Earthworks, palisades, and some structures remain. Today it is the site of a memorial to prisoners of war. *I–75S from Macon to Rte. 26, then east to Oglethorpe, then Rte. 49 to Andersonville,* ☎ *912/924–0343.* ☛ *Free.* ☉ *Daily 8–5.*

Athens. The home of the University of Georgia, this college town has an appeal that's a cross between Mayberry R.F.D. and M-TV—the latter owing to its reputation as a breeding ground for new and alternative music. Athens has several splendid Greek Revival buildings, including, on campus, the **University Chapel** (built in 1832) and the **University President's House,** built in the late 1850s (570 Prince Ave.,

☎ 706/354–4096; open by appointment). The **Taylor-Grady House** (634 Prince Ave., ☎ 706/549–8688; ☛ $2.50; open Tues.–Fri. 10–3:30), down the street, was constructed in 1844. The **Franklin Hotel** (480 E. Broad St.), also built in 1844, was recently restored and reopened as an office building. Contact the **Athens Convention and Visitors Bureau** (☎ 706/546–1805).

Barnsley Gardens, near Adairsville. The Civil War halted construction of Godfrey Barnsley's 26-room Italianate house, and in 1988 the estate and its gardens lay in ruins. A German prince, Hubertus Fugger-Babenhausen, and his wife, Princess Alexandra, bought it and started work on restoration. Today there are 30 acres of shrubbery, trees, ponds, fountains, and flowers, designed in the style of Mr. Barnsley's time. At press time, a restaurant was planned. *Barnsley Gardens Rd. off Hall Station Rd., ☎ 404/773–7480. ☛ $6.50 adults, $5.75 senior citizens, children under 12 free. ☉ Tues.–Sat. 10–6, Sun. noon–6.*

Callaway Gardens, in Pine Mountain. This 14,000-acre family-style golf and tennis resort is best known for its impressive gardens and its not-to-be-missed butterfly conservatory. The gardens were developed in the 1930s by a couple determined to breathe new life into the area's dormant cotton fields. On the grounds are four nationally recognized golf courses, 17 tennis courts, bicycling trails, and a lakefront beach. The **Day Butterfly Center** contains more than 1,000 varieties flying free. Mountain Creek Lake is well stocked with large-mouth bass and bream. If you visit here in the height of the spring season or during the garden's annual holiday light spectacular in December, you may find yourself in a traffic jam in the middle of rural Georgia. *U.S. 27S, ☎ 706/663–2281 or 800/282–8181. ☛ $7.50 adults, $1.50 children 6–11, children under 6 free. ☉ Daily 7–6.*

Chickamauga and Chattanooga National Military Park. Established in 1890 and the nation's first military park, this was the site of one of the Civil War's bloodiest battles; casualties totaled more than 30,000. Though the Confederates routed the Federals early, General Ulysses Grant eventually broke the siege of Chattanooga and secured the city as a base for Sherman's march through Atlanta and on to the sea. Monuments, battlements, and weapons adorn the road that traverses the 8,000-acre park, with markers explaining the action. *U.S. 27 off I–75, south of Chattanooga, ☎ 706/866–9241. ☛ Free. ☉ Daily 8–4:45.*

Clayton. This unassuming mountain town is near spectacular Tallulah Gorge, the deepest canyon in the U.S. besides the Grand Canyon, and a popular turn-of-the-century destination for Atlantans. The state of Georgia recently acquired the site for a state park, and vast improvements are planned. In Clayton, the **Main Street Gallery** (☎ 706/782–2440), one of the state's best sources for folk art, features works by regional artists such as O.L. Samuels, Sarah Rakes, and Jay Schuette, and North Carolina's reclusive James Harold Jennings. About 10 miles north of Clayton on U.S. 441 is the **Dillard House**, justifiably famous for its spread of country food served family-style. ☎ 706/746–5348 or 800/541–0671. *No early breakfast Sun.*

Dahlonega. Gold was mined here before the Civil War, and a U.S. mint operated in this modest boom town from 1838 to 1861. In the present-day courthouse on the town square is the Gold Museum, with coins, tools, and a 5½-ounce nugget. The square is ringed with a mixture of tourist-oriented boutiques and old small-town businesses. *About 55 mi northeast of Atlanta, ☎ 706/864–2257. ☛ $2 adults, $1 children under 18. ☉ Daily.*

Fort Mountain State Park. Amid the deep woods and spectacular views in this out-of-the-way park in the Chattahoochee National Forest, nature is the main attraction, with a wide variety of trees and other flora. *Rte. 52 east of Chatsworth,* ☎ *706/695–2621.* ☛ *$2 per vehicle, free on Wed.* ☉ *Sat.–Thurs. 8–5, Fri. 8–10.*

Macon. This antebellum town features more than 100,000 flowering cherry trees. The Hay House (1860), considered one of the South's finest Italianate villas, contains 19 marble mantlepieces and other fine architectural detailing. *934 Georgia Ave.,* ☎ *912/742–8155.* ☛ *$6.30 adults, $5.25 senior citizens, $2.10 children 12–18, $1.05 children 6–12.* ☉ *Mon.–Sat. 10–5, Sun. 1–5; last tour 4:30.*

The **Harriet Tubman African American Museum** is a tribute to the former slave who led more than 300 people to freedom as one of the "conductors" on the Underground Railroad. A mural that spans two walls and several centuries depicts black history and culture. The museum also has an African artifacts gallery and regularly changing exhibits. *340 Walnut St.,* ☎ *912/743–8544.* ☛ *$2 adults, $1 children 6–18.* ☉ *Mon.–Sat. 10–5, Sun. 2–5.*

Madison. This town remains virtually unchanged architecturally from the 1830s. The **Madison-Morgan Cultural Center** is housed in a turn-of-the-century schoolhouse built in Romanesque Revival style. Besides a restored classroom of the period, the center contains artifacts and information and printed guides for other historic sites in town. *434 S. Main St.,* ☎ *706/342–4743.* ☛ *$2.50 adults, $1.50 students.* ☉ *Tues.–Sat. 10–4:30, Sun. 2–5.*

New Echota State Historic Site. From 1825 to 1838, New Echota was the capital of the Cherokee nation, whose constitution was patterned after that of the United States. There was a courthouse, a Supreme Court building, and the *Cherokee Phoenix,* a newspaper that utilized the Cherokee alphabet developed by Sequoyah. Some buildings have been reconstructed. *Rte. 225, 1 mi east of I–75N, near Calhoun,* ☎ *706/629–8151.* ☛ *$2 adults, $1 children 6–18, under 5 free.* ☉ *Tues.–Sat. 9–5, Sun. 2–5:30.*

Ocmulgee National Monument. This archaeological site, occupied for more than 10,000 years, was at its peak under the Mississippian peoples who lived here between 900 and 1100. There's a reconstructed earth lodge and displays of pottery, effigies, and jewelry of copper and shells discovered in the burial mound. *Rte. 80 just east of Macon,* ☎ *912/752–8257.* ☛ *Free.* ☉ *Daily 9–5.*

Spring Place. Chief James Vann, a leader of the Cherokee Nation around 1800, hired Moravian artisans to build this two-story brick house in 1805. The interior is intricately carved and beautifully restored. *Rte. 52A just west of Chatsworth,* ☎ *706/695–2598.* ☛ *$2 adults, $1.50 children 6–18, under 6 free.* ☉ *Tues.–Sat. 9–5, Sun. 2–5:30.*

Summerville. Paradise Garden is the vision-come-to-life of the Rev. Howard Finster, preacher and folk artist. His artwork has been used for album covers by Talking Heads and R.E.M., and his eccentric visions are also in the collection of Atlanta's High Museum of Art. The garden, which occupies several city blocks, is dominated by the chapel built by Finster and members of his family. A tower built of old bicycle parts serves as a sentry for the spectacle. Artwork is for sale in the shop. *Off U.S. 27, near Pennville,* ☎ *706/857–2926.* ☛ *Free, donations accepted.* ☉ *Daily 10–6.*

Warm Springs. President Franklin Delano Roosevelt first visited here in 1924 and in 1932 built the "Little White House," a simple, three-bedroom house where he stayed when taking the therapeutic hot waters of the area. Now restored, it contains two hand-operated automobiles among his personal effects. *Rte. 85 W,* ☎ *706/655–5870.* ☛ *$4 adults, $2 children 6–18, under 6 free.* ☺ *Daily 9–5.*

3 North Carolina

Historic sights and natural wonders galore accent North Carolina, from Old Salem, where the 1700s spring to life today, to the Great Smoky and Blue Ridge Mountains, where waterfalls cascade over high cliffs into gorges thick with evergreens, to the Cape Hatteras and Cape Lookout national seashores, where tides wash over shipwrecks and lighthouses stand as they have for 200 years. Here, too, you'll find sophisticated cities like Charlotte, first-class golf in the Pinehurst Sandhills, and fields of tobacco in the Piedmont.

NORTH CAROLINA MAY NOT HAVE IT ALL, but don't try telling that to a North Carolinian. Any native will point to its mountains, some of the tallest in the east, which are laced with waterfalls cascading over rocky cliffs into gorges thick with evergreens. He or she will tell you about Cape Hatteras and Cape Lookout national seashores, where tides wash over the wooden beams of ancient shipwrecks, and lighthouses have stood for 200 years. You'll be invited to Charlotte, the state's largest city, where banking and professional basketball draw national attention, and to the Research Triangle Park, at which the technology of virtual reality got a trial run.

By Carol Timblin

Updated by Susan Ladd

North Carolina geography has carved out three distinct regions: The mountains, the Piedmont, and the coast. The Great Smoky and Blue Ridge mountain ranges create the rough, slanted border of western North Carolina. The mountains taper off into foothills and then into the Piedmont, a gently rolling landscape characterized by rich farmlands to the north, red clay soil in the center, and sandy pine forests to the south. Most major cities have grown up in the center of the state, built primarily by the textile, furniture, and tobacco industries. The rolling hills of the Piedmont level off into the rich soil of the coastal plain. Much of eastern North Carolina remains agricultural and rural. Wilmington is a bustling port city, in sharp contrast to the tranquil villages along the Outer Banks.

Golf is the recreational focus in the Sandhills, while skiing has taken hold in the High Country (Alleghany, Ashe, Avery, Mitchell, and Watauga counties). Asheville has maintained its status as a resort city for more than 100 years and continues to grow in popularity.

North Carolina has courted visitors since the first English settlers arrived in 1584. Since the Depression of the 1930s, when the state began to realize the importance of tourism, the welcome mat has been out. The Blue Ridge Parkway was built largely by the CCC (Civilian Conservation Corps), as were many state park facilities. Cape Hatteras was declared a national seashore—the country's first—in 1953. A good highway system and several airports were built, and now eight welcome centers greet visitors at state borders. People come to North Carolina for its historic sites and natural wonders, its sports, resorts, and down-home cooking, not to mention its legendary barbecue. And tourism today, after tobacco and textiles, is the state's largest industry.

CHARLOTTE

Charlotte, once a sleepy Southern crossroads, has grown up to be quite a sophisticated city—with luxury hotels, excellent restaurants, sporting events, and varied cultural activities. The acquisition of a professional football franchise is the city's most recent achievement, and Carolina Panthers mania is already sweeping the state. The Charlotte Hornets basketball team has been setting NBA attendance and merchandise sales records since the team was formed in 1988.

Though Charlotte dates to Revolutionary War times (it is named for King George III's wife, Queen Charlotte), its Uptown is distinctively New South. The NationsBank Corporate Center, a 60-story skyscraper designed by Cesar Pelli, dominates the skyline. The Queen City is the largest city in the Carolinas, the third largest banking center in the nation, and a major trade and distribution center.

North Carolina

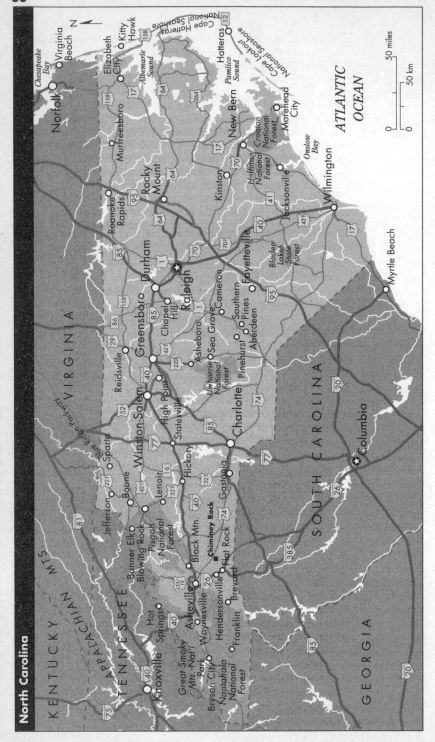

N

Chesapeake Bay
Virginia Beach
Norfolk
158
Kitty Hawk
158
Elizabeth City
Murfreesboro
17
Albemarle Sound
64
264
Cape Hatteras National Seashore
12
Hatteras
Pamlico Sound
Rocky Mount
95
64
Roanoke Rapids
New Bern
Kinston
17
70
Croatan National Forest
Morehead City
Cape Lookout National Seashore

VIRGINIA

85
Durham
1
Raleigh
70
701
Hoffman National Forest
Jacksonville
41
Wilmington
40
421
158
86
Greensboro
85
Chapel Hill
1
421
Reidsville
29
40
Asheboro
Sea Grove
220
Southern Pines
Cameron
Fayetteville
Bladen Lakes State Forest
95
Myrtle Beach
17

52
Winston-Salem
40
High Point
Statesville
Uwharrie National Forest
Pinehurst
Aberdeen

Sparta
221
Boone
421
52
77
Hickory
16
321
Lenoir
Charlotte
74
85
77

Blue Ridge Parkway
KENTUCKY MTS.
81
Jefferson
Banner Elk
Blowing Rock
Pisgah National Forest
221
19
Black Mtn.
40
Gastonia
321
74
77
26

APPALACHIAN
TENNESSEE
Hot Springs
40
Asheville
221
19
26
Chimney Rock
Flat Rock
Brevard

Knoxville
75
40
Great Smoky Mts. Nat'l Park
Bryson City
Nantahala National Forest
Waynesville
Hendersonville
Franklin

SOUTH CAROLINA

Columbia
20
26
385

GEORGIA
85
20

ATLANTIC OCEAN

Onslow Bay

50 miles
50 km

Heavy development has created some typical urban problems. Outdated road systems make traffic a nightmare during rush hour, and virtually all the city's restaurants are packed on weekends. But the southern courtesy of the locals is contagious, and people still love the traditional pleasure of picnicking in Freedom Park.

Exploring

Uptown Charlotte Walking Tour

Numbers in the margin correspond to points of interest on the Charlotte map.

Uptown Charlotte is ideal for walking, and buses are adequate for getting around within the city limits; otherwise, you will need a car. The city was laid out in four wards from the Square, at Trade and Tryon streets. Stop first at **Info Charlotte** on South Tryon Street (*see* Visitor Information, *below*) for information on a self-guided walking tour of Fourth Ward (*see below*) and a historic tour of Uptown, as well as maps and brochures. You can park your car in an open lot a few blocks east of the Square, where Trade and Tryon intersect.

Take a stroll down **Tryon Street** and enjoy the ambience of this revitalized area, noting the outdoor sculptures on the plazas and the creative architecture of some of the newer buildings, among them the

❶ **NationsBank Corporate Center,** a 60-story structure with a crownlike top designed by Pelli, which opened in late 1992. Its main attraction is three philosophical frescoes by Ben Long that symbolize the city's past, present, and future. Also housed in the tower are the **North Carolina Blumenthal Performing Arts Center** and **Founders Hall,** a complex of restaurants and shops.

❷ From the bank, head north on North Tryon Street to **Discovery Place,** the city's premier attraction. Make the wonderful hands-on Science Museum a priority, and allow at least two hours for the aquariums, the rain forest, the Omnimax theater, and Kelly Space Voyager Planetarium. Check the schedule for special exhibits. *301 N. Tryon St.,* ☎ *704/372–6261 or 800/935–0553.* ☛ *$5.50–$8.50 adults, $4.50–$7.50 senior citizens and students, $2.75–$5.50 children 3–5.* ☉ *Mon.–Sat. 9–6, Sun. 1–6.*

❸ **Fourth Ward,** Charlotte's new "old" city, which lies just north of Discovery Place, offers a refreshing change from the newly developed parts of town. The self-guided tour brochure available at Info Charlotte (330 S. Tryon St.) that includes house numbers, points to 18 historic sites in the area. Be sure to stop by **Old Settlers Cemetery,** behind the **First Presbyterian Church,** which contains stones that date to the 1700s. The church, which takes up a city block and faces West Trade Street, reflects the prosperity of the early settlers and their descendants. By the turn of the last century, they had built this Gothic Revival complex with stained glass to replace a much simpler meeting house. **Fourth Ward Park** is an oasis in the middle of the city. **Alexander Michael's** (401 W. Ninth St., ☎ 704/332–6789) is a favorite eatery. **Poplar Street Books** is housed in the Victorian Young-Morrison House (226 W. Tenth St.). U.S. President Taft spent the night in the **Liddell-McNinch House** (511 N. Church St.), now a restaurant, when he visited Charlotte in 1909. **Spirit Square** (345 N. College St.), in a former church, includes galleries, a performing arts center, and classrooms that used to be the sanctuary for the First Baptist Church. The **public library** (310 N. Tryon St.), which contains a mural reproducing a Romare Bearden painting, is open weekdays 9–9, Saturday 9–6, and Sunday 2–6.

Charlotte

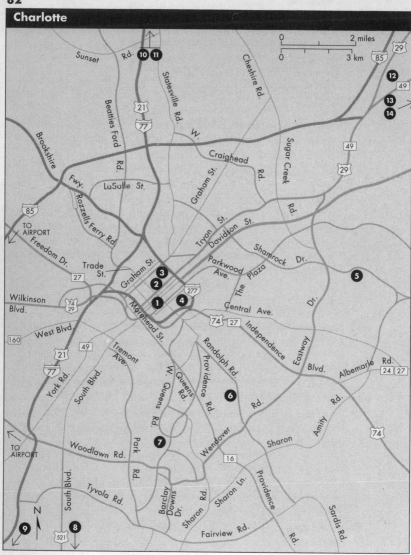

0   2 miles
0   3 km

Afro-American
Cultural Center, **4**

Backing Up Classics
Memory Lane Motor
Car Museum, **14**

Charlotte Motor
Speedway, **13**

Discovery Place, **2**

Energy Explorium, **11**

Fourth Ward, **3**

Hezekiah Alexander
Homesite and History
Museum, **5**

James K. Polk
Memorial, **8**

Latta Plantation
Park, **10**

Mint Museum of Art, **6**

NationsBank
Corporate Center, **1**

New Heritage USA, **9**

UNC Charlotte
Botanical Garden and
Sculpture Garden, **12**

Wing Haven Gardens
and Bird Sanctuary, **7**

Other Area Attractions

You can reach the Afro-American Cultural Center, Hezekiah Alexander Homesite, Mint Museum, and Charlotte Nature Museum by city bus; for visits elsewhere, a car is needed.

❹ From Uptown Charlotte, follow Seventh Street east to North Myers Street. The **Afro-American Cultural Center,** an arts center that has galleries and a theater, is housed in the former Little Rock AME Zion Church. *401 N. Meyers St.,* ☎ *704/374–1565.* ☛ *Free.* ☉ *Tues.–Sat. 10–6, Sun. 1–5.*

❺ From Seventh Street, go east on Central Avenue to Eastway Drive, north to Shamrock Drive, and east to the **Hezekiah Alexander Homesite and Charlotte History Museum.** The stone house, built in 1774, is the oldest dwelling in the county. Here, Alexander and his wife, Mary, reared 10 children and farmed the land. Costumed docents give guided tours, and seasonal events commemorate the early days. *3500 Shamrock Dr.,* ☎ *704/568–1774.* ☛ *$4 adults, $3 senior citizens, $2 children 6–12.* ☉ *Tues.–Fri. 10–5, weekends 2–5.*

★ ❻ Follow Eastway Drive (Charlotte 4) south to Randolph Road and turn right to the **Mint Museum of Art.** Built in 1837 as a U.S. Mint, it has served as a home for art since 1936, attracting such visiting exhibits as "Classical Taste in America." *2730 Randolph Rd.,* ☎ *704/337– 2000.* ☛ *$4 adults, $3 senior citizens, $2 students 13 and older, children under 12 free.* ☉ *Tues. 10–10, Wed.–Sat. 10–5, Sun. noon–5. Closed major holidays.*

❼ Continue on Charlotte 4 (Wendover Rd.) for a visit to **Wing Haven Gardens and Bird Sanctuary** in Myers Park, one of Charlotte's loveliest neighborhoods. The 3-acre garden, developed by the Clarkson family, is home to more than 135 species of birds. *248 Ridgewood Ave.,* ☎ *704/331–0664.* ☛ *Free.* ☉ *Sun. 2–5, Tues.–Wed. 3–5 or by appointment.*

❽ The **James K. Polk Memorial,** now a state historic site, marks the humble 1795 birthplace of the 11th president. Guided tours of the log cabins are available, and exhibits in the center depict early life in Mecklenburg County. *U.S. 521, Pineville,* ☎ *704/889–7145.* ☛ *Free.* ☉ *Apr.–Oct., Mon.–Sat. 9–5, Sun. 1–5; Nov.–Mar., Tues.–Sat. 10– 4, Sun. 1–4.*

❾ Head south on I–77 for about 12 miles to **New Heritage USA,** on the South Carolina line, the 2,200-acre Christian theme park once owned by Jim and Tammy Bakker's PTL television ministry. It's a very pleasant place, with an elaborate water park (open mid-May–Labor Day), paddle boats, farm animals, bike rentals, horseback riding, and shops. You can also visit Billy Graham's boyhood home, which was moved to the site. *3000 Heritage Pkwy., Fort Mill, SC,* ☎ *803/548–7800 or 800/374–1234.* ☛ *Free to the park and Graham house; attractions cost $1–$13.*

❿ **Latta Plantation Park,** northwest of town (off I–77, near Huntersville), centers on Latta Place, a Catawba River plantation house built by merchant James Latta in the early 1800s. Costumed guides give tours of the house. The park also has farm animals, an equestrian center, and the Carolina Raptor Center, a unique nonprofit facility where injured raptors are rehabilitated and then released. Those unable to return to the wild are cared for and used to educate visitors about the importance of bald eagles, owls, and other birds of prey. *5225 Sample Rd., Huntersville,* ☎ *704/875–2312 (Latta Place), 704/875–1391 (park),* or 704/875–6521 (Carolina Raptor Center). ☛ House tour $2 adults, $1.50 senior citizens, $1 children. ☛ Raptor Center $2 adults, $1 students 6 and older. Park ☉ Daily 7 AM–dark; Carolina Raptor Center ☉ Tues.–Sun. 10–5; house tours Tues.–Fri. at 1:30 and 3:30, weekends at 1:30, 2:30, 3:30.

⑪ Continue on I–77N to the **Energy Explorium,** operated by Duke Power Company on Lake Norman. Hands-on exhibits let you simulate the creation of nuclear power and other kinds of energy. A wildflower garden and picnic area offer diversion of a different kind. McGuire Nuclear Site, off I–77 and NC 73, Huntersville, ☎ 704/875–5600 or 800/777–0003. ☛ Free. ☉ Mon.–Sat. 9–5, Sun. noon–5. Closed major holidays.

⑫ The **UNC Charlotte Botanical Garden and Sculpture Garden,** on Route 49 off I–85, has a rhododendron garden and greenhouse with a rain forest, orchids, carnivorous plants, and cacti. Sculptures are constantly being added to the adjoining Sculpture Garden. Rte. 49, ☎ 704/547–4286. ☛ Free. ☉ Gardens daylight–dark, greenhouse weekdays 8–5 and weekends by appointment.

⑬ Northeast of town on Route 29, you'll come to the **Charlotte Motor Speedway.** Learn all about racing at this state-of-the-art facility (which has condos overlooking the first turn), browse through the gift shop, or even take a lesson at the track through the Richard Petty Driving School (☎ 704/455–9443) or Fast Track Driving School (☎ 704/455–1700). Rte. 29 at Concord, ☎ 704/455–3200. ☛ Tour $3, children under 3 free. ☉ Mon.–Sat. 9–4, Sun. 1–4.

⑭ At the **Backing Up Classics Memory Lane Museum** (we're not making this up), you can see up close some of the '50s race and muscle cars that have been the workhorses of stock-car racing. 4545 Hwy. 29, Harrisburg, ☎ 704/788–9494. ☛ $4.50 adults, $4 senior citizens and students, children 6 and under free. ☉ Weekdays 9–5:30, Sat. 9–5, Sun. noon–5.

What to See and Do with Children

At **Celebration Station,** a commercial park, you can play miniature golf, ride in go-carts and bumper boats, try your skill at arcade games, stuff yourself, and watch mechanical cartoon characters entertain you. 10400 Cadillac St., Pineville, ☎ 704/552–7888. ☛ $3–$4 per attraction. ☉ Mon.–Thurs. 4–9, Fri. 4–11, Sat. 10 AM–11 PM, Sun. 10–9. Closed Thanksgiving and Dec. 25.

Paramount's Carowinds, off I–77, a 91-acre theme amusement park on the South Carolina state line, has taken on a new image since its acquisition by the movie studio and the addition of new attractions based on films. Costumed movie characters and actors greet visitors to the park, and the Paladium offers musical concerts with star entertainers. Carowinds Blvd., ☎ 704/588–2600 or 800/888–4386. ☛ $25.95 adults, $13.50 senior citizens over 60 and children 4–6. ☉ June–Aug., daily; mid-Mar.–May. and Sept.–mid-Oct., weekends only; the park usually opens around 10 AM, closing hours vary.

The **Charlotte Nature Museum** has live animals, nature trails, hands-on exhibits, and nature films. 1658 Sterling Rd. (next to Freedom Park), ☎ 704/337–2660. ☛ $1, under 3 free. ☉ Weekdays 9–5, Sat. 10–5, Sun. 1–5. Closed major holidays.

Reed Gold Mine, east of Charlotte in Cabarrus County, is where America's first gold rush began following Conrad Reed's discovery of a 17-

pound nugget in 1799. Visitors may explore the underground mine shaft and gold holes, pan for gold during the summer months, learn about the history of gold mining, or enjoy a picnic. *Take NC 24/27 to Locust and follow the signs,* ☎ 704/786–8337. ☛ *Free, but gold panning is $3 (group rate $1 per person).* ☉ *Apr.–Oct., Mon.–Sat. 9–5, Sun. 1–5; Nov.–Mar., Tues.–Sat. 10–4, Sun. 1–4.*

At the **N.C. Transportation Museum,** north of Salisbury, once a railway repair facility, a restored train takes passengers on a 45-minute ride over the 57-acre complex, with a stop at the round house. The museum, a state historic site, traces the development of transportation in North Carolina from Indian times to the present. The gift shop sells some unique train memorabilia. *Off I–85 at Spencer,* ☎ 704/636–2889. ☛ *Free, train rides $2.50–$3.50.* ☉ *Apr.–Oct., Mon.–Sat. 9–5, Sun. 1–5; Nov.–Mar., Tues.–Sat. 10–4, Sun. 1–4.*

Shopping

Charlotte is the largest retail center in the Carolinas, with the majority of stores in suburban malls. Villages and towns in outlying areas offer some regional specialties. Uptown shops are open 10–5:30 daily except Sunday. Malls are open Monday–Saturday 10–9 and Sunday 1–6. Sales tax is 6%.

Shopping Districts

You can buy well-known brands at a discount in outlets in **Midtown Square** (401 S. Independence Blvd.) near Uptown, **Windsor Square** (9915 E. Independence Blvd.) near Matthews, or **Outlet Marketplace,** (off I–77, Ft. Mill, SC).

Carolina Place Mall (11025 Carolina Place Pkwy., off I-277 at Pineville; 704/543–9300) is the newest mall in the area, with Belk, Dillard's, Hecht's, and JC Penney as anchors. **SouthPark Mall** (4400 Sharon Rd., ☎ 704/364–4411) in the most affluent section of the city, caters to upscale customers. Belk, Dillard's, Hecht's, Montaldo's, and Sears are here. The main attraction at **Eastland Mall** (5431 Central Ave., ☎ 704/537–2626), on the east side of town, is an ice-skating rink. Dillard's, Belk, JC Penney, Sears, and other retail stores are also located here.

Specialty Stores

ANTIQUES

The towns of Waxhaw, Pineville, and Matthews are the best places to find antiques. Each has a number of shops, and Waxhaw sponsors an annual antiques fair each February. Shops are usually open Monday through Saturday in Pineville and Matthews. In Waxhaw, some shops are open on Sunday but closed on Monday. You can find a good selection of antiques at the **Metrolina Expo** (off I–77N at 7100 Statesville Rd.) on the first and third weekends of the month.

BOOKS

There are some excellent bookshops in Charlotte. **Little Professor Book Center** (Park Road Shopping Center, ☎ 704/525–9239; South Lake Shopping Center, Lake Norman, ☎ 704/896–7323) has a nice selection of contemporary fiction and classics. **Barnes & Noble Bookstore** (5837 E. Independence Blvd., ☎ 704/535–9810; 10701 Centrum Pkwy., Pineville, ☎ 704/541–1425) is an upscale chain with more than 100,000 titles. The **Intimate Bookshop** (South Park Mall, ☎ 704/366–6400; Eastland Mall, ☎ 704/568–3600; University Place, ☎ 704/547–7400) is a locally based chain with a fine selection and warm atmosphere.

Borders Books & Music (4500 Sharon Rd., ☎ 704/365–6261), the newest contender in the Charlotte book market, has 100,000 titles and a built-in espresso bar where you can mull over the choices. **Newsstand International** (5636 E. Independence Blvd., ☎ 704/365–0910) carries 5,000 newspapers, maps, and magazines from around the world.

CRAFTS

The best buys are in the **Metrolina Expo** (*see* Antiques, *above*). At the **Carolina Craft Shows,** held in the fall and spring at the Convention Center, as well as the **Southern Christmas Show** and the **Southern Spring Show** at the Merchandise Mart, you can buy a wide variety.

FOOD AND PLANTS

Try the **Charlotte Regional Farmers Market** (1715 Yorkmount Rd.) for fresh produce and fish, plants, and crafts. The **Harris-Teeter** grocery store in Morrocroft Village (6701 Morrison Blvd., ☎ 704/364–1245) is a white-columned showplace with a staff chef who oversees an elaborate dine-in deli and the two other stores.

Participant Sports and Outdoor Activities

Bicycling

North Carolina has designated bike tour routes stretching from the coast to the mountains. There is one between Southpark and Uptown Charlotte. Route maps are available from the NC Department of Transportation (Box 25201, Raleigh 27611).

Camping

Near Charlotte, try McDowell Park and Nature Reserve (15222 York Rd., ☎ 704/588–5224), Carowinds (*see above*), and Duke Power State Park(Rte. 2, Box 224–M, Troutman, ☎ 704/528–6350).

Canoeing

Inlets on Lake Norman and Lake Wylie are ideal for canoeing, as are some spots of the Catawba River. The Pee Dee River east of Charlotte and the New River in the mountains offer other options.

Fishing

There's good fishing in Charlotte's neighboring lakes and streams. A mandatory state license can be bought at local bait and tackle shops or over the phone (with a credit card) from the North Carolina Wildlife Commission (☎ 919/715–4091).

Golf

There are 23 public and 31 private courses in the Charlotte area. The *Metrolina Golf Guide,* a free publication available at the visitor center, has a complete list. **Crystal Springs Golf Club** (NC 51, Pineville, ☎ 704/588–2640) is an 18-hole championship course with restaurant and lounge. **Highland Creek Golf Club** (7001 Highland Creek Pkwy., ☎ 704/875–9000), an 18-hole course with a driving range, is considered by some to be the best public course in Charlotte. **Larkhaven Golf Club** (4801 Camp Stewart Rd., ☎ 704/545–4653) is an 18-hole championship course with club house and pro shop. **Paradise Valley Golf Center** (9309 N. Tryon St., ☎ 704/547–0222), in the University area, has a 9-hole regulation course and a 9-hole par-three course. The driving range is down the street (9615 N. Tryon St., ☎ 704/548–8114). The **Peninsula Club** (19101 Peninsula Club Dr., Davidson, ☎ 704/896–7080) recently hosted the Carolinas LPGA. **Woodbridge Golf Links** (922 New

Camp Creek Church Rd., Kings Mountain., ☎ 704/482–0353), an attractive course featuring covered cart bridges, has 18 holes and a driving range.

Hiking

Crowder's Mountain and Kings Mountain near Gastonia and the Uwharrie Mountains east of Charlotte offer plenty of varied terrain and challenge for hikers.

Jogging

Jogging trails and tracks can be found in most city and county parks and at many local schools. Contact the Mecklenburg County Parks and Recreation Department (☎ 704/336–3854). The **Charlotte Track Club** (☎ 704/358–0713) meets monthly and holds regular group runs Sundays at 7:30 AM at McAlpine Creek Park.

Swimming

The **Mecklenburg County Aquatic Center** (800 E. 2nd St., ☎ 704/336–3483) has a 50-meter lap pool, hydrotherapy pool, fitness room, and whirlpool. It is open daily to local residents and visitors. ☞ *$4 nonresident adults, $3 children under 19.*

Tennis

Courts are available in several city parks, including Freedom, Hornet's Nest, Park Road, and Veterans. A growing number of hotels and motels provide courts as well. For details, call the Charlotte Park and Recreation Department (☎ 704/336–3854).

Spectator Sports

Baseball

The **Charlotte Knights** play from April through August at Knights Castle (I–77 and Gold Hill Rd., SC, ☎ 704/357–8071 or 803/548–8050).

Basketball

The **Charlotte Hornets** play from November to April at the Charlotte Coliseum (Tyvola Rd., off the Billy Graham Pkwy., ☎ 704/357–0489).

Football

The **Carolina Panthers** NFL team plays September–January at the new Carolinas Stadium downtown (S. Tryon St., ☎ 704/358–7800).

Hockey

The **Charlotte Checkers** play from mid-October to mid-March at Independence Arena (2700 E. Independence Blvd., ☎ 704/342–4423).

Racing

NASCAR races, such as the **Coca-Cola 600** and **Mello Yello 500,** draw huge crowds at the Charlotte Motor Speedway near Concord. For tickets, call 704/455–3200.

Dining

If there is one sure indication of Charlotte's transformation from Southern town to big city, it's the restaurant scene. Risotto and dim sum are becoming as common as grits and cornbread. These days, it's probably easier to find a good Thai restaurant than it is to find barbecue. Ethnic specialties of all kinds are available, as well as American nouvelle cuisine and various upscale chain restaurants. But if it's good old-fashioned Southern cooking you want, you can still find that, too. Dress is casual unless otherwise noted.

CATEGORY	COST*
$$$$	over $20
$$$	$15–$20
$$	$10–$15
$	under $10

per person for a three-course meal, excluding drinks, service, and 6% sales tax

American

$$$–$$$$ Townhouse. American cuisine with a French twist is exquisitely prepared and served in an atmosphere of casual elegance. Choose from appetizers such as spinach lasagna with snails and garlic cream and entrées such as carmelized salmon, or let the chef compose a five-course "chef's choice" menu for $45 per person. ✕ *1011 Providence Rd.,* ☎ *704/335–1546. Reservations accepted. AE, DC, MC, V. Closed Sun.*

$$–$$$ Newmarket Grille. You can enjoy a variety of moderately priced dishes, including soups, sandwiches, salads, pastas, steak, and fish, within the rich mahogany walls of this restaurant in the Arboretum Shopping Center on the south side. Outdoor dining is also an option, and there's a cozy, dark bar for getting together with friends. ✕ *8136 Providence Rd.,* ☎ *704/543–4656. No reservations. AE, DC, MC, V.*

$$–$$$ Providence Café. Many of the dishes (especially the sandwiches) served in this chic, contemporary eatery decorated with neon and original art center around the focaccia that is baked daily on the premises. The eclectic menu also includes chicken, steaks, and seafood grilled over green hickory wood. It's a great place for Sunday brunch and after-hours desserts with cappuccino or espresso. ✕ *110 Perrin Pl.,* ☎ *704/376–2008. No reservations on weekends. AE, D, MC, V.*

$–$$ Grady's American Grill. Packed every night of the week, this restaurant has earned praise from patrons for its friendly service and excellent food. Favorites are the greenhouse salad served with honey-mustard dressing, the mesquite-grilled chicken or fish, and the hot chocolate bar cake. There's usually a wait of 30 minutes to an hour, but the time passes quickly at the lively bar. ✕ *5546 Albemarle Rd.,* ☎ *704/537–4663. No reservations. AE, DC, MC, V.*

$ Landmark Restaurant-Diner. This New York–style eatery in the Eastland Mall neighborhood is a cut above most inexpensive restaurants, and it's open until 3 AM on weeknights and 24 hours on weekends. Decorated in contemporary colors, this spacious restaurant is a good place for an informal breakfast, lunch, dinner, or after-hours dessert. (Ask for the New York–style cheesecake from the in-house bakery.) ✕ *4429 Central Ave.,* ☎ *704/532–1153. Reservations accepted for parties of 8 or more. AE, MC, V. Closed Dec. 25.*

Chinese

$$ Ginger Root. Relaxation is guaranteed the moment you step into the quiet, peaceful atmosphere of this Uptown restaurant, convenient to the art centers and galleries. Ideal for lunch or dinner, the restaurant offers pork, chicken, beef, and seafood dishes, served Huñan, Szechuan, Yu Shawn, or Kao Pao style. There's also a comfortable bar. ✕ *201 E. 5th St.,* ☎ *704/377–9429. Reservations advised. AE, DC, MC, V.*

Continental

$$$$ Lamplighter. You don't have to go abroad to find gourmet cuisine served
★ in an elegant setting. Just step into the softly lit, sophisticated atmosphere of the Lamplighter, in an old Dilworth home. The trio combination entrées (beef, veal, and lamb, or different seafoods) are
exceptional, and the wine list is extensive. There's a quiet, intimate lounge
for cocktails. ✗ *1065 E. Morehead St.,* ☎ *704/372–5343. Reservations advised. Jacket required. AE, DC, MC, V.*

$$ Pewter Rose Bistro. In a renovated textile mill in historic Dilworth, 5
★ minutes from Uptown, the Pewter Rose Bistro is a favorite hangout
for Charlotte's young professionals. Lace curtains and plants decorate
the dining room, and the kitchen specializes in fresh seasonal foods,
plus a variety of chicken and seafood dishes. You can order pasta with
feta cheese, sun-dried tomatoes and olives vegetarian or add chicken
for a heartier meal. A nice place to go for Sunday brunch. ✗ *1820 South
Blvd.,* ☎ *704/332–8149. Reservations for parties of 6 or more. AE,
D, MC, V. Closed Mon.*

Italian

$$$$ Bravo! Authentic classic Italian cuisine is served in a Mediterranean-
style atmosphere at this hotel restaurant, the "in" place for special cel-
ebrations and Sunday brunches. The professionally trained singing
waitresses and waiters never seem to tire of performing or graciously
serving. ✗ *Adams Mark Hotel, 555 S. McDowell St.,* ☎ *704/372–5440.
Reservations advised. Jacket required. AE, D, MC, V.*

$$–$$$ Cafe 521. Put on your Doc Maartens and join the Generation Xers for
excellent Northern Italian cuisine at one of the city's coolest restau-
rants. Don't miss the zesty minestrone. Industrial looking on the out-
side, the restaurant is painted with funky murals on the inside. ✗ *521
N. College St.,* ☎ *704/377–9100. Reservations accepted. AE, D, MC,
V.*

$–$$ PizZarrelli Trattoria. The secret to the unique flavor of the made-from-
scratch pizzas is in the wood-burning brick ovens, built by Italian ma-
sons. The menu also features calzone, lasagna, spaghetti, and other
Southern Italian dishes—all family recipes and especially good when
served with the mellow house wine. The tables are covered with red-
checked gingham, and the walls are adorned with posters and photographs that chronicle the professional singing career of owner Neal
Zarrelli, a former opera star who often sings for his customers. ✗ *9101
Pineville-Matthews Rd., Pineville,* ☎ *704/543–0647. Reservations
accepted. MC, V.*

Thai

$$–$$$ Thai House. Fiery pleasure awaits the adventurous diner who samples
from a selection of vegetarian, seafood, and classic Thai dishes. Regarded by many as the best Thai food in town, this restaurant is open
daily for lunch and dinner. The satay and Phad Thai noodles are mild
enough for any taste buds, but many other classic dishes are prepared
as firey as you request. ✗ *3210 N. Sharon Amity Rd.,* ☎ *704/532–
6868. Reservations advised for parties of 6 or more. AE, D, MC, V.*

Lodging

Approximately 14,000 hotel rooms are available in the Charlotte area,
from economy motels to convention hotels or bed-and-breakfast houses.
Most of the major chains are represented, from Hilton, Hyatt, and Sheraton, to EconoLodge, Days Inn, and Motel 6. Some hotels offer great
weekend packages. A 6% accommodations tax and 6% sales tax are

added to every room charge. Pick up the "Charlotte Visitors Guide" for a more comprehensive list.

CATEGORY	COST*
$$$$	over $100
$$$	$60–$100
$$	$30–$60
$	under $30

All prices are for a standard double room, excluding 12% tax

Hotels

$$$ **Dunhill.** Charlotte's oldest and most historic hotel (built in 1929) fea-
★ tures artwork by Philip Moose and 18th- and 19th-century reproduc-
tion furniture in the lobby, restaurant, and guest rooms. The restaurant,
Monticello's, gets rave reviews for its beautifully presented American
cuisine. ⌖ 237 N. Tryon St., 28202, ☎ 704/332–4141 or 800/354–
4141, FAX 704/376–4117. 59 rooms and 1 penthouse with Jacuzzi.
Restaurant, lounge. AE, D, DC, MC, V.

$$$ **Embassy Suites.** An eight-story atrium and three glass elevators dis-
tinguish this all-suite hotel, near the airport and the Coliseum. Guests
have the option of regular suites (which have two rooms, plus a cof-
feemaker, refrigerator, microwave, and regular amenities) or 12 executive suites, four of which have Jacuzzis. Guests are served a
cooked-to-order full breakfast and are treated to an afternoon reception. ⌖ 4800 S. Tryon St., 28217, ☎ 704/527–8400 or 800/362–2779,
FAX 704/527–7035. 274 suites. Restaurant, lounge, indoor pool, hot
tub, sauna, health club, meeting rooms, airport shuttle. AE, D, DC,
MC, V.

$$$ **Hilton at University Place.** This high-rise with a three-story atrium
dominates the European-style shopping and entertainment village near
the University of North Carolina at Charlotte. Movies, restaurants, shops,
a bank, and even a hospital are just a few steps from the hotel door.
Dining is offered in the Lakefront Café. ⌖ 8629 J.M. Keynes Blvd.,
28262, ☎ 704/547–7444 or 800/445–8667, FAX 704/548–1081. 240
rooms, 3 suites. Restaurant, bar, pool, exercise room, beach, meeting
rooms. AE, D, DC, MC, V.

$$$ **Hyatt Charlotte SouthPark.** The focal point of the four-story atrium is
a Mexican water fountain surrounded by 25-foot olive trees. Guest rooms
are equipped with data ports for laptop computers and fax machines.
Meeting rooms and the lower lobby give onto the open-air courtyard.
Scalini's restaurant serves Northern Italian cuisine; the Club piano bar
is a favorite with the after-hours crowd. ⌖ 5501 Carnegie Blvd.,
28209-3462, ☎ 704/554–1234 or 800/233–1234, FAX 704/554–8319.
258 rooms, 4 suites. Restaurant, indoor pool, hot tub, sauna, health
club, meeting rooms, airport shuttle. AE, D, DC, MC, V.

$$$ **Omni Charlotte Hotel.** The pink marble used in the public rooms
makes this one of Charlotte's classiest Uptown hotels. Guests can
enjoy the ambience of C. Banknight's Bistro and Bar and then work
out with Charlotte's movers and shakers in the adjoining 50,000-
square-foot YMCA, which includes an indoor track and a lap pool.
For special pampering, stay on the Club levels or in the Presidential
Suite. ⌖ 222 E. 3rd St., 28202, ☎ 704/377–6664 or 800/843–6664,
FAX 704/377–4143. 392 rooms, 18 suites. Restaurant, bar, indoor pool,
health club, meeting rooms. AE, D, DC, MC, V.

$$$ **Radisson Plaza Hotel.** Convenience and contemporary elegance are
yours at this property just steps from the Square and the center of Up-
town. It's also connected to the Overstreet Mall, a complex of shops
and restaurants. Try dining at the Azaleas American Grill. All guests

get complimentary newspapers and free parking. ⌖ *1 Radisson Plaza, 101 S. Tryon St., 28280,* ☎ *704/377–0400 or 800/333–3333,* FAX *704/347–0649. 361 rooms, 4 suites. Restaurant, bar, pool, sauna, health club, meeting rooms, airport shuttle. AE, D, DC, MC, V.*

$ **Comfort Inn–Lake Norman.** This economy motel, north of Charlotte on I–77 near Lake Norman, offers complimentary breakfast and rooms with refrigerators and coffeemakers. Some rooms also have VCRs, microwaves, and whirlpool baths. ⌖ *20740 Torrence Chapel Rd., Davidson 28036,* ☎ *704/892–3500 or 800/484–9751,* FAX *704/892–6473. 90 rooms. Pool, coin laundry. AE, D, DC, MC, V.*

Bed-and-Breakfasts

$$$–$$$$ **Inn Uptown.** This 1891 brick château on the edge of the historic 4th Ward neighborhood is popular with business and leisure travelers because of its proximity to Uptown businesses and attractions. Deep green wallpaper and a green-and-white-striped bedspread lend formal elegance to one room; some rooms have whirlpools and fireplaces. A complimentary full breakfast is served, and there is turn-down service. ⌖ *129 Poplar and 5th St., 28202,* ☎ *704/342–2800 or 800/959–1990,* FAX *704/342–2222. 6 rooms. In-room modem lines. AE, D, DC, MC, V.*

$$$ **Homeplace.** This spotless turn-of-the-century Victorian gem is now a
★ bed-and-breakfast inn filled with antiques and memorabilia from yesteryear. The inn's guest rooms all have private baths, and breakfast is prepared by owners Peggy and Frank Darien. The Homeplace is in a residential neighborhood. ⌖ *5901 Sardis Rd., 28270,* ☎ *704/365–1936. 2 rooms and 1 2-bedroom suite. AE, MC, V.*

$$$ **Morehead Inn.** Though it's a commercial venture catering to corporate clients, this Dilworth inn has all the comforts of a beautiful home. Wedding parties find it ideal. A Continental breakfast comes with the room. ⌖ *1122 E. Morehead St., 28204,* ☎ *704/376–3357,* FAX *704/335–1110. 11 rooms. Meeting rooms. AE, DC, MC, V.*

Nightlife

Bailey's Sports Bar & Grille. (5873 Albemarle Rd., ☎ 704/532–1005; 8500 Pineville-Matthews Rd., ☎ 704/541–0794) offers billiards in an upscale setting, big screen TV, and deli-style food.

Blockbuster Pavilion (707 Blockbuster Blvd., ☎ 704/549–1292) and the **Paladium Amphitheater** at Paramount's Carowinds (14523 Carowinds Blvd., ☎ 704/588–2600 or 800/888–4386) present stars in concert mid-spring through mid-fall. Ticket prices vary.

Comedy Zone (5317 E. Independence Blvd., ☎ 704/568–4242) showcases live comedy nightly except Monday, with two shows nightly Friday and Saturday.

Dilworth Brewing Company (1301 East Blvd., ☎ 704/377–2739) features rock bands on Friday and Saturday nights, plus several varieties of excellent beer made on the premises.

Edge Nitelife (4369 South Tryon St., ☎ 704/525–3343) is a progressive dance club for the younger set.

Lizzie's (4809 S. Tryon St., ☎ 704/527–3064), a restaurant on the south side, is best known for its piano bar, occasionally featuring owner Liz King.

Charlotte Essentials

Arriving and Departing

BY BUS
Greyhound Lines (601 W. Trade St., ☎ 800/231–2222) serves the Charlotte area.

BY CAR
Charlotte is a transportation hub; I–85 and I–77, north–south routes, run through, and I–40, east–west, is 40 miles to the north. U.S. 74, a major east–west route, also serves the city. I–277 and Charlotte 4 are inner-city loops. I–485, a planned outer loop, has one completed link between I–77 and Elm Street south of Charlotte.

BY PLANE
Charlotte-Douglas International Airport (☎ 704/359–4013) is west of the city off I–85. Carriers include American, British Airways, Delta, Northwest, TWA, United, USAir, and their local affiliates. Direct service is available to London, Frankfurt, Nassau, Grand Cayman, Montego Bay, and Puerto Rico.

Taxis cost about $12 ($2 each additional person), and airport vans are approximately $5 per person. Most major hotels provide complimentary transportation. By car, take the Billy Graham Parkway, then Wilkinson Boulevard (U.S. 74) east to I–277, which leads to the heart of Uptown.

BY TRAIN
Amtrak (1914 N. Tryon St., ☎ 704/376–4416 or 800/872–7245) offers daily service to Washington, DC, Atlanta, GA, and points beyond, and there's daily service to Raleigh.

Getting Around

BY BUS
Charlotte Transit (☎ 704/336–3366) provides public transportation throughout the city. The Transit Mall has bus shelters on Trade and Tryon streets in Uptown. Fares are 80¢ for local rides and $1.15 for express service; senior citizens with ID cards pay 30¢ between 9 and 3, after 6, and on weekends. Free bus service is available between Mint and Kings Drive on Trade and between Stonewall and 11th on Tryon weekdays 9–3.

BY TAXI
Yellow Cab (☎ 704/332–6161) has cars and airport vans. The **University Shuttle** (☎ 704/553–2424) caters to business travelers. Passengers pay a set flat rate.

Guided Tours
Guided tours are given by **Gray Line** (☎ 704/359–8687), **Adam's Stage Lines** (☎ 704/537–5342), and **Queens Carriages** (☎ 704/391–1232). The *Catawba Queen* paddle wheeler (☎ 704/663–2628) gives dinner cruises and tours on Lake Norman.

Several balloon companies give aerial tours, which end with champagne: **Balloons Over Charlotte** (☎ 704/541–7058), **Adventures Aloft of Charlotte** (☎ 704/545–6418), and **Fantasy Flights** (☎ 704/552–0469).

Important Addresses and Numbers

EMERGENCIES
Dial 911 for **police** and **ambulance** in an emergency.

PHYSICIANS
Care Connection, operated by Presbyterian Hospital, will give physician referrals and make appointments (☎ 704/384–4111, open weekdays 8:30–4:30). **Healthfinder,** run by Mercy Hospital, is a similar operation offering recorded information (☎ 704/379–6100). The **Mecklenburg County Medical Society** also gives physician referrals (☎ 704/376–3688, ☉ Weekdays 9–1).

RADIO STATIONS
AM: WAQS 610, sports, talk; WBT 1110, sports, talk, country; WGSP 1310, Christian. **FM:** WSOC 103.7, country; WFAE 90.7, National Public Radio; WWMG 96, oldies; WXRC 95.7, rock; WMXC 104.7, adult contemporary.

24-HOUR PHARMACY
Eckerd Drugs (Park Road Shopping Center, ☎ 704/523–3031; 3740 E. Independence Blvd., ☎ 704/536–3600).

VISITOR INFORMATION
Info Charlotte (330 S. Tryon St., ☎ 704/331–2700 or 800/231–4636) is open weekdays 8:30–5, Sat. 10–4, and Sun. 1–4. Parking is available. The **N.C. Welcome Center** (on I–77 northbound at the South Carolina line, ☎ 704/588–2660) is open daily 8–5 except Christmas Eve, Christmas Day, New Year's Day, and Thanksgiving. The **Charlotte-Douglas International Airport** has a welcome center in the baggage claim area that's open daily, 7 AM–11 PM.

THE TRIANGLE

The cities of Raleigh, Durham, and Chapel Hill make up "The Triangle," so called because together they form a triangle, with Raleigh to the east, Durham to the north, and Chapel Hill to the west, and because of the Research Triangle Park—a complex of public and private research facilities between the three cities that attracts scientists from all over the world. Although the cities lie within 30 miles of each other and all three can be cursorily visited in one day, plan to spend at least a day in each because of their unique character.

Raleigh is Old South and New South, down-home and upscale, all in one. Named for Sir Walter Raleigh (who established the first English colony on the coast in 1585), Raleigh is the state capital and the largest and busiest of the three cities. The state's largest and best museums are here, as are North Carolina State University and six other universities and colleges.

Durham, a tobacco town for decades (and once called Bull Durham, after one of the many brands of tobacco manufactured here), is now known as the City of Medicine, for the nationally known medical and research centers at Duke University. With more than 20,000 employees, Duke is not only the largest employer in Durham, it's one of the largest employers in the state.

Chapel Hill may be the smallest city in The Triangle, but its reputation as a seat of learning—and of liberalism—looms large indeed. The home of the nation's first state university, the University of North Carolina, Chapel Hill remains a quiet, tree-shaded small town that is crowded with students and retirees.

Politics and basketball are always hot topics throughout The Triangle. The NCAA basketball championship has traded hands among the area's three schools often in the last decade.

Exploring

Raleigh

Raleigh is spread out, so a car is almost a necessity unless you limit your sightseeing to downtown, where the streets are laid out in an orderly grid fashion with the State Capitol as the hub. Most of the attractions in the downtown Raleigh walking tour are state government and historic buildings and are free to the public. You'll need several hours just to hit the high spots, even more time if you tend to get hooked on museums (which are also free).

STATE CAPITOL WALKING TOUR

After stopping in at the Capital Area Visitor Center to pick up maps and brochures, begin your tour at the **State Capitol,** a beautifully preserved example of Greek Revival architecture, which once housed all the functions of state government. Finished in 1840 and restored during the 1976 Bicentennial, its rich wood furnishings and elaborate decoration give it a special warmth not found in the more contemporary 1960s State Legislative Building. *Capitol Sq.,* ☎ *919/733–4994.* ☉ *Weekdays 8–5, Sat. 9–5, Sun. 1–5. Closed certain holidays.*

The **State Legislative Building,** on the corner of Salisbury and Jones streets, sits one block north of the Capitol building. When the legislature is in session, it hums with lawmakers and lobbyists, and it's fun to watch from the gallery. A free guided tour is available through the Visitor Center (*see below*). *Salisbury and Jones Sts.,* ☎ *919/733–7928.* ☉ *Weekdays 8–5, Sat. 9–5, Sun. 1–5.*

A half block away is the **North Carolina Museum of Natural Sciences,** where you can check out the massive skeletons of whales and dinosaurs or watch volunteers cleaning fossil bones. The gift shop sells some unusual souvenirs. *102 N. Salisbury St.,* ☎ *919/733–7450.* ☉ *Mon.–Sat. 9–5, Sun. 1–5.*

Adjacent to the Museum of Natural Sciences, on Bicentennial Plaza, is the **North Carolina Museum of History.** Founded in 1898, the museum recently opened a new, state-of-the-art facility that combines artifacts, audiovisual programs, and interactive exhibits to bring the state's history to life. Exhibits include the N.C. Sports Hall of Fame, N.C. Folklife, and Women Making History. *1 East Edenton St.,* ☎ *919/715–0200.* ☉ *Tues.–Sat. 9–5, Sun. 1–6.*

The **Executive Mansion** (200 N. Blount St., ☎ 919/733–3456) is a brick turn-of-the-century Queen Anne cottage-style structure with gingerbread trim. Tour hours vary; check with the Capital Area Visitor Center. A stroll through the nearby **Oakwood Historic District** will introduce you to more fine examples of Victorian architecture.

The revitalized **City Market** (Martin St. and Moore Sq.) is home to specialty shops, art galleries, restaurants, and **Playspace,** a children's educational play center. Trolleys shuttle between downtown and the market at lunchtime; the fare is only 10¢. ☎ *919/828–4555.* ☉ *Stores Mon.–Sat. 10–5:30; restaurants, Mon.–Sat. 7 AM–1 AM and Sun. 11:30–10.*

Fayetteville Street Mall extends from the State Capitol to the Raleigh Civic and Convention Center. Open to pedestrians only, it has a variety of shops, a couple of restaurants, and a bronze statue of Sir Walter Raleigh.

The **North Carolina Museum of Art** (Hillsborough St. W) exhibits art from ancient Egyptian times to the present, from the Old World and the New. The **Museum Café** is open for lunch Tuesday–Sunday, with live entertainment Friday evening. *2110 Blue Ridge Blvd.,* ☎ *919/833–1935 (restaurant* ☎ *919/833–3548). Free guided tours daily at 1:30* PM. ☉ *Tues.–Thurs. and Sat. 9–5, Fri. 9–9, Sun. 11–6.*

From downtown, follow Hargett St. east to the **Wakefield/Joel Lane House.** The oldest dwelling in Raleigh and the home of the landowner "father of Raleigh" dates to the 1760s. *720 W. Hargett at St. Mary's St.,* ☎ *919/833–3431.* ☞ *Free.* ☉ *Mar.–mid-Dec., Tues., Thurs., and Fri. 10–2.*

Return on Hargett Street through downtown to Person Street and then take it north to **Mordecai Historic Park** to see some early buildings that were moved within the park, including a house dating to 1785 and the house where President Andrew Johnson was born. One-hour guided tours are given. *One Mimosa St.,* ☎ *919/834–4844. Tour: $3 adults, $1 children 7–17* ☉ *Weekdays 10–3, weekends 1:30–3:30.*

Durham

From Raleigh, take I–40 west to the Durham Freeway (NC 147), which brings you into downtown Durham and **Duke University.** A stroll along the beautiful tree-lined streets of the campus, which are dominated by Gothic-style buildings, is a lovely way to spend a few hours.

A right onto Anderson Street from the Durham Freeway brings you to the 55-acre **Sarah P. Duke Gardens,** complete with a wisteria-draped gazebo and a Japanese garden with a lily pond teeming with fat goldfish. *Main entrance on Anderson St., West Campus,* ☎ *919/684–3698.* ☉ *Daily 8* AM *to dusk.*

Head west on Campus Drive to Chapel Drive. The Gothic-style **Duke Chapel,** built in the early 1930s, is the centerpiece of the campus. Modeled after Canterbury Cathedral, it has 77 stained glass windows and a 210-foot bell tower. *West Campus,* ☎ *919/681–1704.* ☉ *During daylight hours.*

TIME OUT Return to Anderson Street, head north on Anderson to Hillsborough Road, and take Hillsborough east to 9th Street. At **McDonald's Drug Store** (732 9th St., ☎ 919/286–2770), an old-fashioned soda fountain serves up the best milkshakes in town.

African-American art is showcased at the **North Carolina Central University Art Museum,** south of the Durham Freeway on Fayetteville Street. *1801 Fayetteville St.,* ☎ *919/560–6211.* ☞ *Free.* ☉ *Tues.–Fri. 9–5, Sun. 2–5.*

From the Durham Freeway, take U.S. 501N (Roxboro Rd.) to **West Point on the Eno.** On the banks of the Eno River, this city park has a 19th-century blacksmith shop, 1880s home, and a restored mill dating from 1778. *5101 N. Roxboro Rd.,* ☎ *919/471–1623.* ☞ *Free.* ☉ *Daily 8* AM*–sunset (historic buildings open weekends only).*

West of the park on Cole Mill Road, the 2,064-acre **Eno River State Park** has hiking trails, historic homes and mills, and Class II rapids. *Rte. 2, Box 436-C, 27705,* ☎ *919/383–1686.* ☞ *Free.* ☉ *Daily 8* AM*–sunset.*

Chapel Hill

U.S. 15–501 takes you from Durham into Chapel Hill. **Morehead Planetarium,** where the original Apollo astronauts and many since have trained, was the first planetarium in the state. Visitors can learn about the constellations and take in laser light shows. *E. Franklin St.,* ☎ *919/549–6863 or 919/962–1247.* ☛ *$3 adults, $2.50 children, students, and senior citizens.* ☉ *Sun.–Fri. 12:30–5 and 7 PM–9:45 PM, Sat. 10–5 and 7 PM–9:45 PM. Closed Dec. 24–25.*

After leaving the planetarium, walk left on E. Franklin Street a couple of blocks, into the heart of downtown Chapel Hill. **Franklin Street,** lined with bicycle shops, bookstores, clothing stores, restaurants and coffee shops, and flower vendors on the sidewalk, runs along the northern edge of the **University of North Carolina** campus, which is dotted with oak-shaded courtyards and stately old buildings.

Follow U.S. 15–501 Bypass south to the **N.C. Botanical Garden,** known as the largest natural botanical garden in the Southeast. Two miles of nature trails wind through a 300-acre Piedmont forest; there's also a legendary herb garden and carnivorous plant collection. *Old Mason Farm Rd., 27599,* ☎ *919/962–0522.* ☛ *Free.* ☉ *Mar.–mid-Nov., daily 8–5; mid-Nov.–Feb., weekdays 8–5.*

What to See and Do with Children

Pullen Park (520 Ashe Ave., near NCSU, ☎ 919/831–6468 or 919/831–6640) attracts large crowds during the summer to its 1911 Dentzel carousel and train ride. You can swim here, too, and enjoy an arts and crafts center and the Theater in the Park.

The **ArtsCenter** (300G E. Main St. in Carrboro near Chapel Hill, ☎ 919/929–2787) offers classes of all kinds for children, as well as entertainment.

At the **North Carolina Museum of Life and Science,** you can create a 15-foot tornado, pilot an Apollo capsule, encounter near life-size models of dinosaurs on the nature trail, and ride a train through a 78-acre wildlife sanctuary. The nature center has such native North Carolina animals as flying squirrels. *433 Murray Ave., off I–85 in Durham,* ☎ *919/220–5429.* ☛ *$5.50 adults, $3.50 senior citizens and children 3–12, under 3 free.* ☉ *Mon.–Sat. 10–5, Sun. 1–5.*

Off the Beaten Path

Bennett Place State Historic Site. In this farmhouse in Durham in April 1865, Confederate General Joseph E. Johnston surrendered to U.S. General William T. Sherman. The two generals then set forth the terms for a "permanent peace" between the South and the North. Historic reenactments are held annually. *4409 Bennett Memorial Rd., Durham 27705,* ☎ *919/383–4345.* ☛ *Free.* ☉ *Apr.–Oct., Mon.–Sat. 9–5, Sun. 1–5; Nov.–Mar., Tues.–Sat. 10–4, Sun. 1–4.*

Shopping

Shopping Districts

Fearrington Village, a planned community 8 miles south of Chapel Hill on U.S. 15–501, has a number of upscale shops selling art, garden items, handmade jewelry, and more. **Franklin Street** in Chapel Hill has a wonderful collection of shops, including bookstores, art galleries, crafts shops, and clothing stores. Durham's **9th Street** has funky shops and restaurants that cater to the hip student crowd.

Shopping Malls

Brightleaf Square (905 W. Main St., Durham) is an upscale shopping-entertainment complex housed in old tobacco warehouses in the heart of downtown.

Cameron Village Shopping Center (1900 Cameron St.), Raleigh's oldest shopping center and one of the first in the Southeast, features specialty shops and upscale boutiques.

Cary Towne Center (1105 Walnut St., Cary), located in a suburb of Raleigh just off I–40, features five department stores as well as 125 specialty shops and restaurants.

Crabtree Valley Mall (Glenwood Ave.; U.S. 70) is Raleigh's largest enclosed mall. Stores include Belk, Sears, and Hecht's.

North Hills Mall (Six Forks Rd. and Beltline) offers the latest in high fashion. Stores include Montaldo's, Tyler House, and Dillard's.

Specialty Stores

ART AND ANTIQUES

City Market (Martin St. at Moore Sq., ☎ 919/828–4555) is a revitalized shopping area with a number of shops selling antiques and art. Check out Artspace, a gallery where you can watch artists at work in their glassed-in studios.

BOOKS

The **Intimate Bookshop** (119 E. Franklin St., Chapel Hill, ☎ 919/929–0411), a town mainstay for years, has now spawned a regional chain. This is the original store owned by Wallace Kuralt (brother of former CBS commentator Charles Kuralt, one of UNC's most famous graduates).

At **McIntyre's Fine Books** (Fearrington Village, ☎ 919/542–3030), you can curl up and read in an armchair by the fire in one of the cozy library rooms.

FLEA MARKETS

The **Raleigh Flea Market Mall** offers antiques, knickknacks, and more. *1924 Capital Blvd.,* ☎ *919/839–0038.* ⊘ *Weekends 9–5.*

FOOD

State Farmer's Market. This 60-acre market includes a garden center and a down-home-style restaurant. *Lake Wheeler Rd. and I–40,* ☎ *919/733–7417 (market) or 919/833–7973 (restaurant).* ⊘ *June–Sept., daily 8–7:30; Oct.–May, daily 8–6.*

9th Street Bakery (776 9th St., Durham, ☎ 919/286–0303) is earning a reputation throughout the state for its baked goods.

A Southern Season (Eastgate Mall, Chapel Hill, ☎ 919/929–7133 or 800/253–3663) offers such Tar Heel treats as cheese, wine, barbecue sauces, peanuts, turkeys, and hams.

Wellspring Grocery (737 9th St., Durham, ☎ 919/286–2290; 81 S. Elliott Rd., Chapel Hill, ☎ 919/968–1983; 3540 Wade Ave., Raleigh, ☎ 919/828–5805) has outstanding fresh produce and the widest selection of health foods in town.

MEN'S CLOTHING

Julian's College Shop (140 E. Franklin St., Chapel Hill, ☎ 919/942–4563) is owned by the mother of designer Alexander Julian, a Chapel Hill native.

Participant Sports and Outdoor Activities

Bicycling

Raleigh has more than 25 miles of greenways for biking, and maps are available at Raleigh Parks and Recreation (☎ 919/831–6640). Chapel Hill is a great town for biking; for a bicycling map, contact the Chapel Hill/Orange County Visitors Bureau (*see* Visitor Information, *below*).

Camping

Try the North Carolina State Fairgrounds, William B. Umstead State Park, Eno River State Park at Durham, Clemmons State Forest near Clayton, or Jordan Lake between Apex and Pittsboro. Other options are Lake Gaston and Kerr Lake near the Virginia line. *For details, call the Greater Raleigh Convention and Visitors Bureau, ☎ 919/834–5900 or 800/849–8499, or the North Carolina Division of Travel and Tourism, ☎ 919/733–4171 or 800/847–4862.*

Canoeing

Lake Wheeler and Shelley Lake are the best places for canoeing. The Eno River State Park near Durham is another option. The Haw River is popular as well, but can be treacherous after a heavy rain.

Fishing

Jordan Lake, a 13,900-acre reservoir in Apex, is a favorite fishing spot. Others are Lake Wheeler in Raleigh and the Falls Lake State Recreation Area in Wake Forest. You can buy a fishing license at local bait-and-tackle shops or over the phone (with a credit card) from the North Carolina Wildlife Commission (☎ 919/715–4091).

Fitness

The **YMCA** (1601 Hillsborough St., ☎ 919/832–6601) will permit visitors to use their facilities for $3–$10, provided they have a YMCA membership elsewhere. The Y also accepts guests staying at certain local hotels. Hotels with fitness centers are noted in the accommodations listings.

Golf

There are 14 golf courses within a half-hour drive of downtown Raleigh. Durham has four public courses, and Chapel Hill has one. **Cheviott Hills Golf Course** (7301 Capitol Blvd., Raleigh, ☎ 919/876–9920) is an 18-hole championship course. **Devil's Ridge Golf Club** (Holly Springs Rd., Cary, ☎ 919/557–6100), about 15 miles from Raleigh, is a challenging course with large, rolling greens. **Duke University Golf Course** (Cameron Blvd. and Science Dr., Durham, ☎ 919/681–2288) has a newly renovated Robert Trent Jones course. **Finley Golf Course** (Finley Golf Course Rd., Chapel Hill, ☎ 919/962–2349), on the UNC campus, has an 18-hole course, driving range, putting green, and lessons. **Hillandale Golf Course** (Hillandale Rd., Durham, ☎ 919/286–4211) has an 18-hole George Cobb course. The **Neuse Golf Club** (Hwy. 42E, Clayton, ☎ 919/550–0550) is an attractive course located on the banks of the Neuse River. **Lochmere Golf Club** (Kildare

Farms Rd., Cary, ☎ 919/851–0611) provides a friendly atmosphere and good value.

Hiking

Jordan Lake, Lake Wheeler, and William B. Umstead State Park in Raleigh, and Eno River State Park and Duke Forest in Durham, offer thousands of acres for hiking. For trail information, call the North Carolina Division of Travel and Tourism (☎ 919/733–4171 or 800/847–4862).

Jogging

Runners frequent Shelley Lake, the track at NCSU, and the Capitol Area Greenway system.

River Rafting

You can shoot the rapids at Eno River State Park (*see* Exploring Durham, *above*).

Tennis

More than 80 courts in Raleigh city parks are available for use. Millbrook Exchange Park (1905 Spring Forest Rd.) holds city tournaments. (For more details on tennis courts in Raleigh, call 919/876–2616.) For information on Durham's six public courts, call the Parks and Recreation Department (☎ 919/560–4355). For information on Chapel Hill tennis courts, call the Chapel Hill Parks and Recreation Department (☎ 919/968–2784) or the Orange County Parks and Recreation Department (☎ 919/732–8181).

Spectator Sports

Baseball

The **Carolina Mudcats** play at Five County Stadium in Zebulon, east of Raleigh (☎ 919/269–2287).

The **Durham Bulls** play at their brand new stadium near downtown Durham (200 Willard St., ☎ 919/688–8211).

Basketball

The Triangle is basketball heaven, with three Atlantic Coast Conference teams: Duke's **Blue Devils** (☎ 919/681–2583), the University of North Carolina's **Tarheels** (☎ 919/962–2296), and North Carolina State University's **Wolfpack** (☎ 919/515–2106).

Ice Hockey

The **Raleigh Icecaps** compete in Dorton Arena at the NC State Fairgrounds (☎ 919/755–0022).

Soccer

The **Raleigh Flyers,** the city's first professional soccer team, competes in the Interregional Soccer League (☎ 919/890–6026).

Dining

Dining in the Triangle is both sophisticated and down-home. There are many upscale restaurants, as well as informal places where barbecue, Brunswick stew, fried chicken, and lots of country vegetables are served in great quantities for very low prices. Dress is usually casual.

CATEGORY	COST*
$$$$	over $25
$$$	$15–$25
$$	$8–$15
$	under $8

per person for a three-course meal, excluding drinks, service, and 6% sales tax

Chapel Hill

$$–$$$ **Aurora.** In a historic textile mill in nearby Carrboro, Aurora specializes in northern Italian cuisine. The changing menu sometimes includes succulent sea scallops and shiitake mushrooms sautéed in rosemary and white wine, fresh chive pasta stuffed with four cheeses and tossed with walnut sauce, and veal sautéed with Golden Delicious apples. ✕ *Carr Mill Mall, Carrboro,* ☎ *919/942–2400. Reservations accepted. AE, MC, V.*

$$–$$$ **Pyewacket Restaurant.** What began as a hole-in-the-wall vegetarian restaurant in 1977 has become one of Chapel Hill's most popular restaurants. Now in bigger digs and offering courtyard dining, Pyewacket has added seafood and pasta specialties to its former vegetarian repertoire. Appetizers include smoked trout paté; entrées range from Southwest grilled seafood to spinach lasagna. ✕ *431 West Franklin St.,* ☎ *919/929–0297. Reservations accepted. AE, DC, MC, V.*

$$ **Crook's Corner.** If there's such a thing as chic Southern cooking, Crook's produces it. Particularly famous for its barbecue, the restaurant also turns out such regional Southern specialties as hoppin' John, hot pepper jelly, collards, crab gumbo, cheese grits, and buttermilk pie. One of the joys of summer is lunching on Crook's patio, under the huge pig sculpture that sparked a local debate when erected but is now a beloved local landmark. ✕ *610 West Franklin St.,* ☎ *919/929–7643. Reservations accepted. AE, MC, V.*

Durham

$$ **Bullock's Bar-B-Cue.** If you want to experience local cuisine, try the Brunswick stew, barbecue, southern fried chicken, and hush puppies at this casual eatery that offers eat-in or carry-out service. It's first-come, first-served, so come early. ✕ *3330 Wortham St.,* ☎ *919/383–3211. No credit cards. Closed Sun.*

$$ **Cafe Parizäde.** This Erwin Square Mediterranean restaurant gets high marks for its food, service, and atmosphere (soft lighting and white tablecloths give the place an elegant feel, even at lunch). Start with grilled bread soaked in garlic oil, fresh tomatoes and eggplant relish, or fried calamari with jalapeno-tomato salsa. Then choose among such entrées as fettucine with fresh salmon and black pepper dill cream, sesame pasta with scallops, and roasted duck with fresh vegetables. ✕ *2200 West Main St.,* ☎ *919/286–9712. Reservations accepted. Closed Sun. AE, MC, V.*

Raleigh

$$$ **Angus Barn, Ltd.** This Raleigh tradition is housed in a huge rustic barn. Gingham- and denim-clad waiters and waitresses add authenticity to the farmlike scene. The astonishing wine and beer list covers 35 pages of the menu. The restaurant serves the best steaks, baby back ribs, and prime rib, plus fresh seafood, for miles around. Desserts are heavenly. ✕ *U.S. 70W at Airport Rd.,* ☎ *919/781–2444. Reservations advised. AE, DC, MC, V.*

No matter where you go, travel is easier when you know the code.^{SM}

dial 1 8 0 0
C A L L
A T T®

Dial 1 800 CALL ATT and you'll always get through from any phone with any card* and you'll always get AT&T's best deal.** It's the one number to remember when calling away from home.

*Other long distance company calling cards excluded.
**Additional discounts available.

AT&T
Your True Choice

All the best trips start with **Fodor's**.

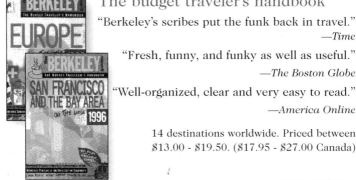

$$$ **42nd St. Oyster Bar.** This much talked-about restaurant is the place to see and be seen in Raleigh. Politicians, businessmen, and laborers sit side by side downing succulent oysters and other seafood. There's live jazz on Friday and Saturday evenings. ✗ *508 W. Jones St.,* ☎ *919/831– 2811. No reservations. AE, DC, MC, V.*

$$–$$$ **Jean Claude's Café.** Casual and chic, this restaurant on the north side features authentic French cuisine, including such specials as veal sweetbreads, braised scallops, and smoked salmon. ✗ *6111 Falls of Neuse Rd.,* ☎ *919/872–6224. Reservations accepted. MC, V. Closed Mon.*

$$ **Est Est Est Trattoria.** The best place in town for authentic northern Italian pasta. ✗ *19 W. Hargett St.,* ☎ *919/832–8899. Reservations accepted for parties of 6 or more. AE, MC, V. Closed Sun.*

$ **Big Ed's City Market Restaurant.** A must for breakfast, this Raleigh favorite in the City Market serves three home-cooked meals. ✗ *220 Wolfe St.,* ☎ *919/836–9909. Reservations not required. No credit cards. Closed Sun.*

$ **Greenshields Brewery & Pub.** Enjoy beer and ale brewed on the spot with your soups, salads, sandwiches, and such entrées as fish and chips, shepherd's pie, and steak in this English-type pub in the City Market. ✗ *214 E. Martin St., City Market,* ☎ *919/829–0214. Reservations accepted. AE, D, MC, V.*

Lodging

The Triangle has lodgings in all price ranges—from convention hotels to bed-and-breakfast houses to economy chains. Major hotel chains represented here are Holiday Inn, Hilton, Radisson, Marriott, Embassy Suites, and Sheraton. Inexpensive lodging is offered by Comfort Inn, EconoLodge, Crickett Inn, Days Inn, and Hampton Inn. Since Raleigh is a business town, many hotels and motels advertise special weekend rates.

CATEGORY	COST*
$$$$	over $100
$$$	$60–$100
$$	$30–$60
$	under $30

All prices are for a standard double room, excluding 8% tax

Chapel Hill

$$$$ **Fearrington House.** This French-style country inn is a member of the
★ prestigious Relais & Chateaux group. The 200-year-old farm has been remade into a residential community that looks like an English country village. Modern guest rooms, furnished in English pine, floral print fabrics, and dried flower arrangements, are situated around a garden courtyard. The farmhouse restaurant, done up in green ivy and delicate peach prints, serves regional food prepared in a classic manner; Carolina crab cakes with mustard mayonnaise and beef tenderloin with merlot and peppercorn sauce are favorites here. Afternoon tea and breakfast are included in the rate. ⌂ *8 mi south of Chapel Hill on U.S. 15– 501 (postal address: Fearrington Village Center, Pittsboro 27312),* ☎ *919/542–2121,* ℻ *919/542–4202. 15 double rooms with baths, 9 suites. AE, MC, V.*

Durham

$$$$ **Washington Duke Hotel & Golf Club.** On the campus of Duke University, this luxurious inn overlooks the Robert Trent Jones golf course. On display in the public rooms are memorabilia belonging to the Duke family for whom the hotel and university are named. The bar is called

the Bull Durham. ☎ *3001 Cameron Blvd., 27706,* ☎ *919/490–0999 or 800/443–3853,* ℻ *919/688–0105. 171 rooms, 7 suites. Restaurant, bar, pool, 18-hole golf course, jogging. AE, DC, MC, V.*

$$$–$$$$ **Arrowhead Inn.** This bed-and-breakfast inn, in an 18th-century white clapboard farmhouse with black shutters, has brick chimneys and tall Doric columns. It's a few miles outside Durham and offers a homelike setting with antiques, old plantings, and a log cabin in the garden. Guests are served a hearty breakfast. ☎ *106 Mason Rd., 27712,* ☎ ℻ *919/477–8430. 8 rooms, 6 with private bath. AE, D, DC, MC, V.*

$$$–$$$$ **Blooming Garden Inn.** This B&B is truly a bright spot in the Holloway
★ Historic District. With yellow paint on the exterior, the inn explodes inside with color and warmth, thanks to exuberant hosts Dolly and Frank Pokrass. For breakfast you might have walnut crepes with ricotta cheese and warm raspberry sauce. ☎ *513 Holloway St., 27701,* ☎ *919/687–0801. 5 rooms with private baths. AE, D, DC, MC, V.*

Raleigh

$$$ **Courtyard by Marriott–Airport.** Convenient to the airport and the Research Triangle Park, this chain offers many luxuries, including a Continental breakfast, without hefty rates. Rooms are predictably modern, as you would expect from this chain, and some have refrigerators. ☎ *2001 Hospitality Ct., 27560,* ☎ *919/467–9444 or 800/321–2211,* ℻ *919/467–9332. 152 rooms. Facilities: dining room, pool, hot tub, exercise room, coin laundry, airport shuttle. AE, D, DC, MC, V.*

$$$ **North Raleigh Hilton.** This is a favorite capital city spot for corporate meetings. The Tower Suites offer a complimentary Continental breakfast, free hors d'oeuvres, concierge, newspapers, and secretarial service if wanted. Guests enjoy dining in Lofton's restaurant and listening to the piano afterward in the lobby bar. Bowties is one of the city's hottest nightspots. ☎ *3415 Wake Forest Rd., 27609,* ☎ *919/872–2323 or 800/445–8667,* ℻ *919/876–0890. 330 rooms, 7 suites. Restaurant, indoor pool, health club, nightclub, meeting rooms, airport shuttle. AE, D, DC, MC, V.*

$$$ **Oakwood Inn.** In Historic Oakwood, one of the city's oldest downtown neighborhoods, this is an alternative to hotel/motel living. Built in 1871 and now on the National Register of Historic Places, the inn is furnished with Victorian period pieces. Guests are served a sumptuous complimentary breakfast and assisted with dinner reservations and evening entertainment plans. ☎ *411 N. Bloodworth St., 27604,* ☎ *919/832–9712 or 800/267–9712,* ℻ *919/836–9263. 6 rooms with bath. AE, D, DC, MC, V.*

$$$ **Raleigh Marriott Crabtree Valley.** This is one of the city's most luxurious hotels. Fresh floral arrangements adorn the elegantly decorated public rooms. Guests enjoy the intimacy of the Scotch Bonnets restaurant, the family atmosphere of Allie's, and Champions Sports Bar. The concierge floor offers complimentary Continental breakfast and hors d'oeuvres. ☎ *4500 Marriott Dr. (U.S. 70W near Crabtree Valley Mall), 27612,* ☎ *919/781–7000 or 800/228–9290,* ℻ *919/781–3059. 372 rooms, 3 suites. Restaurant, bar, indoor/outdoor pool, hot tub, exercise room, recreation room, airport shuttle. AE, D, DC, MC, V.*

$$$ **Velvet Cloak Inn.** This hotel is in a class of its own. Local brides have wedding receptions in the tropical garden around the enclosed pool, and politicians frequent the bar at Baron's Lounge. The Charter Room, an elegant restaurant, often has live entertainment. Afternoon tea and cookies are served in the lobby. Rooms in the brick structure, decorated with delicate wrought iron, are frequently refurbished. ☎ *1505 Hillsborough St., 27605,* ☎ *919/828–0333 or 800/334–4372; in NC,*

800/662–8829; FAX *919/828–2656. 168 rooms, 4 suites. 2 restaurants, lounge, meeting rooms, airport shuttle. AE, D, DC, MC, V.*

$$–$$$ **Quality Suites Hotel.** Minutes from downtown, this hotel offers luxurious two-room suites equipped with VCRs, cassette stereos, microwaves, wet bars, and refrigerators. The manager's evening reception and the cooked-to-order breakfast are included in the rate. ☎ *4400 Capital Blvd., 27604,* ☎ *919/876–2211 or 800/543–5497,* FAX *919/790–1352. 114 suites. Pool, exercise room, meeting rooms. AE, D, DC, MC, V.*

$$–$$$ **Ramada Inn Crabtree.** This hotel gets the award for being the friendliest motel in town, and rooms are comfortable and clean at this link in the familiar chain. It's also where football and basketball teams like to stay when they're here for a game, as evidenced by the helmet collection and other sports memorabilia in the Brass Bell Lounge. ☎ *3920 Arrow Dr. (U.S. 70 and Beltline), 27612,* ☎ *919/782–7525 or 800/441–4712. 174 rooms and suites. Restaurant, lounge, pool, jogging, meeting rooms, airport shuttle. AE, D, DC, MC, V.*

$$ **Hampton Inn North Raleigh.** This budget motel offers inexpensive rates without sacrificing quality. A Continental breakfast, local calls, and in-room movies are available at no extra charge. ☎ *1001 Wake Towne Dr., 27609,* ☎ *919/828–1813 or 800/426–7866,* FAX *919/834–2672. 131 rooms. Pool, meeting rooms. AE, D, DC, MC, V.*

The Arts

The **North Carolina Theatre** (One E. South St., Raleigh, ☎ 919/831–6916), the state's only professional nonprofit theater, produces five Broadway shows a year. Durham's newly renovated, 1926 Beaux Arts **Carolina Theatre** (309 Morgan St., ☎ 919/560–3060) hosts the city's symphony and opera company, as well as the International Jazz Festival in March and the American Dance Festival in June. The **North Carolina Symphony** (2 E. South St., Raleigh, ☎ 919/733–2750) gives more than 200 concerts in the state annually.

Playmakers Repertory Company (CB 3235 Graham Memorial, Chapel Hill, ☎ 919/962–7529) performs six plays annually at the Paul Green Theatre. Jazz and folk music, dance and theater are all offered at the **ArtsCenter** (300G E. Main St., Carrboro, ☎ 919/929–2787).

Nightlife

Much of Raleigh's nightlife is centered in the larger hotels, such as the Hilton or the Marriott. **Bowties** (North Raleigh Hilton, 3415 Wake Forest Rd., ☎ 919/878–4917) is a popular after-hours spot. **Charlie Goodnight's Comedy Club** (861 W. Morgan St., ☎ 919/828–5233) combines dinner with a night of laughs. Another option is **Comedy Sportz** (204 Wolfe St., City Market, Raleigh, ☎ 919/829–0822; Omni Europa, U.S. 15–501, Chapel Hill, ☎ 919/968–4900). Chapel Hill is the place to hear live rock and alternative bands. **Cat's Cradle** (206 W. Franklin St., ☎ 919/967–9053) features entertainment nightly. **He's Not Here** (112½ W. Franklin St., ☎ 919/942–7939) features live music Friday and Saturday nights, with concerts outdoors in warm weather.

Triangle Essentials

Arriving and Departing

BY BUS

Carolina Trailways/Greyhound Lines (☎ 800/231–2222) serves Raleigh, Durham, and Chapel Hill.

I–440 forms a perimeter route around Raleigh. I–40 runs west of downtown (to Durham and Chapel Hill), joining I–85 on the west side and crossing I–95 on the east side. U.S. 1, which runs north and south, also links to I–85 going northeast. U.S. 64 and U.S. 70 run east–west through Raleigh.

BY PLANE
The **Raleigh–Durham International Airport** (RDU, ☎ 919/840–2123), between the two cities off I–40, is served by American, Delta, Northwest, TWA, United, USAir, and Midway, with flights to London, Cancun, Bermuda, Puerto Rico, Nassau, and the U.S. Virgin Islands. If you're driving to Raleigh, take I–40 east to Exit 285; for Chapel Hill, take I–40 west to exits 273, 270, and 266; for Durham, also take I–40 west to NC 147. It takes about 20 minutes to get to any of the three cities.

BY TRAIN
Amtrak (320 W. Cabarrus St., ☎ 919/833–7594 or 800/872–7245) has one daily train northbound and one southbound, with stops in Raleigh and Durham. Service to Charlotte is also offered daily.

Getting Around
BY BUS
Capital Area Transit (☎ 919/833–5701) is Raleigh's public transport system. Fares are 50¢. Children under 4 ride free.

Chapel Hill Transit (☎ 919/968–2769) buses serve the city as well as Research Triangle Park and Duke University.

Triangle Transit Authority (☎ 919/549–9999), which links downtown Raleigh with the Research Triangle Park, Durham, and Chapel Hill, runs weekdays except major holidays. Fares: $1 for a 10-mile trip, $1.50 for 15 miles, and $2 for 20 miles. Senior citizens and riders with disabilities pay half fare.

BY TAXI
Approximately 28 taxi companies serve The Triangle; contact City Taxi (Raleigh, ☎ 919/832–1489), **National Cab** (Raleigh–Durham Airport, ☎ 919/469–1333), or Orange Cab (Durham, ☎ 919/682–6111) for service. Fares are calculated by the mile.

BY TROLLEY
The **Trolley Through Raleigh** (☎ 919/833–5701) makes six stops around the city, including City Market and the Capital Area Visitor Center. Trolleys run weekdays 11:20–2 and the fare is 10¢. From noon to 4 PM on the third Saturday of each month, Mordecai Historic Park (*see above*) runs a **historic trolley tour** of Raleigh (fare: $3 adults, $1 children 7–17), with a pickup at the Amtrak station by advance arrangement.

Chapel Hill Trolley (☎ 919/968–2769) serves downtown Chapel Hill, UNC Hospitals and campus, plus Franklin and Rosemary Street businesses. Trolleys run weekdays 11:30–2:30, and the fare is 25¢. The **Historic Chapel Hill/UNC Trolley Tour** (☎ 919/942–7818) operates April–June and September–November, Wednesdays at 3 PM. The fare is $3 adults, $1 children under 12.

Guided Tours
Capital Area Visitor Center provides maps, brochures, and free tours of the executive mansion, state capitol, legislative building, and other

government buildings. *301 N. Blount St.,* ☎ *919/733–3456.* ☉ *Weekdays 8–5, Sat. 9–5, Sun. 1–5.*

UNC Visitors Center offers information about the University, campus parking, and conducts tours of the campus, highlighting its many historic buildings and monuments. *Morehead Planetarium, Franklin St.,* ☎ *919/962–1630.* ☉ *Weekdays 10–5.*

Important Addresses and Numbers

EMERGENCIES
Dial 911 for **police** or **ambulance** in an emergency. Hospital emergency rooms are open 24 hours a day. For minor emergencies, go to one of the many urgent-care centers in Raleigh, Durham, and Chapel Hill. The **Wake County Medical Society** (☎ 919/821–2227) can refer you to a doctor.

PHARMACIES
Kerr Drug Store (Lake Boone Shopping Center, 2462 Wycliff Rd., Raleigh, ☎ 919/781–4070) is open 24 hours. **Eckerd Drugs** (3527 Hillsborough Rd., Durham, ☎ 919/383–5591) is open 7 AM–midnight.

RADIO STATIONS
AM: WPTF 680, news, talk; WKIX 850, country. **FM:** WCPE 89.7, classical; WQDR 94.7, country; WUNC 91.5, National Public Radio; WRAL 101.5, adult contemporary; WDUR 104, urban contemporary.

VISITOR INFORMATION
The **Greater Raleigh Convention and Visitors Bureau** offers information on the area. *225 Hillsborough St., Suite 400,* ☎ *919/834–5900 or 800/849–8499.*

The **Durham Convention & Visitors Bureau** (101 E. Morgan St., Durham 27701, ☎ 919/687–0288 or 800/446–8604) provides information on that city. The **Durham Bullhorn** provides 24-hour recorded information on events and activities (☎ 919/688–2855 or 800/772–2855).

Chapel Hill/Orange County Visitors Bureau (Box 600, Chapel Hill 27514, ☎ 919/968–2060). The **Downtown Chapel Hill Welcome Center** provides maps, brochures, and flyers on attractions, accommodations, and services. Volunteers are usually on hand to answer questions. *113 W. Franklin St.,* ☎ *919/929–9700.* ☉ *Tues.–Sat. 10–4.*

THE SOUTHERN PINES AND PINEHURST SANDHILLS

Because of their sandy soil—once the beaches of the Atlantic Ocean— the Sandhills weren't of much use to early farmers, most of whom switched to lumbering and making turpentine for a livelihood. Since the turn of the century, however, this area has proven ideal for golf and tennis. Today promoters call it the Golf Capital of the World; the Tufts Archives honors the sport and the founding of Pinehurst. First-class resorts are centered around more than three dozen golf courses, including the famed Pinehurst Number 2 and several spectacular new courses.

The Highland Scots, who settled the area, left a rich heritage perpetuated through festivals and gatherings. In Colonial times, English potters were attracted to the rich clay deposits in the soil, and today their descendants and others turn out beautiful wares that are sold in more than 40 local shops.

Exploring

Southern Pines

Southern Pines, the center of the Sandhills, is a good place to start a tour. The **Shaw House,** the oldest structure in town (circa 1840), serves as headquarters for the Moore County Historical Association. *S. W. Broad St. and Morganton Rd.,* ☎ *910/692–2051.* ☛ *Free.* ⊘ *Wed.–Sun. 1–4.*

Weymouth Center, former home of author James Boyd, hosts numerous music, lecture, and holiday events. *E. Vermont Ext.,* ☎ *910/692–6261.* ☛ *Free. Call ahead to arrange tours.* ⊘ *Weekdays 10–noon, 2–4.*

Weymouth Woods Nature Preserve, on the eastern outskirts of town, is a 571-acre wildlife preserve with 4 miles of hiking trails, a beaver pond, and a naturalist on staff. *400 N. Ft. Bragg Rd. (off U.S. 1),* ☎ *910/692–2167.* ☛ *Free.* ⊘ *Mon.–Sat. 9–6, Sun. noon–5.*

PINEHURST

Pinehurst lies 8 miles west of Southern Pines via U.S. 15–501, or Midland Road. The New England–style village, with its quiet, shaded streets and immaculately kept cottages, was laid out in the late 1800s in a wagon-wheel fashion, by landscape genius Frederick Law Olmsted. It is a mecca for sports enthusiasts, retirees, and tourists.

Tufts Archives recounts the founding of Pinehurst in the letters, pictures, and news clippings, dating from 1895, of James Walker Tufts. Golf memorabilia is also on display. *Given Memorial Library, Pinehurst,* ☎ *910/295–6022 or 910/295–3642.* ⊘ *Weekdays 9:30 AM–12:30 PM and 2–5 PM; Sat. 9:30 AM–12:30 PM.*

Aberdeen

In **Aberdeen,** a town of Scottish ancestry south of Pinehurst, there's a beautifully restored turn-of-the-century train station, and on Bethesda Road east of town, the **Bethesda Presbyterian Church,** founded in 1790. The present wooden structure, which is used for weddings, funerals, and reunions, was built in the 1860s, and has bullet holes from a Civil War battle. The cemetery, where many early settlers are buried, is always open. Continue on Bethesda Road to the **Malcolm Blue Farm,** featuring farm buildings and an old grist mill. A September festival recalls life here in the 1800s. *Bethesda Rd.,* ☎ *910/944–7558.* ⊘ *By appointment only.*

Asheboro

Follow U.S. 220 north to NC 159, which leads to the ★**North Carolina Zoological Park** at Asheboro. This 1,400-acre natural habitat for animals is one of the up-and-coming zoos of the late 20th century. The park includes the African Pavilion, an aviary, a gorilla habitat, a Sonora Desert habitat, and a new North American habitat with polar bears and sea lions. ☎ *910/879–7000 or 800/488–0444.* ☛ *Including tram ride: $6 adults, $4 senior citizens and children 2–12.* ⊘ *Daily 9–5.*

Shopping

Antiques

Shop for antiques in **Cameron,** which hasn't changed much since the 19th century. Approximately 60 antiques dealers operate out of several stores. The town itself has been declared a historic district. *Off U.S. 1, 10 mi north of Southern Pines,* ☎ *910/245–7001.* ☉ *Most shops Wed.–Sat. 10–5, Sun. 1–5.*

Herbs and Wildflowers

Sandhill Farms, 12 miles east of Cameron off Highway 24, is a one-of-a-kind operation offering herbs, wildflowers, wreaths, crafts, and oils. ☎ *919/499–4753.* ☉ *Weekdays 1–5. Closed Jan.–Feb. except by appointment.*

Pottery

Mugs, bowls, pitchers, platters, and sometimes clay voodoo heads can be found in about 60 shops scattered along and off Route 705 and U.S. 220 in Seagrove. The work of some local potters is exhibited in national museums, including the Smithsonian. A map locating the various pottery studios is available at most shops and at the guild headquarters in downtown Seagrove. *124 E. Main St.,* ☎ *910/873–7887.* ☉ *Most shops Tues.–Sat. 10–5.*

Participant Sports

Golf

The Sandhills doesn't call itself the Golf Capitol of the World for nothing. More than three dozen courses await you in this golfers' paradise. Several of the area's courses host the biggest tournaments in the sport. A complete list of golf courses and their fee ranges is available from the Pinehurst Area Convention and Visitors Bureau (*see* Visitor Information, *below*).

Pinehurst Resort and Country Club (Carolina Vista, Pinehurst, ☎ 910/295–6811 or 800/487–4653) celebrated its 100th birthday in 1995. It boasts eight courses designed by masters like Donald Ross, including the famed Number 2, rated second-best resort course in America by *Golf Digest*. Number 7 is also highly ranked. The U.S. Open will be played here in 1999. **Pine Needles Resort** (Box 88, Southern Pines, ☎ 910/692–7111) has a Donald Ross–designed course that will host the 1996 U.S. Women's Open.

The **Pit Golf Links** (Hwy. 5, Box 5789, Pinehurst, ☎ 910/944–1600 or 800/574–4653) is ranked among America's 75 best public courses by *Golf Digest*. The eighth hole is ranked by *Golf Magazine* as one of the 50 best holes open to the public. **Mid-Pines Resort** (1010 Midland Rd., Southern Pines, ☎ 910/692–2114 or 800/323–2114) is a quieter golf getaway with a Donald Ross–designed course. **Legacy Golf Links** (U.S. 15–501 South, Aberdeen, ☎ 910/944–8825 or 800/344–8825) has the first American course designed by Jack Nicklaus Jr. **Club at Longleaf** (Box 5789, Pinehurst, ☎ 910/692–6100 or 800/889–5323) was built on a former horse farm. The front nine plays through posts, rails, and turns of the old race track. **Talamore at Pinehurst** (1595 Midland Rd., Southern Pines, ☎ 910/692–5884 or 800/552–6292), designed by Rees Jones, was ranked 14th in the state by *Golf Digest*. It's most unusual feature is llama caddies.

Horseback and Carriage Riding

Riding instruction and carriage rides are available by appointment at **Pinehurst Stables** (Hwy. 5, ☎ 910/295–8456).

Tennis

The **Lawn and Tennis Club of North Carolina** (☎ 910/692–7270) and **Pinehurst Resort and Country Club** (☎ 910/295–6811) are known for their clinics. Public courts can be found in **Aberdeen, Carthage, Pinebluff,** and **Southern Pines** and at **Sandhills Community College.** For details, contact the Pinehurst Area Convention and Visitors Bureau (*see* Visitor Information, *below*) or the Moore County Parks and Recreation Department (☎ 910/947–2504).

Dining and Lodging

Dining

No particular local cuisine typifies the Sandhills, but the area has a number of sophisticated restaurants. Casual but neat clothing and golf wear are suitable anywhere in the Sandhills.

CATEGORY	COST*
$$$$	over $25
$$$	$15–$25
$$	$8–$15
$	under $8

per person for a three-course meal, excluding drinks, service, and 6% sales tax

Lodging

Most lodging options in the Sandhills are in the luxury resort category, featuring full amenities and services. However, there are a few chain motels in Southern Pines, as well as several bed-and-breakfasts in the area.

CATEGORY	COST*
$$$$	over $100
$$$	$60–$100
$$	$30–$60
$	under $30

All prices are for a standard double room, excluding 8% tax

Aberdeen

LODGING

$$–$$$ **Inn at Bryant House.** Downtown, one block off U.S. 1, this charming B&B is like a home away from home. The inn offers golf packages and arranges tennis and horseback riding. ⊡ *214 N. Poplar St., 28315,* ☎ *910/944–3300 or 800/453–4019,* FAX *910/944–8898. 9 rooms, most with private bath. AE, D, MC, V.*

Cameron

DINING

$ **Dewberry Deli.** Housed in the Old Hardware, this eatery is a wonderful place for a sandwich or salad after shopping for antiques. ✕ *Carthage St.,* ☎ *910/245–3697. No reservations. No credit cards.* ☉ *Tues.–Sat. 11–4:30.*

Eagle Springs

LODGING

$$$ **Inn at Eagle Springs.** A private girls' school during the 1920s, this B&B, amid the pines in a remote area 15 miles from Pinehurst, is great for golfers who want rest and quiet. The action-oriented might be bored,

however. A full breakfast is always provided, and other meals can be arranged ahead. ☎ *1813 Samarcand Rd., Box 56, 27242,* ☎ *910/673– 2722,* FAX *910/673–7740. 6 rooms. No credit cards.*

Pinehurst
DINING

$ **Pinehurst Playhouse Restaurant.** This casual eatery housed in an old theater is in the heart of the village and is *the* place to meet for soups and sandwiches. ✕ *Theater Bldg., W. Village Green.,* ☎ *910/295–8873. No reservations. No credit cards.* ◷ *Weekdays 9–4, Sat. 11–4.*

DINING AND LODGING

$$$$ **Holly Inn.** This renovated wooden inn, built in 1895, is testimony to James Tufts' success as a hotelier. It was so popular that he was forced to build a bigger structure—now the Pinehurst Resort. ☎ *Cherokee Rd., Box 2300, 28374,* ☎ *910/295–2300 or, in NC, 800/682–6901,* FAX *910/295–0988. 77 rooms and suites. Restaurant, lounge, pool. AE, DC, MC, V.*

$$$$ **Magnolia Inn.** Once just a hangout for golfing buddies, this Old South inn is now tastefully decorated with fresh paint and unusual antiques. The inn's dining room serves superb grilled Norwegian salmon and roasted herb-crusted rack of lamb, among other delectables—there's also an English pub, where you can discuss your golf game. ☎ *Magnolia and Chinquapin Rds., Box 818, 28374,* ☎ *910/295–6900 or 800/526–5562,* FAX *910/215–0858. 12 double rooms. Restaurant, pub, pool. AE, MC, V.*

$$$$ **Pinehurst Resort and Country Club.** This venerable resort hotel, in operation for nearly a century, has never lost the charm that founder James Tufts intended it to have. Civilized decorum rules in the spacious public rooms, on the rocker-lined wide verandas, and amid the lush gardens of the surrounding grounds. Guests can play lawn croquet, shoot skeet, or tee off on one of seven premier golf courses. The Carolina Dining Room is known for its gourmet cuisine. ☎ *Carolina Vista, Box 4000, 28374,* ☎ *910/295–6811 or 800/487–4653,* FAX *910/295– 8503. 310 rooms, 125 condos. Dining room, pool, 7 18-hole golf courses, 20 tennis courts, croquet, windsurfing, boating, fishing, bicycles, children's programs, meeting rooms, airport shuttle. AE, D, DC, MC, V.*

$$$ **Pine Crest Inn.** After an extensive remodeling, this small village inn, once owned by golfing great Donald Ross, sports chintz and mahogany in its rooms. Chefs Carl and Peter Jackson whip up some great dishes, including homemade soups; fresh seafood dishes; and the house special, stuffed pork chops. Mr. B's Bar is the liveliest nightspot in town. Guests have golf and tennis privileges at local clubs. Rates include two meals per day. ☎ *Dogwood Rd., Box 879, 28374,* ☎ *910/295–6121,* FAX *910/295–4880. 40 rooms, 3 suites. AE, D, DC, MC, V.*

Southern Pines
DINING

$$$ **Mannie's Dinner Theater.** Guests can see musicals here on Saturday evening, after a dinner of prime rib or shrimp scampi. ✕ *210 W. Penn. Ave.,* ☎ *910/692–8400. Reservations required for dinner theater. AE, MC, V. Closed Sun.*

$$–$$$ **Lob Steer Inn.** Come hungry for broiled seafood and prime rib dinners, complemented by salad and dessert bars. The restaurant is upscale. ✕ *U.S. 1, Southern Pines,* ☎ *910/692–3503. Reservations advised on weekends. AE, DC, MC, V. No lunch.*

$–$$ **Silver Bucket Restaurant.** You can order just about any kind of fish—plus steaks, ribs, barbecue, and some Italian dishes—for a tasty and satisfying meal. The atmosphere is très casual. ✕ *S.E. Broad St.,* ☎ *910/692–6227. Reservations accepted. MC, V. Closed Mon.*

$ **Whiskey NcNeill's Restaurant.** Diners fill up on soups, sandwiches, salads, and a variety of entrées (from grilled sirloin to pork chops) over what used to be a grease pit of a downtown filling station but is now a fabulous spot for lunch and dinner. Stare closely at the building, and you can practically imagine pulling up to the pump in your '57 Chevy. ✕ *181 N.E. Broad St.,* ☎ *910/692–5440. Reservations accepted. MC, V.*

LODGING

$$$–$$$$ **Pine Needles Resort and Country Club.** One of the bonuses of staying at this informal lodge is the chance to meet Peggy Kirk Bell, a champion golfer and golf instructor. She built the resort with her late husband, and she continues to help run it. The rooms of the spacious lodge are done in a rustic style, with exposed beams in many rooms. ⚑ *1005 Midland Rd., Box 88, Southern Pines 28387,* ☎ *910/692–7111 or 800/747–7272,* FAX *910/692–5349. 71 rooms. Restaurant, pool, hot tub, sauna, whirlpool, 18-hole golf course, 2 tennis courts, airport shuttle. AE, MC, V.*

$$$ **Mid Pines Inn and Golf Club.** This resort community includes an 18-hole golf course designed by Donald Ross that has been the site of numerous tournaments. ⚑ *1010 Midland Rd., Southern Pines 28387,* ☎ *910/692–2114 or 800/323–2114,* FAX *910/692–4615. 118 rooms. Restaurant, lounge, pool, 18-hole golf course, 4 tennis courts, game room, meeting rooms, airport shuttle. AE, DC, MC, V.*

Southern Pines and Pinehurst Sandhills Essentials

Arriving and Departing, Getting Around

BY CAR

U.S. 1 runs north–south through the Sandhills and is the recommended route from the Raleigh–Durham area, a distance of about 70 miles. Another alternate is U.S. 15–501 from Chapel Hill. U.S. 74 from Charlotte intersects U.S. 1 at Rockingham, about 25 miles south of Southern Pines.

BY PLANE

Visitors arrive via USAir Express (☎ 800/428–4322) from **Charlotte–Douglas International Airport** or they fly into the **Raleigh–Durham Airport** or the **Piedmont Triad International Airport** and rent a car.

BY TRAIN

Amtrak (☎ 910/692–6305 or 800/872–7245) southbound and northbound trains, one daily from each direction, stop in Southern Pines.

Important Addresses and Numbers

EMERGENCIES

Dial 911 for **police** or **ambulance** in an emergency. For medical care, go to the emergency room of the **Moore Regional Hospital** (Memorial Dr., Pinehurst, ☎ 910/215–1111).

RADIO STATIONS

AM: WQNX 1350, talk; WKHO 550, easy listening; WEEB 990, news, talk. **FM:** WIOZ 107, easy listening.

VISITOR INFORMATION
Pinehurst Area Convention and Visitors Bureau (1480 Hwy. 15–501 N, Box 2270, Southern Pines 28388, ☎ 910/692–3330 or 800/346–5362). For details on local events, call 910/692–1600.

WINSTON-SALEM

The manufacture of cigarettes, textiles, and furniture built a solid economic base in the Winston-Salem area; major area employers today also include USAir, Wachovia Bank, the Bowman Gray School of Medicine, and N.C. Baptist Hospital. Winston-Salem residents' donations to the arts are among the highest per capita in the nation, and the North Carolina School of the Arts commands international attention. Wake Forest University, where writer Maya Angelou teaches, is also here. Old Salem, a restored 18th-century Moravian town within the city of Winston-Salem, has been drawing tourists since the early 1950s.

Exploring

Begin your tour of the city at the **Winston-Salem Visitor Center** (*see* Visitor Information, *below*), where you'll see a 12-minute film on the area.

★ **Old Salem** is just a few blocks from downtown Winston-Salem and only a stone's throw from Business I–40 (take the Old Salem/Salem College exit). The 1700s live again in this village of 80 original brick and wooden structures. The aromas of freshly baked bread, sugar cakes, and ginger snaps mix with those of beeswax candles and newly dyed flax. Tradesmen work in their shops making pewterware, cooking utensils, and other items, while the womenfolk embroider and weave cloth. There are African-American interpretations at each site. The Moravians, a Protestant sect, fled to Georgia to find religious freedom; from there they went to Bethlehem, Pennsylvania, finally settling here. In 1753, they built Bethabara (on Bethabara Rd., off University Pkwy.) and in 1766 built Salem. Tour tickets will get you into several restored buildings at Old Salem, but you may wander through the streets free of charge. Old Salem will undergo expansion over the next few years. *600 S. Main St., 27101,* ☎ *910/721–7300 or 800/441–5305.* ☛ *$12 adults, $6 children ages 6–14; combination ticket with MESDA (see below), $16 adults, $8 children.* ⊙ *Mon.–Sat. 9:30–4:30, Sun. 1:30–4:30.*

TIME OUT   **Winkler Bakery** will satisfy your craving for hot, freshly baked Moravian sugar cake. *525 S. Main St.,* ☎ *910/721-7302.* ⊙ *Mon.–Sat. 9–5, Sun. 1:30–5.*

Another way to step back in time is to enter the **Museum of Early Southern Decorative Arts (MESDA).** Six galleries and 19 rooms decorated with period furnishings are augmented with a new discovery center. *924 S. Main St.,* ☎ *910/721–7360.* ☛ *$6 adults, $3 children, ages 6–14; combination ticket with Old Salem, $16 adults, $8 children.* ⊙ *Mon.–Sat. 10:30–4:30, Sun. 1:30–4:30.*

Stroh Brewery, approximately 5 miles south of downtown via U.S. 52, rolls out 5.5 million barrels of beer a year as the second-largest brewery in the country. A single machine can fill and seal up to 1,500 12-ounce cans of beer per minute. You can see it made and enjoy a complimentary drink. *Schlitz Ave., U.S. 52S at S. Main St.,* ☎ *910/788–6710.* ☛ *Free.* ⊙ *Weekdays 1–4, with tours conducted on the hour.*

R. J. Reynolds Whitaker Park is one of the world's largest and most modern cigarette manufacturing centers. On the guided tour you see how 8,000 are produced every minute. *1100 Reynolds Blvd.,* ☎ *910/741–5718.* ☞ *Free.* ⊙ *Late Sept.–Apr., weekdays 8–6; late May–early Sept., weekdays 8–8.*

Historic **Bethabara Park** is another vision from the 1700s. You can explore the foundations of the town, as well as the three remaining buildings. Kids love the reconstructed Indian fort. A greenway now connects the park to another restoration of a 1700s mill, fort, and village. *2147 Bethabara Rd.,* ☎ *910/924–8191.* ☞ *Free.* ⊙ *Weekdays 9:30– 4:30, weekends 1:30–4:30. Guided tours Apr.–Nov. or by appointment. Brochures for a self-guided walking tour are available year-round at the visitor center.*

The **Museum of Anthropology,** the only one in the state, displays objects from cultures around the globe. *Wake Forest University,* ☎ *910/759–5282.* ☞ *Free.* ⊙ *Tues.–Sat. 10–4:30.*

Reynolda House Museum of American Art, formerly the home of tobacco magnate R. J. Reynolds, contains an outstanding collection of American art, a costume collection, and clothing and toys used by the Reynolds children. In Reynolda Village, on the estate, there are shops and restaurants. *Reynolda Rd.,* ☎ *910/725–5325.* ☞ *$6 adults, $3 students, $5 senior citizens.* ⊙ *Tues.–Sat. 9:30–4:30.*

The **Southeastern Center for Contemporary Art (SECCA),** near Reynolda House, is the place to see the latest in Southern painting, sculpture, and printmaking. *750 Marguerite Dr.,* ☎ *910/725–1904.* ☞ *$3 adults, $2 students and senior citizens, children under 12 free.* ⊙ *Tues.–Sat. 10–5, Sun. 2–5.*

The manor house at **Tanglewood Park,** the former home of the late William and Kate Reynolds, has just been spruced up with antiques and furnishings of the 1920s and now takes overnight guests. The public park has riding, golf, tennis, boating, camping, and PGA golf. *Hwy. 158 off I–40, Clemmons,* ☎ *910/766–0591.* ☞ *$2 per car, plus separate fees for each activity.*

Chinqua–Penn Plantation, 40 miles north of Winston-Salem on NC 158, is a National Register English country mansion built by Jeff and Betsy Penn in 1925. The Penns were world travelers, and filled the house with an eclectic collection of artifacts representing 30 countries. The estate also has a Chinese pagoda, three-story clock tower, greenhouses, and formal gardens. *2138 Wentworth St., Reidsville 27320,* ☎ *910/349– 4576.* ☞ *$7 adults, $6 seniors citizens, $2.50 students.* ⊙ *Tues.–Sat. 10–6, Sun. 1–6. Closed Jan.–Feb.*

What to See and Do with Children

Bethabara Park (*see* Exploring, *above*).

SciWorks. Look at the stars, handle live starfish in the tidal pool, pet the lambs and goats, and make discoveries at this hands-on museum. The complex includes the museum, an outdoor park, and a planetarium. *400 W. Hanes Mill Rd., Winston-Salem 27105,* ☎ *910/767–6730.* ☞ *Museum $4 adults, $2.50 students and senior citizens, children under 5 free.* ☞ *The "Works" (planetarium, park, and museum): $7 adults, $5 students and senior citizens.* ⊙ *Mon.–Sat. 10–5, Sun. 1–5.*

Shopping

Shopping Districts
Hanes Mall (Silas Creek Pkwy. and Hanes Mall Blvd.) is one of the finest malls in the region, with such major department stores as Hecht's and Dillards and specialty stores like the Nature Company and Banana Republic.

Outlets
This is a textile center, so there are many clothing outlets clustered along the interstates. **Marketplace Mall** (2101 Peters Creek Pkwy., ☎ 910/759–9889) has 36 outlet stores under one roof, including specialty shops, shoes, and apparel. The 100 stores in **Burlington Manufacturers Outlet Center** (☎ 910/227–2872) make the area off I–85 near Burlington a mecca for dedicated shoppers. ⊘ *Most stores Mon.–Sat. 10–9, Sun. 1–6.*

Books
Rainbow News & Cafe (712 Brookstown Ave., ☎ 910/723–0858) is a wonderful place where book lovers can browse for days through several converted old homes filled to the rafters with new and used books, then read their choice over a bowl of the best homemade soup in the city.

Crafts
The *New York Times* called the **Piedmont Craftsmen's Shop and Gallery** a "showcase for Southern crafts." *1204 Reynolda Rd., ☎ 910/725–1516. ⊘ Tues.–Sat. 10–6, Sun. 1–5.*

Participant Sports

Golf
Bryan Park and Golf Club (6275 Bryan Park Rd., Brown Summit, ☎ 910/375–2200) is a highly regarded course east of Winston-Salem. Its Champions Course was runner-up for best new public course of 1990 by *Golf Digest*. **Oak Hollow Park Golf Course** (1400 Oakview Rd., High Point, ☎ 910/883–3260), south of Winston-Salem, was ranked among America's 75 best public courses by *Golf Digest*. **Tanglewood Park Golf Club** (NC 158, Clemmons, ☎ 910/766–5082) has two fine 18-hole courses; the Reynolds Course and the Championship Course, where the Vantage Championship is played each year.

Dining

Traditional dining in these parts is Southern—fried chicken, ham, vegetables, biscuits, fruit cobblers, and the like. Chopped or sliced pork barbecue is also a big item. Nowadays, however, there's a growing number of gourmet restaurants. Unless otherwise noted, casual wear is acceptable throughout the region.

CATEGORY	COST*
$$$	$15–$25
$$	$8–$15
$	under $8

per person for a three-course meal, excluding drinks, service, and 6% tax

$$$ **Leon's Café.** This casual eatery in a renovated building near Old Salem serves some of the best gourmet food in town—fresh seafood, chicken breasts with raspberry sauce, lamb, and other specialties. The restaurant's dark colors are set off by artworks and lacy window treatments. ✕ *924 S. Marshall St.,* ☏ *910/725–9593. Reservations advised. AE, MC, V.*

$$–$$$ **Noble's Grille.** This upscale French restaurant serves a variety of entrées grilled or roasted over an oak-and-hickory fire, including braised rabbit with black-pepper fettuccine and Carolina *poussin* with polenta. Decorated in an airy style with tall windows and track lighting, the dining room affords a view of the kitchen's wood-burning grill. ✕ *380 Knollwood St.,* ☏ *910/777–8477. Reservations advised. Jacket and tie. AE, DC, MC, V.*

$$–$$$ **Old Salem Tavern Dining Room.** Eat Moravian food in a Moravian setting served by waiters in Moravian costumes. Standard menu items are chicken pie (excellent choice!), ragout of beef, and rack of lamb. From April through October you can dine outside under the arbor. ✕ *736 S. Main St.,* ☏ *910/748–8585. Reservations advised. AE, MC, V.*

$$ **Café Piaf.** Inside the Stevens Center, a restored Art Deco performing-arts space, the café offers pasta primavera, chicken Piaf (mushroom pâté and chicken breast in puff pastry with champagne or mushroom cream sauce), and other French entrées. Dessert and coffee follow performances. ✕ *401 W. 4th St.,* ☏ *910/750–0855. Reservations advised. AE, DC, MC, V.*

$$ **Maze.** Innovative American fare, such as chicken with black-eyed-pea salad or eggplant sandwiches draw diners to this restaurant in Reynolda Village. ✕ *120 Reynolda Rd.,* ☏ *910/748–0269. Reservations advised for parties of 6 or more. AE, MC, V.*

$$ **Newmarket Grille.** Fresh vegetables and meats, plus homemade breads and desserts, make this establishment a winner. The varied menu includes fresh grilled fish, poultry, beef, and pork dishes, as well as some stir-fry items, plus burgers and sandwiches. The bar is a popular gathering spot for the city's movers and shakers. ✕ *300 S. Stratford Rd., 27103,* ☏ *910/724–5220. No reservations. AE, DC, MC, V.*

Lodging

CATEGORY	COST*
$$$$	over $100
$$$	$60–$100
$$	$30–$60
$	under $30

All prices are for a standard double room, excluding 8% service charge.

$$$$ **Brookstown Inn.** Sleep under a comfy handmade quilt in front of the fireplace or enjoy wine and cheese in the spacious lobby of this unusual bed-and-breakfast hotel, built in 1837 as one of the first textile mills in the South. Some rooms have whirlpools. Breakfast is Continental. ▦ *200 Brookstown Ave., 27101,* ☏ *910/725–1120 or 800/845–4262,* FAX *910/773–0147. 71 rooms. Meeting rooms. AE, MC, V.*

$$$–$$$$ **Adam's Mark Winston Plaza Hotel.** Centrally located off I–40, this elegant hotel, Winston's premier lodging, has a marble lobby, traditional furnishings, and almost 10,000 square feet of meeting space. ▦ *425 N. Cherry St., 27101,* ☏ *910/725–3500 or 800/444–2326,* FAX *910/721–2240. 317 rooms. 2 restaurants, bar, pool, sauna, steam room, gift shop, recreation room. AE, D, DC, MC, V.*

$$$-$$$$ **Henry F. Shaffner House.** Accessible to downtown and Old Salem, this B&B is a favorite with business travelers and honeymoon couples. The rooms in the restored English Tudor house are furnished in 19th-century Victorian elegance. In addition to a complimentary Continental breakfast, there's afternoon tea and evening wine and cheese. ⌨ *150 S. Marshall St., 27101, ☎ 910/777–0052, ℻ 910/777–1188. 8 rooms with bath. AE, MC, V.*

$$$-$$$$ **Tanglewood Manor House.** This former home of a branch of the Reynolds family provides bed-and-breakfast guests with 10 rooms in the antiques-filled manor house, 18 lodge rooms, and four cottages on Mallard Lake in Tanglewood Park. Continental breakfast, admissions to the park, swimming, and fishing are included in the cost. ⌨ *Hwy. 158 off I–40, Clemmons 27012, ☎ 910/766–0591, ℻ 910/766–1571. 32 rooms. AE, DC, MC, V.*

$$$ **Comfort Inn–Cloverdale Place.** Off I–40 near downtown and Old Salem, this immaculately kept inn offers a free Continental breakfast. ⌨ *110 Miller St., 27103, ☎ 910/721–0220 or 800/228–5150, ℻ 910/723–2117. 122 rooms. Pool, health club, meeting room. AE, D, DC, MC, V.*

Winston-Salem Essentials

Arriving and Departing, Getting Around

BY BUS
Contact **Greyhound Lines** (☎ 910/723–3663 or 800/231–2222).

BY PLANE
Continental Airlines has a hub at **Piedmont Triad International Airport** (☎ 910/665–5666). It is also served by American, Delta, United, and USAir.

BY TRAIN
Amtrak serves Greensboro (☎ 910/855–3382 or 800/872–7245), about 25 miles away.

BY TROLLEY
Trolleys run throughout downtown. The fare is 10¢.

Guided Tours
Contact **Carolina Treasures and Tours** (1031 Burke St., Winston-Salem 27101, ☎ 910/631–9144) or **Margaret Glenn Tours** (Box 11342, Winston-Salem 27116, ☎ 910/724–6547).

Important Addresses and Numbers

EMERGENCIES
Dial 911 for **police** and **ambulance** in an emergency.

RADIO STATIONS
AM: WSJS 600, news, talk; WSMX 1500, gospel; WAAA 980, urban contemporary. **FM:** WXRA 94.6, alternative rock; WMAG 99.5, adult contemporary; WBFJ 89.3, Christian; WFDD 88.5, National Public Radio; WJMH 102, urban contemporary; WTQR 104.1, country.

VISITOR INFORMATION
Winston-Salem Convention & Visitors Bureau (Box 1408, Winston-Salem 27102, ☎ 910/725–2361 or 800/331–7018). A visitor's **reception center** in the City Market building (601 N. Cherry St., Suite 100, ☎ 910/777–3796) is open daily.

THE OUTER BANKS

North Carolina's Outer Banks, a series of barrier islands, stretch from the Virginia state line south to Cape Lookout. Throughout history the nemesis of shipping, these waters have been called the "Graveyard of the Atlantic"; a network of lighthouses and lifesaving stations was built, which draws visitors today, and the many submerged wrecks attract scuba divers. English settlers landed here in 1587 and attempted to colonize the region, but the colony—known today as "The Lost Colony"—disappeared without a trace. The islands' coves and inlets offered privacy to pirates—the notorious Blackbeard lived and died here. For many years the Outer Banks remained isolated, home only to a few families who made their living by fishing. Today the islands, linked by bridges and ferries, have become popular tourist destinations. Much of the area is included in the Cape Hatteras and Cape Lookout national seashores. The largest towns are Kitty Hawk, Kill Devil Hills, Nags Head, and Manteo.

On the inland side of the Outer Banks is the historic Albemarle region, a remote area of small villages and towns surrounding Albemarle Sound. Edenton was the Colonial capital for a while, and many of its early structures are preserved.

Exploring

Numbers in the margin correspond to points of interest on the Outer Banks map.

You can tour the Outer Banks from the southern end or, as in the following route, from the northern end. You can drive the 70-mile stretch in a day, but be sure to allow plenty of time in summer to wait for the ferry connecting the islands, and to explore the undeveloped beaches, historic lifesaving stations, and charming beach communities stretched

★ along the **Cape Hatteras** and **Cape Lookout National seashores.** Rentals are available from Corolla to Ocracoke, with the highest concentration of accommodations in the area from Kill Devil Hills to Nags Head. Be aware that during major storms and hurricanes the roads and bridges become clogged with traffic. In that case, follow the blue-and-white evacuation signs.

The small settlements of **Corolla** and **Duck** are largely seasonal residential enclaves full of summer rental condominiums with, in Duck, a growing number of restaurants and shopping outlets. Drive slowly in Corolla; wild ponies wander free here and always have the right of way. **Kitty Hawk,** with 1,672 permanent residents, is among the quieter of the beach communities, with fewer rental accommodations.

❶ **Kill Devil Hills,** on U.S. 158 Bypass, has been the site of rapid development over the last decade. Its population explodes in summer, and though many businesses are seasonal, you can find anything you need here year round. It's also the windswept site of man's first motorized

★ flight. The **Wright Brothers National Memorial,** a granite monument that resembles the tail of an airplane, stands as a tribute to Wilbur and Orville Wright, two bicycle mechanics from Ohio who took to the air on December 17, 1903. You can see a replica of *The Flyer* and stand on the exact spot where it made four takeoffs and landings, the longest being a distance of 852 feet. Exhibits and an entertaining, informative talk by a National Park Service ranger make the event come to life again. The Wrights had to bring in the unassembled airplane by boat and also all their food and supplies for building a camp. They made four trips to the site, beginning in 1900. The First Flight is commemorated annually. ☎ *919/441–7430.* ☛ *$4 per carload or $2 per person, children under 16 free.* ☉ *Daily 9–5; extended hours in summer. Closed Dec. 25.*

A few miles south of Kill Devil Hills, via U.S. 158 Bypass, is **Jockey's Ridge State Park,** the tallest sand dune in the East and a popular spot for hang gliding and kite flying. You can join in the activities and have a picnic here. *Rte. 158 Bypass, MM 12,* ☎ *919/441–7132.* ☛ *Free.* ☉ *Daily 8 AM–sunset.*

Nags Head got its name because Outer Bankers hoping for shipwrecks would tie lanterns around the heads of their horses to deceive merchant ships about the location of the shoals, thus profiting from the cargo that washed ashore. It is the most commercial area, with restaurants, motels, and hotels.

❷ ❸ Take U.S. 64/264 from U.S. 158 Bypass to reach the appealing town of **Manteo** on **Roanoke Island.** Clustered together on the other side of Manteo you'll find the lush **Elizabethan Gardens,** which were established as a memorial to the first English colonists. They are impeccably maintained by the Garden Club of North Carolina and are a fine site for a leisurely stroll. *U.S. 64, Manteo,* ☎ *919/473–3234.* ☛ *$2 adults, children under 12 free when accompanied by an adult.* ☉ *Mar.–Nov., daily 9–5; Dec.–Jan., weekdays 9–4.*

Fort Raleigh National Historic Site is a reconstruction of what is thought to be the original fort of the first Carolinian colonists. Be sure to see the orientation film and then take a guided tour of the fort. A nature trail leads to an outlook over Roanoke Sound. On special occasions, musicians play 16th-century music in the visitor center. *U.S. 64/264, 3 mi north of Manteo,* ☎ *919/473–5772.* ☛ *Free.* ☉ *Daily 9–5; extended hours in summer.*

The Lost Colony, an outdoor drama staged at the Waterside Amphitheatre, reenacts the story of the first colonists who settled here in 1587 and then disappeared. *1409 U.S. 64/264,* ☎ *919/473–3414 or 800/488–5012.* ☛ *$12 adults, $11 senior citizens, $6 children under 12. Reservations advised. Performances mid-June–late Aug., Sun.–Fri. at 8:30 PM.*

A short drive away (right next to the Dare County Regional Airport) is the **North Carolina Aquarium/Roanoke Island,** one of three in the state. The aquarium features a new shark exhibit, and children love the unusual hands-on exhibit that is the aquatic equivalent of a petting zoo. *Airport Rd. (off U.S. 64), Manteo,* ☎ *919/473–3493.* ☛ *$3 adults, $2 senior citizens and active military personnel, $1 children 6–17.* ☉ *Mon.–Sat. 9–5, Sun. 1–5.*

Back in Manteo, across a short bridge next to the Tranquil House Inn, is the **Elizabeth II State Historic Site,** a 16th-century vessel re-created to commemorate the 400th anniversary of the landing of the first colonists on Roanoke Island. A visitor center has exhibits on exploration and shipboard life. Historical interpretations are given by costumed guides during the summer. *Downtown Manteo,* ☎ *919/473–1144.* ☛ *$3 adults, $2 senior citizens, $1.50 students (any age), children 5 and under free.* ☉ *Nov.–Mar., Tues.–Sun. 10–4; Apr.–Oct., daily 10–6.*

Resume your journey southward on Route 12. On the way you will pass over **Herbert C. Bonner Bridge,** which arches for three miles over

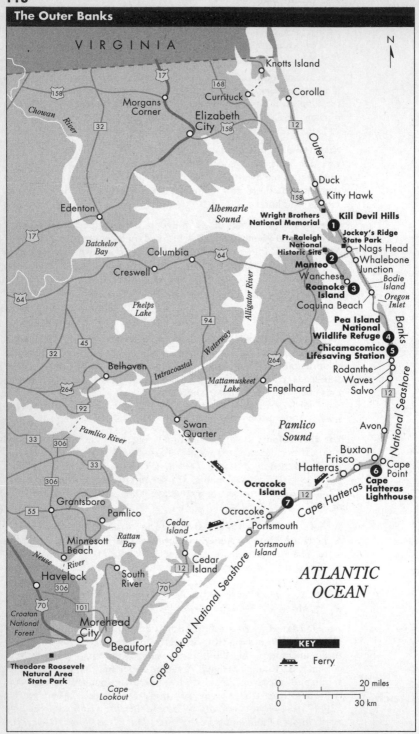

VIRGINIA

Knotts Island

17

168

Currituck

Corolla

158

Morgans
Corner

Chowan River

32

Elizabeth
City

12

Outer

158

Duck

Kitty Hawk

Edenton

Albemarle
Sound

Wright Brothers
National Memorial

Kill Devil Hills

1

17

Batchelor
Bay

Columbia

64

Ft. Raleigh
National
Historic Site

Manteo

2

Jockey's Ridge
State Park

Nags Head

Whalebone
Junction

Creswell

Wanchese

*Bodie
Island*

64

Phelps
Lake

94

Alligator River

**Roanoke
Island**

3

Coquina Beach

*Oregon
Inlet*

Banks

45

32

Waterway

264

**Pea Island
National
Wildlife Refuge**

4

**Chicamacomico
Lifesaving Station**

5

Belhaven

Intracoastal

Mattamuskeet
Lake

Engelhard

Rodanthe

Waves

Salvo

National Seashore

264

92

12

33

306

Pamlico River

Swan
Quarter

*Pamlico
Sound*

Avon

33

306

Grantsboro

Buxton

Frisco

**Cape
Point**

6

55

Pamlico

Hatteras

**Cape
Hatteras
Lighthouse**

Minnesott
Beach

*Rattan
Bay*

**Ocracoke
Island**

7

12

Cape Hatteras

Neuse River

*Cedar
Island*

Ocracoke

Portsmouth

South
River

*Portsmouth
Island*

Havelock

12

Cedar
Island

70

**ATLANTIC
OCEAN**

306

101

70

*Croatan
National
Forest*

**Morehead
City**

Cape Lookout National Seashore

Beaufort

*Cape
Lookout*

KEY

Ferry

0   20 miles

0   30 km

Oregon Inlet and carries traffic to Hatteras Island, the "Blue Marlin Capital of the World."

❹ Pea Island National Wildlife Refuge, between Oregon Inlet and Rodanthe, is made up of more than 5,000 acres of marsh. On the Atlantic Flyway, it's a birder's paradise: More than 265 species are spotted regularly, including endangered peregrine falcons and piping plovers. *Pea Island Refuge Headquarters,* ☎ *919/473–1131.* ☞ *Free.* ☉ *Apr.–Nov., weekdays 8–4.*

❺ Rodanthe is the site of the 1911 **Chicamacomico Lifesaving Station.** Now restored, the museum tells the story of the 24 stations that once lined the Outer Banks. Living-history reenactments are performed June–August. ☎ *919/987–2203.* ☞ *Free.* ☉ *May–Oct., Tues., Thurs., and Sat. 11–5.*

❻ Cape Hatteras Lighthouse, about 30 miles south of Rodanthe, sits as a beacon to ships offshore. The 208-foot lighthouse is the tallest in the East, and is open for climbing in summer months. Offshore lie the remains of the *Monitor,* a Confederate ironclad ship that sank in 1862. The visitor center offers information on the national seashore. *Hatteras Island Visitor Center,* ☎ *919/995–4474.* ☞ *Free.* ☉ *Daily 9–5.*

At Hatteras, board the free ferry to Ocracoke Island. Boats leave every
❼ half hour, and the journey takes 40 minutes. **Ocracoke Island** was cut off from the world for so long that native residents still speak in quasi-Elizabethan accents; today, however, the island is a refuge for tourists. There is a village of shops, motels, and restaurants around Silver Lake Harbor, which is where the infamous pirate Blackbeard met his death in 1718. The Ocracoke Lighthouse is a photographer's dream. *Ocracoke Visitor Center,* ☎ *919/928–4531.*

Cape Lookout National Seashore (☎ 919/728–2250) extends for 55 miles from Portsmouth Island to Shackleford Banks. It includes 28,400 acres of uninhabited land and marsh, accessible only by boat or ferry. Portsmouth, a deserted village that was inhabited from 1753 until 1984, is being restored, and wild ponies roam the Shackleford Banks.

Off the Beaten Path

Merchants Millpond State Park. A 170-year-old millpond and an ancient Southern swamp comprise one of the state's rarest ecosystems. Cypress and gum trees hung with Spanish moss reach out of the still, dark waters, which are ideal for canoeing. Fishing, hiking, and camping are also available. *Rte. 1, Box 141-A, Gatesville 27938,* ☎ *919/357–1191.* ☞ *Free.* ☉ *Sept.–May, daily 8–8; June–Aug., daily 8 AM–9 PM.*

Somerset Place. The Collins family kept meticulous records on the 300 slaves that worked this plantation on Albemarle Sound (now a state historic site) in the 1800s. The slaves' descendants still hold family reunions here. *Off U.S. 64 at Creswell,* ☎ *919/797–4560.* ☞ *Free.* ☉ *Apr.–Oct., Mon.–Sat. 9–5, Sun. 1–5; Nov.–Mar., Tues.–Sat. 10–4, Sun. 1–4.*

Beaches

Kill Devil Hills has 5 miles of beach with 27 public access areas with limited parking off NC 12. Some have off-road vehicle access. Because of the large number of rental cottages and hotels, this beach tends to have a higher number of people, but it is seldom uncomfortably crowded, even at the height of the season.

Nags Head has 11 miles of beach with 33 public access areas, all with parking and some with rest rooms and showers. You'll usually have company on this beach as well. One point of interest is mile marker 11.5, site of the first North Carolina Historic Shipwreck Site. The USS *Huron* lies in 20 feet of water roughly even with the Nags Head pier.

Cape Hatteras National Seashore offers more than 70 miles of unspoiled beaches stretching from Nags Head to Ocracoke Island. Preserved as Cape Hatteras National Seashore, this coastal area is ideal for swimming, surfing, windsurfing, diving, boating, and any number of water activities. It's easy to find a slice of beach all your own as you drive south down NC 12, but park only in designated areas. If you want to swim, beware of strong tides and currents—there are no lifeguard stations. Fishing piers are located in Rodanthe, Avon, and Frisco.

Coquina Beach (off NC 12, 8 mi south of U.S. 158) on the Cape Hatteras National Seashore, is considered by some to be the best swimming hole on the Outer Banks. The wide-beamed ribs of the shipwreck *Laura Barnes* rest in the dunes here, and facilities include picnic shelters, rest rooms, showers, and bath houses.

Ocracoke Island beaches are among the least populated and most beautiful on the Cape Hatteras National Seashore. There are 4 public access areas with parking, as well as off-road vehicle access. Be sure to stop at the Ocracoke Pony Pen, where you can see direct descendants of Spanish mustangs that once roamed wild on the island.

Participant Sports and Outdoor Activities

Camping
Camping is permitted in designated areas all along the Cape Hatteras National Seashore (Rte. 1, Box 675, Manteo 27954, ☎ 919/473–2111). All campgrounds in the park have cold showers, drinking water, tables, grills, and rest rooms (except Ocracoke, which has pit toilets). Sanitary stations for recreational vehicles are at Oregon Inlet, Cape Point at Cape Hatteras, and Ocracoke. Oregon Inlet, Cape Point, and Ocracoke are open from mid-April through mid-October; Frisco, mid-June to late August. Be sure to take along extra-long tent stakes for sand, and don't forget the insect repellent. All sites are available on a first-come, first-served basis (except Ocracoke, where reservations are accepted). There are also many private campgrounds scattered along the Outer Banks. For information about these, contact the Dare County Tourist Bureau (☎ 919/473–2138).

Fishing
This area is a paradise for anglers who enjoy surf casting or deep-sea fishing. You can board a charter boat or head your own craft out of **Oregon Inlet Fishing Center** (☎ 919/441–6301 or 800/272–5199) or **Pirates Cove Yacht Club** (☎ 919/473–5577 or 800/367–4728) in Manteo. You don't need a license for saltwater fishing.

Hang Gliding
Only a few miles from where Wilbur and Orville Wright first took flight, you can try your hand at hang gliding. The giant sand dune at Jockey's Ridge State Park is where national champions gather every May for the Hang Gliding Spectacular. Lessons are given by **Kitty Hawk Kites** (U.S. 158 at MM 13, Nags Head, ☎ 919/441–4124 or 800/334–4777) and by **Corolla Flight** (Box 1021, Kitty Hawk 27949, ☎ 919/453–4800).

Golf

Nags Head Golf Links (MM 15, Nags Head, ☎ 919/441–8074 or 800/851–9404) offers ocean views and a Scottish feel. **Sea Scape Golf Course** (Kitty Hawk, ☎ 919/261–2158) is an authentic links course set amid the dunes.

Scuba Diving

With over 600 known shipwrecks off the coast of the Outer Banks, diving opportunities are virtually unlimited. The *Monitor* is off-limits, however. The **USS *Huron* Historic Shipwreck Preserve,** which lies offshore between mile markers 11 and 12, is a popular diving site. Dive shops include: **Hatteras Divers** (☎ 919/986–2557) and **Nags Head Pro Dive Shop** (☎ 919/441–7594).

Surfing and Windsurfing

The Outer Banks offer ideal conditions for these sports. Contact **Kitty Hawk Sports** (U.S. 158 at MM 13, ☎ 919/441–6800 or 800/334–4777) or **Bert's Surf Shop** (MM 10, Nags Head, ☎ 919/441–1939; MM 4, Kitty Hawk, ☎ 919/261–7584). A favorite spot for windsurfing on the Pamlico Sound between Buxton and Avon is known as **Canadian Hole** for all the northern visitors who congregate here to catch the wind.

Dining and Lodging

While you can find fancy restaurants catering to tourists in the major towns, by far the best fare around here is the fresh seafood. There are plenty of raw bars featuring oysters and clams on the half shell, and seafood houses offering fresh crabs (soft-shells in season, early in the summer) and whatever local fish—tuna, wahoo, dolphin (mahi-mahi, not Flipper)—has been hauled in that day. Competition keeps them on their toes, so the cooking is good. Dress is usually casual.

CATEGORY	COST*
$$$$	over $25
$$$	$15–$25
$$	$8–$15
$	under $8

per person for a three-course meal, excluding drinks, service, and 6% sales tax

The majority of motels and hotels are clustered in the Nags Head–Manteo area, with rental properties in all the towns that dot the Cape Hatteras National Seashore. There are 60 cottages for rent on Ocracoke Island, plus a dozen or so motels and inns. The Dare County Tourist Bureau (☎ 919/473–2138) can steer you in the direction of agencies to arrange weekly or monthly rentals.

CATEGORY	COST*
$$$$	over $100
$$$	$60–$100
$$	$30–$60
$	under $30

All prices are for a standard double room, excluding 8% tax

Buxton

DINING

$$$ Great Salt Marsh. A clean, well-lighted place with a black-and-white checkered art-deco look, the restaurant serves lunch and dinner to regulars and the passers-through. Among the imaginative appetizers are

fresh green beans sautéed and served with Parmesan cheese, and such
entrées as Pamlico crab cakes with "absolutely no filler" and soft
crabs served on a bed of garlic-laced spinach. It has a splendid wine
list. ✕ *Osprey Shopping Center, Hwy. 12,* ☎ *919/995–6200. Reservations strongly advised. AE, D, DC, MC, V.*

Duck

DINING AND LODGING

$$$$ **Sanderling Inn and Restaurant.** If you enjoy being pampered, come to
this inn on a remote beach north of Duck. Guests are treated to afternoon tea. For recreation you can play tennis, go swimming, or take
a nature walk through the Pine Island Sanctuary and then curl up with
a good book from the inn's library—or enjoy a videotape. Though it
was built in 1985 and has all the contemporary conveniences, the inn
has the stately, mellow look of old Nags Head. Ceiling fans, wicker,
and neutral tones give rooms a cool and casual feel. The ambitious but
unexceptional restaurant is in a beautifully renovated lifesaving station. It serves three meals a day, and reservations are required for dinner. ⊡ *1461 Duck Rd., 27949,* ☎ *919/261–4111 or 800/701–4111.
60 rooms and 28 efficiencies. Restaurant, pool, hot tub, 2 tennis
courts, health club, meeting rooms. AE, D, MC, V.*

Kill Devil Hills

DINING

$$–$$$ **Etheridge Seafood Restaurant.** The fish comes straight from the boat
to the kitchen at this family-owned seafood house, in operation for over
half a century. It's decorated with Etheridge family memorabilia, depicting their successful fishing and warehousing operation. ✕ *U.S. 158
Bypass at MM 9.5,* ☎ *919/441–2645. No reservations. MC, V. Closed
Nov.–Feb.*

LODGING

$$$–$$$$ **Ramada Inn.** Rooms in this convention-style hotel have ocean views
and come with refrigerators and microwave ovens. Peppercorns restaurant, overlooking the ocean, serves breakfast and dinner, and lunch is
available on the sun deck next to the pool. ⊡ *U.S. 158, MM 9.5, Box
2716, 27948,* ☎ *919/441–2151 or 800/635–1824,* ℻ *919/441–
1830. 172 rooms. Pool, hot tub, meeting rooms. AE, D, DC, MC, V.*

Nags Head

DINING

$$$ **Owens' Restaurant.** Housed in an old Nags Head–style clapboard
cottage, Owens' has been in the same family since 1946. The seafood
is outstanding—especially the coconut shrimp and lobster bisque.
Nightly entertainment is offered in the brass-and-glass Station Keeper's
Lounge. ✕ *U.S. 158, MM 17,* ☎ *919/441–7309. Reservations accepted
for large parties only. AE, DC, MC, V. No lunch. Closed Jan.–Mar.*

$$–$$$ **Lance's Seafood Bar & Market.** You can contemplate the fishing and
hunting memorabilia while you dine on steamed or raw seafood and
then drop the shells through the hole in the table. ✕ *U.S. 158 Bypass,
MM 14,* ☎ *919/441–7501. AE, MC, V. Closed Dec. 25.*

LODGING

$$$–$$$$ **First Colony Inn.** The rooms in this historic inn near the ocean are fur-
★ nished with four-poster and canopied beds, hand-crafted armoires, and
English antiques. The suites have wet bars, kitchenettes, and Jacuzzis.
A Continental breakfast and afternoon tea come with the room. ⊡ *6720
S. Virginia Dare Trail, 27959,* ☎ *919/441–2343 or 800/368–9390.
26 rooms. Refrigerators, pool, coin laundry. D, MC, V.*

Ocracoke

DINING AND LODGING

$$–$$$ **Island Inn and Dining Room.** The inn was built as a private lodge back in 1901. It shows its age a bit, but is full of Outer Banks character and is being upgraded a step at a time. The large rooms in the Crow's Nest on the third floor are the best; they have cathedral ceilings and look out over the island. The dining room is known for its oyster omelet, crab cakes, and hush puppies. Reservations are advised, particularly for dinner. ⊞ *Rte. 12, Box 9, 27960,* ☎ *919/928–4351 (inn) or 919/928–7821 (dining room). 35 rooms. Pool. D, MC, V.*

Roanoke Island

DINING

$$$ **Queen Anne's Revenge.** This stately old home expanded into a restaurant serves some of the best seafood on the coast from a secluded location in the woods of Wanchese. Nightly specials, like marinated grilled tuna, are always fresh and well-prepared; even the side dishes are impressive. ✕ *1 mi off U.S. 64, Wanchese,* ☎ *919/473–5166. Reservations accepted for parties of 8 or more. AE, D, DC, MC, V. Closed Tues. Nov.–Mar.*

$$ **Weeping Radish Brewery and Restaurant.** Waiters dressed in Bavarian costumes serve German dishes while German music plays in the background. Tours of the brewery are given upon request. The beer is superb, but this isn't the place for seafood. ✕ *U.S. 64, Manteo,* ☎ *919/473–1157. Reservations advised for parties of 6 or more. MC, V. Closed major holidays.*

DINING AND LODGING

$$$$ **Tranquil House Inn.** This 19th-century-style waterfront inn is only a few steps from shops, restaurants, and the Elizabeth II State Historic Site, but bikes are provided for adventures beyond. Handmade comforters in designer fabrics give rooms a cozy feel. Some of the bathroom mirrors are hand-stenciled to match the flowers in the wallpaper. A Continental breakfast and wine and cheese each evening is on the house. The new restaurant, 1587, serves inventive entrées like sesame-crusted tuna with wasabi vinaigrette and shiitake mushrooms. ⊞ *Queen Elizabeth Ave., the Waterfront, Box 2045, Manteo 27954,* ☎ *919/473–1404 or 800/458–7069,* ℻ *919/473–1526. 25 rooms. AE, D, MC, V.*

Outer Bank Essentials

Arriving and Departing, Getting Around

BY BOAT

Seagoing visitors travel the Intracoastal Waterway through the Outer Banks and Albemarle region. Boats may dock at Elizabeth City (☎ 919/338–2886), Manteo Waterfront Docks (☎ 919/473–3320), Park Service Docks at Ocracoke (☎ 919/928–5111), and other ports. For a complete list of facilities, see the North Carolina Coastal Boating Guide compiled by the North Carolina Department of Transportation (☎ 919/733–2520).

BY CAR

U.S. 158 links the Outer Banks with U.S. 17 leading to Norfolk and other places north. U.S. 64, 70, and 264 are western routes. Route 12 goes south toward Ocracoke Island and north toward Corolla. Toll ferries connect Ocracoke to Cedar Island and Swan Quarter. For reservations, call 800/293–3779). There is a free ferry across Hatteras

Inlet. On summer weekends, traffic waiting for the Hatteras Inlet ferry can be backed up for hours.

BY PLANE

The closest commercial airports are the **Raleigh–Durham International Airport** (☎ 919/840–2123) and **Norfolk International** (☎ 804/857–3340), both of which are served by major carriers, including American, Continental, Delta, and USAir. Southeast Airlines (☎ 919/473–3222) provides charter service between the **Dare County Regional Airport** (919/473–2600) at Manteo and major cities along the East Coast.

BY TAXI

Beach Cabs (☎ 919/441–2500), based in Nags Head, offers 24-hour service from Norfolk to Ocracoke and towns in between. Another option is **Outer Banks Limousine Service** (☎ 919/261–3133).

BY TRAIN

Amtrak service (☎ 800/872–7245) is available to Norfolk, VA, about 75 miles to the north.

Guided Tours

Historic Albemarle Tour, Inc. (Box 759, Edenton 27932, ☎ 919/482–4747) offers guided tours of Edenton and publishes a brochure on a self-guided tour of the Albemarle Region.

Kitty Hawk AeroTours leave from the First Flight Airstrip or from Manteo for Kitty Hawk, Corolla, Cape Hatteras, Ocracoke, Portsmouth Island, and other areas along the Outer Banks. ☎ *919/441–4460. Tours run Mar.–Labor Day.*

The **North Carolina Aquarium/Roanoke Island** (Box 967, Airport Rd., Manteo 27954, ☎ 919/473–3493) sponsors summer boat tours of the estuary and the sound.

Ocracoke Trolley Tours (of Ocracoke Island) depart from Trolley Stop One in Ocracoke. *NC 12, Ocracoke, ☎ 919/928–6711. Tours run Easter–Labor Day, Mon.–Sat.*

Important Addresses and Numbers

EMERGENCIES

Dial 911 for Oregon Inlet, Roanoke Island, Hatteras Island, and Ocracoke Island. For non-emergency care, contact **Ocracoke Health Center** (☎ 919/928–1511). The **Outer Banks Medical Center** (☎ 919/441–7111) at Nags Head is open 24 hours a day. For Coast Guard assistance, dial ☎ 919/995–6411.

RADIO STATIONS

AM: WOBR 1530, vacation information, news, weather; WGAI 560, adult contemporary. **FM:** WNHW 92, country; WOBR 95.3, adult contemporary; WRSF 105.7, country; WVOD 99.1, beach, Top 40; WCXL 104.1, adult contemporary.

VISITOR INFORMATION

Dare County Tourist Bureau (Box 399, Manteo, 27954, ☎ 919/473–2138). **Historic Albemarle Tour, Inc.** (Box 759, Edenton 27932, ☎ 919/482–7325).

WILMINGTON AND THE CAPE FEAR COAST

The old seaport town of Wilmington has much to celebrate these days. Thanks to efforts led by the Downtown Area Revitalization Effort (DARE), the once-decadent downtown has been reborn. *Henrietta II,* a paddle wheeler similar to those that used to ply the waters of the Cape Fear River, has been put into service as a tourist vessel. Visitors are drawn to the Coast Line Convention Center complex, reminiscent of old railroad days, and to the charms of Chandler's, the Cotton Exchange, and Water Street Market, now shopping and entertainment centers. They also come to Wilmington for special annual events such as the Azalea Festival, North Carolina Jazz Festival, Christmas candlelight tours, and fishing tournaments. And on the surrounding Cape Fear Coast visitors tour old plantation houses and azalea gardens, study sea life at the state aquarium, and bask in the sun at nearby beaches.

Exploring

Wilmington

USS *North Carolina* Battleship Memorial, a top tourist priority, can be reached by car or by taking the river taxi from Riverfront Park. The ship participated in every major naval offensive in the Pacific during World War II. The self-guided tour takes about two hours, and a 10-minute film is shown throughout the day. Narrated tours on cassette are available for rent, and a 70-minute sound-and-light spectacular, "The Immortal Showboat," is presented nightly at 9 from early June until Labor Day. *Box 480, Wilmington 28402,* ☎ *910/251–5797.* ☛ *$6 adults, $3 children 6–11; sound-and-light show $3.50 adults, $1.75 children.* ☉ *Daily 8–sunset.*

The **Wilmington Railroad Museum,** at the corner of Red Cross and Water streets, focuses on the days of the Wilmington and Weldon Railroad (circa 1840) to the present. Children love climbing on the steam locomotive and caboose. ☎ *910/763–2634.* ☛ *$2 adults, $1 children 6–11.* ☉ *Tues.–Sat. 10–5, Sun. 1–5.*

From the museum, follow Red Cross Street one block toward downtown and turn right on Front Street. On the second block is the **Cotton Exchange,** a shopping-dining complex housed in restored buildings that have flourished as a trading center since the pre–Civil War days. ☎ *910/343–9896.* ☉ *Mon.–Sat. 10–5:30, some stores open evenings and Sun. 1–5.*

From Front Street, go to Grace Street, head east until you reach Third Street, and then go south to Chestnut Street, to the **New Hanover County Public Library.** The North Carolina Room in the library attracts researchers and genealogists from all over the country. *201 Chestnut St.,* ☎ *910/341–4394.* ☛ *Free.* ☉ *Mon.–Thurs. 9–9, Fri. 9–6, Sat. 9–5, Sun. 1–5.*

Follow Chestnut Street to 4th Street, then go two blocks to Market Street. On that corner is the **St. James Graveyard,** which contains the headstones of many early settlers. In the next block of South Fourth Street is the **Temple of Israel,** the oldest Jewish place of worship in the state.

Continue several blocks north on Market Street to the **Cape Fear Museum,** which traces the natural, cultural, and social history of Cape Fear

River Country from its beginnings to the present day. *814 Market St.,* ☎ *910/341–7413. ☛ $2 adults, $1 students, senior citizens, and children 5–17. ☯ Tues.–Sat. 9–5, Sun. 2–5. Closed holidays.*

Several blocks west on Market Street at the corner of Third is the **Burgwin-Wright House,** built in 1770 on the foundations of a jail. This colonial restoration, which includes a period garden, is maintained by the National Society of the Colonial Dames of America and by the state of North Carolina. *224 Market St.,* ☎ *910/762–0570. ☛ $3 adults, $1 children. ☯ Tues.–Sat. 10–3:30.*

Go two blocks south on Third Street, where you'll find the **Zebulon Latimer House,** built in 1852 in the Italianate style. *126 S. 3rd St.,* ☎ *910/762–0492. ☛ $3 adults, $1 children. ☯ Tues.–Sat. 10–4.*

Wind up your tour at **Chandler's Wharf** on Water Street. Originally a complex of warehouses, it now contains shops and some good seafood restaurants like Elijah's. This is a great place to conclude your tour of downtown Wilmington.

Cape Fear Coast

Go three blocks east to U.S. 17. On the way out of town, stop at **Greenfield Lake and Gardens,** on South Third Street (U.S. 421). The park offers picnicking and canoe and paddle-boat rentals on a scenic 180-acre lake bordered by cypress trees laden with Spanish moss. ☎ *910/763–9371. ☛ Free. ☯ Daily.*

Follow U.S. 17 northeast for 9 miles until you reach **Poplar Grove Historic Plantation.** The home of the Foy family for generations, the 1850 Greek Revival plantation was opened to the public in 1980. You can tour the manor house and outbuildings, see craft demonstrations, shop in the country store, and pet the farm animals. *9 mi northeast of Wilmington on U.S. 17,* ☎ *910/686–9989 (restaurant 910/686–9503). Guided tours Feb.–Dec.: $6 adults, $5 senior citizens, $3 students and children 5–16. ☯ Mon.–Sat. 9–5, Sun. noon–5. Closed Jan.*

Now head south on U.S. 17 until you reach Military Cut-off Road, which becomes Oleander Drive and leads to **Airlie Gardens** (8 mi east). The gardens are open from March through September. *Airlie Rd. off Rte. 74/76,* ☎ *910/763–4646. ☛ $6 adults, $5 senior citizens ($1 less May–Oct.), children under 10 free.*

Take Route 76 west to Route 421 south and follow it to the **Southport–Fort Fisher Ferry** (☎ 910/458–3329), some 20 miles south of Wilmington. On the way, stop at **Fort Fisher State Historic Park** and the **North Carolina Aquarium** (*see* What to See and Do with Children, *below*). The car-ferry trip is an enjoyable river ride between Old Federal Point at the tip of the spit and the quaint town of Southport. You can see the "Old Baldy" lighthouse en route. *Ferries run every 50 min between 8:50 and 6:50. Fare: $3 per car. The privately owned passenger ferry to Bald Head Island,* ☎ *910/457–5003, runs from Southport on the hour (except noon) 8–6; fare: $15 adults, $8 children.*

After you get off the ferry in Southport, take Route 87 north to the **Carolina Power and Light Company Visitors Center.** Here you can learn about nuclear power through exhibits and movies and then use the picnic area. ☎ *910/457–6041. ☛ Free. ☯ June–Aug., weekdays 9–4, Sun. and July 4 1–4; Sept.–May, weekdays 9–4.*

Continue north on Route 87/133, and you will arrive at **Orton Plantation Gardens.** The house is not open to the public, but the gardens may be toured anytime. ☎ *910/371–6851.* ☛ *$8 adults, $4 children 6–12.* ⊙ *Mar.–Aug., daily 8–6, Sept.–Nov., daily 10–5.*

Take a short detour off Route 133 to **Brunswick Town State Historic Site,** where you can explore the excavations of a colonial town, see Fort Anderson, a Civil War earthworks fort, and have a picnic. ☎ *910/371– 6613.* ☛ *Free.* ⊙ *Apr.–Oct., Mon.–Sat. 9–5, Sun. 1–5; Nov.–Mar., Tues.–Sat. 10–4, Sun. 1–4.*

What to See and Do with Children

Fort Fisher State Historic Site was the largest and one of the most important earthwork fortifications in the South during the Civil War. Visitors enjoy the reconstructed battery and Civil War relics and artifacts from sunken blockade-runners. *U.S. 421 at Kure Beach,* ☎ *910/458– 5538.* ☛ *Free.* ⊙ *Apr.–Oct., Mon.–Sat. 9–5, Sun. 1–5; Nov.–Mar., Tues.–Sat. 10–4, Sun. 1–4.*

The **North Carolina Aquarium at Fort Fisher,** one of three state aquariums, has a 20,000-gallon shark tank, a touch pool (where you can handle starfish, sea urchins, and the like), a whale exhibit, and a new alligator exhibit. The park is also a natural area where wildflowers, birds, and small animals thrive. You can also visit the World War II bunker that stood guard against sea attacks from the Atlantic. Field trips and workshops for groups can be arranged. *U.S. 421 at Kure Beach,* ☎ *910/458–8257.* ☛ *$3 adults, $2 senior citizens and active military, $1 students 6–17.* ⊙ *Mon.–Sat. 9–5, Sun. 1–5. Closed major holidays.*

The **Wilmington Railroad Museum** (*see* Exploring, *above*).

Off the Beaten Path

Military history buffs get a bang out of **Moore's Creek National Battlefield,** where American patriots defeated the Loyalists in 1776. *20 mi northwest of Wilmington on Rte. 210,* ☎ *910/283–5591.* ☛ *Free.* ⊙ *Daily 8–5.*

★ A visit to **Tryon Palace at New Bern,** about 150 miles from the Outer Banks, 100 miles north of Raleigh, and 80 miles from Wilmington, is an ideal overnight trip. The reconstructed Georgian palace, considered the most elegant government building in the country in its time, was the colonial capitol and the home of Royal Governor William Tryon in the 1770s. It was rebuilt according to architectural drawings of the original palace and furnished in English and American antiques as listed in Governor Tryon's inventory. Costumed interpreters give tours of the house; tours of the 18th-century formal gardens are self-guided. During the summer, actors in period dress give monologues describing a day in the life of Governor Tryon. Special events are held periodically throughout the year, and craft demonstrations are given daily. The stately John Wright Stanly House (circa 1783), Dixon-Stevenson House (circa 1826), and the recently restored New Bern Academy (circa 1809) are a part of the Tryon Palace Complex. An audiovisual orientation is offered in the Visitor Reception Center. *610 Pollock St., New Bern 28560,* ☎ *919/638–1560.* ☛ *Palace and gardens only, $8 adults, $4 students 6–17; garden tour only, $4 adults, $2 students; combination tour of all buildings and gardens, $12 adults, $6 students.* ⊙ *Mon.–Sat. 9:30–4, Sun. 1–4. Closed major holidays.*

Shopping

Visitors will find it easy to restrict their shopping to Chandler's Wharf, the Cotton Exchange, and the Water Street Market, but the city also offers many unique shops in the Historic District, as well as shopping malls and discount outlets.

Beaches

Three beaches—**Wrightsville, Carolina,** and **Kure**—are within a short drive from Wilmington, and miles and miles of sand stretch northward to the Outer Banks and southward to South Carolina. The beaches offer a full gamut of activities, from fishing to sunbathing to scuba diving, and a choice of accommodations, including weathered cottages, resorts, condos, and motels. There are approximately 100 points of public access along the shoreline. Marked by orange-and-blue signs, these points offer parking, rest rooms, and outdoor showers. Some of the smaller beaches have lifeguards on duty, and many are accessible to people with disabilities. A number of fishing piers are also open to the public.

Wrightsville, about 5 miles east of Wilmington, is a posh and popular beach with a number of outstanding restaurants nearby. **Carolina Beach,** about 12 miles south, caters to families. Camping, fishing, swimming, and picnicking are permitted at **Carolina Beach State Park** (☎ 910/458–8206, marina 910/458–7770). **Kure Beach** is a quiet family enclave with historic sites like Fort Fisher and attractions like the North Carolina Aquarium (*see* What to See and Do With Children, *above*). In some places, twisted live oaks still grow behind the dunes.

Participant Sports

Fishing
Surf fishing is popular on the piers that dot the coast. Charter boats and headboats are available for off-shore fishing. Four major fishing tournaments, for substantial prize money, are held each year—the **Cape Fear Marlin Tournament,** the **Wrightsville Beach King Mackerel Tournament, the East Coast Open King Mackerel Tournament,** and the **U.S. Open King Mackerel Tournament.** For more information on these tournaments, contact the Cape Fear Coast Convention and Visitors Bureau (*see* Visitor Information, *below*).

Golf
There are 10 public and semi-private courses in the Greater Wilmington area, and South Brunswick County is golf heaven, especially the areas around Calabash, Sunset Beach, and Ocean Isle. A few top choices are listed below, but for more information on golf, call the Cape Fear Coast Convention and Visitors Bureau (*see* Visitor Information, *below*) or the South Brunswick Islands Chamber of Commerce (Box 1380, Shalotte, 28459, ☎ 910/754–6644).

Bald Head Island Club (Bald Head Island, ☎ 910/457–5000 or 800/234–1666) is a George Cobb–designed course in a beautiful setting of tropical forest and marsh. **Beau Rivage Plantation Golf Club** (6230 Carolina Beach Rd., Wilmington, 910/392–9022) is an 18-hole course in a natural links setting. The **Cape Golf & Racquet Club** (535 The Cape Blvd., Wilmington, ☎ 910/799–3110) is an 18-hole resort course with driving range. The **Gauntlet at St. James Plantation** (Hwy. 211, Southport, ☎ 910/253–3008 or 800/247–4806) lives up to its name as a challenging course. **Lockwood Folly Golf Links** (100 Club House Dr.,

Holden Beach, ☎ 910/842–5666 or 800/443–7891) is a highly rated resort course. **Marsh Harbour Golf Links** (Hwy. 179, Calabash, ☎ 910/579–3161 or 800/552–2660) was rated one of the best 75 public courses in America by *Golf Digest*. **Oyster Bay Golf Links** (Hwy. 179, Sunset Beach, ☎ 910/579–3528 or 800/552–2660) was selected "best new resort course of 1983" by *Golf Digest* and is known for its oyster shell hazards and gator sightings. **Sea Trail Plantation** (211 Clubhouse Rd., Sunset Beach, ☎ 910/579–4350 or 800/624–6601) features three courses designed by Dan Maples, Rees Jones, and Willard Byrd. These are great courses and a good value.

Scuba Diving

Wrecks such as the World War II tanker *John D. Gill* make for exciting diving off the coast. **Aquatic Safaris** (5751–4 Oleander Dr., Wilmington, ☎ 910/392–4386) rents equipment and leads trips.

Surfing and Board Sailing

These sports are popular at area beaches, and rentals are available at shops in Wilmington, Wrightsville Beach, and Carolina Beach.

Triathlon

Those who enjoy jogging, swimming, and bicycling can join in the annual **Wilmington Triathlon** in the fall. Participants swim across Banks Channel to Wrightsville Beach, then bicycle to Carolina Beach and back to Wilmington, and then run from there back to Wrightsville Beach.

Spectator Sports

College Sports

Local fans support the University of North Carolina at Wilmington's Seahawk basketball, baseball, and swimming teams. The school belongs to the NCAA Division I Colonial Athletic Association. *For tickets*, ☎ 910/395–3233.

Rugby

The **Cape Fear Rugby Tournament** (☎ 910/395–3233) is an annual July 4th event, held at UNC-W.

Dining and Lodging

Dining

Local cuisine is simply seafood. Shrimp (this is where the shrimp boats come in), oysters, Atlantic blue crab, and king mackerel—and lots of it—are prepared in a variety of ways. Homegrown fruits and vegetables, too, are used extensively in local cooking. Barbecued pork is another popular dish. International cuisines—from Mexican to Japanese to German—are also represented. Dress at these restaurants is neat but casual.

CATEGORY	COST*
$$$$	over $25
$$$	$15–$25
$$	$8–$15
$	under $8

per person for a three-course meal, excluding drinks, service, and 6% sales tax

$$-$$$ **Market Street Casual Dining.** This always-busy eatery offers a wide variety of sandwiches and entrées, including seafood and steaks, served in a casual atmosphere. There's also a bar on the premises. ✕ *6309 Market St.,* ☎ *910/395–2488. No reservations. AE, D, MC, V.*

$$-$$$ **Ocean Terrace Restaurant.** Part of the Blockade Runner Resort (*see* Lodging, *below*), this restaurant attracts large crowds to its Friday lobster night, Saturday seafood buffet, and Sunday brunch. Regular dishes here include grilled New York strip steak with bourbon-shallot butter; sautéed, almond-breaded flounder with shrimp; and sautéed chicken breast with toasted pecans, pears, and apples. ✕ *Blockade Runner Resort Hotel and Conference Center, 275 Waynick Blvd., Wrightsville Beach,* ☎ *910/256–2251 or 800/541–1161. Reservations advised. AE, D, DC, MC, V.*

$$-$$$ **Oceanic Restaurant and Grill.** Its Oceanic Pier location gives patrons the top panoramic view of the Atlantic for miles around—a wonderful backdrop for the fresh seafood, steaks, and chicken served here. ✕ *703 S. Lumina St., Wrightsville Beach,* ☎ *910/256–5551. Reservations advised for large parties. AE, MC, V.*

$$-$$$ **Pilot House.** At this Chandler's Wharf restaurant, known for its seafood, pastas, and fresh vegetables, you can now dine outdoors overlooking the Cape Fear River. The Sunday Brunch (Apr.–Oct.), featuring Low Country Southern food, is the most popular in town. ✕ *2 Ann St.,* ☎ *910/343–0200. Reservations advised. AE, D, MC, V.*

$–$$ **Ken and Art's Studio Café.** This restaurant is where you might spot a star when they're filming on location in Wilmington. The menu features a mixture of California, New York, and Carolinas cuisine, served amid movie memorabilia. ✕ *North Carolina Film Studios, 1223 N. 23rd St.,* ☎ *910/343–3708. Reservations advised. No credit cards. No dinner.*

$ **Water Street Restaurant and Sidewalk Café.** Housed in a restored two-story brick waterfront warehouse that dates to 1835, this outdoor café and restaurant serves up Greek, Mexican, Middle Eastern, and other ethnic cooking. ✕ *5 Water St.,* ☎ *910/343–0042. Reservations not required. MC, V.*

Lodging

Visitors to Wilmington and Cape Fear Coast can choose among 6,000 rooms. The selection includes a variety of chains, condos, and resorts overlooking the ocean, and in-town guest houses. In addition to in-town properties, there are many accommodations at Carolina, Kure, and Wrightsville beaches. A complete list is included in the *Accommodations Guide,* available from the Convention and Visitors Bureau.

CATEGORY	COST*
$$$$	over $100
$$$	$60–$100
$$	$30–$60
$	under $30

*All prices are for a standard double room, excluding 9% tax

$$$$ **Bald Head Island Resort.** Accessible only by ferry (☎ 910/457–5003; fare: $15 adults, $8 children) from Southport, this resort offers privacy in a luxurious isolated setting. Despite the quiet surroundings, there's always something to do on the resort island: Activities include golf, tennis, sailing, and fishing. Other favorite pastimes are watching the loggerhead turtles, and taking a tour led by a naturalist. Accommo-

dations include rental condos, cottages, and bed-and-breakfast inns; a two-night minimum stay is required. ⊠ *Bald Head Island, 28461,* ☎ *910/457–5000 or 800/234–1666,* FAX *910/457–9232. Over 100 rental condos and beach houses. 3 restaurants, pool, boating, shops. AE, DC, MC, V.*

$$$–$$$$ **Blockade Runner Resort Hotel and Conference Center.** This extensive complex is widely known for both its food (*see* Dining, *above*) and lodging. Rooms overlook either the inlet or the ocean. ⊠ *275 Waynick Blvd., Wrightsville Beach 28480,* ☎ *910/256–2251 or 800/541–1161,* FAX *910/256–2251, ext. 404. 150 rooms and suites. Restaurant, pool, health club, boating, bicycles, meeting rooms. AE, D, DC, MC, V.*

$$$–$$$$ **Inn at St. Thomas Court.** Guests are pampered yet enjoy total privacy at this small luxurious apartment-type house, which has one- and two-bedroom suites furnished in a traditional style in keeping with the surrounding historic district. A Continental breakfast is included in the rate. ⊠ *101 S. 2nd St., 28401,* ☎ *910/343–1800 or 800/525–0909,* FAX *910/251–1149. 34 units. AE, DC, MC, V.*

$$$ **Catherine's Inn.** Built in 1883 and in the historic district overlooking the Cape Fear River, this two-story Italianate home, now a B&B, has hardwood floors, a sunken garden, four-poster and canopy beds, and claw-foot tubs—many items collected by the innkeepers over the years. ⊠ *410 S. Front St., 28401,* ☎ *910/251–0863 or 800/476–0723. 3 rooms. AE, MC, V.*

$$$ **Docksider Inn.** In a class of its own, this waterfront hotel in the heart of Kure Beach is nautical both outside and in. Gray with navy shutters, the inn is furnished in light-colored beachy furniture and enhanced with marine art and artifacts, including a set of 1930s British Admiralty signal flags. Each bathroom has an original watercolor. The third floor is being converted into "Captain's Cabins" for those seeking a romantic getaway. ⊠ *202 Fort Fisher Blvd. (U.S. 421), 28449,* ☎ *910/458–4200,* FAX *910/458–6468. 34 rooms. Pool. AE, DC, D, MC, V.*

$$$ **Wilmington Hilton Inn.** Overlooking the Cape Fear River on one side and the city on the other, this is one of the most convenient places to stay in town. The spacious inn has a dining room and lounge. ⊠ *301 N. Water St., Wilmington 28401,* ☎ *910/763–5900 or 800/445–8667,* FAX *910/763–0038. 168 rooms, 10 suites. Pool, meeting rooms, airport shuttle. AE, DC, D, MC, V.*

$$ **Hampton Inn.** This economy chain motel, 3 miles from downtown, is not luxurious but offers such extras as complimentary Continental breakfast, in-room movies, and free local calls. ⊠ *5107 Market St., 28403,* ☎ *910/395–5045 or 800/426–7866,* FAX *910/799–1971. 118 rooms. Facilities: pool. AE, D, DC, MC, V.*

The Arts and Nightlife

The arts are very much a part of Wilmington life. Theatrical productions are staged by the **Thalian Association, Opera House Productions,** and **Tapestry Players.** The city has its own symphony orchestra, oratorio society, civic ballet, and concert association; and the **North Carolina Symphony** makes four appearances here each year. The annual **Wilmington Jazz Festival,** held in February, and the **Blues Festival,** in August, draw big crowds.

The Arts

St. John's Museum of Art is known for its 13 prints by Cassatt, as well as for its works by North Carolina artists. The museum is housed in three buildings, including the 1804 Masonic Lodge Building, the oldest such lodge in the state. There is also a sculpture garden. *114 Orange St.,* ☎ *910/763–0281.* ☛ *$2 adults, $1 students under 18, children under 5 free.* ☼ *Tues.–Sat. 10–5, Sun. noon–4.*

Museum of World Cultures (601 S. College Rd., ☎ 910/395–3411 or 910/350–4007), at the University of North Carolina at Wilmington, exhibits its collections of African art, pre-Columbian textiles, Chinese ceramics, and Middle Eastern artifacts at various locations around the campus.

Thalian Hall, a magnificent opera house built in 1858 and refurbished in 1990 to the tune of $5 million, is the site of theater, dance, and musical performances. *310 Chestnut St.,* ☎ *910/343–3664 or 800/523–2820. The hall is open for self-guided tours Mon.–Sat. noon–5, as permitted by performance schedules.*

Nightlife

Wilmington nightlife is centered in hotel lounges. The **Ocean Terrace Restaurant** in the Blockade Runner Hotel (*see* Dining and Lodging, *above*) offers live entertainment Thursday through Sunday, with nationally known acts in the **Comedy Zone** March–November. **Ice House Beer Garden** (115 S. Water St., ☎ 910/251–1158 or 910/763–2084) serves food and beer and showcases a different music group nightly. **Johnny Rockit's** (5025 Market St., ☎ 910/791–2001) is known for rock music.

Wilmington and the Cape Fear Coast Essentials

Arriving and Departing, Getting Around

Visitors can get to Wilmington and the Cape Fear Coast via car, plane, bus, or boat. Several cruise lines dock here on their way to Bermuda or the Caribbean.

BY BOAT

Public boat access is offered at Atlantic Marina, Carolina Beach State Park, Masonboro Boat Yard and Marina, Seapath Transient Dock, Wrightsville Gulf Terminal, and Wrightsville Marina. The Wilmington Hilton, Blockade Runner, Harbor Inn, and Summer Sands provide docking facilities for their guests. A river taxi runs (mid-June—Labor Day) across the Cape Fear River between the USS *North Carolina Battleship Memorial* and downtown Wilmington. The fare is $1 round-trip. A state-run car ferry connects Fort Fisher with Southport on the coast.

BY BUS

Greyhound Lines serves the Union Bus Terminal (201 Harnett St., ☎ 910/762–6625 or 800/231–2222). The **Wilmington Transit Authority** (☎ 910/343–0106) provides service every day except Sunday. There is also taxi service.

BY CAR

U.S. Highways 421, 74, 76, 17, and 117 serve Wilmington. I–40 now links the city with I–95.

BY PLANE

USAir (☎ 800/428–4322) and ASA Delta Connection (to Atlanta; ☎ 800/282–3424) serve the **New Hanover International Airport** (☎ 910/341–4333), ½ mile from downtown Wilmington.

Guided Tours

The **"Guide Map of Historic Wilmington and the Cape Fear Coast"** is available from the Cape Fear Coast Convention and Visitors Bureau in the restored New Hanover County Courthouse and at the Visitor Information Booth at the foot of Market Street (in the summer). The bureau can suggest itineraries and arrange tours of local industries upon advance request.

Wilmington Adventure Walking Tours, run by Bob Jenkins, will guide you around old Wilmington. *Tours operate Apr. 1–Nov. 1.,* ☎ *910/763–1785.* ☛ *$10 adults, $5 children 6–12.*

Walk and Talk Tour, offered by the Lower Cape Fear Historical Society, covers 12 blocks in downtown Wilmington. *Tours operate Feb.–Dec., Wed. only. Depart from Latimer House, 126 S. 3rd St.,* ☎ *910/762–0492.* ☛ *$5 ($6, including Latimer House).*

Sightseeing Tours by Horse Drawn Carriage, given by John and Janet Pucci of Springbrook Farms Tuesday through Sunday during the summer and on weekends off-season, depart from Water & Market streets. ☎ *910/251–8889.* ☛ *$7 adults, $4 children under 12.*

Cape Fear Riverboats, Inc., operated by Capt. Carl Marshburn, offers a variety of cruises aboard a stern-wheel riverboat that departs from Riverfront Park. ☎ *910/343–1611 or 800/676–0162. Sightseeing tours: $9 adults, $4 children. Entertainment/dinner cruises: $29–$32.50 per person. Sunset dinner cruises: $22 adults, $15 children. Moonlight cruises: $9 adults, $5 children (call for boarding times).*

The **Captain J. N. Maffitt Harbor Tour** (☎ 910/343–1611 or 800/676–0162) runs cruises and shuttles passengers between Riverfront Park and the USS *North Carolina Battleship Memorial. Shuttle: every 30 min 10–5 except during tours. Fare: $2. Cruises: $5 adults, $3 children.*

Cape Fear Tours (☎ 910/686–7744) offers walking and driving tours of the Wilmington Historic District, mansions, and the beaches for individuals and groups by reservation. Individual tours are $20 per hour.

Important Addresses and Numbers

EMERGENCIES

Dial 911 for **police** and **ambulance.** For Coast Guard assistance, dial ☎ 910/343–4881. Emergency medical attention is available round the clock at the **Cape Fear Memorial Hospital** (5301 Wrightsville Ave., ☎ 910/452–8100) and the **New Hanover Regional Medical Center** (2131 S. 17th St., ☎ 910/343–7000); both hospitals have 24-hour pharmacies as well.

RADIO STATIONS

AM: WAAV 980, news, talk; WBMS 1340, urban contemporary. **FM:** WHQR 91.3, National Public Radio; WKOO 98.7, oldies; WGNI 102.7, adult contemporary; WWQQ 101.3, country; COAST 97.3, urban contemporary; WSFM 107.5, classic rock.

VISITOR INFORMATION

Cape Fear Coast Convention and Visitors Bureau (24 N. 3rd St., Wilmington 28401, ☎ 910/341–4030 or 800/222–4757).

NORTH CAROLINA HIGH COUNTRY, INCLUDING ASHEVILLE

The majestic peaks, meadows, and valleys of the Appalachian, Blue Ridge, and Smoky mountains characterize the High Country in the western corner of the state. National parks and forests and the Blue Ridge Parkway are the region's main attractions, providing prime opportunities for skiing, hiking, bicycling, camping, fishing, and canoeing, or just taking in the breathtaking views.

The largest and most cosmopolitan city in High Country, Asheville has been a retreat for the wealthy and famous for decades. In recent years this mountain city has been rated, among cities of its size, as America's number-one favorite place to live. It has scenic beauty, low levels of pollution, a good airport and road system, a moderate four-season climate, a variety of hotels and restaurants, and a thriving arts community. Banjo pickers are as revered as violinists, mountain folks mix with city slickers, and everyone loves where they live.

Cities like Boone, Blowing Rock, and Banner Elk have boomed in the 30 years since the introduction of snowmaking equipment. Luxury resorts now dot the valleys and mountaintops. Visitors to the hills take advantage of the many crafts shops, music festivals, theater offerings, and such special events as the Grandfather Mountain Highland Games. The passing of each season is a special visual event here, and autumn is the star.

Exploring

Asheville

Downtown Asheville is noted for its eclectic architecture. The **Battery Park Hotel,** built in 1924, is neo-Georgian; the **Flatiron Building** (1924) is neo-classical; the **Basilica of St. Lawrence** (1912) is Spanish Baroque; **Old Pack Library** (1925) is in Italian Renaissance–style; the **S & W Cafeteria** (1929) is Art Deco. In fact, the city has the largest collection of Art Deco buildings outside of Miami.

Pack Place Education, Arts & Science Center houses the Asheville Art Museum, Colburn Gem & Mineral Museum, Health Adventure, YMI Cultural Center, and the Diana Wortham Theatre. *2 S. Pack Sq.,* ☎ *704/257–4500.* ☛ *Fees vary.* ☉ *June–Oct., Tues.–Sat. 10–5, Sun. 1–5; Nov.–May, Tues.–Sat. 10–5.*

The **Thomas Wolfe Memorial,** built in 1880 in the Queen Anne style, is one of the oldest houses in downtown Asheville. Wolfe's mother ran a boarding house here for years, and he used it as the setting for his novel *Look Homeward, Angel.* Family pictures, clothing, and original furnishings fill the house, now a state historic site. Guided tours are available. *48 Spruce St.,* ☎ *704/253–8304.* ☛ *$1 adults, 50¢ students.* ☉ *Apr.–Oct., Mon.–Sat. 9–5, Sun. 1–5; Nov.–Mar., Tues.–Sat. 10–4, Sun. 1–4.*

From downtown, take U.S. 25 south. The entrance to the architecturally ★ famous **Biltmore Estate** faces Biltmore Village, about three blocks from the interstate. Built as the private home of George Vanderbilt, the 255-room French Renaissance château is America's largest private residence (Vanderbilt's descendants still live in the mansion, but open the bulk of the home and grounds to visitors). Richard Morris Hunt designed it, and Frederick Law Olmsted landscaped the original 125,000-acre estate (now 8,000 acres). It took 1,000 men five years to complete the gargantuan project. On view are the priceless antiques and art collected by the Vanderbilts, and 17 acres of gardens. Visitors can also see the state-of-the-art winery and take Christmas candlelight tours of the house. Allow a full day to tour the house and grounds. ☎ *704/255–1700 or 800/543–2961.* ☛ *$24.95 adults, $18.75 students ages 10–15, accompanied children under 10 free.* ☯ *Daily 9–5 except Thanksgiving, Dec. 25, and Jan. 1.*

Weaverville

Take U.S. 19–23 Bypass north about 18 miles to Weaverville and the **Zebulon B. Vance Birthplace** state historic site, with a two-story log cabin and several outbuildings, where North Carolina's governor during the Civil War grew up. Crafts and chores typical of his period are often demonstrated. Picnic facilities are available. *Reems Creek Rd. (Rte. 1103),* ☎ *704/645–6706.* ☛ *Free.* ☯ *Apr.–Oct., Mon.–Sat. 9–5, Sun. 1–5; Nov.–Mar., Tues.–Sat. 10–4, Sun. 1–4.*

Blue Ridge Parkway

★ The most direct route from Asheville to the Boone–Blowing Rock area is the **Blue Ridge Parkway,** a 469-mile stunningly beautiful road that gently winds through mountains and meadows and crosses mountain streams on its way from Cherokee, North Carolina, to Waynesboro, Virginia. To get onto the Parkway from the Vance Birthplace, follow Reems Creek Road west, turn onto Ox Creek Road, and follow it 3 miles to the Parkway entrance. The Parkway is generally open year-round but often closes during heavy snows. Maps and information are available at visitor centers along the highway. *Superintendent, Blue Ridge Pkwy., BB & T Bldg., 1 Pack Sq., Asheville 28801,* ☎ *704/298–0398.*

The **Folk Art Center** (MM 382 on the Blue Ridge Pkwy.) sells authentic mountain crafts made by members of the Southern Highland Handicraft Guild. ☎ *704/298–7928.* ☯ *Daily except major holidays.*

About 65 miles north of the Folk Art Center, just off the parkway on U.S. 221, is **Linville Caverns,** the only caverns in the Carolinas. They go 2,000 feet underground and have a year-round temperature of 51 degrees. ☎ *704/756–4171.* ☛ *$4 adults, $2.50 children 5–12.* ☯ *June–Labor Day, daily 9–6; Apr.–May and Sept.–Oct., daily 9–5; Nov. and Mar., daily 9–4:30; Dec.–Feb., weekends only 9–4:30.*

About a mile farther north along the Parkway is **Linville Falls** (MMDM 316.3), one of North Carolina's most frequently photographed waterfalls. An easy trail winds through evergreens and rhododendrons to overlooks where you can get wonderful views of the series of cascades tumbling into Linville Gorge. There's also a visitor center, a campground, and a picnic area.

Just off the parkway at mile marker 305 is **Grandfather Mountain,** famous for its Mile-High Swinging Bridge, a 228-foot-long bridge that sways over a 1,000-foot drop into the Linville Valley. Sweaty-palmed tourists have crossed it since 1952. A Natural History Museum has exhibits on native minerals, flora and fauna, and pioneer life. The annual Singing on the Mountain in June is an opportunity to hear old-time gospel music and preaching, and the Highland Games in July brings together Scottish clans from all over North America for athletic events and Highland dancing. There's also hiking, picnicking, and an environmental habitat. *Blue Ridge Pkwy. and U.S. 221, Linville 28646,* ☎ *704/733–4337.* ☛ *$9 adults, $5 children 4–12.* ☯ *Apr.–mid-Nov., 8–dusk; mid-Nov.–Mar., 9–4, weather permitting.*

Parks along the parkway include **Julian Price Park** (MM 298–295.1), which offers hiking, canoeing on a mountain lake, trout fishing, and camping, and **Moses H. Cone Park** (MM 292.7–295), which has a turn-of-the-century manor house that's now the **Parkway Craft Center.**

Blowing Rock

Just north of the entrance to Moses H. Cone Park, take U.S. 221/321 to Blowing Rock, a tourist mecca since the 1880s, which has retained the flavor of a quiet mountain village. Only a few hundred people are permanent residents, but the population swells each summer. The **Blowing Rock,** considered the state's oldest tourist attraction, looms 4,000 feet over the Johns River Gorge. If you throw your hat over the sheer precipice, it may come back to you, should the wind gods be playful. The story goes that a Cherokee brave and a Chickasaw maiden fell in love. Torn between his tribe and his love, he jumped from the cliff, but she prayed to the Great Spirit and he was blown safely back to her. It's more or less a gimmick, but the view from the observation tower is nice, and there's a garden landscaped with mountain laurel, rhododendron, and other native plants. *Off U.S. 321,* ☎ *704/295–7111.* ☛ *$4 adults, $1 children 6–11.* ☉ *Summer 8–8, winter 10–5.*

Head north toward Boone on U.S. 321, until you come to **Tweetsie Railroad,** a popular theme park where visitors can ride a train beset by train robbers and Indians. The park also has a petting zoo, country fair (May–Oct.), rides, gold panning, a saloon show, and concessions. ☎ *704/264–9061 or 800/526–5740.* ☛ *$14.95 adults, $12.95 children 4–12 and senior citizens 60 years and older.* ☉ *Late May–Oct. 31, daily 9–6.*

Boone

Boone, named for frontiersman Daniel Boone, is a city of several thousand residents at the convergence of three major highways—U.S. 321, U.S. 421, and NC 105. **"Horn in the West,"** a project of the Southern Highlands Historical Association, is an outdoor drama that traces the story of Boone's life. *Amphitheater off U.S. 321,* ☎ *704/264–2120.* ☛ *$9 (reserved) or $8 (general admission) adults, $4.50 children under 13. Performances nightly at 8:30, except Mon. mid-June–mid-Aug.*

Boone's **Appalachian Cultural Museum** showcases the successes of such mountain residents as stock-car racer Junior Johnson and country singers Lula Belle and Scotty Wiseman, and exhibits a vast collection of antique quilts, fiddles, and handcrafted furniture. *University Hall near Greene's Motel, U.S. 321,* ☎ *704/262–3117.* ☛ *$2 adults, $1.75 senior citizens, $1 children 12–18.* ☉ *Tues.–Sat. 10–5, Sun. 1–5.*

Banner Elk

From Boone, take U.S. 321 west and NC 194 south to Banner Elk, a popular ski resort town surrounded by the lofty peaks of Grandfather, Hanging Rock, Beech, and Sugar mountains.

Ashe County

North of Boone in Ashe County, past Blue Ridge Parkway mile marker 258.6, are the **Blue Ridge Mountain Frescoes.** North Carolina artist Ben Long painted four big-as-life frescoes in two abandoned churches here in the '70s. *The Last Supper* (measuring 17 × 19.5 feet) is in the Glendale Springs Holy Trinity Church. The others are in St. Mary's Episcopal Church at Beaver Creek, including *Mary, Great with Child,* which won the Leonardo da Vinci International Award. Signs from the highway lead to the churches. ☎ 910/982–3076. ☛ *Free.* ☉ *24 hours a day; staffed 10–4. Guide service available with prior arrangements.*

What to See and Do with Children

Tour an underground mine or dig for gems of your own at **Emerald Village,** an old mine. *McKinney Mine Rd. at Blue Ridge Pkwy., MM 334,* ☎ *704/765–6463.* ☛ *Museum $3.50 adults, $2.50 students, $3 senior citizens, plus cost of gem bucket chosen ($3–$100). A $50 bucket guarantees you a stone, which will be cut free of charge, $100 guarantees two.* ☉ *June–Labor Day, daily 9–6, May and Sept.–Oct., daily 9–5.*

Sliding Rock. In summer, you can skid 150 feet on a natural water slide in Pisgah National Forest. Wear old jeans and tennis shoes, and bring a towel. *Pisgah National Forest, north of Brevard, off U.S. 276,* ☎ *704/877–3265.* ☛ *Free.* ☉ *Daily.*

Tweetsie Railroad (*see* Exploring, *above*).

Off the Beaten Path

At **Chimney Rock Park,** about 25 miles southeast of Asheville on U.S. 64/74–A, you can ride an elevator up through a 26-story shaft of rock for a staggering view of Hickory Nut Gorge and the surrounding Blue Ridge Mountains. Trails, open spring–fall, lead to 400-foot Hickory Nut Falls, where *The Last of the Mohicans* was filmed. ☎ *704/625–9611 or 800/277–9611.* ☛ *$9 adults, $4.50 children 6–15.* ☉ *Mid-Oct.–Apr., daily 8:30–4:30, May–mid-Oct., daily 8:30–5:30.*

About 25 miles south of Asheville via I–26 is **Flat Rock,** the town to which the poet and Lincoln biographer Carl Sandburg moved with his wife, Lilian, in 1945. Guided tours of their house, **Connemara,** where Sandburg's papers still lie scattered on his desk, are given by the National Park Service. In summer, "The World of Carl Sandburg" and "Rootabaga Stories" are presented at the amphitheater. ☎ *704/693–4178.* ☛ *$2 adults, children 16 and under free.* ☉ *Daily 9–5.*

You'll find everything from ribbons and calico to brogans and overalls in the **Mast General Store,** ten miles northwest of Boone in the tiny town of Valle Crucis. Built in 1882, the store has plank floors worn to a soft sheen and a potbellied stove that's still fired up on chilly mornings. (The company operates a similar store in downtown Boone: Old Boone Mercantile, 104 E. King St., Boone, ☎ 704/262–0000; ☉ Mon.–Sat. 10–6, Sun. 1–6.) *NC 194, Valle Crucis,* ☎ *704/963–6511.* ☉ *Mon.–Sat. 6:30–6:30, Sun. 1–6.*

Shopping

Groovewood Gallery at the Homespun Shops, on the grounds of the Grove Park Inn and established by Mrs. George Vanderbilt, sells woven goods, such as blankets, shawls, and baskets, made on the premises. *111 Groovewood Rd., Asheville,* ☎ *704/253–7651.* ☉ *Nov.–May, Mon.–Sat. 10–5; June–Oct., Mon.–Sat. 10–5, Sun. 1–5.*

Bolick Pottery sells mountain crafts and pottery, handcrafted on the spot by Glenn and Lula Bolick; Glenn will even throw in a mountain tale, a buck dance, or a tune on his saw free of charge. *Off U.S. 321, Rte. 8, Box 285–A, Lenoir,* ☎ *704/295–3862.* ☉ *Mon.–Sat. 9–5, Sun. 1–6.*

Goodwin Weavers sell bedspreads, afghans, and other woven goods, as well as home furnishings designed by North Carolina artist Bob Timberlake. *Off U.S. 321 Bypass, Blowing Rock,* ☎ *704/295–3394.* ☉ *June–Dec., daily 9–5, Jan.–May, daily 10–4:30.*

Qualla Arts and Crafts has authentic Cherokee Indian crafts and items from other American tribes. *U.S. 441 and Drama Rd., Cherokee,* ☎ *704/497–3103.* ☉ *June–Aug., Mon.–Sat. 8–8, Sun. 8–5; Sept.–May, weekdays 8–4:30, Sat. 9–4:30.*

Participant Sports

Canoeing and Whitewater Rafting
In the Asheville area, the Chattooga, Nolichucky, French Broad, Nantahala, Ocoee, and Green rivers offer Class I–V rapids. Outfitters include **Carolina Wilderness** (Box 488, Hot Springs 28743, ☎ 704/622–3535 or 800/872–7437) and **Nantahala Outdoor Center** (13077 Hwy. 19W, Box 41, Bryson City 28713, ☎ 704/488–2175 or 800/232–7238).

Near Boone and Blowing Rock, the wild and scenic New River (Class I and II) provides hours of excitement, as do the Nolichucky River, the Watauga River, Wilson Creek, and Toe River. Outfitters include **Edge of the World Outfitters** (Hwy. 184, Box 1137, Banner Elk 28604, ☎ 704/898–9550 or 800/789–3343) and **Wahoo's Adventures** (Box 1915, Boone 28607, ☎ 704/262–5774 or 800/444–7238).

Golf
Western North Carolina offers many challenging courses. For a complete listing of public courses in Asheville, Black Mountain, Brevard, Hendersonville, Lake Lure, Old Fort, and Waynesville, contact Asheville's Visitor Information Center (*see* Visitor Information, *below*). North Carolina High Country Host (*see* Visitor Information, *below*) has information on public courses in Boone, Seven Devils, Newland, and West Jefferson.

Boone Golf Club (Fairway Dr., Boone, ☎ 704/264–8760) is a good 18-hole course for the whole family. **Colony Lake Lure Golf Resort** (201 Blvd. of the Mtns., Lake Lure, ☎ 704/625–2888), located five miles from Asheville, has two 18-hole courses known for their beauty. **Etowah Valley Country Club** (U.S. 64, Etowah, ☎ 704/891–7141 or 800/451–8174), about 20 miles from Asheville, has three very different 9-hole courses with good package deals. **Grove Park Inn** (290 Macon Ave., Asheville, ☎ 704/252–2711 or 800/438–5800) has a beautiful 18-hole course. **Hound Ears Club** (NC 105, Boone, ☎ 704/963–4312) has an 18-hole course with great mountain views. **Linville Golf Club** (Linville, ☎ 704/733–4363), located 17 miles from Boone, has a highly rated Donald Ross course. **Reems Creek Golf Club** (Weaverville, ☎ 704/645–4393), about 12 miles from Asheville, offers what some consider to be perfect mountain golf.

Hiking
More than 100 trails lead off the Blue Ridge Parkway, from easy strolls to strenuous hikes. The **Bluff Mountain Trail** at Doughton Park (MM 238.5) is a moderately strenuous 7.5-mile trail winding through forests, pastures, and valleys, and along the mountainside. Moses H. Cone Memorial Park's (MM 292.7) **Figure 8 Trail** is an easy and beautiful trail that the Cones designed specifically for their morning walks. The half-mile loop winds through a tunnel of rhododendron and a hard-

wood forest lined with moss-covered rocks, wildflowers, and lush green ferns. Those who tackle the half-mile, strenuous **Waterrock Knob Trail** (MM 451.2), near the southern end of the parkway, will be rewarded with spectacular views from the 6,400-foot-high Waterrock Knob summit. For more information on parkway trails, contact the Blue Ridge Parkway (*see* Exploring, *above*). Another good source is *Walking the Blue Ridge: a Guide to the Trails of the Blue Ridge Parkway* by Leonard Adkins (UNC Press, $11.95), available at most parkway visitor center gift shops.

Trails abound in **Great Smoky Mountains National Park.** For trail maps, contact the Superintendent (Great Smoky Mountains National Park, Gatlinburg, TN 37738, ☎ 615/436–5615). The park maintains an information bulletin board with basic trail information at the entrance at the junction of mile marker 469.1 and U.S. 441.

Serious hikers wishing to explore the **Appalachian Trail,** which runs along the crest of the Appalachian Mountains at the North Carolina–Tennessee border, can pick it up at several points, including at the Newfound Gap Parking Area in Great Smoky Mountains National Park (☎ 615/436–5615) and at Grandfather Mountain (☎ 704/733–4337), where you can get trail maps.

Horseback Riding and Trekking
Trail rides are offered by several Asheville area stables, including **Pisgah View Ranch** (Rte. 1, Candler 28715, ☎ 704/667–9100) and **Cataloochee Ranch** (Rte. 1, Box 500, Maggie Valley 28751, ☎ 704/926–1401 or 800/868–1401). In the Boone–Blowing Rock area, trail rides are offered by **Blowing Rock Stables** (U.S. 221, Blowing Rock, ☎ 704/295–7847), **Elk Creek Stables** (NC 268, Ferguson, ☎ 910/973–8635), and **Banner Elk Riding Stables** (NC 184, Banner Elk, ☎ 704/898–5424). You can hike with llamas carrying your pack into the Pisgah National Forest on day and overnight trips with **Windsong Llama Treks, Ltd.** (120 Ferguson Ridge Rd., Clyde 28721, ☎ 704/627–6111). In Asheville, contact **Avalon Llama Trek** (310 Wilson Cove Rd., Swannanoa, ☎ 704/298–5637).

Rock Climbing
One of the most challenging climbs in the country is the Linville Gorge (MM 317, Blue Ridge Pkwy.). Permits are available from the District Forest Ranger's Office in Marion (☎ 704/652–2144) or from the Linville Falls Texaco Station on U.S. 221. **Edge of the World Outfitters in Banner Elk** (☎ 704/898–9550) provides instruction and guided trips.

Skiing
Ski resorts in the Asheville area include **Cataloochee** (Rte. 1, Box 500, Maggie Valley 28751, ☎ 704/926–0285 or 800/768–0285), **Fairfield–Sapphire Valley** (4000 U.S. 64W, Sapphire Valley 28774, ☎ 704/743–3441 or 800/533–8268), and **Wolf Laurel** (Rte. 3, Mars Hill 28754, ☎ 704/689–4111).

The Boone–Blowing Rock area offers downhill skiing at **Appalachian Ski Mountain** (Box 106, Blowing Rock 28605, ☎ 704/295–7828 or 800/322–2372), **Ski Beech** (Box 1118, Beech Mountain 28604, ☎ 704/387–2011 or 800/438–2093), **Sugar Mountain** (Box 369, Banner Elk 28604, ☎ 704/898–4521), and **Hawksnest Golf and Ski Resort** (1800 Skyland Dr., Seven Devils, 28604, ☎ 704/963–6561 or 800/822–4295). For ski conditions, call 800/962–2322. Cross-country skiing is offered at **Moses H. Cone Park** and at **Linville Falls** on the Blue Ridge Parkway (☎ 704/295–7591), and **Roan Mountain** (☎ 615/772–3303). Tours and equipment are available from **High Country Ski Shop** in Pineola (☎ 704/733–2008).

Dining and Lodging

Dining
Dining choices in Asheville are many: upscale gourmet restaurants, middle-of-the-road country fare, and fast-food eateries. In the past 30 years, High Country towns outside Asheville have seen a tremendous increase in restaurants. Fresh mountain trout, as well as such game meats as pheasant and venison, are regional specialties. Beer, wine, and liquor by the drink are permitted in Blowing Rock, Banner, Elk, and Beech Mountain; beer and wine only in Boone. Dress is usually casual.

CATEGORY	COST*
$$$$	over $25
$$$	$15–$25
$$	$8–$15
$	under $8

per person for a three-course meal, excluding drinks, service, and 6% sales tax

Lodging
Lodging options range from posh resorts to mountain cabins, country inns, and economy chain motels. There's a bed for virtually every pocketbook.

CATEGORY	COST*
$$$$	over $100
$$$	$60–$100
$$	$30–$60
$	under $30

All prices are for a standard double room, excluding 8% tax

Asheville
DINING
$$$$ Market Place on Wall Street. Nouvelle cuisine is served in a relaxed atmosphere. Vegetables and herbs are regionally grown, and bread, pasta, and pastries are made on the premises. The Grill and Patio, a new addition, provides a lower-cost dining alternative, specializing in American and ethnic dishes. ✗ 20 Wall St., ☎ 704/252–4162. Reservations advised. AE, DC, MC, V. No lunch. Closed Sun.

$$ Blue Moon Bakery. Chris and Margaret Kobler offer a variety of pastries and breads made on site, as well as sandwiches and salads for lunch, at their European-style bakery. ✗ 60 Biltmore Ave., ☎ 704/252–6063. No reservations. MC, V.

$$ West Side Grill. Have a country-style meal of meatloaf, turkey, roast beef, or baked chicken, with all the trimmings, at this '50s-style diner. Salads and vegetarian fare are also offered. ✗ 1190 Patton Ave., ☎ 704/252–9605. No reservations. AE, MC, V.

$$ Windmill European Grill/Il Pescatore. As the name implies, the menu is international—this cool, dark, and cozy cellar restaurant even serves Asian dishes. There's also an extensive wine list. ✗ 85 Tunnel Rd., ☎ 704/253–5285. Reservations advised. AE, MC, V. No lunch Tues.–Sat.

DINING AND LODGING

$$$$ **Richmond Hill Inn.** Once a private residence, this elegant Victorian man-
★   sion is on the National Register of Historic Places. Rooms in the mansion feature canopy beds, Victorian sofas and other antiques, while the
more modern cottages have contemporary pine poster beds. Gabrielle's
(reservations advised, jacket required), named for the former mistress
of the house—wife of congressman and ambassador Richmond Pear-
son—is known for innovative cuisine such as grilled medallions of antelope with wild boar sausage; the restaurant is only open to the public
for dinner and Sunday brunch. ☏ *87 Richmond Hill Dr., 28806,* ☎
704/252–7313 or 800/545–9238, FAX *704/252–8726. 12 rooms, 9 cottages. Restaurant, croquet, meeting rooms. AE, MC, V.*

LODGING

$$$$ **Grove Park Inn.** This is Asheville's premier resort, and it's just as beau-
★   tiful and exciting as it was the day it opened in 1913. The guest list
has included Henry Ford, Thomas Edison, Harvey Firestone, and Warren G. Harding. Novelist F. Scott Fitzgerald stayed here while his wife,
Zelda, was in a nearby sanitarium. In the past five years the hotel has
been completely renovated. The two newer wings are in keeping with
the original design. ☏ *290 Macon Ave., 28804,* ☎ *704/252–2711 or
800/438–5800,* FAX *704/253–7053 (guests) or 704/252–6102 (reservations). 486 rooms, 24 suites. 4 restaurants, 2 pools, sauna, hot tub,
18-hole golf course, 12 tennis courts, health club, racquetball, children's
programs, meeting rooms, airport shuttle. AE, D, DC, MC, V.*

$$$$ **Haywood Park Hotel.** Imagine yourself the star in "Are You Being
Served?" at this downtown contemporary hotel that was once a department store. Twenty-Three Page, the hotel's elegant restaurant,
serves seafood and game, and a free Continental breakfast is delivered
to your room. A shopping galleria adjoins the property. ☏ *One Battery Park Ave., 28801,* ☎ *704/252–2522 or 800/228–2522,* FAX
*704/253–0481. 33 rooms, some with refrigerator and whirlpool bath.
2 restaurants, sauna, exercise room. AE, D, DC, MC, V.*

$$$ **Quality Inn Biltmore.** Built on the grounds of the old Biltmore Dairy,
this hotel is especially convenient for Biltmore Estate visitors. It is at-
tached to the Biltmore Dairy Bar, a popular restaurant that offers
sandwiches and ice cream, and adjacent to the Criterion Grill, a full-
service restaurant and lounge. ☏ *115 Hendersonville Rd., 28803,* ☎
704/274–1800 or 800/221–2222, FAX *704/274–5960. 160 rooms.
Pool, meeting rooms. AE, D, DC, MC, V.*

$$–$$$ **Cedar Crest Victorian Inn.** This beautiful cottage was constructed by
Biltmore craftsmen as a private residence around the turn of the cen-
tury. Lovingly restored as a bed-and-breakfast inn, it's filled with Vic-
torian antiques. Guests are treated to afternoon tea; evening coffee or
chocolate; and a breakfast of fruit, pastry, and coffee. ☏ *674 Biltmore
Ave., 28803,* ☎ *704/252–1389 or 800/252–0310,* FAX *704/252–7667.
13 rooms. AE, MC, V.*

$$–$$$ **Hampton Inn.** Guests can swim in the enclosed pool and then relax be-
side the fire in the lobby at this economy motel off I–26 that's conve-
nient to downtown. Some guest rooms have whirlpool baths. ☏ *One
Rocky Ridge Rd., 28806,* ☎ *704/667–2022 or 800/426–7866,* FAX
*704/665–9680. 121 rooms. Pool, sauna, exercise room, airport shut-
tle. AE, D, DC, MC, V.*

Banner Elk

DINING

$$$ **Heidi's Swiss Inn.** Authentic Swiss-German cuisine is served up at this unique mountain farmhouse-turned-restaurant. ✗ *Rte. 184,* ☎ *704/898–5020. Reservations required. D, MC, V. No lunch. Closed Sun.–Mon.*

$$$ **Stonewalls.** This contemporary rustic restaurant enjoys one of the best views of Beech Mountain. Fare includes steak, prime rib, fresh seafood, chicken, and homemade desserts. ✗ *Hwy. 194,* ☎ *704/898–5550. No reservations. AE, D, MC, V. No lunch.*

LODGING

$$$ **Beech Alpen Inn.** Guests have a view of the slopes or the Blue Ridge Mountains at this friendly country inn. Some rooms have fireplaces. A Continental breakfast is included in the rate. ☎ *700 Beech Mountain Pkwy., Banner Elk 28604,* ☎ *704/387–2252. 25 rooms. AE, MC, V.*

Blowing Rock

DINING AND LODGING

$$$$ **Hound Ears Club.** This Alpine inn, overlooking Grandfather Mountain and a lush golf course, offers comfortable, well-kept rooms dressed in Waverly print fabrics. From April through October, the room rate includes breakfast and dinner. ☎ *Off NC 105, 6 mi from Boone; Box 188, 28605,* ☎ *704/963–4321,* FAX *704/963–8030. 29 rooms. Restaurant, pool, 18-hole golf course, tennis court. AE, MC, V.*

$$$–$$$$ **Chetola Resort.** This small resort of about 70 acres grew out of a turn-of-the-century stone-and-wood lodge that overlooks Chetola Lake. The original building now houses the resort's restaurant and meeting rooms and is adjacent to the 1988 lodge, which contains the accommodations. The best rooms have balconies facing the lake, and there are whirlpools in the suites. The property adjoins Moses Cone H. Park, part of the Blue Ridge Parkway system, with hiking trails and riding facilities. ☎ *Box 17, 28605,* ☎ *704/295–9301 or 800/243–8652,* FAX *704/295–5529. 37 rooms, 5 suites. Restaurant, indoor pool, hot tub, sauna, 2 tennis courts, exercise room, hiking, racquetball, boating, meeting rooms. AE, D, MC, V.*

$$$ **Green Park Inn.** This 100-year-plus Victorian charmer on the eastern continental divide offers spacious rooms, wide porches with rocking chairs, and large public rooms decorated in greens and maroons. The bilevel restaurant has won high praise for its French-inspired cuisine and extensive walk-through wine cellar. ☎ *U.S. 321, Box 7, 28605,* ☎ FAX *704/295–3141 or 800/852–2462. 85 rooms. Pool, 18-hole golf course, 4 tennis courts, meeting rooms. AE, D, MC, V.*

Boone

DINING

$$ **Mike's Inland Seafood.** Calabash-style (lightly battered and fried) or broiled, the seafood here couldn't taste better if it were served at the ocean. (There's another one in Banner Elk.) ✗ *U.S. 321, Boone,* ☎ *704/262–5605. Reservations accepted. AE, DC, MC, V. Closed Mon.*

$$ **Shadrack's.** Barbecue and seafood are featured at this all-you-can-eat buffet. Patrons also love the live music and square dancing. This is a fun place for a family meal. ✗ *1980 Blowing Rock Rd.,* ☎ *704/264–1737. Reservations advised. D, MC, V.* ☉ *Fri.–Sat. dinner only, Thurs.–Sat. dinner during summer.*

DINING AND LODGING

$$–$$$ Smoketree Lodge. Enjoy grand views of Grandfather Mountain, indoor swimming, and great food at this mountain inn near the ski slopes with fully equipped efficiencies. ☎ *Hwy. 105, Box 3407, 28607,* ☎ *704/963–6505 or 800/843–5581 in NC,* FAX *704/963–7815. 40 units. Restaurant, picnic area, indoor pool, hot tub, sauna, exercise room, recreation room, coin laundry. AE, D, MC, V.*

$$ Broyhill Inn. Though primarily a conference center, this contemporary hotel on the ASU campus is attractive to individual travelers who enjoy a university atmosphere. The dining room offers a great view of the mountains and hearty Southern cuisine. ☎ *775 Bodenheimer Dr., 28607,* ☎ *704/262–2204 or 800/951–6048,* FAX *704/262–2946. 76 rooms, 7 suites. Restaurant, meeting rooms. AE, MC, V.*

Linville

DINING AND LODGING

$$$$ Eseeola Lodge and Restaurant. Built in the 1880s, this lodge is the cornerstone of Linville. Rich chestnut paneling and stonework grace the interior rooms. ☎ *U.S. 221, 28646,* ☎ *704/733–4311,* FAX *704/733–3227. 28 rooms. Restaurant, lounge, pool, 18-hole golf course, 8 tennis courts. MC, V. Closed Labor Day–May.*

Little Switzerland

DINING AND LODGING

$$$–$$$$ Switzerland Inn and Chalet Restaurant. This Swiss-style lodge overlooking the mountains offers lodge rooms, parlor-bedroom suites, and a lovely honeymoon cottage with a fireplace. A full breakfast served in the restaurant is included in the room rate. The prime rib and seafood buffet served each Friday night is a big draw. ☎ *MM 334, off Blue Ridge Pkwy., Box 399, 28749,* ☎ *704/765–2153 or 800/654–4026,* FAX *704/765–0049. 66 rooms. Pool, lounge, 2 tennis courts, shuffleboard, 6 shops. AE, D, MC, V. Closed Nov.–Apr. Dining reservations accepted for 5 or more.*

Valle Crucis

DINING AND LODGING

$$$$ Mast Farm Inn. You can turn back the clock and still enjoy modern amenities at this charming pastoral inn. Guests have a choice of rooms in the farmhouse or in the log out-buildings. Breakfast and dinner are included in the rate. ☎ *Box 704, 28691,* ☎ *704/963–5857,* FAX *704/963–6404. 12 rooms. Closed early Mar.–late Apr., Dec., and weekdays in Nov. MC, V.*

North Carolina High Country Essentials

Arriving and Departing, Getting Around

BY BUS

Greyhound Lines (☎ 704/253–5353 or 800/231–2222) serves Asheville.

BY CAR

I–40 runs east and west through Asheville. I–26 runs from Charleston, SC, to Asheville. I–240 forms a perimeter around the city. U.S. 23–19A is a major north and west route. The Blue Ridge Parkway runs northeast from Great Smoky Mountains National Park to Shenandoah National Park in Virginia. U.S. 221 runs north from Little Switzerland to the Virginia border through Blowing Rock and Boone and intersects I–40 at Marion. U.S. 321 intersects I–40 at Hickory and heads to Blowing Rock/Boone.

Asheville Regional Airport (☎ 704/684–2226) is served by American Eagle, Atlantic Southeast Airlines, ComAir, Delta, and USAir. USAir Express (☎ 800/428–4322) serves the **Hickory Airport,** about 40 miles from Blowing Rock.

Guided Tours
Travel Professionals, Inc. (☎ 704/298–3438), **Western Carolina Tours** (☎ 704/254–4603), and **Young Transportation** (☎ 704/258–0084 or 800/622–5444) provide group tours of Asheville.
A brochure entitled **"The Asheville Urban Trail"** (available at the Downtown Welcome Center and many other locations) provides a self-guided walking tour. **Tour Services of Historic Asheville** (☎ 704/255–1093) conducts 2-hour walking tours of downtown, March–December; tours leave from Pack Place. The **Preservation Society of Asheville** has produced a walking tour cassette ($10), available at Pack Place.

Important Addresses and Numbers
EMERGENCIES
Dial 911 for **police** and **ambulance,** or head to **Watauga Medical Center** (☎ 704/262–4100) in Boone or **Cannon Memorial Hospital** (☎ 704/898–5111) in Banner Elk for emergency medical attention.

RADIO STATIONS
AM: WZQR 1350, country; WFGW 1010, Christian; WSKY 1230, talk. **FM:** WCQS 88.1, National Public Radio; WSPA 98.9, easy listening; WMIT 106.9, Christian; WKSF 99.9, country.

VISITOR INFORMATION
The **Visitor Information Center** (151 Haywood St., Asheville 28801, ☎ 704/258–6100) and the **Asheville Travel and Tourism Office** (Box 1010, Asheville 28802, ☎ 800/257–1300). The **Downtown Welcome Center** (14 Battery Park, Asheville, ☎ 704/255–1093) can answer questions and provide maps. **North Carolina High Country Host** (1701 Blowing Rock Rd., Boone 28607, ☎ 704/264–1299 or 800/438–7500).

4 South Carolina

South Carolina's scenic Low Country shoreline is punctuated by the lively port city of Charleston, decked out with fine museums, and the recreational resorts of Myrtle Beach and Hilton Head at each end of the coast. The state capital of Columbia is set in the fertile interior of the state, which stretches toward the Blue Ridge Mountains. Also to the west are the rolling fields of Thoroughbred country and Upcountry South Carolina, at the northwestern tip of the state, noted for incredible mountain scenery and whitewater rafting.

By Edgar and
Patricia
Cheatham

Updated by
Patricia
Cheatham

FROM ITS LOW COUNTRY SHORELINE, with wide sand beaches, spacious bays, and forests of palmettos and moss-strewn live oaks, South Carolina extends into an undulating interior region rich with fertile farmlands, then reaches toward the Blue Ridge Mountains, studded with scenic lakes, forests, and wilderness hideaways. What this smallest of Southern states lacks in land area it makes up for in diversity.

The historic port city of Charleston, lovingly preserved, links past with present. Many of its treasured double-galleried antebellum homes are now authentically furnished house museums. Culturally vibrant, the city nurtures theater, dance, music, and visual arts, showcased each spring during the internationally acclaimed Spoleto Festival USA.

Myrtle Beach is the hub of the Grand Strand, a 60-mile stretch of wide golden-sand beaches and recreational activities (especially golf, a top attraction throughout the state). To the south, tasteful, low-key Hilton Head—a sea island tucked between the Intracoastal Waterway and the ocean and divided into several sophisticated, self-contained resorts— also offers beautiful beaches and wonderful golf and tennis. Nearby is the port city of Beaufort (pronounced *Bew*fort), where the most re- warding activity is wandering the lovely streets dotted with preserved 18th-century homes, live oaks, and palmettos.

Columbia, the state capital, is a lively (and, of course, historic) city cleaved by a rushing river. In addition to several museums and a good minor- league baseball team, the city has one of the country's top zoos. It is also home to the State Museum and the fine new Koger Center for Per- forming Arts. Nearby lakes and state parks offer abundant outdoor recreation and first-rate fishing.

Thoroughbred Country, centered around the town of Aiken, is a peace- ful area of rolling pastures where top race horses are trained. It is also notable for magnificent mansions built by wealthy Northerners who vacationed here at the turn of the century. Upcountry South Carolina, at the northwestern tip of the state, is less visited than the rest of the state but well repays time spent there with dramatic mountain scenery, excellent hiking, and challenging white-water rafting. Scattered along SC 11 are premier parks, some of which offer luxurious accommoda- tions.

Since 1670, when the British established the first permanent European settlement at Charleston, the history of the Palmetto State has been char- acterized by periods of great prosperity contrasted with eras of dismal depression. This vibrant past is preserved in cherished traditions and an enduring belief in family, which give resonance to the optimism and vitality of today's South Carolina.

CHARLESTON

At first glimpse, Charleston resembles an 18th-century etching come to life. Its low-profile skyline is punctuated with the spires and steeples of 181 churches, representing 25 denominations (Charleston was known for its religious freedom). Parts of the city appear stopped in time because block after block of old downtown structures have been preserved and restored for both residential and commercial use. Charleston has survived three centuries of epidemics, earthquakes, fires, and hurricanes, and it is today one of the South's best-preserved cities.

Along the Battery, on the point of a narrow peninsula bounded by the Ashley and Cooper rivers, handsome mansions in the "Charleston style," surrounded by gardens, face the harbor. Their distinctive look is reminiscent of the West Indies, and for good reason. Before coming to the Carolinas in the late 17th century, many early British colonists had first settled on Barbados and other Caribbean islands where against the warm and humid climate they'd built houses with high ceilings and broad piazzas at each level, to catch the sea breezes. In Charleston, they adapted these designs for other practical reasons. One new type—narrow two- to four-story houses (called single houses) built at right angles to the street—emerged partly because buildings were taxed according to frontage length.

Each year, from mid-March to mid-April, the Historic Charleston Foundation's Festival of Homes and Gardens conducts tours of private homes, gardens, and churches, and celebrates with symphony galas in stately drawing rooms, plantation oyster roasts, and candlelight tours. Each year in May and June, the renowned Spoleto Festival USA and Piccolo Spoleto take place, when hundreds of local and international artists, musicians, and other performers fill the city with sound and spectacle.

Exploring

Numbers in the margin correspond to points of interest on the Charleston map.

If you have just a day to spend in Charleston, you might begin with a carriage tour for the tidbits of history and humor that the driver-guides provide as they take you through the main streets of the historic district. This is the best way to decide where to go on your own. Next, browse through the shops of the Old Market area, where most of the carriage tours begin and end. After that, walk south along East Bay Street, past Rainbow Row (a row of pastel-painted houses near Tradd Street), or along any side streets on your way to your choice of the area's four house museums. Spend the rest of the day wandering the cool, palmetto-shaded streets, discovering all the little surprises that reveal themselves only to those who seek them out.

If you have more time (and you really should), expand your itinerary by adding more sights within the same area; by adding an excursion to the Shops at Charleston Place or along King Street; by including the Marion Square area, which has an excellent art museum and a house museum; or by adding trips to magnificent plantations and gardens west of the Ashley River or to major historic sites east of the Cooper. There are also boat excursions and some very nice beaches.

For a good overview of the city before you begin touring, drop by the **①** **Visitor Information Center,** where there's parking (free for two hours; 50¢ per hour thereafter). Take time to see *Forever Charleston,* a multimedia presentation on the city. *375 Meeting St.,* ☎ *803/853–8000.* ☞ *$2.50 adults, $2 senior citizens, $1 children 6–12, under 6 free. Shown daily 9–5 on the ½ hour.* ☉ *Mar.–Oct., daily 8:30–5:30; Nov.–Feb., daily 8:30–5.*

The Historic District

On Meeting Street, housed in a $6 million contemporary complex, is **★ ②** the oldest city museum in the United States. The **Charleston Museum,**

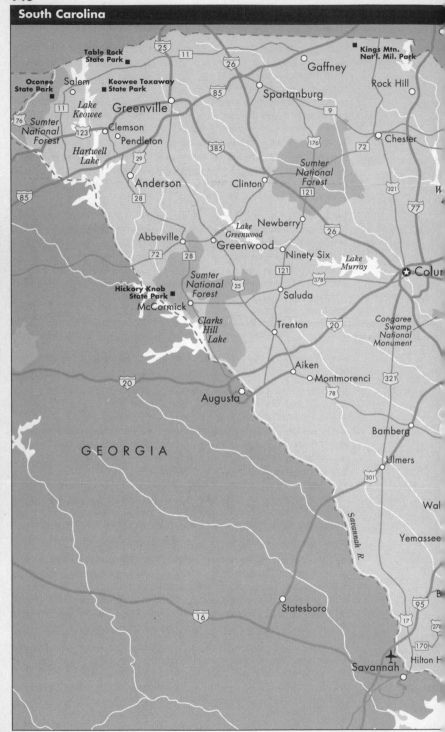

Table Rock
State Park

Kings Mtn.
Nat'l. Mil. Park

Gaffney

Oconee
State Park

Salem

Keowee Toxaway
State Park

Rock Hill

Spartanburg

Greenville

Lake
Keowee

Clemson

Pendleton

Sumter
National
Forest

Hartwell
Lake

Chester

Sumter
National
Forest

Anderson

Clinton

Abbeville

Lake
Greenwood

Newberry

Greenwood

Ninety Six

Lake
Murray

Colu

Sumter
National
Forest

Hickory Knob
State Park

McCormick

Saluda

Trenton

Congaree
Swamp
National
Monument

Clarks
Hill
Lake

Aiken

Montmorenci

Augusta

Bamberg

GEORGIA

Ulmers

Wal

Savannah R.

Yemassee

Statesboro

Hilton H

Savannah

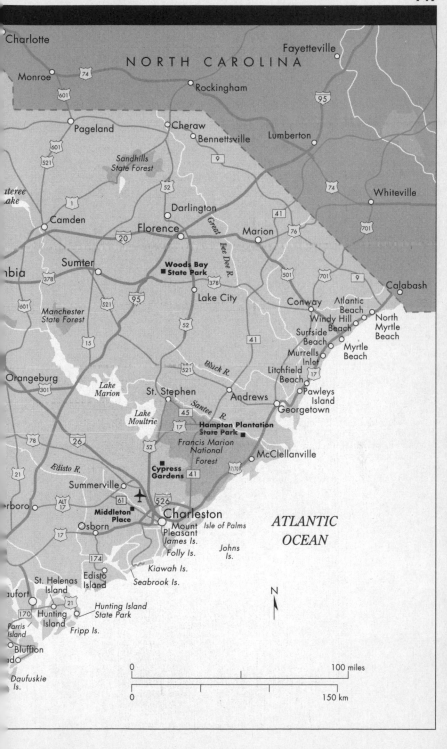

NORTH CAROLINA

Charlotte

Monroe

Fayetteville

Rockingham

74

601

95

Pageland

Cheraw

Bennettsville

Lumberton

601

9

521

Sandhills State Forest

52

Whiteville

1

Darlington

41

74

701

Camden

Florence

Marion

76

20

Great Pee Dee R.

iteree ake

bia

Sumter

Woods Bay State Park

501

701

9

Calabash

378

378

Lake City

Conway

Atlantic Beach

Windy Hill Beach

North Myrtle Beach

601

95

521

52

Manchester State Forest

15

41

Surfside Beach

Myrtle Beach

Murrells Inlet

521

Buck R.

Litchfield Beach

17

Orangeburg

St. Stephen

Santee R.

Andrews

Pawleys Island

Georgetown

301

Lake Marion

45

17

Hampton Plantation State Park

Lake Moultrie

52

Francis Marion National Forest

McClellanville

78

26

Cypress Gardens

41

17/17

Edisto R.

21

Summerville

rboro

ALT 17

61

526

Middleton Place

Osborn

Charleston

Mount Pleasant

Isle of Palms

17

James Is.

Johns Is.

ATLANTIC OCEAN

174

Folly Is.

Edisto Island

Kiawah Is.

St. Helenas Island

Seabrook Is.

ufort

21

N

170

Hunting Island

Hunting Island State Park

Parris Island

ado

Fripp Is.

Bluffton

Daufuskie Is.

0   100 miles

0   150 km

150

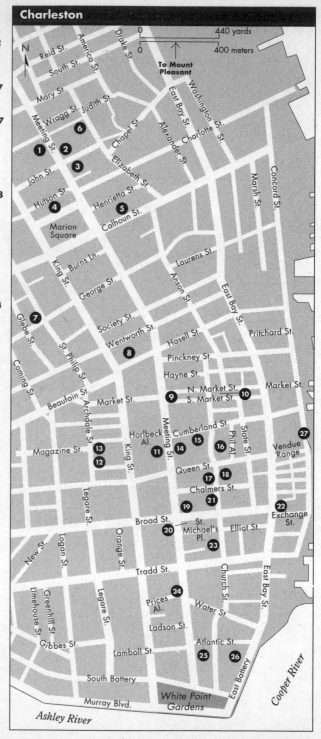

Charleston

founded in 1773, is especially strong on South Carolina decorative arts. The 500,000 items in the collection—in addition to Charleston silver, fashions, toys, snuff boxes, etc.—include objects relating to natural history, archaeology, and ornithology. Three historic homes—the Joseph Manigault Mansion *(see below)*, the Aiken–Rhett House *(see below)*, and the Heyward–Washington House *(see below)*—are part of the museum. *360 Meeting St.,* ☎ *803/722–2996.* ☛ *$6 adults, $3 children 3–12, under 3 free.* ☛ *Combination ticket for museum and houses $15; for just the three houses, $10.* ⊙ *Mon.–Sat. 9–5, Sun. 1–5.*

❸ Across John Street is one of Charleston's fine house museums, and a National Historic Landmark, the **Joseph Manigault Mansion.** An outstanding example of Adam-style architecture, it was designed by Charleston architect Gabriel Manigault in 1803 and is noted for its carved-wood mantels and elaborate plasterwork. Furnishings are British, French, and Charleston antiques, including rare tricolor Wedgwood pieces. *350 Meeting St.,* ☎ *803/723–2926.* ☛ *$6 adults, $3 children 3–12, under 3 free (for combination ticket* see *Charleston Museum,* above*).* ⊙ *Mon.–Sat. 10–5, Sun. 1–5.*

❹ Walk down Meeting Street to Marion Square. Facing the square is the **Old Citadel Building,** built in 1822 to house state troops and arms. Here began the famed South Carolina Military College—the Citadel—now on the Ashley River.

❺ Walk down a block, cross Meeting, and turn east to 110 Calhoun Street to visit **Emanuel African Methodist Episcopal Church,** home of the South's oldest AME congregation, which had its beginnings in 1818. The church was closed in 1822 when authorities learned that Denmark Vesey used the sanctuary to plan his slave insurrection. It was reopened in 1865 at the present site. *Call 803/722–2561 in advance for tour.* ⊙ *Daily 9–4.*

❻ Walk north along Elizabeth Street to see the **Aiken–Rhett House,** the newest addition to the Charleston Museum complex. The stately 1819 mansion, residence of South Carolina Governor William Aiken Jr. from 1833–87, was headquarters of Confederate General P.G.T. Beauregard during his 1864 Civil War defense of Charleston. Original wallpapers, paint colors, and some furnishings are displayed. House, kitchen, slave quarters, stable, and outbuildings are maintained much as they were when the Aiken and Rhett families lived there. *48 Elizabeth St.,* ☎ *803/723–1159.* ☛ *$6 adults, $3 children 3–12, under 3 free (for combination ticket,* see *Charleston Museum,* above*).* ⊙ *Mon.–Sat. 10–5, Sun. 1–5.*

❼ If you've left your car at the visitor center, return now to retrieve it. From here proceed to the lovely **College of Charleston** (founded in 1770), whose graceful main building (1828) was designed by Philadelphia architect William Strickland. The large campus is located at the corner of George and St. Philip's streets. Within the college is the **Avery Research Center for African-American History and Culture,** which traces the heritage of South Carolina Low Country African-Americans. *125 Bull St.,* ☎ *803/727–2009.* ☛ *Free.* ⊙ *Reading room/archives weekdays 1–4:30 or by appointment. Group tours weekdays 2–4 or by appointment.*

❽ Next you can make a shopping tour of King Street, or go directly to the market area and head for one of the many parking garages. Now is the time for a carriage tour, many of which leave from here (*see* Guided Tours, *below*). Our tour picks up again at **Congregation Beth Elohim** (90 Hasell St.), considered one of the nation's finest examples of Greek

Revival architecture. It was constructed in 1840 to replace an earlier temple—the birthplace of American Reform Judaism in 1824—that was destroyed by fire. ☎ *803/723–1090.* ⊘ *Weekdays 10–noon.*

9 Follow Meeting Street south to Market Street, and at the intersection on the left you'll see **Market Hall,** a National Historic Landmark built in 1841 and modeled after the Temple of Nike in Athens. Here you'll find the **Confederate Museum** (88 Meeting St., ☎ 803/723–1541), where the Daughters of the Confederacy preserve and display flags, uniforms, swords, and other memorabilia. The museum is currently closed for renovation and may remain so through 1996; however, costumed guides sometimes stand outside and describe the facility for visitors.

10 Between Market Hall and East Bay Street is **Old City Market,** a series of low sheds that once housed produce and fish markets. The area now has restaurants and shops, along with vegetable and fruit vendors and local "basket ladies" busy weaving and selling distinctive sweet-grass, pine-straw, and palmetto-leaf baskets—a craft inherited from their West African ancestors. *Usually* ⊘ *Daily 9 AM–sunset.*

TIME OUT   This is a great area for some serious time out. Pick up batches of Charleston's famed benne (sesame) seed wafers at **Olde Colony Bakery** (280 King St., ☎ 803/722–2147). Choose from 12 gourmet food stands in the **Gourmetisserie** (☎ 803/722–4455) in the Market Square shopping complex across South Market Street. Or indulge the urge to munch on oysters on the half-shell, steamed mussels, and clams at **A.W. Shucks** (☎ 803/723–1151) in nearby State Street Market.

Across the street is the **Omni Hotel at Charleston Place** (130 Market St.). You might wander over to peer at the lobby or have cocktails or tea in the intimate Lobby Lounge. The city's only world-class hotel is flanked by a four-story complex of upscale boutiques and specialty shops (*see* Shopping, *below*).

11 Heading south on Meeting Street, see the **Gibbes Museum of Art.** Its collection of American art includes notable 18th- and 19th-century portraits of Carolinians and an outstanding group of more than 400 miniature portraits. Don't miss the miniature rooms—intricately detailed with fabrics and furnishings and nicely displayed in shadow boxes inset in dark-paneled walls—or the Tiffany-style stained-glass dome in the rotunda. *135 Meeting St.,* ☎ *803/722–2706.* ☛ *$5 adults, $4 senior citizens, $3 children 6–18, children under 6 free.* ⊘ *Tues.–Sat. 10–5, Sun. and Mon. 1–5.*

12 For a detour, head south on Meeting Street to Queen Street, then west to Archdale. At no. 8 is the **Unitarian Church,** begun in 1772 and completed in 1787. The building was remodeled in the mid-19th century after plans inspired by the Chapel of Henry VII in Westminster Abbey, including the addition of a Gothic fan-tracery ceiling. *8 Archdale St.,* ☎ *803/723–4617 (weekdays 8:30–2:30). Call ahead for visiting hours.*

13 At the corner of Clifford and Archdale streets is the Greek Revival **St. John's Lutheran Church,** built in 1817 for a congregation that celebrated its 250th anniversary in 1992. Notice the fine craftsmanship in the delicate wrought-iron gates and fence. Organ aficionados may be interested in the 1823 Thomas Hall organ case. *5 Clifford St.,* ☎ *803/723–2426.* ⊘ *Weekdays 9:30–3 with advance arrangement.*

14 Back at Meeting Street, across from the Gibbes is the unusual Romanesque **Circular Congregational Church,** its corners rounded off, it's said, so the devil would have no place to hide. The church is simple but pretty with a beamed, vaulted ceiling. *150 Meeting St.,* ☎ *803/577–6400. Tours given Apr.–Oct., weekdays 9–1.*

⓯ On Cumberland Street, one of Charleston's few remaining cobblestone thoroughfares, is the **Old Powder Magazine,** built in 1713, used during the Revolutionary War, and now a museum with costumes, furniture, armor, and other artifacts from 18th-century Charleston. Because the Historic Charleston Foundation is currently restoring the building, visitors should call ahead for information on tours, admission, and opening hours. *79 Cumberland St.,* ☎ *803/723–1623.* ☉ *By appointment.*

⓰ Around the corner on Church Street you come to the graceful late-Georgian **St. Philip's Episcopal Church,** the second on the site, built in 1838 and restored in 1994. In its serene graveyard are buried some legendary native sons, including statesman John C. Calhoun and DuBose Heyward, the author of *Porgy. 146 Church St.,* ☎ *803/722–7734.* ☉ *By appointment.*

⓱ The **Dock Street Theatre,** across Queen Street, was built on the site of one of the nation's first playhouses. It combines the reconstructed early Georgian playhouse and the preserved Old Planter's Hotel (circa 1809). *135 Church St.,* ☎ *803/720–3968.* ☛ *Free tours; call ahead to check ticket prices for performances.* ☉ *Weekdays 10–4.*

⓲ Across the street is the Gothic-style **French Protestant (Huguenot) Church,** the only one in the country still using the original Huguenot liturgy, which can be heard in a special service held each spring. *110 Church St.,* ☎ *803/722–4385. Donations accepted.* ☉ *Weekdays 10–12:30 and 2–4.*

The intersection of Meeting and Broad streets is known as the Four Corners of Law, representing federal, state, city, and religious jurisdiction. ⓳ In the graceful 1801 **City Hall,** on the northeast corner, the second-floor Council Chamber has interesting historical displays and fine portraits, including John Trumbull's 1791 portrait of George Washington and Samuel F. B. Morse's likeness of James Monroe. On the southwest corner, the Old U.S. Post Office building now houses a museum depicting the area's postal history. *80 Broad St.,* ☎ *803/577–6970.* ☛ *Free.* ☉ *Weekdays 10–5.*

⓴ On the last corner is **St. Michael's Episcopal Church,** modeled after London's St. Martin's-in-the-Fields. Completed in 1761, this is Charleston's oldest surviving church. Its steeple clock and bells were imported from England in 1764. *14 St. Michael's Alley,* ☎ *803/723–0603.* ☉ *Weekdays 9–5, Sat. 9–noon.*

From the Four Corners, head east down Broad Street to Church Street. ㉑ The **American Military Museum** displays hundreds of uniforms and artifacts from all branches of service, dating from the Revolutionary War. *40 Pinckney St.,* ☎ *803/723–9620.* ☛ *$2 adults, $1 children under 12, uniformed military personnel free.* ☉ *Mon.–Sat. 10–6, Sun. 1–6.*

㉒ At the corner of East Bay Street stands the **Old Exchange Building/Provost Dungeon,** originally a customs house. The dungeon was used by the British during the Revolutionary War; today, a tableau of lifelike manikins recalls this era. *122 East Bay St.,* ☎ *803/792–5020.* ☛ *$4 adults, $3.50 senior citizens, $2.50 children 7–12, children under 7 free..* ☉ *Daily 9–5.*

Return to Church Street and continue south to the neighborhood known as Cabbage Row, the home of Dubose Heyward and an area central to Charleston's African-American history. At 87 Church Street

㉓   is the **Heyward–Washington House,** built in 1772 by rice king Daniel Heyward, which was also the setting for Dubose Heyward's *Porgy.* President George Washington stayed here during his 1791 visit. The mansion is full of fine period furnishings by such local craftsmen as Thomas Elfe, and its restored 18th-century kitchen is the only one in Charleston open to visitors. ☎ *803/722–0354.* ☛ *$6 adults, $3 children 3–12, under 3 free (for combination ticket, see Charleston Museum, above.)* ⊙ *Mon.–Sat. 10–5, Sun. 1–5.*

★ ㉔   At 51 Meeting Street is the **Nathaniel Russell House,** headquarters of the Historic Charleston Foundation. Built in 1808, it is one of the nation's finest examples of Adams-style architecture. The interior is notable for its ornate detailing, its lavish period furnishings, and a "flying" circular staircase that spirals three stories with no apparent support. ☎ *803/724–8481.* ☛ *$6 adults, children under 7 free; combination ticket with the Edmonston–Alston House, $10.* ⊙ *Mon.–Sat. 10–5, Sun. 2–5.*

㉕   Continuing south, you'll come into an area where somewhat more lavish mansions reflect the wealth of a later era. The **Calhoun Mansion,** at 16 Meeting Street, is opulent by Charleston standards, an interesting example of Victorian taste. Built in 1876, it's notable for ornate plasterwork, fine wood moldings, and a 75-foot domed ceiling. ☎ *803/722–8205.* ☛ *$10 adults, $5 children 6–16, children under 6 free.* ⊙ *Thurs.–Sun. 10–4. Closed Jan.*

㉖   The imposing **Edmondston–Alston House,** with commanding views of Charleston Harbor, was built in 1825 in the late Federal style and transformed into a Greek Revival structure during the 1840s. It is tastefully furnished with antiques, portraits, Piranesi prints, silver, and fine china. *21 E. Battery,* ☎ *803/722–7171 or 803/556–6020.* ☛ *$6 adults, children under 7 free; combination ticket with Nathaniel Russell House, $10.* ⊙ *Tues.–Sat. 10–5, Sun.–Mon. 1:30–5.*

㉗   After all this serious sightseeing, relax in **White Point Gardens,** on Battery Point, facing the harbor, a tranquil spot shaded by palmettos and graceful oaks. Another option is **Waterfront Park,** on the Cooper River in the historic district. It offers beautiful river views, fountains, landscaped gardens, and a fishing pier. ⊙ *Daily 6 AM–midnight.*

East of the Cooper River

Across the Cooper River Bridges, via U.S. 17, is the town of **Mount Pleasant,** named not for anything in the area resembling so much as a hillock, but for a plantation in England from which a number of the area's settlers hailed. Here, along Shem Creek, where the local fishing fleet brings in the daily catch, seafood restaurants attract visitors and

★   locals alike. **Patriots Point,** the world's largest naval and maritime museum, and now home to the Medal of Honor Society, is also in Mount Pleasant. Berthed here are the aircraft carrier *Yorktown,* the World War II submarine *Clamagore,* the destroyer *Laffey,* the nuclear merchant ship *Savannah,* and the cutter *Ingham,* responsible for sinking a U-boat during World War II. Tours are offered in all vessels, the film *The Fighting Lady* is shown regularly aboard the *Yorktown,* and there is a Vietnam exhibit. *Foot of Cooper River Bridges,* ☎ *803/884–2727.* ☛ *$8 adults, $7 senior citizens and active military personnel, $4 children 6–12.* ⊙ *Labor Day–Mar., daily 9–6:30; Apr.–Labor Day, daily 9–7:30.*

★   Fort Sumter Tours' boats leave from the docks here and from Charleston's Municipal Marina for 2¼-hour cruises that include a stop at **Fort Sumter National Monument,** on a man-made island in the harbor. ☎

803/722–1691. Cost: $9 adults, $4.50 children 6–11, under 6 free.
Tours leave from Municipal Marina daily at 9:30, noon, and 2:30. Tours
leave from Patriots Point daily at 10:45 and 1:30; Apr.–Labor Day,
there is an additional tour at 4 pm.

It was at Fort Sumter that the first shot of the Civil War was fired on
April 12, 1861, when Confederate forces at Fort Johnson (now defunct)
across the way opened fire. After a 34-hour bombardment Union
forces surrendered, and Confederate troops occupied Sumter, which
became a symbol of Southern resistance. The Confederacy held the fort—
despite almost continual bombardment—for nearly four years, and when
it was finally evacuated it was a heap of rubble. Today, National Park
Service rangers conduct free guided tours of the restored structure, which
includes a museum (☎ 803/883–3123; ☛ Free) with historical displays
and dioramas.

Continuing north out of Mount Pleasant along U.S. 17, you'll find "basket ladies" at roadside stands. If you have the heart to bargain, you
may be able to purchase the baskets at somewhat lower prices than in
Charleston. SC 703 will take you to **Sullivan's Island** and **Fort Moultrie,** completed in 1809, the third fort on this site. Here Colonel William
Moultrie's South Carolinians repelled a British assault in one of the
first Patriot victories of the Revolutionary War. The interior has been
restored. A film and slide show tell the history of the fort. *W. Middle
St., Sullivan's Island,* ☎ *803/883–3123.* ☛ *Free.* ☉ *Memorial Day–Labor
Day, daily 9–6; Labor Day–Memorial Day, daily 9–5.*

Back on U.S. 17, about 8 miles out of Charleston, is the 1681 **Boone
Hall Plantation,** approached via one of the South's most majestic avenues of oaks. The primary attraction is the grounds, with formal azalea and camellia gardens, as well as the original slave quarters—the
only "slave street" still intact in the Southeast—and the cotton-gin house
used in the made-for-television movies *North and South* and *Queen.*
Visitors may also tour the first floor of the classic columned mansion,
which was built in 1935 incorporating woodwork and flooring from
the original house. ☎ *803/884–4371.* ☛ *$7.50 adults, $6 senior citizens, $3 children 6–12, children under 6 free.* ☉ *Apr.–Labor Day,
Mon.–Sat. 8:30–6:30, Sun. 1–5; Labor Day–Mar., Mon.–Sat. 9–5, Sun.
1–4.*

West of the Ashley River

★ Vestiges of the Old South—and Charleston's beginnings—beckon as
you cross the Ashley River Bridge. Take SC 171 north to reach **Charles
Towne Landing State Park,** commemorating the site of the original
Charleston settlement, begun in 1670. There are a reconstructed village and fortifications, English park gardens with bicycle trails and walkways, and a replica 17th-century vessel moored in the creek. In the animal
park species native to the region three centuries ago roam freely. Bicycle and kayak rentals and cassette and tram tours are available.
1500 Old Towne Rd., ☎ *803/852–4200.* ☛ *$5 adults, $2.50 senior
citizens and children 6–14, children under 6 free.* ☉ *Memorial
Day–Labor Day, daily 9–6; Labor Day–Memorial Day, daily 9–5.*

★ Nine miles west of Charleston via the Ashley River Road (SC 61) is
Drayton Hall, built between 1738 and 1742. A National Historic Landmark, it is considered the nation's finest example of unspoiled Georgian–Palladian architecture. The mansion is the only plantation house
on the Ashley River to have survived the Civil War and serves as an
invaluable lesson in history as well as in architecture. It has been left
unfurnished to highlight the original plaster moldings, opulent hand-

carved woodwork, and other ornamental details. *3380 Ashley River Rd.,* ☎ *803/766–0188.* ☛ *$7 adults, $4 children 6–18, children under 6 free. Guided tours Mar.–Oct., daily 10–4; Nov.–Feb., daily 10–3.*

A mile or so farther north on Ashley River Road (SC 61) is **Magnolia Plantation and Gardens.** The 50-acre informal garden, begun in 1685, has a huge collection of azaleas and camellias and was proclaimed the "most beautiful garden in the world" by John Galsworthy. You can ride a tram for an overall tour with three stops. Nature lovers may canoe through the 125-acre Waterfowl Refuge, explore the 30-acre **Audubon Swamp Garden** along boardwalks and bridges, or walk or bicycle over 500 acres of wildlife trails. Tours of the manor house, built during the Reconstruction period, depict plantation life. You can also see the petting zoo and a mini-horse ranch. ☎ *803/571–1266.* ☛ *$9 adults, $8 senior citizens, $7 children 13–19, $4 children 4–12 (house tour $4 extra; swamp tour $3 extra; tram tour $3 extra; combination tour also available).* ☉ *Daily 8–5:30.*

Middleton Place, 4 miles farther north on SC 61, has the nation's oldest landscaped gardens, dating from 1741. Design highlights of the magnificent gardens—ablaze with camellias, magnolias, azaleas, roses, and flowers of all seasons—are the floral *allées,* terraced lawns, and ornamental lakes. Much of the mansion was destroyed during the Civil War, but the south wing has been restored and houses impressive collections of silver, furniture, paintings, and historic documents. The stableyard is a living outdoor museum: here craftspeople, using authentic tools and equipment, demonstrate spinning, blacksmithing, and other domestic skills from the plantation era. Farm animals, peacocks, and other creatures roam freely. The Middleton Place restaurant serves distinctive Low Country specialties for lunch daily; a gift shop features local arts, crafts, and souvenirs. ☎ *803/556–6020 or 800/782–3608.* ☛ *$10 adults, $5 children 4–12; house tours $6 extra.* ☉ *Daily 9–5; house tours Tues.–Sun. 10–4:30, Mon. 1:30–4:30.*

On the banks of the Old Santee Canal in Moncks Corner is the new **Old Santee Canal State Park,** reached via I–26 and Highway 52. You can explore on foot or take a canoe. There's also an interpretive center. *Rembert C. Dennis Blvd., Moncks Corner,* ☎ *803/899–5200.* ☛ *$3 per car.* ☉ *Daily 9–5, spring and summer until 6.*

The picturesque town of **Summerville,** about 25 miles northwest of Charleston via I–26 (Exit 199), is a pleasant place for a drive or stroll. Built by wealthy planters as an escape from hot-weather malaria, it's a treasure trove of mid-19th-century and Victorian buildings—many of which are listed in the National Register of Historic Places—with colorful gardens of camellias, azaleas, and wisteria. Streets often curve around tall pines, since a local ordinance prohibits cutting them down in this "Flowertown in the Pines." This is a good place for a bit of antiquing in attractive shops. Stop by the **Summerville Chamber of Commerce** (106 E. Doty Ave., Box 670, 29483, ☎ 803/873–2931) to get oriented; they're open weekdays 8:30–12:30 and 1:30–5, Saturday 10–3.

About 24 miles north of Charleston via U.S. 52 is **Cypress Gardens,** a swamp garden created from what was once the freshwater reserve of the vast Dean Hall rice plantation. Explore the inky waters by boat, or walk along paths lined with moss-draped cypress trees, azaleas, camellias, daffodils, wisteria, and dogwood. *3030 Cypress Gardens Rd., Moncks Corner,* ☎ *803/553–0515.* ☛ *$6 adults, $5 senior citizens, $2 children 6–16 (May 1–Feb. 14, $1 less).* ☉ *Daily 9–5.*

What to See and Do with Children

American Military Museum (*see* The Historic District *in* Exploring Charleston, *above*).

Boat Ride to Fort Sumter (*see* East of the Cooper River *in* Exploring Charleston, *above*).

Charles Towne Landing State Park (*see* West of the Ashley River *in* Exploring Charleston, *above*). Birds, alligators, bison, pumas, bears, wolves, and many other animals roam in natural environments. Children's Days are held during the last two weeks of December.

Charleston Museum (*see* The Historic District *in* Exploring Charleston, *above*). The Discover Me Room, designed just for children, has computers and other hands-on exhibits.

Magnolia Plantation and Gardens has a petting zoo and mini-horse ranch (*see* West of the Ashley River *in* Exploring Charleston, *above*).

Middleton Place (*see* West of the Ashley River *in* Exploring Charleston, *above*).

Palmetto Islands County Park. This family-oriented nature park has a Big Toy playground, a two-acre pond, a canoe trail, an observation tower, marsh boardwalks, and a recently added "water island." Bicycles, pedal boats, and canoes can be rented in season. *On U.S. 17N, ½ mi past Snee Farm, turn left onto Long Point Rd.,* ☎ *803/884–0832.* ☛ *$1.* ☉ *Apr., Sept., and Oct., daily 10–6; May–Aug., daily 10–7; Nov.–Mar., daily 10–5.*

Shelling. Kiawah Island has excellent shelling. If you're not staying at the private resort, you can shell at Beachwalker Park, the public beach at the west end of the island. ☎ *803/762–2172. Parking fee: $3.* ☉ *June–Aug., daily 10–7; May and Sept., daily 10–6; Apr. and Oct., weekends 10–6.*

Off the Beaten Path

Angel Oak. Among the continent's oldest and largest oak trees, this 1,500-year-old giant has a 25½-foot circumference and a 151-foot limb spread. *From SC 700 turn left onto Bohicket Rd.; after about ½ mi, turn right at sign and follow dirt road,* ☎ *803/559–3496.* ☛ *Free.* ☉ *Daily 9–5.*

Francis Marion National Forest. About 40 miles north of Charleston via U.S. 52, this site comprises 250,000 acres of swamps, vast oaks and pines, and little lakes thought to have been formed by meteors— a good place for picnicking, camping, boating, and swimming (☎ 803/336–3248). At the park's **Rembert Dennis Wildlife Center** (off U.S. 52 in Bonneau, ☎ 803/825–3387), deer, wild turkey, and striped bass are reared and studied. Admission is free.

At Goose Creek, about 19 miles north of Charleston, is the remarkably well-preserved **St. James United Methodist Church,** built between 1708 and 1719. Not in use since 1808, it retains the original box pews, slave gallery, and pulpit. The British royal arms are still visible above the chancel. The sexton, who lives nearby, will open the church on request. *Off U.S. 78,* ☎ *803/553–3117. Donations accepted.* ☉ *Weekdays 9–noon.*

Shopping

Shopping Districts. Don't miss the colorful produce market in the three-block **Old City Market** at East Bay and Market streets and adjacent to it, the **open-air flea market,** with crafts, antiques, and memorabilia. The **Market** is a complex of specialty shops and restaurants.

Other such complexes in the area are the **Shops at Charleston Place** adjoining the Omni Hotel, **Rainbow Market** (in two interconnected 150-year-old buildings), **Market Square,** and **State Street Market.** Also, some of Charleston's oldest and finest shops are on **King Street.**

Antiques

King Street is the center. **Petterson Antiques** (201 King St., ☎ 803/723–5714) offers books, furniture, porcelain, and glass. **Livingston & Sons Antiques,** dealers in 18th- and 19th-century English and Continental furniture, clocks, and bric-a-brac, has a large shop west of the Ashley (2137 Savannah Hwy., ☎ 803/556–6162) and a smaller one at 163 King Street (☎ 803/723–9697). **Birlant & Co.** (191 King St., ☎ 803/722–3842) offers a fine selection of 18th- and 19th-century English antiques, as well as the famous Charleston Battery bench, identical to those on Charleston Green.

Art and Crafts

The **Birds I View Gallery** (119–A Church St., *n* 803/723–1276) sells bird paintings and prints by Anne Worsham Richardson. At **Birds & Ivy** (235 King St., ☎ 803/853–8534), which sells garden art and accessories of every type, there's a coffee shop in back where you can have a sandwich or a snack. **Charleston Crafts** (38 Queen St., ☎ 803/723–2938) has a fine selection of pottery, quilts, weavings, sculptures, and jewelry fashioned mostly by local artists. The **Elizabeth O'Neill Verner Studio & Museum** (79 Church St., ☎ 803/722–4246), in a 17th-century house, is now open to the public. Prints of Elizabeth O'Neill Verner's pastels and etchings are on sale at adjacent **Tradd Street Press** (38 Tradd St., ☎ 803/722–4246). The **Virginia Fouché Bolton Art Gallery** (127 Meeting St., ☎ 803/577–9351) sells original paintings and limited-edition lithographs of Charleston and Low Country scenes.

Gifts

Charleston Collections (233 King St., ☎ 803/722–7267; at the Straw Market, Kiawah Island Resort, ☎ 803/768–7487; Quadrangle Center, ☎ 803/556–8911) has Charleston chimes, prints, candies, T–shirts, and more. The **Charleston Catalog Company** (139 Market St., ☎ 803/722–6121) also offers merchandise with a Charleston motif. Charleston's and London's own **Ben Silver** (149 King St., ☎ 803/577–4556), premier purveyor of blazer buttons, has over 800 designs, including college and British regimental motifs. He also sells British neckties, embroidered polo shirts, and blazers.

Period Reproductions

Historic Charleston Reproductions (105 Broad St., ☎ 803/723–8292) has superb replicas of Charleston furniture and accessories, all authorized by the Historic Charleston Foundation. Royalties from sales contribute to restoration projects. At the **Old Charleston Joggling Board Co.** (652 King St., ☎ 803/723–4331), these Low Country oddities (on which people bounce) can be purchased.

Sports and the Outdoors

Beaches

The Charleston area's mild climate generally is conducive to swimming from April through October. This is definitely not a "swingles" area; all public and private beaches are family oriented, providing a choice of water sports, sunbathing, shelling, fishing, or a setting for quiet moonlight strolls.

The Charleston County Parks and Recreation Commission operates several public beach facilities. **Beachwalker Park** (☎ 803/762–2172) on the west end of Kiawah Island (which is otherwise a private resort) provides 300 feet of beach frontage, seasonal lifeguard service, rest rooms, outdoor showers, a picnic area, snack bar, and 150-car parking lot. ☛ *$3 per car (up to 8 passengers).* ☉ *June–Aug. daily 10–7; Apr. and Oct., weekends 10–6; May and Sept., daily 10–6.*

Folly Beach County Park (☎ 803/588–2426), located 12 miles from Charleston via U.S. 17 and SC 171 (Folly Rd.), has 4,000 feet of ocean frontage and 2,000 feet of river frontage. Lifeguards are on duty seasonally along a 600-foot section of the beach. Facilities include dressing areas, outdoor showers, rest rooms, picnicking areas, beach chairs, raft and shower rentals, and a 300-vehicle parking lot. Pelican Watch shelter is available year round for group picnics and day or night oyster roasts. ☛ *$3 per car (up to 8 passengers).* ☉ *Aug.–May and Sept.–Oct., daily 10–6; June–Aug., daily 10–7; Nov.–May, daily 10–5.*

Private resorts with extensive beaches and amenities include **Fairfield Ocean Ridge** (☎ 803/869–2561), on Edisto Island; **Kiawah Island** (☎ 903/768–2121 or 800/654–2924); **Seabrook Island** (☎ 803/768–1000 or 800/845–5531); and **Wild Dunes** (☎ 803/886–6000 or 800/845–8880), on the Isle of Palms.

Bicycling

The historic district is ideal for bicycling, and many city parks have biking trails. **Palmetto Islands County Park** also has trails. Bikes can be rented at the **Bicycle Shoppe** (280 Meeting St., ☎ 803/722–8168; on Kiawah Island, ☎ 803/768–9122) and at **Charleston Bicycle Rentals** (26 Cumberland St., ☎ 803/722–7433).

Golf

One of the most appealing aspects of golfing the Charleston area is the relaxing pace. With fewer golfers playing the courses than in destinations that are primarily oriented to golf, golfers find choice starting times and an unhurried atmosphere. For a comprehensive listing of area golf packages, including current rates, contact the Charleston Area Convention and Visitors Bureau (Box 975, Charleston 29402, ☎ 803/853–8000 or 800/868–8118).

Non-guests may play on a space-available basis at private island resorts. The prestigious Pete Dye–designed **Ocean Course at Kiawah Island Resort (**☎ 803/768–7272) was the site of the 1991 Ryder Cup. Other championship Kiawah courses are the Gary Player–designed **Marsh Point** (☎ 803/768–2121); **Osprey Point** (☎ 803/768–2121), by Tom Fazio; and **Turtle Point** (☎ 803/768–2121), a Jack Nicklaus layout. Seabrook Island Resort, a secluded hideaway on Johns Island, offers two more championship courses: **Crooked Oaks** (☎ 803/768–2529) by Robert Trent Jones Sr., and **Ocean Winds** (☎ 803/768–2529), designed by William Byrd. Wild Dunes Resort, on the Isle of Palms, is home to two Tom Fazio designs: the **Links** (☎ 803/886–2180) and **Harbor Course** (☎ 803/886–2301).

Top public courses in the area include **Charleston Municipal** (Charleston, ☎ 803/795–6517), **Charleston National Country Club** (Charleston, ☎ 803/884–7799), the **Dunes West Golf Club** (Mount Pleasant, ☎

803/856–9000), **Links at Stono Ferry** (Hollywood, ☎ 803/763–1817), **Oak Point Golf Course** (Johns Island, ☎ 803/768–7431), **Patriots Point** (Mount Pleasant, ☎ 803/881–0042), and **Shadowmoss Golf Club** (Charleston, ☎ 803/556–8251).

Tennis
Courts are open to the public at **Shadowmoss Plantation** (☎ 803/556–8251), **Kiawah Island** (☎ 803/768–2121), and **Wild Dunes** (☎ 803/886–6000).

Dining

By Eileen Robinson Smith

Updated by Patricia Cheatham

She-crab soup, sautéed shrimp and grits, variations on pecan pie, and other Low Country specialties are served all over the Charleston area, but local chefs whip up some creative contemporary dishes as well. Known for outstanding eateries—ranging from fresh seafood houses to elegant French restaurants—Charleston is a mecca for gastronomes. Across the East Cooper Bridge, in the trendy suburb of Mount Pleasant, there are a number of good restaurants. Dress is casual unless otherwise noted.

CATEGORY	COST*
$$$	over $30
$$	$20–$30
$	under $20

per person for a three-course meal, excluding drinks, service, and 5% tax

American

$$$ **Anson.** After an afternoon of strolling through the Old City Market, you can walk a couple hundred feet up Anson Street to one of the better, and newer, restaurants in town. The softly lit, gilt-trimmed dining room is framed by about a dozen magnificent French windows; booths are anchored by marble-top tables. Anson's serves up dependable American fare—mainly seafood, chicken, and steak selections—with the occasional foreign twist (like the Thai-influenced, cashew-crusted grouper). Desserts are of the rich, southern variety, so save room. ✕ 12 Anson St., ☎ 803/577–0551. Reservations accepted. AE, D, DC, MC, V. No lunch.

$$ **82 Queen.** This popular restaurant, part of a complex of pink stucco
★ buildings dating to the mid-1800s, is the unofficial headquarters for many of the city's annual events; during Spoleto, musicians perform in the courtyard garden. Low Country favorites such as crab cakes are served with sweet red-pepper cream sauce. The traditional mingles with such innovations as roast duck with a blueberry-Cointreau glaze and oysters stuffed with Daufuskie crab. For dessert, choose death by chocolate or the healthy cheesecake. ✕ 82 Queen St., ☎ 803/723–7591. Reservations accepted for dinner. AE, MC, V.

$ **California Dreaming Restaurant & Bar.** The floor-to-ceiling windows of this heavy-volume restaurant, in an impressive stone fort on the Ashley River, look out at night on the lights of the harbor. The crowds come for the great view, low prices, and bountiful platters of food, such as grilled salmon, chicken salads, prime rib, and catch of the day. To make the wait bearable, take to the bar for a frothy piña colada. ✕ 1 Ashley Pointe Dr. (5 min from downtown), ☎ 803/766–1644. No reservations. AE, MC, V.

$ **Mike Calder's Deli & Pub.** Soups, salads, sandwiches, daily specials, and 12 different draft beers are offered in an "Old World" setting, once a

Dining

Anson, **19**
Barbadoes Room, **25**
California Dreaming Restaurant & Bar, **1**
Captain Guilds Cafe, **4**
Carolina's, **30**
82 Queen, **24**
Gaulart and Maliclet Cafe Restaurant, **28**
Louis's Charleston Grill, **16**
Magnolias Uptown/Down South, **21**
Mike Calder's Deli & Pub, **12**
Moultrie Tavern, **22**
Restaurant Million, **29**
Shem Creek Bar & Grill, **2**
Slightly North of Broad, **23**

Lodging

Ansonborough Inn, **15**
Best Western King Charles Inn, **14**
Brasington House Bed & Breakfast, **9**
Cannonboro Inn, **11**
Comfort Inn Riverview, **5**
Days Inn Historic District, **20**
1837 Bed and Breakfast and Tearoom, **13**
Elliott House Inn, **25**
Hampton Inn–Historic District, **6**
Hawthorn Suites Hotel, **18**
Holiday Inn Charleston/Mount Pleasant, **3**
John Rutledge House Inn, **27**
Maison DuPré, **10**
Mills House Hotel, **26**
Omni Hotel at Charleston Place, **16**
Planters Inn, **17**
Quality Inn–Heart of Charleston, **8**
Sheraton Inn Charleston, **7**
Two Meeting Street, **31**

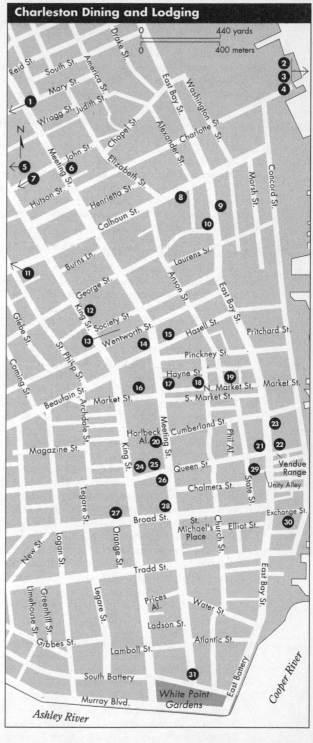

Charleston Dining and Lodging

pharmacy in the historic district. ✕ *288 King St.,* ☎ *803/577–0123. No reservations. D, MC, V. Closed Sun.*

French

$$$ Restaurant Million. This restaurant serves French nouvelle cuisine on Limoges china in a building dating to 1788. The rack of lamb and the five-course ($50) and three-course ($28) prix-fixe meals are outstanding. Downstairs at the casual and inexpensive McCrady's (☎ 803/853–8484), soup, salad, sandwiches, and grills are served. ✕ *2 Unity Alley,* ☎ *803/577–7472. Reservations required. Jacket and tie. AE, DC, MC, V. Restaurant Million: No lunch. Closed Sun. McCrady's: No lunch Sat. Closed Sun.*

$$ Gaulart and Maliclet Cafe Restaurant. This casual, chic eatery serves Continental dishes—breads and pastries, soups, salads, sandwiches, and evening specials like Seafood Normandy and chicken sesame. ✕ *98 Broad St.,* ☎ *803/577–9797. Reservations accepted. AE, DC, MC, V. No lunch Mon. Closed Sun.*

Low Country

$$$ Louis's Charleston Grill. When owner-chef Louis Osteen took over the
★ former Shaftesbury Room in the Omni, he created an elegant low-key ambience, with historic photographs of old Charleston on mahogany-panel walls and wrought-iron chandeliers reflected in gleaming crystal and china. The food is "local, not too fancy," and entrées match a variety of grilled meat and fish fillets with such exotic sauces as pear-walnut conserve and warm cumin vinaigrette. The staff is friendly, not stuffy, and will gladly help you choose from among the wines on its long and distinguished list. ✕ *224 King St. at Charleston Pl.,* ☎ *803/577–4522. Reservations advised. AE, MC, V. No lunch.*

$$ Carolina's. European chic with its black lacquer, white, and peach decor, Carolina's is the brainchild of German restaurateurs Franz Meier and Chris Weihs. Many come here for the "appeteasers" and the late-night (until 1 AM) offerings, which include everything from smoked baby back ribs to pasta with crawfish and tasso (spiced ham) in cream sauce. Dinner entrées are selections from the grill: Carolina quail with goat cheese, sun-dried tomatoes, and basil; salmon with cilantro, ginger, and lime butter; and lamb loin with jalapeño chutney. ✕ *10 Exchange St.,* ☎ *803/724–3800. Reservations advised. D, MC, V. No lunch.*

$$ Moultrie Tavern. This reconverted brick 1883 warehouse is filled with artifacts and artwork from the Civil War era. Chef/owner Robert Bohrn, who greets guests in a Confederate uniform, is a historian and unearths his own relics. The fife-and-drum music plays continuously and the food and spirits are authentically 1860s. Try an early Southern specialty: baked oyster and sausage pie with puff pastry. ✕ *18 Vendue Range,* ☎ *803/723–1862. Dinner reservations advised. AE, D, DC, MC, V.*

$$ Slightly North of Broad. This high-ceilinged haunt with visible air
★ ducts, brick and stucco walls, and red wooden floors opened early in 1994 to a packed house. The best seats are those looking directly into the exposed kitchen. From here you'll see chef Frank Lee laboring over his inventive—but hardly esoteric—dishes: sautéed quail filled with herbed chicken mousse; pad Thai noodles with shrimp, pork, and an authentic fish sauce; and corn-and-crab soup with spinach ravioli. You can order almost every item as either an appetizer or an entrée. The wine list is extensive and moderately priced. ✕ *192 E. Bay St.,* ☎ *803/723–3424. No reservations. AE, MC, V. No lunch Sat. Closed Sun.*

Low Country/Southern
$ **Captain Guilds Cafe.** There are actually two restaurants here: The little downstairs storefront restaurant churns out inexpensive, expertly prepared southern food. The catfish with honey curry butter and the chicken breast breaded with parmesan cornmeal and lemon caper sauce are surprisingly light and tender given the regional tendency to deep fry. For dessert, sample the bread pudding with a brown-sugar cream sauce. Upstairs, formal, prix-fixe, four-course Continental meals ($29) are presented in a grand dining room—the menu changes daily and depends largely on what's fresh that day. ✕ *101 Pitt St., Mount Pleasant,* ☎ *803/884–7009. Reservations required. Jacket and tie. AE, MC, V. Downstairs: No dinner Sun. Closed Mon. Upstairs: No lunch. Closed Sun. and Mon.*

$ **Magnolias Uptown/Down South.** This popular place, in an 1823 ware-
★ house on the site of the old customs house, is cherished by Charlestonians and visitors alike. The magnolia theme is seen throughout, and a custom-built circular bar overlooks the dining room. Specialties include grilled mahimahi fillet topped with succotash of shrimp, butter beans, yellow corn, and fresh spinach. Even the Black Angus strip steak is distinctive, served with fricassee of wild mushrooms, black-eyed peas, and Madeira sauce. Equally innovative appetizers include seared yellow grits cakes with Tasso gravy and yellow corn relish, and the salt-and-pepper fried shrimp with honey mustard–and-horseradish dip. ✕ *185 E. Bay St.,* ☎ *803/577–7771. Reservations advised. AE, MC, V.*

Seafood
$$ **Barbadoes Room.** This large, airy plant- and light-filled space has a sophisticated island look and a view out to a cheery courtyard garden. Entrées include sautéed jumbo shrimp and scallops served with creamy wild mushroom sauce on a bed of fresh spinach; linguini with an assortment of fresh shellfish in a light saffron sauce; and grilled breast of duck served with tarragon pear sauce. There's an elegant and extensive Southern-style breakfast menu and a popular Sunday brunch. ✕ *115 Meeting St., in the Mills House Hotel,* ☎ *803/577–2400. Reservations advised. D, DC, MC, V.*

$ **Shem Creek Bar & Grill.** This pleasant dockside spot is perennially popular for its oyster bar and light fare (until 10 PM Sun.–Thurs., until 1 AM Fri.–Sat.). There's also a wide variety of seafood entrées, including a steam pot—lobsters, clams, oysters, and sausages with melted lemon butter or hot cocktail sauce—big enough for two. ✕ *508 Mill St., Mount Pleasant,* ☎ *803/884–8102. No reservations. AE, D, DC, MC, V.*

Lodging

Rates tend to increase during the Spring Festival of Houses and Spoleto, when reservations are essential. The **Charleston Area Convention and Visitors Bureau** (Box 975, Charleston 29402, ☎ 803/853–8000 or 800/868–8118) distributes a Courtesy Discount Card entitling the bearer to 10%–50% off at many accommodations, restaurants, tours, and shops between mid-November and mid-February. To find rooms in homes, cottages, and carriage houses, try **Charleston East Bed and Breakfast League** (1031 Tall Pine Rd., Mount Pleasant 29464, ☎ 803/884–8208) and **Historic Charleston Bed and Breakfast** (60 Broad St., Charleston 29401, ☎ 803/722–6606). For historic home rentals in Charleston, contact **Charleston Carriage Houses–Oceanfront Realty** (Box 6151, Hilton Head, SC 29938, ☎ 803/785–8161). For condo and house rentals on the Isle of Palms—some with private pools and tennis courts—try **Island Realty** (Box 157, Isle of Palms 29451, ☎ 803/886–8144).

CATEGORY	COST*
$$$$	over $150
$$$	$90–$150
$$	$50–$90
$	under $50

All prices are for a standard double room, excluding 7% tax.

Hotels and Motels

$$$$ **Hawthorn Suites Hotel.** The hotel's spacious suites, all decorated with 18th-century reproductions and canopied beds, include full kitchens or wet bars with microwave ovens and refrigerators. Across from the City Market, the hotel is popular with business people, families, and tour groups. Complimentary full breakfast and afternoon refreshments are included in the rate. ⌸ *181 Church St., 29401,* ☎ *803/577–2644 or 800/527–1133,* ₣₳₭ *803/577–2697. 164 suites. Restaurant, lounge, pool, hot tub, exercise room, business services, meeting rooms. AE, D, DC, MC, V.*

$$$ **Mills House Hotel.** Antique furnishings and period decor give great charm
★ to this luxurious Holiday Inn property, a reconstruction of an old hostelry on its original site in the historic district. There's a lounge with live entertainment, and excellent dining in the Barbadoes Room (*see* Dining, *above*). ⌸ *115 Meeting St., 29401,* ☎ *803/577–2400 or 800/874–9600,* ₣₳₭ *803/722–2712. 214 rooms, 15 suites. Restaurant, 2 lounges, pool. AE, D, DC, MC, V.*

$$$ **Omni Hotel at Charleston Place.** Among the city's most luxurious ho-
★ tels, this graceful, low-rise structure in the historic district is flanked by upscale boutiques and specialty shops. The lobby features a magnificent hand-blown Venetian glass chandelier, an Italian marble floor, and antiques from Sotheby's. Rooms are furnished with period reproductions. ⌸ *130 Market St., 29401,* ☎ *803/722–4900 or 800/843–6664,* ₣₳₭ *803/722–4074. 348 rooms, 46 suites. 2 restaurants, 2 lounges, pool, hot tub, sauna, health club, concierge floor. AE, D, DC, MC, V.*

$$$ **Sheraton Inn Charleston.** Some rooms in this 13-story hotel outside the historic district overlook the Ashley River. Spacious rooms and suites are highlighted with Queen Anne furnishings. There's also concierge service and live entertainment. ⌸ *170 Lockwood Dr., 29403,* ☎ *803/723–3000 or 800/968–3569. 334 rooms, 2 suites. Coffee shop, dining room, lounge, pool, exercise room, meeting rooms. AE, D, DC, MC, V.*

$$–$$$ **Holiday Inn Charleston/Mount Pleasant.** This hotel just over the Cooper River Bridge is a 10-minute drive from the downtown historic district. Everything has been gracefully done: brass lamps, crystal chandeliers, Queen Anne–style furniture. The "high-tech suites" offer PC cable hookups, large working areas, glossy ultramodern furniture, and refrigerators. ⌸ *250 U.S. 17, Mount Pleasant 29464,* ☎ *803/884–6000 or 800/290–4004,* ₣₳₭ *803/744–0942. 158 rooms. Restaurant, lounge, raw bar (they mean fruits, veggies, oyster, steamed shrimp, and clams), pool, sauna, exercise room, concierge floor, meeting rooms. AE, D, DC, MC, V.*

$–$$ **Best Western King Charles Inn.** This inn in the historic district has spacious rooms furnished with 18th-century period reproductions. It's location, convenient to the Charleston Convention Center, is the primary attraction. ⌸ *237 Meeting St., 29401,* ☎ *803/723–7451 or 800/528–*

1234, FAX *803/723–2041. 91 rooms. Dining room, lounge, pool. AE, D, DC, MC, V.*

$–$$ **Comfort Inn Riverview.** Close to the Ashley River, the historic district, and restaurants, this 7-story contemporary inn offers free parking and complimentary Continental breakfast. ☎ *144 Bee St., 29401,* ☎ *803/577–2224 or 800/228–5150,* FAX *803/577–9001. 128 rooms. Pool. AE, DC, MC, V.*

$–$$ **Days Inn Historic District.** Conveniently located near the Gibbes Museum of Art and other historic district attractions, this modest inn features spacious, quiet rooms with king-size beds. A complimentary breakfast of coffee, juice, and doughnuts is available in the lobby. ☎ *155 Meeting St., 29401,* ☎ *803/722–8411 or 800/325–2525,* FAX *803/733–5361. 124 rooms. Dining room, pool. AE, D, DC, MC, V.*

$–$$ **Hampton Inn–Historic District.** This downtown property has hardwood
★ floors in the lobby, extra-light guest rooms furnished in period reproductions, a courtyard garden, and pool. Guests also get a Continental breakfast. This is a front-runner in the economy category. ☎ *345 Meeting St., 29403,* ☎ *803/723–4000 or 800/126 7866,* FAX *803/722–3725. 171 rooms. Pool. AE, DC, MC, V.*

$–$$ **Quality Inn–Heart of Charleston.** A block from the Gaillard Municipal Auditorium and Exhibition Hall, the inn is clean and run by a friendly staff. It draws loyal repeat visitors because of its convenient courtyard parking and location across from the convention center. Rooms are motel modern, as you would expect from this chain. ☎ *125 Calhoun St., 29401,* ☎ *803/722–3391 or 800/845–2504,* FAX *803/577–0361. 126 rooms. Coffee shop, lounge, pool. AE, D, DC, MC, V.*

Inns and Guest Houses

The charms of historic Charleston can be enhanced by a stay at one of its many inns, most in restored structures. Some are reminiscent of European inns; one is tastefully contemporary, tucked away on the grounds of a famous estate.

HISTORIC DISTRICT

$$$$ **John Rutledge House Inn.** This 1763 house, built by John Rutledge,
★ one of the framers of the U.S. Constitution, is one of Charleston's most luxurious inns. Ornate ironwork on the facade has a palmetto tree and eagle motif, signifying Rutledge's service to both his state and his nation. Wine and tea are served in the ballroom, and Continental breakfast and newspapers are delivered to your room. Two charming period carriage houses also accommodate guests. There are whirlpool tubs in some guest rooms. ☎ *116 Broad St., 29401,* ☎ *803/723–7999 or 800/476–9741,* FAX *803720–2615. 11 rooms in mansion, 4 in each carriage house. AE, MC, V.*

$$$ **Ansonborough Inn.** Formerly a turn-of-the-century stationer's warehouse, this spacious all-suite inn is furnished in antique reproductions. It offers hair dryers, irons, off-street parking, a morning newspaper, message service, wine reception, morning newspaper, and Continental breakfast, but it's best known for its friendly staff. ☎ *21 Hasell St., 29401,* ☎ *803/723–1655 or 800/522–2073,* FAX *803/527–6888. 37 suites. Meeting room. AE, MC, V.*

$$$ **Brasington House Bed & Breakfast.** During afternoon tea or at the Continental breakfast, Dalton and Judy Brasington, educators by profession, will advise you on what to see and do in Charleston. The formal dining room of their restored Greek Revival "single house" in the historic district is filled with antiques and treasures from around the

world. ▦ *328 E. Bay St., 29401,* ☎ *803/722–1274 or 800/722–1274,* ☏ *803/722–6785. 4 rooms with private baths. MC, V.*

$$$ **Elliott House Inn.** Listen to the chimes of St. Michael's Episcopal Church as you sip wine in the courtyard of this lovely old inn in the heart of the historic district. Then retreat to a cozy room with period furniture, including canopied four-posters and Oriental carpets. A Continental breakfast is included. ▦ *78 Queen St., 29401,* ☎ *803/723–1855 or 800/729–1855,* ☏ *803/722–1567. 26 rooms. Hot tub, bicycles. AE, D, MC, V.*

$$$ **Maison DuPré.** A quiet retreat off busy East Bay Street, this 1801 inn was created out of three restored homes and two carriage houses. It is filled with antiques, and each room features an original painting by Lucille Mullholland, who operates the inn with her husband Robert. Enjoy a full Low Country tea (cheeses, finger sandwiches, and cakes, with tea), Continental breakfast, and tickets to the Nathaniel Russell house museum—all complimentary. ▦ *317 E. Bay St., 29401,* ☎ *803/723–8691 or 800/844–4667. 12 rooms, 3 suites. AE, MC, V.*

$$$ **Planters Inn.** Rooms and suites here are beautifully appointed with opulent furnishings, including mahogany four-poster beds and marble baths. There's a concierge and 24-hour room service. ▦ *112 N. Market St., 29401,* ☎ *803/722–2345 or 800/845–7082,* ☏ *803/577–2125. 36 rooms, 5 suites. AE, DC, MC, V.*

$$$ **Two Meeting Street.** As pretty as a wedding cake and just as roman-
★ tic, this turn-of-the-century inn near the Battery features Tiffany windows, carved English oak paneling, and a chandelier from Czechoslovakia. There are two very private honeymoon suites. Guests are treated to afternoon sherry and Continental breakfast. ▦ *2 Meeting St., 29401,* ☎ *803/723–7322. 7 rooms, 2 suites. No credit cards.*

$$–$$$ **Cannonboro Inn.** One of the most elegant inns in town, this B&B in the historic district has luxurious rooms, tastefully decorated in period furnishings by owners Bud and Sally Allen. Guests are treated to a complimentary full English breakfast, use of the bicycles, and afternoon sherry. ▦ *184 Ashley Ave., 29403,* ☎ *803/723–8572,* ☏ *803/723–9080. 6 rooms with private baths. Bicycles. MC, V.*

$$ **1837 Bed and Breakfast and Tea Room.** Though it's not as fancy as some of the B&Bs in town, this inn is long on hospitality. Restored and operated by two artists, the home and carriage house feature rooms filled with antiques (including romantic canopied rice beds). A gourmet breakfast of homemade breads and hot entrées such as sausage pie or eggs Benedict is included in the rate, as is the afternoon tea (which is also open to the public for a nominal price). ▦ *126 Wentworth St., 29401,* ☎ *803/723–7166. 8 rooms with baths. AE, MC, V.*

Resort Islands

The semitropical islands dotting the South Carolina coast near Charleston are home to several sumptuous resorts. A wide variety of packages is sold. Peak-season rates (during spring and summer vacations) range from $100 to $250 per day, double occupancy. Costs drop considerably off-season.

$$$$ **Kiawah Island Resort.** Choose from 150 inn rooms, 48 suites, and 300 completely equipped one- to four-bedroom villas in two luxurious resort villages on 10,000 wooded acres. The accommodations and much of the property were refurbished in 1994. There are 10 miles of fine broad beaches and an array of recreational options. Dining options are many and varied: Low Country specialties in the Jasmine Porch and Veranda, Indigo House; Continental cuisine in the Charleston Gallery; lagoonside dining at the Park Cafe; casual dining in the Sand Wedge,

Sundancers, Jonah's. ⊠ *Kiawah Island, Box 12357, Charleston 29422-2357,* ☎ *803/768–2121 or 800/654–2924,* FAX *803/768–9386. 498 units. Restaurants, 4 18-hole golf courses, 28 tennis courts, boating, fishing, shops, children's programs. AE, DC, MC, V.*

$$$$ **Seabrook Island Resort.** There are 360 completely equipped one- to three-bedroom villas, cottages, and beach houses. Beach Club and Island Club, open to all guests, are centers for dining and leisure activities. ⊠ *1002 Landfall Way, Seabrook Island 29455,* ☎ *803/768–1000 or 800/845–2475,* FAX *803/768–4922. 360 units. Restaurants, 4 pools, 2 18-hole golf courses, 13 tennis courts, horseback riding, boating, fishing, bicycles, children's programs. AE, D, MC, V.*

$$$$ **Wild Dunes.** This serene, 1,600-acre resort has 250 one- to three-bedroom villas for rent, each with a kitchen and washer and dryer. There are two widely acclaimed golf courses, a racquet club, a yacht harbor on the Intracoastal Waterway, and a long list of recreational options. Beef specialties are served at the Club House and seafood at the Island House, where all dishes are created by a French master chef. There's a lounge with live entertainment. ⊠ *Box 503, Isle of Palms 29451,* ☎ *803/886–6000 or 800/845–8880,* FAX *803/886–2916. 250 units. 2 restaurants, lounge, 2 18-hole golf courses, 16 tennis courts, water sports, boating, fishing, bicycles, children's programs. AE, MC, V.*

The Arts

Pick up the Schedule of Events at the Visitors Center (375 Meeting St.) or at area hotels, inns, and restaurants. Also see "Tips for Tourists" each Saturday in the *News & Courier/The Evening Post.*

Arts Festivals

Spoleto Festival USA. Founded by the composer Gian Carlo Menotti in 1977, Spoleto has become one of the world's greatest celebrations of the arts. For two weeks, from late May to early June, opera, dance, theater, symphonic and chamber music performances, jazz, and the visual arts are showcased in concert halls, theaters, parks, churches, streets, and gardens throughout the city. For information: Spoleto Festival USA (Box 704, Charleston 29402, ☎ 803/722–2764).

Piccolo Spoleto Festival. The spirited companion festival of Spoleto Festival USA showcases the best in local and regional talent from every artistic discipline. There are about 700 events—from jazz performances to puppet shows—held at 60 sites in 17 days, from mid-May through early June, and most performances are free. For a program, contact the Office of Cultural Affairs, Piccolo Spoleto Festival (133 Church St., Charleston 29401, ☎ 803/724–7305).

During the **Festival of Houses and Gardens,** held during March and April each year, more than 100 private homes, gardens, and historic churches are open to the public. (Contact the Historic Charleston Foundation, Box 1120, 29202, ☎ 803/724–8484.)

Moja Arts Festival. Theater, dance, and music performances, art shows, films, lectures, and tours celebrating the rich heritage of the African continent are held at sites throughout the historic district the first two weeks in October. For information: The Office of Cultural Affairs (133 Church St., Charleston 29401, ☎ 803/724–7305).

Southeastern Wildlife Exposition. Held in mid-February, one of Charleston's biggest annual events features art by renowned wildlife artists. *211 Meeting St., 29401,* ☎ *803/723–1748 or 800/221–5273.*

Concerts

The College of Charleston has a **Monday Night Recital Series.** The **Charleston Symphony Orchestra** (☎ 803/723–7528) presents its Classics Concerts Series at Gaillard Municipal Auditorium (77 Calhoun St., ☎ 803/577–4500). Its Brass Quintet plays at the Charleston Museum Auditorium (360 Meeting St., ☎ 803/722–2996) and the Garden Theatre (☎ 803/577–7400) and at other locations around the city.

Dance

The **Charleston Ballet Theatre** (280 Meeting St., ☎ 803/723–7334) performs everything from contemporary to classical dance. The **Charleston Civic Ballet** (☎ 803/722–8779 or 803/577–4502) performs at the Sotille Theater (☎ 803/953–6340). The **Robert Ivey Ballet Company** (☎ 803/556–1343), a student group at the College of Charleston, gives a fall and spring program of jazz, classical, and modern dance at the **Simons Center for the Arts.**

Theater

Several groups, including the **Footlight Players,** perform at the Dock Street Theatre (135 Church St., ☎ 803/723–5648). Performances by the College of Charleston's drama department and guest theatrical groups are presented during the school year at the **Simons Center for the Arts** (☎ 803/953–5600).

Nightlife

Dancing and Music

Windjammer (☎ 803/886–8596), on the Isle of Palms, is an oceanfront spot featuring live rock music. In the market area, there's the **Jukebox** (4 Vendue Range, ☎ 803/723–3431), where a disc jockey spins oldies and contemporary rock. Amid the shops at Charleston Place is **Louis's Jazz Lounge Grill** (☎ 803/722–4900), an intimate, upscale locale featuring live jazz or performances by harpist or pianist.

Dinner Cruise

For an evening of dining and dancing, climb aboard the luxury yacht, *Spirit of Charleston.* ☎ 803/722–2628. *Reservations required. Closed Sun. and Mon.*

Film

Stage One Cinema (30 Cumberland St. Courtyard, ☎ 803/722–1900) offers films from around the world in an old livery stable, plus wine, beer, coffee, and pastries.

Hotel and Jazz Bars

The Best Friend Lounge (115 Meeting St., ☎ 803/577–2400), in the Mills House Hotel, has a guitarist playing light tunes Monday–Saturday nights. In the **Lobby Lounge** (130 Market St., ☎ 803/722–4900) in the Omni Charleston, cocktails and appetizers are accompanied by piano. Live jazz is offered Friday and Saturday evenings at **Henry's Restaurant** (54 N. Market St., ☎ 803/723–4363).

Restaurant/Lounges

A.W. Shucks (State Street Market, ☎ 803/723–1151) is a popular spot for relaxed evenings set to taped easy-listening music. **J.B. O'Brien's** (139 Calhoun St., ☎ 803723–1558) is an especially lively late night spot. **East Bay Trading Co.** (161 E. Bay St., ☎ 803/722–0722) has a small dance floor in its lively bar and a DJ playing Top 40s Friday and Saturday nights. You find authentic Irish music at **Tommy Condon's Irish Pub & Restaurant** (160 Church St., ☎ 803/577–3818).

Charleston Essentials

Arriving and Departing

BY BOAT
Boaters traveling the Intracoastal Waterway may dock at the **City Marina** (Lockwood Blvd., ☎ 803/724–7357) in the Charleston Harbor or **Wild Dunes Yacht Harbor** (☎ 803/886–5100) on the Isle of Palms.

BY BUS
Greyhound (3610 Dorchester Rd., N. Charleston, ☎ 800/231–2222).

BY CAR
I–26 traverses the state from northwest to southeast and terminates at Charleston. U.S. 17, the coast road, passes through Charleston.

BY PLANE
Charleston International Airport (☎ 803/767–1100) on I–26, 12 miles west of downtown, is served by American, Continental, Delta, United, and USAir.

Low Country Limousine Service (☎ 803/767–7111 or 800/222–4771) charges $9 per person one-way to downtown Charleston, by reservation. By car, take I–26S into the city.

BY TRAIN
Amtrak (4565 Gaynor Ave., N. Charleston, ☎ 803/744–8264 or 800/872–7245).

Getting Around

BY BUS
Regular buses run in most of Charleston from 5:35 am till 10 pm and to North Charleston until 1 am. The cost is 75¢ exact change (free transfers); at off-peak hours (9:30–3:30), senior citizens and people with disabilities pay 25¢. **DASH** (Downtown Area Shuttle) trolley-style buses provide fast service in the main downtown areas. The fare is 75¢; $1 for an all-day pass. For schedule information for buses or DASH, call 803/747–0922.

BY TAXI
Fares within the city average $2–$3 per trip. Companies include **Yellow Cab** (☎ 803/577–6565), **Safety Cab** (☎ 803/722–4066), and **Low Country Limousine Service** (*see* Arriving and Departing *above*).

Guided Tours

BOAT TOURS
Princess Gray Line Harbor Tours (☎ 803/722–1112 or 800/344–4483) **and Charleston Harbor Tour** (☎ 803/722–1691) ply the harbor. **Fort Sumter Tours** (☎ 803/722–1691) includes a stop at Fort Sumter and also offers Starlight Dinner Cruises aboard a luxury yacht.

CARRIAGE TOURS
Charleston Carriage Co. (☎ 803/577–0042), **Old South Carriage Company** (☎ 803/723–9712), and **Palmetto Carriage Works** (☎ 803/723–8145) run approximately one-hour horse- and mule-drawn carriage tours of the historic district, some conducted by guides in Confederate uniforms.

Adventure Sightseeing (☎ 803/762–0088 or 800/722–5394) and **Carolina Lowcountry Tours** (☎ 803/797–1045 or 800/621–7996) offer van or motor-coach tours of the historic district. **Gray Line** (☎ 803/722–4444) offers similar tours, plus seasonal trips to gardens and plantations.

PERSONAL GUIDES
Contact Associated Guides of Historic Charleston (☎ 803/724–6419); **Parker Limousine Service** (☎ 803/723–7601), which offers chauffeur-driven luxury limousine tours; or **Charleston Guide Service** (☎ 803/723–4402), the city's oldest guide service.

SPECIAL-INTEREST
Doin' the Charleston (☎ 803/763–1233 or 800/647–4487) combines its narration with audiovisuals and makes a stop at the Battery.

WALKING TOURS
Guided tours are given by **Historic Charleston Walking Tours** (☎ 803/722–6460); **Charleston Strolls** (☎ 803/884–9505); and **Charleston Tea Party Walking Tour** (☎ 803/577–5896 or 803/722–1779), which includes tea in a private garden.

Important Addresses and Numbers
EMERGENCIES
Dial 911 for police and **ambulance** assistance. The emergency rooms are open all night at **Charleston Memorial Hospital** (326 Calhoun St., ☎ 803/577–0600) and **Roper Hospital** (316 Calhoun St., ☎ 803/724–2000).

RADIO STATIONS
AM: WQIZ 810, gospel; WTMA 1250, talk radio; WXTC 1390, sports. **FM:** WAVF 96, alternative rock; WEZL 104, country; WBUB 107.5, country; WJUK 104.5, music from the 70s; WPAL 99, urban contemporary; WSCI 89.3, news, classical, jazz, information line; WSUY 100.7, light adult contemporary; WWWZ 93, urban contemporary; WXLY 102.5, oldies; WXTC 97, music from the 70s; WYBB 98.1, classic rock.

24-HOUR PHARMACIES
Henry's Conway Drug Store (633 King St., ☎ 803/577–5123), **Super E** (572 Meeting St., ☎ 803/722–0176), **Tellis Pharmacy** (125 King St., ☎ 803/723–0682).

VISITOR INFORMATION
Charleston Area Convention & Visitors Bureau (Box 975, Charleston 29402, ☎ 803/853–8000 or 800/868–8118) has information also on Kiawah Island, Seabrook Island, Mount Pleasant, North Charleston, Edisto Island, Summerville, and the Isle of Palms. **Historic Charleston Foundation** (Box 1120, Charleston 29402, ☎ 803/723–1623) has information on house tours.

MYRTLE BEACH AND THE GRAND STRAND

The lively, family-oriented Grand Strand, a booming resort area along the South Carolina coast, is one of the Eastern Seaboard's mega-vacation centers. Myrtle Beach alone accounts for about 40% of the state's tourism revenue. The main attraction, of course, is the broad, beckoning beach—60 miles of it, stretching from the North Carolina border south to Georgetown, with Myrtle Beach at the hub. But the Strand has something for everyone: more than 80 championship golf courses, designed by Arnold Palmer, Robert Trent Jones, Jack Nicklaus, and Tom and George Fazio, among others; excellent seafood restaurants; giant shopping malls and factory outlets; amusement parks, water slides, and arcades; a dozen shipwrecks for divers to explore; fine fishing; campgrounds, most on the beach; plus antique-car and wax museums, the world's largest outdoor sculpture garden, a half dozen country music shows, an antique pipe organ and merry-go-round, and a museum dedicated entirely to rice.

Exploring

Myrtle Beach—whose population of 26,000 explodes to about 350,000 in summer—is the center of activity on the Grand Strand. It is here that you find the amusement parks and other children's activities that make the area so popular with families, as well as most of the nightlife that keeps parents and teenagers happy into the wee hours. If the younger generation can't be amused and entertained here it might as well stay at home! In 1993, the city put up dozens of colorful street-light displays around major intersections, adding yet a few more volts of energy to the already pulsating scene. On the North Strand, there is Little River, with a thriving fishing and charter industry, and the several communities that make up North Myrtle Beach. On the South Strand, the family retreats of Surfside Beach and Garden City offer more summer homes and condominiums. Farther south are Murrells Inlet, once a pirate's haven and now a popular fishing port, and Pawleys Island, one of the East Coast's oldest resorts. Historic Georgetown forms the southern tip.

Our tour begins at the **Myrtle Beach Pavilion Amusement Park**, which underwent a major renovation and expansion in 1994. Here families while away the days enjoying thrill and kiddie rides, the Carolinas' largest flume, video games, a teen nightclub, specialty shops, antique cars, and sidewalk cafés. *Ninth Ave. N and Ocean Blvd.,* ☎ *803/448–6456. Fees for individual attractions; family discount book available.* ☉ *Mar.–May and Sept.–Oct., weekdays 6 PM–midnight, weekends 1 PM–midnight; June–Sept., daily 1 PM–midnight.*

More of the unusual awaits at **Ripleys Believe It or Not Museum.** Among the more than 750 exhibits is an 8-foot, 11-inch wax replica of the world's tallest man. *901 N. Ocean Blvd.,* ☎ *803/448–2331.* ☛ *$6.50 adults, $3.50 children 6–12.* ☉ *Daily 10–10.*

Drama, sound, and animation highlight religious, historical, and entertainment sections in the **Myrtle Beach National Wax Museum.** *1000 N. Ocean Blvd.,* ☎ *803/448–9921.* ☛ *$5 adults, $3 children 5–12, under 5 free.* ☉ *Late Feb.–mid-Oct., daily 9 AM–11 PM; in summer months, daily 9 AM–midnight.*

When your family's appetite for more raucous amusements has been sated, it's time to head out of town. Going south on U.S. 17 for about 20 miles brings you to **Murrells Inlet,** a picturesque little fishing village with popular seafood restaurants that's also a great place for chartering a fishing boat or joining a group excursion.

Three miles south, on the grounds of a Colonial rice plantation, is the largest outdoor collection of American sculpture, with works by such artists as Frederic Remington and Daniel Chester French. ★**Brookgreen Gardens** was begun in 1931 by railroad magnate/philanthropist Archer Huntington and his wife, Anna, herself a sculptor. Today, more than

500 works are set amid beautifully landscaped grounds, with avenues of live oaks, reflecting pools, and over 2,000 plant species. Also on the site is a wildlife park, an aviary, a cypress swamp, nature trails, and an education center. *18 mi south of Myrtle Beach off U.S. 17,* ☎ *803/237–4218.* ☛ *$6.50 adults, $3 children 6–12, children under 6 free.* ◔ *Daily 9:30–5:30.*

Across the highway is **Huntington Beach State Park,** the Huntingtons' 2,500-acre former estate. The park's focal point is Atalaya (circa 1933), their Moorish-style, 30-room home, open to visitors in season. In addition to the splendid beach, there are surf fishing, nature trails, an interpretive center, a salt-marsh boardwalk, picnic areas, a playground, concessions, and a campground. ☎ *803/237–4440.* ☛ *Free; parking fee in peak months.* ◔ *Daily dawn to dusk.*

Farther south is **Pawleys Island,** 4 miles long and a half-mile wide, which began as a resort before the Civil War, when wealthy planters and their families summered here. It's mostly made up of weathered old summer cottages nestled in groves of oleander and oak trees. You can watch the famous Pawleys Island hammocks being made here (*see* Shopping, *below*), but there's little else to do.

Bellefield Nature Center Museum, south on U.S. 17 near Georgetown, is at the entrance of Hobcaw Barony, on the vast estate of the late Bernard M. Baruch. Here such guests as Franklin D. Roosevelt and Winston Churchill came to confer with him. The museum, run by the Belle W. Baruch Foundation, is used for teaching and research in forestry and marine biology. There are aquariums, touch tanks, and video presentations. ☎ *803/546–4623.* ☛ *To museum free.* ◔ *Weekdays 10–5, Sat. 1–5. A variety of nature tours and estate tours are given year-round; call at least 1 month in advance for schedules and fees.*

Georgetown, on Winyah Bay, founded in 1729 by a Baptist minister, soon became the center of America's Colonial rice empire. A rich plantation culture took root here and developed on a scale comparable to Charleston's. Today, oceangoing vessels still come to Georgetown's busy port, and the **Harbor Walk,** the restored waterfront, hums with activity. Georgetown's historic district—among the prettiest in the state north of Charleston—encompasses more than 50 homes and other buildings and can be walked in a couple of hours.

The graceful market–meeting building in the heart of town, topped by an 1842 clock and tower, has been converted into the **Rice Museum,** with maps, tools, and dioramas. *Front and Screven Sts.,* ☎ *803/546–7423.* ☛ *$2 adults, children under 18 and students free.* ◔ *Mon.–Sat. 9:30–4:30.*

Nearby, **Prince George Winyah Episcopal Church** (named after King George II) still serves the congregation established in 1721. It was built in 1737 with bricks brought from England. *Broad and Highmarket Sts.,* ☎ *803/546–4358. Donation suggested.* ◔ *Mar.–Oct., weekdays 11:30–4:30.*

Overlooking the Sampit River from a bluff is the **Harold Kaminski House** (circa 1760). It's especially notable for its collections of regional antiques and furnishings, its Chippendale and Duncan Phyfe furniture, Royal Doulton vases, and silver. *1003 Front St.,* ☎ *803/546–7706.* ☛ *$4 adults, $2 children under 13.* ◔ *Mon.–Sat. 10–5, Sun. 1–4.*

Twelve miles south of Georgetown lies **Hopsewee Plantation,** surrounded by moss-draped live oaks, magnolias, and tree-size camellias, overlooking the North Santee River. The mansion has a fine Georgian staircase and hand-carved Adam candlelight moldings. *U.S. 17,* ☎ *803/546–7891.* ☛ *To mansion: $5 adults, $2 children 5–17, under 5 free.* ☛ *To grounds: $2 per car. Mansion open Mar.–Oct., Tues.–Fri. 10–4.* ☉ *Grounds, including nature trail, year-round, daily dawn–dusk.*

Hampton Plantation State Park, at the edge of the Francis Marion National Forest (*see* Off the Beaten Path *in* Charleston section, *above*), preserves the home of Archibald Rutledge, poet laureate of South Carolina for 39 years until his death in 1973. The 18th-century plantation house is a fine example of a Low Country mansion. The exterior has been restored; cutaway sections in the finely crafted interior show the changes made through the centuries. The grounds are landscaped and there are picnic areas. *Off U.S. 17,* ☎ *803/546–9361.* ☛ *Mansion $2 adults.* ☛ *To grounds free.* ☉ *Mansion Apr.–Labor Day, Thurs.–Mon. 1–4; Labor Day–Mar., weekends 1–4.* ☉ *Grounds Thurs.–Mon. 9–6.*

What to See and Do with Children

Brookgreen Gardens (*see* Exploring, *above*).

Myrtle Beach is the minigolf capital of the world, and **Hawaiian Rumble** is its crown jewel, featuring a smoking mountain that erupts fire and rumbles at timed intervals. *3210 33rd Ave. S, U.S. 17, Myrtle Beach,* ☎ *803/272–7812.* ☛ *$4 all day (9–5), $4 per round 5–midnight. Closed Jan.–Feb.*

Huntington Beach State Park (*see* Exploring, *above*).

Myrtle Beach Grand Prix. Auto-mania heaven, it offers Formula 1 race cars, go-carts, bumper boats, mini-go-carts, kiddie cars, and mini-bumper boats for adults and children age 3 and up. *Two locations: 3201 Hwy. 17, Myrtle Beach,* ☎ *803/238–2421; Windy Hill, U.S. 17N, N. Myrtle Beach,* ☎ *803/272–6010. Rides priced individually, $2–$5.50.* ☉ *Mar. 10–Oct. 31, daily 10 AM–11 PM.*

Myrtle Beach Pavilion and Amusement Park (*see* Exploring, *above*).

Myrtle Waves Water Park. There's splashy family fun for all ages in 17 rides and activities. *U.S. 17 Bypass and 10th Ave. N, Myrtle Beach,* ☎ *803/448–1026 or 800/524–9283.* ☛ *$10.95, $8.45 after 3 PM, $5.95 spectators and over 54, children under 3 free.* ☉ *Memorial Day Weekend–Labor Day, daily 10–6 (Tues.–Thurs. until 8); May and Sept., weekends 10–5.*

Shopping

Discount Outlets

Off-price shopping outlets abound in the Grand Strand. At **Waccamaw Pottery and Outlet Park** (U.S. 501 at the Waterway, Myrtle Beach, ☎ 803/236–1100) over 3 miles of shelves in several buildings are stocked with china, glassware, wicker, brass, pewter, and countless other items, and about 50 factory outlets sell clothing, furniture, books, jewelry, and more. **Hathaway/Olga Warner** (☎ 803/236–4200), across from Waccamaw, offers menswear by Chaps, Ralph Lauren, Speedo, and Jack Nicklaus, and women's lingerie.

Malls

Myrtle Square Mall (2501 N. Kings Hwy., Myrtle Beach, ☎ 803/448–2513) has 71 upscale stores and restaurants, and a food court. **Barefoot Landing** in North Myrtle Beach (4898 S. Kings Hwy., ☎

803/272–8349) is a unique complex built over marshland and water. **Briarcliffe Mall** (10177 N. Kings Hwy., Myrtle Beach, ☎ 803/272–4040) has 100 specialty shops. Malls are generally open Monday–Saturday 10–9, Sunday 1–6.

Specialty Stores

The **Hammock Shops at Pawleys Island** (☎ 803/237–8448) is a handsome complex of approximately two-dozen boutiques, gift shops, and restaurants nestled amid moss-draped live oak trees and built with old beams, timber, and ballast brick. Just outside the Original Hammock Shop, in the Hammock Weavers' Pavilion, skilled craftsfolk demonstrate the more than 100-year-old art of weaving the famous cotton-rope Pawleys Island hammocks. In one shop, rope hammocks are being made as they have been since 1880. Others sell jewelry, toys, antiques, and designer fashions.

Beaches

The broad 60-mile-long swath of South Carolina's Atlantic beach known as the **Grand Strand** extends from Little River near the North Carolina line down to Georgetown and its tidelands. All the region's beaches are family oriented, and most are public. The widest expanses are in **North Myrtle Beach,** where, at low tide, the sand stretches up to an eighth of a mile from the dunes to the water. Those who wish to combine their sunning with nightlife and amusement park attractions can enjoy it all at **Myrtle Beach,** the Strand's longtime hub. Vacationers seeking a quieter day in the sun head for the **South Strand** communities of Surfside Beach and Garden City or historic **Pawleys Island.** All along the Strand you can enjoy shell hunting, fishing, swimming, sunbathing, sailing, surfing, jogging, or just strolling.

Participant Sports

Fishing

The Gulf Stream makes fishing usually good from early spring through December. Anglers can fish from 10 piers and jetties for amberjack, sea trout, and king mackerel. Surfcasters may snare bluefish, whiting, flounder, pompano, and channel bass. In the South Strand, salt marshes, inlets, and tidal creeks yield flounder, blues, croakers, spots, shrimp, clams, oysters, and blue crabs. **Capt. Dick's** (U.S. 17 Bus., Murrells Inlet, ☎ 803/651–3676) and **Hague Marina** (Hwy. 707, Myrtle Beach, ☎ 803/293–2141) offer half- and full-day fishing and sightseeing trips. The annual **Grand Strand Fishing Rodeo** (☎ 803/626–7444, Apr.–Oct.) features a "fish of the month" contest, with prizes for the largest catch of a designated species.

Golf

Many of the Grand Strand's 86 courses are championship layouts; most are public. Spring and fall, with off-season rates, are the busiest seasons, and there are many packages (call **Golf Holiday,** ☎ 803/448–5942 or 800/845–4653). Popular courses include: in Myrtle Beach, **Arcadian Shores Golf Club** (☎ 803/449–5217) and **Myrtle Beach National Golf Club** (☎ 803/448–2308 or 800/344–5590); in North Myrtle Beach, **Bay Tree Golf Plantation** (☎ 803/249–1487 or 800/845–6191), **Gator Hole** (☎ 803/249–3543 or 800/447–2668), **Heather Glen Golf Links** (☎ 803/249–9000), and **Robbers Roost Golf Club** (☎ 803/249–2085 or 800/352–2384); near Surfside Beach, **Blackmoor Golf Club** (☎ 803/650–5555); in Cherry Grove Beach, the much touted **Tidewater**

(☎ 803/249–6675); on Pawleys Island, **Litchfield Beach and Golf Resort** (☎ 803/237–3000 or 800/849–1897), **Litchfield Plantation** (☎ 803/237–9121 or 800/869–1410), and **Pawleys Plantation Golf & Country Club** (☎ 803/237–8497 or 800/367–9959).

Scuba Diving

In summer, a wide variety of warm-water tropical fish finds its way to the area from the Gulf Stream. Off the coast of Little River, rock and coral ledges teem with coral, sea fans, sponges, reef fish, anemones, urchins, arrow crabs, and stone crabs. Several outlying shipwrecks are home to schools of spadefish, amberjack, grouper, and barracuda. Instruction and equipment rentals are available from **Scuba Syndrome** (2718 Hwy. 501, Myrtle Beach, ☎ 803/626–6740).

Tennis

There are more than 150 courts on the Grand Strand. Facilities include hotel and resort courts, as well as free municipal courts in Myrtle Beach, North Myrtle Beach, and Surfside Beach. Among tennis clubs offering court time, rental equipment, and instruction are **Myrtle Beach Racquet Club** (☎ 803/449–4031), **Myrtle Beach Tennis and Swim Club** (☎ 803/449–4486), and **Litchfield Country Club** (☎ 803/237–3411).

Water Sports

Surfboards, Hobie Cats, Jet Skis, Windsurfers, and sailboats are available for rent at **Downwind Sails** (Ocean Blvd. at 29th Ave. S, Myrtle Beach, ☎ 803/448 7245) and **Myrtle Beach Yacht Club** (Coquina Harbor, N. Myrtle Beach, ☎ 803/249–5376).

Dining

Coastal South Carolina serves traditionally prepared seafood in lavish portions, garnished with hush puppies, coleslaw, and fresh vegetables. Myrtle Beach's mile-long "Restaurant Row" stretches along U.S. 17 from the city's northernmost limits. Here you'll find every type of cuisine imaginable, but you won't find the gourmet cooking of Charleston and Hilton Head; instead, expect family-style restaurants with predictable, but dependable, menus. Dress is casual unless otherwise noted.

CATEGORY	COST*
$$$$	over $25
$$$	$15–$25
$$	$7–$15
$	under $7

*per person for a three-course meal, excluding drinks, service, and 5% sales tax

Georgetown

$$ ★ **Rice Paddy.** This cozy Low Country restaurant is apt to be crowded at lunch, when local solons flock in for homemade vegetable soup, garden-fresh salads, and sandwiches. Dinner is more relaxed, and the menu might have broiled fresh seafood, crabmeat casserole, or veal scaloppine. ✕ 408 Duke St., ☎ 803/546–2021. Reservations accepted. AE, MC, V. Closed Sun.

$$ **River Room.** This restaurant on the Sampit River specializes in chargrilled fish, seafood pastas, and steaks. For lunch you can have shrimp and grits or a variety of sandwiches and salads. It's especially romantic at night when the oil lamps and brass fixtures cast a warm glow on

the dark wood and brick interior of the turn-of-the-century building. ✕ *801 Front St.,* ☎ *803/527–4110. No reservations. AE, MC, V. Closed Sun.*

Murrells Inlet

$$ **Planter's Back Porch.** Sip cool drinks in the spring house of a turn-of-
★ the-century farmhouse, then have dinner in a garden setting. Black wrought-iron chandeliers are suspended from high white beams, and hanging baskets of greenery decorate white latticework archways separating the fireplace-centered main dining room and the airy, glass-enclosed porch. You can't go wrong with baked whole flounder, panned lump crabmeat, or the hearty inlet dinner with several types of fish. ✕ *U.S. 17 and Wachesaw Rd.,* ☎ *803/651–5263. Reservations accepted. AE, D, MC, V. Closed Dec.–mid-Mar.*

Myrtle Beach

$$–$$$ **Crab House.** In this sprawling, two-level dining room with beamed ceil-
★ ings, plank floors, and marine artifacts adorning the walls, the emphasis is on crabs steamed with garlic and other fresh local seafood. There's an extensive all-you-can-eat seafood, salad, and raw bar. The entire top floor is no-smoking. ✕ *Barefoot Landing, 4744 U.S. 17S, N. Myrtle Beach,* ☎ *803/272–1062. Reservations accepted. AE, MC, V.*

$$ **Rice Planters.** Dine on fresh seafood, quail, or steaks grilled to order
★ in a homey setting enhanced by candlelight, Low Country antiques, and rice-plantation tools and artifacts. Shrimp Creole is a house specialty; among the appetizers, don't miss the crab fingers! The bread and the pecan pie are home-baked. ✕ *6707 N. Kings Hwy.,* ☎ *803/449–3456. Reservations accepted. AE, D, MC, V.*

$$ **Sea Captain's House.** At this picturesque restaurant with nautical
★ decor, the best seats are in the windowed porch room, which overlooks the ocean. The fireplace in the wood-paneled dining room inside is warmly welcoming on cool off-season evenings. Menu highlights include she-crab soup, Low Country crab casserole, and avocado-seafood salad. The breads and desserts are baked here. ✕ *3002 N. Ocean Blvd.,* ☎ *803/448–8082. AE, D, MC, V.*

$$ **Southern Suppers.** Here's hearty family dining in a cozy farmhouse filled with country primitive art; handmade quilts line the walls. The menu features an all-you-can-eat seafood buffet and such down-home Southern specialties as fried chicken, country-fried steak, and country ham with red-eye gravy and grits. ✕ *5301 U.S. 17, midway between Myrtle Beach and Surfside Beach,* ☎ *803/238–4557. MC, V. Closed Oct.–Mar.*

North Myrtle Beach

$$–$$$ **Oak Harbor Inn.** Located on a quieter, northern stretch of the beach, this airy, open restaurant overlooks picturesque Vereen's Marina. It's a great local favorite. Specialties include chicken Annie, a boneless breast of chicken in puff pastry laced with ham, Swiss, and blue cheeses, drizzled with Parmesan and Mornay sauce. ✕ *1407 13th Ave. N,* ☎ *803/249–4737. Reservations accepted. AE, D, MC, V.*

$$ **Horst Gausthaus.** Dine on knockwurst, bratwurst, sauerbraten, and other traditional German foods at this Bavarian-style restaurant, where there's oom-pah-pah music every night but Sunday. ✕ *802 37th Ave. S,* ☎ *803/272–3351. Reservations advised. AE, MC, V.*

AFLOAT
Dinner cruises aboard the cruise ship *Hurricane* (☎ 803/249–3571) and yachts of the Neptune's pleasure fleet (☎ 803/280–4100) depart

from Vereen's Marina (U.S. 17N and 11th Ave.). The *Barefoot Princess* (☎ 803/272–7743 or 800/685–6601), a replica of a sidewheel riverboat, offers dinner, sunset, and sightseeing cruises along the Intracoastal Waterway from Barefoot Landing (4898 U.S. 17S).

Pawleys Island
$$ Tyler's Cove. This restaurant specializes in such unusual Low Country fare as fried Carolina alligator, seasoned with buttermilk batter, and spicy Cajun chicken tossed in a salad of lettuce, cabbage, and jalapeño honey dressing. Sunday brunch is served. ✕ *Hammock Shops, U.S. 17,* ☎ *803/237–4848. Reservations advised. AE, D, MC, V.*

Lodging

With about 55,000 rooms available along the Grand Strand, it's never difficult to find a place to stay, and discounting is rampant. Package deals are offered year-round, the most attractive of them between Labor Day and spring break. Among other lodgings options, condominiums are popular, combining spaciousness and modern amenities and appealing especially to families. You can choose among cottages, villas, and hotel-style high-rise units. Maid service is frequently available. For the free directories *Grand Hotel and Motel Accommodations* and *Grand Condominium and Cottage Accommodations,* write to the Myrtle Beach Area Convention Bureau (710 21st Ave. N, Suite J, Myrtle Beach, SC 29577, ☎ 803/448–1629 or 800/356–3016).

CATEGORY	COST*
$$$$	over $100
$$$	$65–$100
$$	$45–$65
$	under $45

All prices are for a standard double room, excluding 7% tax.

Georgetown
$$–$$$ 1790 House. This lovely restored house, redecorated in 1993 by new owners Patricia and John Wiley, is in the center of the historic district. Built after the Revolution, when Georgetown's rice culture was at its peak, it contains Colonial furnishings suitable to its age. Guests are treated to gourmet breakfasts, evening refreshments, and the use of bicycles. For a romantic hideaway, request the private carriage house. 🏠 *630 Highmarket St., 29440,* ☎ *803/546–4821. 6 rooms with baths. AE, MC, V.*

McClellanville
$$$ Laurel Hill Plantation. This Low Country plantation bed-and-breakfast house, overlooking the marsh near the Intracoastal Waterway, has been rebuilt after its destruction by Hurricane Hugo (ask to see the scrapbooks of the storm). Owners Lee and Jackie Morrison have furnished it with country antiques. Guests can read a book in the hammock, go fishing or crabbing, take a boat ride, or watch the birds. The Morrisons serve a full breakfast and complimentary afternoon refreshments. 🏠 *8913 N. Hwy. 17, Box 190, 29458,* ☎ *803/887–3708. 4 rooms with bath. No credit cards.*

Myrtle Beach
$$$$ Kingston Plantation: A Radisson Resort. The Grand Strand's most lux-
★ urious property, this 20-story glass-sheathed tower is part of a complex of shops, restaurants, hotels, and condominiums set amid 145 acres of oceanside woodlands. Guest rooms are highlighted by bleached-wood

furnishings and attractive art. The balconied one-bedroom suites have kitchenettes. ⌧ *9800 Lake Dr., 29572,* ☎ *803/449–0006 or 800/876–0010,* FAX *803/497–1110. 614 suites. 2 restaurants, lounge, pool, 2 tennis courts, health club. AE, D, DC, MC, V.*

$$$–$$$$ **Best Western/Landmark.** The rooms in this high-rise oceanfront resort hotel are tastefully decorated in a modern style. Some have balconies and refrigerators. ⌧ *1501 S. Ocean Blvd., 29577,* ☎ *803/448–9441 or 800/845–0658,* FAX *803/626–1501. 313 rooms, 14 suites. Restaurant, pub, pool bar, lounges, pool, nightclub, recreation room, children's program. AE, D, DC, MC, V.*

$$$–$$$$ **Breakers Resort Hotel.** The rooms in this recently renovated oceanfront hotel are airy and spacious, with contemporary decor. Many have balconies and refrigerators. ⌧ *2006 N. Ocean Blvd., Box 485, 29578-0485,* ☎ *803/444–4444 or 800/845–0688,* FAX *803/626–5000. 204 rooms, 186 suites. Restaurant, lounge, 3 pools, 2 hot tubs, 3 saunas, exercise room, children's programs, laundry service. AE, D, DC, MC, V.*

$$$–$$$$ **Sheraton Myrtle Beach Resort.** All rooms and suites have a fresh, contemporary look. Oceanfront Lounge, highlighted by tropical colors and rattan furnishings, is a lively evening gathering spot. ⌧ *2701 S. Ocean Blvd., 29577,* ☎ *803/448–2518 or 800/992–1055,* FAX *803/449–1879. 211 rooms, 8 suites. Restaurant, indoor and outdoor pools, health club, arcade. AE, D, DC, MC, V.*

$$$ **Chesterfield Inn.** A remnant from the past, this oceanfront brick inn, hidden beneath the towers of Myrtle Beach's more glitzy hotels, has been in operation for over half a century. The rooms in the old part are simple and plain, but many guests prefer them to the ones in the newer wing. Family-style meals are served on starched white tablecloths in the paneled dining room. ⌧ *700 N. Ocean Blvd., 29578,* ☎ *803/448–3177,* FAX *803/626–4736. 57 rooms, 6 kitchenette units. Restaurant, pool, shuffleboard. AE, D, DC, MC V.*

$$$ **Driftwood on the Oceanfront.** Under the same ownership for more than 50 years, this facility is popular with families. Some rooms are oceanfront; all are decorated in sea, sky, or earth tones. ⌧ *1600 N. Ocean Blvd., Box 275, 29578,* ☎ *803/448–1544 or 800/942–3456,* FAX *803/448–2917. 90 rooms. 2 pools, exercise room, recreation room. AE, D, DC, MC, V.*

$$$ **Holiday Inn Oceanfront.** This oceanfront inn is right at the heart of the action. The spacious rooms are decorated in cool sea tones. After beach basking, you can prolong the mood in the inn's spacious, plant-bedecked indoor recreation center, which comprises an indoor pool, exercise room, game room, and gift shop. ⌧ *415 S. Ocean Blvd., 29577,* ☎ *803/448–4481 or 800/845–0313,* FAX *803/448–0086. 311 rooms. 2 restaurants, 2 lounges, snack bar, outdoor and indoor pools, hot tub, sauna, recreation room. AE, D, DC, MC, V.*

$$–$$$ **Comfort Inn.** This chain motel, 400 yards from the ocean, is clean, predictably furnished, and well maintained. ⌧ *2801 S. Kings Hwy., 29577,* ☎ *803/626–4444 or 800/228–5150,* FAX *803/626–0753. 139 rooms, 14 suites. Restaurant, pool, health club. AE, D, DC, MC, V.*

North Myrtle Beach

$ **Days Inn at Waccamaw.** Relax by the pool or in the gazebo after a full day of shopping at the nearby Waccamaw Pottery and Outlet Park. The theaters of the Fantasy Harbour complex are also close at hand. Rooms here are clean and functional, filled with contemporary furnishings, and most are equipped with a refrigerator. ⌧ *3650 Hwy. 501,*

29577, ☎ 803/236–1950 or 800/325–2525, ℻ 803/236–9415. *160 rooms. Restaurant, lounge, pool, hot tub. AE, D, DC, MC, V.*

Pawleys Island

$$$$ **Litchfield by the Sea Beach and Golf Resort.** Contemporary gray-blue wood suite units, a short walk from the beach, nestle amid 4,500-acre gardenlike grounds, which include three private golf clubs and a racquet club open to guests. All suites, tastefully decorated in pastel tones and light woods, feature marble baths, wet bars, refrigerators, and microwave ovens. Similarly furnished one- and two-bedroom units in the new five-story Bridgewater complex have private balconies overlooking the pool and Atlantic Ocean. "Country Club" cottages and marshside villas are ideal for families or couples seeking extra privacy. ⌖ *U.S. 17, 2 mi north of Pawleys Island, Drawer 320, 29585, ☎ 803/237– 3000 or 800/845–1897, ℻ 803/237–4282. 96 hotel suites; 120 condominium, cottage, and villa units. Restaurant, lounge, indoor and outdoor pools, sauna, hot tub, 3 18-hole golf courses, 19 tennis courts, exercise room, racquetball, conference center. AE, MC, V.*

$$$$ **Litchfield Plantation.** Period furnishings adorn four spacious suites of this impeccably restored 1750 rice plantation manor-house-turned-country-inn fronted by a majestic avenue of live oaks. Guests may also stay in retreat cottages scattered about the grounds. Golf and tennis privileges at the adjacent country club are part of the package here, as is a complimentary Continental breakfast. The resort is approximately 2 miles south of Brookgreen Gardens on U.S. 17 (turn right at the Litchfield Country Club entrance and follow the signs to the plantation). ⌖ *River Rd., Box 290, 29585, ☎ 803/237–9121 or 800/869–1410. 20 rooms, 6 2-and 3-bedroom cottages. Restaurant, pool, 2 tennis courts, horseback riding, boating, concierge. AE, MC, V.*

$$ **Ramada Inn Seagull.** This is a very well-maintained inn on a golf course (excellent golf packages are available). Outfitted with motel-modern furnishings, the rooms are spacious, bright, and airy. ⌖ *U.S. 17S, Box 2217, 29585, ☎ 803/237–4261 or 800/272–6232, ℻ 803/237–9708. 99 rooms. Dining room, lounge, pool. AE, DC, MC, V.*

The Arts

Theater productions, concerts, art exhibits, and other cultural events are regularly offered at the **Myrtle Beach Convention Center** (Oak and 21st Ave. N, Myrtle Beach, ☎ 803/448–7166). The **Atalaya Arts Festival** at Huntington Beach State Park in the fall is a big draw; phone 803/237–4440 for more information. **Art in the Park,** featuring arts and crafts, is staged in Myrtle Beach's Chapin Park three times during the summer season (call 803/626–7444 for details).

Nightlife

Clubs offer varying fare, including beach music, the Grand Strand's unique '50s-style sound. During summer, sophisticated live entertainment is featured nightly at some clubs and resorts. Some hotels and resorts also have piano bars or lounges featuring easy-listening music.

In Myrtle Beach: **Sandals** (500 Shore Dr., ☎ 803/449–6461) is an intimate lounge with live entertainment. **Coquina Club,** at the Best Western Landmark Resort Hotel (☎ 803/448–9441), features beach-music bands. The shag (the state dance) is popular at **Studebaker's** (2000 N. Kings Hwy., ☎ 803/448–9747 or 803/626–3855) and **Duck's** (229 Main St., N. Myrtle Beach, ☎ 803/249–3858). At the Breakers Hotel, **At-**

lantis Nightlife (Hwy. 501, ☎ 803/448–4200) is three nightclubs in one: a high-energy dance club, live entertainment and music, and a quiet patio lounge. At the **Afterdeck,** enjoy live bands, dancing, and comedy at an open-air club along the Intracoastal Waterway (Hwy. 17, Restaurant Row, ☎ 803/449–1550).

In Murrells Inlet: **Drunken Jack's** (☎ 803/651–2044 or 803/651–3232) is a popular restaurant with a lounge overlooking the docks and fishing fleets.

Country-western shows and other live acts have added a new dimension to Grand Strand entertainment. Currently, music lovers have 10 family-oriented shows to choose from: the 2,250-seat **Alabama Theater** (Barefoot Landing, 4750 U.S. 17, N. Myrtle Beach, tel 803/272–1111); **Carolina Opry** (82nd Ave. N, Myrtle Beach, ☎ 803/238–8888 or 800/843–6779); **Dolly Parton's Dixie Stampede** (next door to Carolina Opry, 8901-B U.S. 17 Bus., Myrtle Beach, ☎ 803/497–9700); **Dixie Jubilee** (701 Main St., N. Myrtle Beach, ☎ 803/238–8888 or 800/843–6779); **Southern Country Nights** (301 U.S. 17 Bus., Surfside Beach, ☎ 803/238–8888 or 800/843–6779).

The **Fantasy Harbor** complex (Hwy. 51 across from the Waccamaw Outlet Mall) includes five theaters: 200-seat **Gatlin Brothers Theatre** (☎ 803/395–6802 or 800/681–7469); **Euro Circus: The Russian Fantasy** (☎ 803/236–8500 or 800/830–3876); **Magic on Ice** (☎ 803/236–8500 or 800/395–6802); **Medieval Times Dinner & Tournment** (☎ 803/236–8080 or 800/436–4386), which opened early in 1995; and the 2000-seat **Ronnie Milsap Theatre** (☎ 803/236–8500).

Myrtle Beach and the Strand Essentials

Arriving and Departing, Getting Around

BY BOAT
Boaters traveling the Intracoastal Waterway may dock at **Hague Marina** (Hwy. 707, Myrtle Beach, ☎ 803/293–2141).

BY BUS
Greyhound Bus Lines (☎ 800/231–2222) serves Myrtle Beach.

BY CAR
Midway between New York and Miami, the Grand Strand can be reached from all directions via Interstates 20, 26, 40, 77, 85, and 95, which connect with U.S. 17, the major north–south coastal route through the Strand.

BY PLANE
The **Myrtle Beach Jetport** (☎ 803/448–1589) is served by American, American and its American Eagle affiliate, Delta and its Atlantic Southeast Airlines affiliate, and USAir.

BY TAXI
Service is provided by **Coastal Cab Service** in Myrtle Beach (☎ 803/448–3360 or 803/448–4444).

BY TRAIN
Amtrak (☎ 800/872–7245) service for the Grand Strand is available through a terminal in Florence. Buses connect with Amtrak there for the 65-mile drive to Myrtle Beach.

Guided Tours

Palmetto Tour & Travel (☎ 803/626–2660) and **Leisure Time Unlimited/Gray Line** (☎ 803/448–9483), both in Myrtle Beach, offer tour packages, guide services, and charter services. At the **Georgetown County Chamber of Commerce and Information Center** (102 Broad St., ☎ 803/546–8436 or 800/777–7705), you can take tours of historic areas (Mar.–Oct.) by tram, by 1840 horse-drawn carriage, or by boat. You can also rent cassette walking tours and pick up free driving- and walking-tour maps. **Georgetown Tour Company** (627 Front St., ☎ 803/546–9812 or 803/546–6827) offers tram tours of the historic district, a Ghostbusting Tour, and an afternoon Tea 'n Tour.

Important Addresses and Numbers

EMERGENCIES
Dial 911 for emergency assistance. The emergency room is open 24 hours a day at the **Grand Strand General Hospital** (off U.S. 17 at 809 82nd Pkwy., Myrtle Beach, ☎ 803/449–4411).

PHARMACY
The only all-night pharmacy in the area is located at the **Grand Strand General Hospital** (*above*).

RADIO STATIONS
FM: WDAI 98.5, light rock; WJXY 93.9, country; WJYR 92.1, easy listening; WKZQ 101.7, rock and roll; WNMB 105.9, best of the 60's–80's; WRNN 94.5, talk; WSYN 106.5, oldies; WYAK 103.1, country; WYAV 104, classic rock.

VISITOR INFORMATION
Georgetown County Chamber of Commerce and Information Center (*see* Guided Tours, *above*). **Myrtle Beach Area Chamber of Commerce and Information Center** (1301 N. Kings Hwy., Box 2115, Myrtle Beach 29578, ☎ 803/626–7444 or 800/356–3016, for brochures only).

HILTON HEAD AND BEYOND

Anchoring the southern tip of South Carolina's coastline is 42-square-mile Hilton Head Island, named after English sea captain William Hilton, who claimed it for England in 1663. It was settled by planters in the 1700s and flourished until the Civil War. Thereafter, the economy declined and the island languished until Charles E. Fraser, a visionary South Carolina attorney, began developing the Sea Pines resort in 1956. Other developments followed, and today Hilton Head's casual pace, broad beaches, myriad activities, and genteel good life make it one of the East Coast's most popular vacation getaways.

Beaufort (pronounced "Bewfort") is a graceful antebellum town with a compact historic district preserving lavish 18th- and 19th-century homes. Southeast, on the ocean, lies Fripp Island, a self-contained resort with controlled access. And midway between Beaufort and Charleston is Edisto ("ED–is–toh") Island, settled in 1690 and once notable for its silky Sea Island cotton. Some of its elaborate mansions have been restored; others brood in disrepair.

Exploring

Lined by towering pines, wind-sculpted live oaks, and palmettos, Hilton Head's 12 miles of beaches are a major attraction, and the semitropical barrier island also has oak and pine woodlands and meandering lagoons. Choice stretches are occupied by various resorts, or "plantations," among them Sea Pines, Shipyard, Palmetto Dunes, Port Royal, and Hilton Head. In these areas, accommodations range from rental villas and lavish private houses to luxury hotels (except Hilton Head, which has no rentals). The resorts are also private residential communities, although many have public restaurants, marinas, shopping areas, and recreational facilities. All are secured, and visitors cannot tour them unless arrangements are made at the visitor office near the main gate of each plantation.

In the south of the island, at the **Audubon–Newhall Preserve,** you'll find unusual native plant life identified and tagged in a pristine 50-acre site. There are trails, a self-guided tour, and seasonal plant walks. *Palmetto Bay Rd.,* ☎ *803/671–2008.* ☛ *Free.* ☉ *Dawn to dusk.*

Also in the south is the **Sea Pines Forest Preserve,** a 605-acre public wilderness tract with walking trails, a well-stocked fishing pond, a waterfowl pond, and a 3,400-year-old Indian shell ring. Both guided and self-guided tours are available. Sea Pines is located at the southwest tip of the island, accessible via US 278 (also called William Hilton Parkway). ☎ *803/842–1449.* ☛ *To Sea Pines Plantation: $3 per car for nonguests; this allows free access to preserve.* ☉ *Daily 7–4. Closed during the Heritage Golf Classic in Apr.*

The **Museum of Hilton Head Island**'s permanent collection consists of a diorama depicting Indian life on Hilton Head in the 15th century AD; the museum also hosts changing exhibits. Beach walks are conducted on weekdays, and tours of Indian sites, forts, and plantations randomly in season. *100 William Hilton Pkwy.,* ☎ *803/689–6767.* ☛ *Free.* ☉ *Mon.–Sat. 10–5, Sun. noon–4.*

Three miles west of the island, there's the **James M. Waddell Jr. Mariculture Research & Development Center,** where methods of raising seafood commercially are studied. Visitors may tour its 24 ponds and research building to see work in progress. *Sawmill Creek Rd., near the intersection of U.S. 278 and SC 46,* ☎ *803/837–3795.* ☛ *Free. Tours weekdays at 10 AM and by appointment.*

Beaufort

North of here is the waterfront city of **Beaufort,** established in 1710. It achieved immense prosperity toward the close of the 18th century when Sea Island cotton was introduced, and many of its lavish houses— with wide balconies, high ceilings, and luxurious appointments—remain today. Although many private houses in **Old Point,** the historic district, are not usually open to visitors, some may be on the annual Fall House Tour in mid-October, and the Spring Tour of Homes and Gardens, in April or May. The Greater Beaufort Chamber of Commerce (☎ 803/524–3163) can provide more information about house tour schedules. The rest of the year, you'll have to content yourself with appreciating the fine exteriors.

Across the street from the Chamber of Commerce is the **George Elliot House Museum,** which served as a Union hospital during the Civil War. It was built in 1840 in Greek Revival style, with leaded-glass fanlights, pine floors, and rococo ceilings. The furnishings include some fine early Victorian pieces. *1001 Bay St.,* ☎ *803/524–6334.* ☛ *$3 adults, $2 children under 15.* ☉ *Weekdays 11–3. Closed Jan.–early Feb.*

Nearby, the **John Mark Verdier House Museum,** built about 1790 in the Federal style, has been restored and furnished as it would have been between 1790 and the visit of Lafayette in 1825. It was headquarters for Union forces during the Civil War. *801 Bay St.,* ☎ *803/524–6334.* ☞ *$4 adults, $2 children under 15.* ⊘ *Tues.–Sat. 11–4.*

Built in 1795 and remodeled in 1852, the Gothic-style arsenal that was home of the Beaufort Volunteer Artillery now houses the **Beaufort Museum,** with prehistoric relics, Indian pottery, and Revolutionary and Civil War exhibits. *713 Craven St.,* ☎ *803/525–7077.* ☞ *$2 adults, 50¢ students and children 6–18.* ⊘ *Mon.–Tues. and Thurs.–Sat. 10–5, Sun. 1–5.*

St. Helena's Episcopal Church, dating from 1724, was also touched by the Civil War: It was turned into a hospital and gravestones were brought inside to serve as operating tables. *501 Church St.,* ☎ *803/522–1712.* ⊘ *Mon.–Sat. 10–4.*

Before setting off to explore outlying areas, pause in the **Henry C. Chambers Waterfront Park** off Bay Street to rest and survey the scene. Barbara Streisand filmed *Prince of Tides* here. Its seven landscaped acres along the Beaufort River, part of the Intracoastal Waterway, include a seawall promenade, a crafts market, gardens, and a marina. Some events of the popular mid-July Beaufort Water Festival, as well as a seasonal farmers'/crafts market, take place here.

On the Coast

Nine miles southeast of Beaufort via U.S. 21 is **St. Helena's Island,** site of the **Penn Center Historic District** and **York W. Bailey Museum.** Penn Center, established in the middle of the Civil War as the South's first school for freed slaves, today provides community services. The museum (formerly Dr. Bailey's clinic) has displays reflecting the heritage of sea island blacks. *Land's End Rd., St. Helena's Island,* ☎ *803/838–2432. Donation suggested.* ⊘ *Tues.–Fri. 11–4 and by appointment.*

Nine miles farther east via U.S. 21 is **Hunting Island State Park,** a secluded domain of beach, nature trails, and varied fishing. The 1,120-foot fishing pier is among the longest on the East Coast. If you climb the 181 steps of the photogenic 140-foot **Hunting Island Lighthouse** (built in 1859 and abandoned in 1933) you'll be rewarded with sweeping views. ☎ *803/838–2011.* ☞ *$3 per car Mar.–Oct.; free rest of year. For cabin and camping reservations, write to Hunting Island State Park, 1775 Sea Island Pkwy., St. Helena 29920.*

Heading north from Beaufort on U.S. 21 to Gardens Corner, take Routes 17N and S-7-21 to the ruins of the **Sheldon Church,** built in 1753 and burned in 1779 and 1865. Only the brick walls and columns remain beside the old cemetery. Get back on Route 17N and then follow Route 174 to **Edisto Island** (80 miles from Beaufort). Here, magnificent stands of age-old oaks festooned with Spanish moss border quiet streams and side roads; wild turkeys still may be spotted on open grasslands and amid palmetto palms. Many of the island's inhabitants are descendants of former slaves. **Edisto Beach State Park** has 3 miles of beach with excellent shelling, housekeeping cabins by the marsh, and campsites by the ocean. Luxury resort development have also recently begun to encroach upon the scene. For camping reservations, call 803/869–2156 or 803/869–3396.

What to See and Do with Children

On Hilton Head Island, all major hotels offer **summer youth activities,** some have full-scale youth programs. The Island Recreation Center (Wilborn Rd.) runs a summer camp that visiting youngsters can join.

Hilton Head Island Recreation Association, Box 22593, Hilton Head Island 29925, ☎ *803/681–7273.* ⊙ *Camp mid-June–late Aug., weekdays.*

Off the Beaten Path

From Hilton Head, you can go by boat to **Daufuskie Island,** the setting for Pat Conroy's novel *The Water Is Wide,* which was made into the movie *Conrack.* Most inhabitants, descendants of former slaves, live on small farms among remnants of churches, homes, and schools—reminders of prosperous antebellum times. With its unspoiled live oaks, pines, and palmettos, Daufuskie won't remain off the beaten track for long. Excursions to the island are run out of Hilton Head by **Adventure Cruises** (Shelter Cove Marina, ☎ 803/785–4558), **Vagabond Cruises** (Harbour Town Marina, ☎ 803/842–4155), and **Calibogue Cruises** (164-B Palmetto Bay Rd., ☎ 803/785–8242). You can arrange kayak nature trips at Shelter Cove Marina (☎ 803/384–8125) and South Beach Marina (☎ 803/671–2643).

At **Parris Island,** 10 miles south of Beaufort via SC 802, visitors are welcome to observe U.S. Marine Corps recruit training and take a guided tour or drive through in their own vehicles. There's a replica of the Iwo Jima flag-raising monument on the base. The **Parris Island Museum** exhibits vintage uniforms, photographs, and weapons. ☎ *803/525–2951.* ☛ *Free.* ⊙ *Fri.–Wed. 10–4:30, Thurs. 10–7.*

Shopping

Malls and Outlets

Major Hilton Head Island shopping sites include the **Mall at Shelter Cove** (Hwy. 278, ½ mi north of Palmetto Dunes Resort, ☎ 803/686–3090), with 55 shops and four restaurants; and **Coligny Plaza** (Coligny Circle, ☎ 803/842–6050), with 60-plus shops, restaurants, a movie theater, and a supermarket. **Shoppes on the Parkway** (Hwy. 278, 1 mi south of Palmetto Dunes Resort, ☎ 803/686–6233) comprises nearly 30 outlets, including Dansk, Gorham, Aileen, and Van Heusen. **Low Country Factory Outlet Village** (Hwy. 278 at the island gateway, ☎ 803/837–4339) has 40 outlets selling clothing, shoes, and housewares.

Antiques

Den of Antiquity (Hwy. 170, Beaufort, ☎ 803/842–6711), the area's largest antiques shop, carries a wide assortment of Low Country and nautical pieces. **Harbour Town Antiques** (Harbour Town, Hilton Head, ☎ 803/671–5999) carries American and English furniture and unusual Oriental and English porcelain.

Art Galleries

In Hilton Head, the **Red Piano Art Gallery** (220 Cordillo Pkwy., ☎ 803/785–2318) showcases works by island artists and craftspeople. In Beaufort, the **Rhett Gallery** (901 Bay St., ☎ 803/524–3339) sells Low Country art by members of the Rhett family and Stephen Webb.

Jewelry

On Hilton Head, the **Bird's Nest** (Coligny Plaza, ☎ 803/785–3737) sells locally made shell and sand-dollar jewelry. The **Goldsmith Shop** (3 Lagoon Rd., ☎ 803/785–2538) features classic jewelry, island charms, custom designs, and repairs. **Touch of Turquoise** (Mall at Shelter Cove, ☎ 803/842–3880) showcases creations in silver and turquoise.

In Beaufort, the **Craftseller** (813 Bay St., ☎ 803/525–6104) showcases jewelry and other items by Southern craftsfolk.

Nature

The **Audubon Nature Store** (The Village at Wexford, ☎ 803/785–4311) and the **Hammock Company** (Coligny Plaza, ☎ 803/686–3636 or 800/344–4264) sell gift items and other things with a nature theme.

Beaches

Although the resort beaches are reserved for guests and residents, there are four public entrances to Hilton Head's 12 miles of ocean beach. Two main parking and changing areas are at Coligny Circle, near the Holiday Inn, and on Folly Field Road, off U.S. 278. Signs along U.S. 278 point the way to Bradley and Singleton beaches, where parking space is limited. **Hunting Island State Park** and **Edisto Beach State Park** each have about 3 miles of public beach.

Sports

Bicycling

There are pathways in several areas of Hilton Head (many in the resorts), and pedaling is popular along the firmly packed beach. Bicycles can be rented at most hotels and resorts and at **Harbour Town Bicycles** (Heritage Plaza, ☎ 803/785–3546), **South Beach Cycles** (Sea Pines Plantation, ☎ 803/671–2453), and **Fish Landing Creek** (Palmetto Dunes, ☎ 803/785–2021).

Fishing

On Hilton Head, you can pick oysters, dig for clams, or cast for shrimp; supplies are available at **Shelter Cove Marina** at Palmetto Dunes (☎ 803/842–7001). Local marinas offer in-shore and deep-sea fishing charters. Each year a billfishing tournament and two king mackerel tournaments attract anglers.

Golf

Many of Hilton Head's 28 championship courses are open to the public, including **Palmetto Dunes** (☎ 803/785–1138), **Sea Pines** (☎ 803/842–8484), **Port Royal and Shipyard** (☎ 803/689–5600), **Island West Golf Course** (Hwy. 278, ☎ 803/689–6660), and **Old South Golf Links** (Hwy. 278, ☎ 803/785–5353). **Harbour Town Golf Links at Sea Pines** hosts the MCI Classic (☎ 803/671–2448) every spring.

Horseback Riding

Many trails wind through woods and nature preserves. Some stables in and near Hilton Head are: **Lawton Stables** (Sea Pines, ☎ 803/671–2586), **Rose Hill Plantation Stables** (Bluffton, ☎ 803/757–3082), and **Sandy Creek Stables** (near Spanish Wells, ☎ 803/689–3423).

Polo

There are matches every other Sunday during spring and fall at **Rose Hill Plantation** (Bluffton, ☎ 803/757–4945).

Tennis

There are more than 300 courts on Hilton Head. **Sea Pines Racquet Club** (☎ 803/842–8484), home of the Family Circle Tournament; **Shipyard** (☎ 803/686–8804); and **Port Royal** (☎ 803/686–8803) are highly rated. Clubs that welcome guests include **Palmetto Dunes** (☎ 803/785–1152) and **Van der Meer Tennis Center** (☎ 803/785–8388).

Windsurfing

Lessons and rentals are available from **Outside Hilton Head** at Sea Pines Resort's South Beach Marina (☎ 803/671–2643) and at Shelter Cove Plaza (☎ 803/686–6996).

Dining

Hilton Head serves South Carolina seafood, of course, but this cosmopolitan island has restaurants to suit every palate. Dress is casual unless otherwise noted.

CATEGORY	COST*
$$$$	over $25
$$$	$15–$25
$$	$7–$15
$	under $7

per person for a three-course meal, excluding drinks, service, and 5% tax

Beaufort
LOW COUNTRY

$$ New Gadsby Tavern. Dine on fresh seafood and Low Country specials in any of three dining areas overlooking Beaufort's Waterfront Park and bay. The formal dining room and taproom are noted for Italian specialties and great European desserts. On the terrace, you can feast on tapas or selections from a fresh raw bar. ✕ *822 Bay St.,* ☎ *803/525–1800. Reservations advised. AE, D, MC, V.*

Edisto Island
LOW COUNTRY

$$–$$$ Old Post Office. Try the veal Edistonian, the fussed-over pork chop, or ★ the blue-crab-and-asparagus pie, served with the house salad, vegetables, and freshly baked bread, at this island restaurant on Shore Creek. The house specialty is shrimp and grits. Originally Bailey's General Store and U.S. Post Office, the renovated building contains the original post office boxes and window. ✕ *Hwy. 174, 5 mi from Edisto Beach,* ☎ *803/869–2339. Reservations advised. MC, V. Closed Sun. June–Sept., Sun. and Mon. Oct.–May. No lunch.*

Hilton Head
CONTINENTAL

$$$$ Harbourmaster's. With sweeping views of the harbor, this spacious, multilevel dining room offers such dishes as chateaubriand and New Zealand rack of lamb laced with a brandy demiglaze. Service is deft. Prix-fixe early dinners ($16.95) are offered daily except Sunday. ✕ *Shelter Cove Marina, off U.S. 278,* ☎ *803/785–3030. Reservations required. Jacket required at dinner. AE, DC, MC, V. No lunch. Closed Sun. and Jan.*

$$$–$$$$ Barony Grill. A series of softly lighted seating areas with upscale country ★ French decor lead off the main dining room, which is centered with a display of drop-dead desserts, marzipan flowers, and exotic cheese and bread. Try an elegant low-calorie dish like chilled coconut-pineapple soup, asparagus salad with quail eggs, poached fillet of Dover sole with seafood mousse, or macédoine of fresh fruit with raspberry sauce.

✕ *Westin Resort, 135 S. Port Royal Dr.,* ☎ *803/681–4000. Reservations required. AE, D, DC, MC, V. No lunch.*

LOW COUNTRY

$$ Old Fort Pub. Tucked away in a quiet site overlooking Skull Creek and beside the Civil War ruins of Fort Mitchell, this rustic restaurant specializes in such dishes as oyster pie, oysters wrapped in Smithfield ham, Savannah chicken-fried steak with onion gravy, and hoppin' john (a Southern concoction of black-eyed peas and rice seasoned with ham hocks and Tabasco). ✕ *Hilton Head Plantation,* ☎ *803/681–2386. Reservations advised. AE, D, DC, MC, V. No lunch Sun.*

SEAFOOD

$$ Crazy Crab. This casual eatery serves seafood as fresh as you can get it—steamed, fried, baked, or broiled—at two locations overlooking the water. They're famous for their steamed seafood pot and Crazy Crab boil. ✕ *U.S. 278,* ☎ *803/681–5021 (no lunch); Harbour Town Yacht Basin,* ☎ *803/363–2722. No reservations. AE, D, MC, V.*

$$ Hemingway's. This oceanfront restaurant serves pompano *en papillote,* trout almandine with herbed lemon-butter sauce, fresh grilled seafoods, and steaks in a relaxed, Key West–type atmosphere. ✕ *Hyatt Regency Hilton Head, Palmetto Dunes Resort,* ☎ *803/785–1234. Reservations advised. AE, D, DC, MC, V. No lunch.*

$$ Hudson's on the Docks and **Carmine's.** Hudson's on the Docks is a huge, airy, family-owned restaurant with its own fishing fleet; freshly caught fish is rushed straight to the kitchens. The dining room seems always to be full, but service is quick and friendly, and diners never feel rushed. There's also an oyster bar. Next door is Carmine's, which specializes in steaks and ribs, as well as serving seafood. A third branch, **Hudson's on the Beach,** nearby at Coligny Place, also emphasizes seafood. ✕ *Hudson's on the Docks and Carmine's: The Landing,* ☎ *803/681–2772. Hudson's on the Beach: Coligny Place,* ☎ *803/842–4888. All three: No reservations. AE, MC, V. Carmine's: No lunch. Closed Sun. Hudson's on the Beach: No lunch Sun.*

Lodging

Sea Pines, the oldest and best-known of Hilton Head's resort developments, or plantations, occupies 4,500 thickly wooded acres with three golf courses, a fine beach, tennis clubs, stables, and shopping plazas. The focus of Sea Pines is **Harbour Town,** built around the charming marina, which has shops, restaurants, some condominiums, and the landmark Hilton Head lighthouse. Accommodations are in luxurious houses and villas facing the ocean or the golf courses.

The Crystal Sands–Crowne Plaza Resort is the oceanfront centerpiece of **Shipyard Plantation,** which also has villa condominiums, three nine-hole courses, a tennis club, and a small beach club. **Palmetto Dunes Resort** has the oceanfront Hyatt Regency Hilton Head, the Hilton Resort and other accommodations, the renowned Rod Laver Tennis Center, a good stretch of beach, three golf courses, and several oceanfront rental villa complexes. At **Port Royal Plantation** there's the posh Westin Resort, which is on the beach and has three golf courses and a tennis club.

Hilton Head Central Reservations (Box 5312, Hilton Head Island 29938, ☎ 803/785–9050 or 800/845–7018, ℻ 803/686-3255) represents almost every hotel, motel, and rental agency on the island. Other options are available through the **Hilton Head Condo Hotline** (☎ 803/785–2939 or 800/258–5852, ext. 53) and **Hilton Head Reserva-**

tions and Golf Line (☎ 803/444–4772). Rates drop appreciably in the off-season (Nov.–Mar.), and package plans are available year-round.

CATEGORY	COST*
$$$$	over $145
$$$	$95–$145
$$	$55–$95
$	under $50

All prices are for a standard double room, excluding 7% tax

Beaufort

$$$ **Rhett House Inn.** True southern hospitality can be had at this story-
★ book inn in the heart of the historic district. Art and antiques fill the rooms, and guests are served breakfast and afternoon tea. The restaurant, which is open to the public by reservation, serves such excellent Continental fare as leek-and-goat cheese tarts, seared veal chops in a green peppercorn sauce, and chicken fricassee with quenelles. ☎ *1009 Craven St., 29902, ☎ 803/524–9030, FAX 803/524–1310. 9 rooms with bath, 1 suite. Bicycles, billiards. MC, V.*

$$$ **Two Suns Inn.** Guests at this B&B, a restored 1917 Neoclassical house overlooking the Beaufort River, enjoy large rooms, afternoon tea-and-toddy hour, and a full breakfast. The inn also has an extensive business center and extremely down-to-earth and friendly hosts, making this a great spot for business travelers after companionship and computer modems. ☎ *1705 Bay St., 29902, ☎ FAX 803/522–1122, ☎ 800/552–4244. 5 rooms with baths. AE, MC, V.*

$$ **Best Western Sea Island Inn.** At this well-maintained resort inn in the downtown historic district, rooms feature period decor. ☎ *1015 Bay St., Box 532, 29902, ☎ 803/524–4121 or 800/528–1234, FAX 803/524–9396. 43 rooms. Restaurant, lounge, pool. AE, DC, MC, V.*

Edisto Island

$$$ **Cassina Point Plantation.** You can live out your fantasies about the antebellum days at this authentically restored plantation house, now a bed-and-breakfast inn, surrounded by fields that used to be planted in Sea Island cotton. Federal troops who occupied the house for three years left their graffiti in the basement. Guests may fish in the creek (watch for the playful porpoises), go crabbing or shrimping, watch birds, or take a stroll. A fruit bowl, beverages, and full breakfast come with the room. ☎ *1642 Clark Rd., Box 535, 29438, ☎ 803/869–2535. 4 rooms with half baths (2 full hall baths). Croquet, boating. No credit cards.*

$$–$$$ **Fairfield Ocean Ridge Resort.** This is a good choice for vacationers seeking to combine all the resort amenities with a get-away-from-it-all setting. There are accommodations in well-furnished two- and three-bedroom villa units tastefully decorated in contemporary style. ☎ *1 King Cotton Rd., Box 27, 29438, ☎ 803/869–2561 or 800/845–8500, FAX 803/869–2384. 100 units. Restaurant, lounge, pool, wading pool, 18-hole golf course, miniature golf, 4 tennis courts, hiking trails, beach, boating, fishing. AE, D, MC, V.*

Fripp Island

$$–$$$ **Fripp Island Resort.** The resort encompasses the entire island, and access is limited to guests only. The two- and three-bedroom villas are contemporary in decor. ☎ *19 mi south of Beaufort via U.S. 21, 1 Tarpon Blvd., 29920, ☎ 803/838–3535 or 800/845–4100, FAX 803/828–2733. 133 units. 3 restaurants, 6 pools, 18-hole golf course, 10 tennis courts, jogging, boating, rental bikes and bike paths. AE, MC, V.*

Hilton Head Island

$$$$ **Hyatt Regency Hilton Head Resort.** Recent renovation added 150 rooms to the island's largest oceanfront resort property. Spacious rooms are in pastel tones; some have balconies. Guests have golf and tennis privileges at the nearby Palmetto Dunes Resort. ⚎ *U.S. 278, Box 6167, 29938,* ☎ *803/785–1234 or 800/233–1234,* FAX *803/842–4695. 475 rooms, 30 suites. 3 restaurants, lounge, indoor and outdoor pools (one each), health club, beach, boating, concierge floor, convention facilities. AE, DC, MC, V.*

$$$$ **Westin Resort, Hilton Head Island.** This horseshoe-shaped hotel sprawls
★ in a lushly landscaped oceanfront setting. The expansive guest rooms, most with ocean views, are furnished in a mix of period reproduction and contemporary furnishings. All have comfortable seating areas and desks. Public areas display fine Oriental porcelains, screens, and paintings. ⚎ *2 Grass Lawn Ave., 29928,* ☎ *803/681–4000 or 800/228–3000,* FAX *803/681–1087. 415 rooms, 38 suites. 3 restaurants, 3 lounges, pool, health club. AE, DC, MC, V.*

$$$–$$$$ **Crystal Sands–Crowne Plaza Resort.** Holiday Inn Worldwide's first property of this caliber in the United States, this oceanfront resort (formerly Marriott's Hilton Head) opened in 1993. Decorated in a nautical theme and set in a luxuriant garden, it offers all the amenities of Shipyard Plantation. ⚎ *130 Shipyard Dr., 29928,* ☎ *803/842–2400 or 800/465–4329,* FAX *803/785–8463. 313 rooms, 25 suites. 2 restaurants, pub, indoor and outdoor pools, spa, 9- and 18-hole golf courses, racquetball, health club, business services, meeting rooms. AE, D, DC, MC, V.*

$$$–$$$$ **Hilton Head Island Resort.** There's a Caribbean feel to this five-story resort hotel. The grounds are beautifully landscaped, and the rooms, all oceanside, are spacious and colorfully decorated in a modern style. ⚎ *23 Ocean La., Box 6165, 29938,* ☎ *803/842–8000 or 800/845–8001,* FAX *803/842–4988. 303 rooms, 20 suites. Restaurant, pool, hot tub, sauna, health club, volleyball, boating, fishing, bicycles. AE, DC, MC, V.*

$$$–$$$$ **Marriott's Grande Ocean Resort.** Though built as a time-share property, this beautiful oceanfront condo development, within walking distance of shops and restaurants, offers a limited number of rentals. The fully furnished two-bedroom, two-bath luxurious villas come with kitchens, large whirlpool tubs, and maid service. ⚎ *51 S. Forest Beach Dr., 29929,* ☎ *803/785–2000 or 800/473–6674,* FAX *803/842–3413. 140 villas. Deli, lounge, indoor pool, exercise room. AE, MC, V.*

$$$ **Holiday Inn Oceanfront Resort.** This handsome high-rise motor hotel is on a broad, quiet stretch of beach. The rooms are spacious and well furnished in a contemporary style. ⚎ *S. Forest Beach Dr., Box 5728, 29938,* ☎ *803/785–5126 or 800/465–4329,* FAX *803/785–6678. 249 rooms. Restaurant, 2 lounges, pool. AE, D, DC, MC, V.*

$–$$ **Red Roof Inn.** This budget-priced, two-story inn is especially popular with families. Clean and functional rooms are just a short drive from the public beaches. ⚎ *5 Regency Pkwy. (U.S. 278), 29928,* ☎ *803/686–6808 or 800/843–7663,* FAX *803/842–3352. 112 rooms. AE, D, DC, MC, V.*

The Arts

The **Cultural Council of Hilton Head** (☎ 803/686–3945) has details on Hilton Head arts events. **Community Playhouse** (Arrow Rd., ☎ 803/785–4878) presents up to 10 musicals or plays each year and has a young people's theater program. In warm weather, free outdoor concerts are held at **Harbour Town** and **Shelter Cove.** Concerts, plays, films, art shows, theater, sporting events, food fairs, and minitournaments make up Hilton Head's **SpringFest,** (☎ 803/686–4944), which runs for the month of March.

Nightlife

Dancing

Club Indigo (☎ 803/785–1234), a large cabaret downstairs at the Hyatt Regency Hilton Head, has dancing and two shows nightly Monday through Saturday. **Regatta** (☎ 803/842–8000), a sophisticated oceanfront night spot in the Hilton Resort, features smooth jazz nightly. **Robber's Row** (☎ 803/785–5126), a locally popular lounge in the Holiday Inn Oceanfront Resort, has nightly entertainment, as does **Signals** (☎ 803/842–2400), in the Crystal Sands–Crowne Plaza Resort.

Easy Listening

Cafe Europa (☎ 803/671–3399), at the Lighthouse in Harbour Town, has nightly piano entertainment. **Hemingway's Lounge** (☎ 803/785–1234) at the Hyatt Regency Hilton Head has live entertainment in a casually elegant setting Tuesday through Saturday. The **Pelican Poolside** (☎ 803/681–4000), an oceanfront lounge at the Westin Resort, has informal entertainment every night but Sunday. **Playful Pelican** (☎ 803/681–4000), the pool bar at the same location, has a live calypso band Tuesday through Sunday from 1 to 4 PM.

Hilton Head Essentials

Arriving and Departing, Getting Around

BY BOAT

Hilton Head is accessible via the Intracoastal Waterway, with docking available at **Shelter Cove Marina** (☎ 803/842–7001), **Harbour Town Marina** (☎ 803/671–2704), and **Schilling Boathouse** (☎ 803/681–2628).

BY CAR

The island is 40 miles east of I–95 (Exit 28 off I–95S, Exit 5 off I–95N).

BY PLANE

Hilton Head Island Airport (no ☎) is served by USAir Express. Most travelers use the **Savannah International Airport** (☎ 912/964–0514), about an hour from Hilton Head, which is served by Delta, United, USAir, and ValuJet.

BY TAXI

Yellow Cab (☎ 803/686–6666) and **Low Country Taxi and Limousine Service** (☎ 803/681–8294) provide service in Hilton Head.

Guided Tours

Low Country Adventures (☎ 803/681–8212) offers tours of Hilton Head, Beaufort, and Charleston. **Discover Hilton Head** (☎ 803/842–9217) gives daily historical tours of the island. Hilton Head's **Adventure Cruises** (☎ 803/785–4558) offers dinner, sightseeing, and murder-mystery cruises. Several companies, including **Harbour Town Charters** (☎ 803/363–2628), run dolphin sightseeing and feeding trips. Call the **Greater Beaufort Chamber of Commerce** (☎ 803/524–3163) to find out about self-guided walking or driving tours of Beaufort.

Important Addresses and Numbers

EMERGENCIES

Dial 911 for police, fire, and ambulance assistance. Emergency medical service is available at the **Hilton Head Hospital** (Hospital Center Blvd., ☎ 803/681–6122).

RADIO STATIONS

AM: WFXH 1130, sports talk. **FM:** WFXH 106.1, classic rock; WAEV 97.3, adult contemporary; WLVH 101.1, soft soul; WJCL 96.5, country; WOCW 92.1, oldies; WNCK 99.7, beach, boogie, and blues.

VISITOR INFORMATION

Greater Beaufort Chamber of Commerce (Box 910, 1006 Bay St., Beaufort 29901-0910, ☎ 803/524–3163). In Hilton Head, your best bet for tourist information is to stop by the **Welcome Center and Museum of Hilton Head** (100 William Hilton Pkwy.; calls automatically go to the Hilton Head Island Chamber of Commerce, ☎ 803/785–3673), which opened in 1994. You can also write to the **Hilton Head Island Chamber of Commerce** (Box 5647, Hilton Head 29938, ☎ 803/785–3673). The two **Hilton Head Welcome Centers,** run by a private real estate firm, are on Route 278 next to the bridge to Hilton Head and at 6 Lagoon Road at the south end of the island. In addition to providing tourism information about the island, these centers attempt to entice you into purchasing real estate on Hilton Head.

THE HEARTLAND

South Carolina's Heartland, between the coastal Low Country and the mountains, is a varied region of swamps and flowing rivers, fertile farmland, and vast forests of pines and hardwoods. Lakes Murray, Marion, and Moultrie offer wonderful fishing, and the many state parks are popular for hunting, hiking, swimming, and camping. At the center of the region is the state capital, Columbia, an engaging contemporary city superimposed on cherished historic remnants. It's a city of restored mansions, several museums, a university, a variety of dining, a lively arts scene, and one of the country's best zoos.

In Aiken, the center of South Carolina's Thoroughbred Country, such champions as Kelso and Pleasant Colony were trained. The beautiful scenery is studded with the fine mansions of such wealthy Northerners as the Vanderbilts and Whitneys. Throughout the region, towns like Ninety Six, Sumter, and Camden preserve and interpret the past, with historic re-creations, exhibits, and restorations. Several splendid public gardens provide islands of color during much of the year.

Exploring

Columbia

In 1786, South Carolina's capital was moved from Charleston to Columbia, in the center of the state along the banks of the Congaree River. One of the nation's first planned cities, Columbia's streets are among the widest in America—designed this way because it was then thought that stagnant air fostered the spread of malaria. The city soon grew into a center of political, commercial, cultural, and social activity. But in early 1865 General William Tecumseh Sherman invaded South Carolina with a destructive determination described by a New York newspaper as 50 times worse than the earlier march through Georgia. Two-thirds of Columbia was incinerated, though a few homes and public buildings were spared. Today the city is a sprawling blend of modern office blocks, suburban neighborhoods, and the occasional ante-bellum home.

Our tour begins at the **State House.** Started in 1855 and completed in 1950, the Capitol is made of native blue granite in the Italian-Renaissance style. Six bronze stars on the outer western wall mark direct hits by Sherman's cannons. The interior is richly appointed with brass, marble, mahogany, and artworks, and a replica of Jean Antoine Houdon's statue of George Washington is on the grounds. The building was closed in 1995 for three years of extensive renovation. *Main and Gervais Sts.,* ☏ *803/734–2430.* ☛ *Free.*

The **Fort Jackson Museum,** on the grounds of the U.S. Army Training Center, displays armaments, heavy equipment from the two world wars, and exhibits on the life of Andrew Jackson. *Bldg. 4442, Jackson Blvd.,* ☏ *803/751–7419.* ☛ *Free.* ☉ *Tues.–Fri. 10–4, weekends 1–4.*

The **Columbia Museum of Art and Gibbes Planetarium** contains the Kress Foundation Collection of Renaissance and Baroque treasures, sculpture, decorative arts, and European and American paintings, with special emphasis on works by Southeastern artists. *1112 Bull St.,* ☏ *803/799–2810.* ☛ *Free; planetarium shows: $2.50 adults, $1.50 children under 18 and senior citizens.* ☉ *Tues.–Fri. 10–5, weekends 12:30–5. Planetarium shows weekends at 2, 3, and 4.*

Exhibits at the **South Carolina State Museum,** in a large, refurbished textile mill, interpret the state's natural history, archaeology, historical development, technological and artistic accomplishments. A permanent exhibit portrays noted black astronauts (dedicated to South Carolina native Dr. Ronald McNair, who died on the *Challenger*), and another focuses on the cotton industry and slavery. An iron gate made for the museum by Phillip Simmons, the "dean of Charleston Blacksmiths," is also on display. *301 Gervais St.,* ☏ *803/737–4921.* ☛ *$4 adults, $3 senior citizens, $1.50 children 6–17.* ☉ *Mon.–Sat. 10–5, Sun. 1–5.*

TIME OUT   For a quick and tasty break, check out the **Gourmet Shop Cafe** (724 Saluda Ave., ☏ 803/799-3705), in the heart of the Five Points Shopping District (*see* Shopping, *below*). You can choose from among dozens of fancy sandwiches and salads here. The Amaretto cheesecake is memorable.

Stop by the Museum Shop at Taylor and Henderson Streets in the historic district to get a map and buy tickets to tour the four Columbia houses that have been restored and opened to the public. The **Hampton–Preston Mansion** (1615 Blanding St., ☏ 803/252–1770), dating from 1818, is filled with lavish furnishings collected by three generations of two influential families. The classic, columned 1823 **Robert Mills House** (1616 Blanding St., ☏ 803/252–1770) was named for its architect who later designed the Washington Monument. It has opulent Regency furniture, marble mantels, silver doorknobs, and spacious grounds. **Mann–Simons Cottage-Museum of African-American Cultures** (1403 Richland St., ☏ 803/252–1770) was the home of Celia Mann, one of only 200 free African-Americans in Columbia in the mid-1800s. The nearby **Woodrow Wilson Boyhood Home** (1705 Hampton St., ☏ 803/252–1770) displays the gaslights, arched doorways, and ornate furnishings of the Victorian period. ☛ *To each house: $3 adults, $1.50 students; combination ticket to all four houses: $10 adults, $5 students.* ☉ *All houses Tues.–Sat. 10:15–3:15, Sun. 1:15–4:15.*

Riverfront Park and Historic Columbia Canal, where the Broad and Saluda rivers meet, is made around the city's original waterworks and hydroelectric plant. Interpretive markers describe the area's plant and animal life and tell the history of the buildings. *312 Laurel St.,* ☎ *803/733–8613.* ☛ *Free.* ☉ *Daily dawn to dusk.*

★ **Riverbanks Zoological Park and Botanical Gardens** contains more than 2,000 animals and birds, some endangered, in natural habitats. Walk along pathways and through landscaped gardens to see polar bears, Siberian tigers, and American bald eagles. The South American primate collection has won international acclaim, and the park is noted for its success in breeding endangered and fragile species. There's also an aquarium-reptile complex, whose four habitats exhibit South Carolina, desert, tropical, and marine specimens. In June 1995 a new 70-acre Botanical Garden was added on the west bank of the Saluda River, doubling the size of the facility. *I–126 and U.S. 76 at Greystone Riverbanks exit,* ☎ *803/779–8717 or 803/779–8730.* ☛ *$4.75 adults, $3.25 senior citizens, $2.25 children 3–12.* ☉ *9–4 weekdays, 9–5 summer weekends.*

Camden

From Columbia, drive northeast on I–20 for 32 miles to charming **Camden,** a town with a horsy history and grand Southern Colonial homes. Camden's fanciest roads remain unpaved for the sake of the hooves of the horses who regularly trot over them. A center of textile trade from the late 19th century through the 1940s, Camden attracted Northerners escaping the cold winters; one of its early prominent families, the DuPonts, is today one of Camden's major employers. Because General Sherman spared the town during the War Between the States, most of its antebellum homes still stand. It's South Carolina's oldest inland town, dating to 1732. British General Lord Cornwallis established a garrison here during the Revolutionary War, and burned most of Camden before evacuating it. Today, the **Historic Camden Revolutionary War Site** re-creates the British occupation of 1780 on the site of the early 19th-century village. Several house restorations display period furnishings, including Cornwallis's headquarters, the **Kershaw–Cornwallis House** (circa 1770). Nature trails, fortifications, a powder magazine, a picnic area, and a crafts shop are also here. *U.S. 521, 1.4 mi north of I–20,* ☎ *803/432–9841.* ☛ *$4.50 adults, $4 senior citizens, $1.50 children.* ☉ *For guided tours Tues.–Sat. 10–4, Sun. 1–4. Museum shop open daily 10–5.*

Sumter

From Camden, drive southeast on U.S. 521 for 30 miles to **Sumter.** Named for the Revolutionary War hero and statesman General Thomas Sumter, the city was settled about 1740 as the center of a cultivated plantation district. Today it is home to varied industries, lumbering, agricultural marketing, and nearby Shaw Air Force Base. The **Sumter County Museum and Archives** (headquarters of the Sumter County Historical Society), in a lovely 1845 Victorian Gothic house, exhibits fine period furnishings, Oriental carpeting, vintage carriages, dolls, and various memorabilia. Archival records are valuable for tracing family roots. *122 N. Washington St.,* ☎ *803/775–0908.* ☛ *Free.* ☉ *Museum Tues.–Sat. 10–5, Sun. 2–5;* ☉ *archives Tues.–Sat. 10–5.*

Swan Lake Iris Gardens is like Eden when its 6 million irises are in bloom. Royal-white-mute, black-necked, coscoroba, whooper, trumpeter, and black Australian swans paddle leisurely around the 45-acre lake. The 150-acre park also includes walking trails, picnic areas, tennis courts, a playground, and concessions. *W. Liberty St.,* ☎ *803/775–3304.* ☛ *Free.* ⊙ *Daily 8–sunset.*

Aiken and Beyond

Head south along U.S. 301/601, then west on U.S. 78 to **Aiken,** in Thoroughbred Country, about 64 miles altogether. Aiken's fame began during the 1890s, when wealthy Northerners wintering here built stately mansions and entertained each other with lavish parties, horse shows, and hunts. Many of the mansions—some with up to 90 rooms—remain as testament to this era of opulence. Since those days, the area's horse farms have produced many national champions, which are commemorated at the **Aiken Racing Hall of Fame** with exhibitions of horse-related decorations, paintings, and sculptures, plus racing silks and trophies. The Hall of Fame is on the grounds of the 14-acre **Hopeland Gardens,** with winding paths, quiet terraces, and reflecting pools. There's a Touch and Scent Trail with Braille plaques. Open-air free concerts and plays are presented on Monday evenings mid-July–August. *Corner of Dupree Pl. and Whiskey Rd.,* ☎ *803/642–7630.* ☛ *Free.* ⊙ *Museum fall–spring, Tues.–Sun. 2–5;* ⊙ *grounds daily sunrise–sunset.*

TIME OUT The who's who of Aiken's horsy set can be found most mornings feasting in the **Track Kitchen** (Mead Ave., ☎ 803/641–9628) on the heavy and hearty cooking of Carol and Pockets Curtis. The small dining room is quite unpretentious, with walls of mint-green cinder block and simple formica counters. The best time to people-watch is at about 4 AM.

The **Aiken County Historical Museum,** devoted to early regional culture, has Native American artifacts, firearms, an authentically furnished 1808 log cabin, and a one-room schoolhouse. *433 Newberry St. SW,* ☎ *803/642–2015. Donations accepted.* ⊙ *Tues.–Fri. 9:30–4:30, first Sun. of each month 2–5.*

Aiken surrounds the serene and wild **Hitchcock Woods** (enter from the junction of Clark Road and Whitney Drive, Berrie Road, and Dibble Road), a 2,000-acre tract of southern forest traversed by hiking trails and bridal paths.

About 64 miles northwest of Aiken is **Hickory Knob State Resort Park,** which has everything for a complete vacation. Take SC 19 and U.S. 25 to U.S. 378, drive west to the town of McCormick, then south until you see signs for the park on the shore of Strom Thurmond Lake. There's fishing, waterskiing, sailing, motorboating, a swimming pool, boat slips and a launch, a tackle shop, nature trails, an 18-hole championship golf course, a fully equipped pro shop, tennis courts, and skeet and archery ranges. If none of these is to your liking, bring your favorite canine for a training session on the 4-mile bird-dog field-trial area. An 80-room lodge, nine duplex lakeside cottages, campgrounds, and a restaurant round out Hickory Knob's offerings. *Rte. 1, Box 199B, McCormick 29835,* ☎ *803/391–2450.* ⊙ *Office daily 7 AM–11 PM.*

Abbeville

Return to McCormick via U.S. 378, then drive northwest 30 miles on SC 28 and SC 72 to **Abbeville.** This may well be one of inland South Carolina's most satisfying, though lesser-known, small towns. In Abbeville the "Southern cause" was born and died, for here the first organized secession meeting was held, and here on May 2, 1865, Confederate President Jefferson Davis officially disbanded the defeated armies of the South in the last meeting of his war council. The 1830 house

where the council met is the **Burt Stark Mansion** (306 N. Main St., ☎
803/459–4297 or 803/459–2181). ☛ *$3.* ☼ *Fri.–Sat. 1–5 or by ap-
pointment.*

In the **Abbeville Educational Garden** are the 1837 log cabin home of
Marie Cromer Siegler, founder of 4–H clubs, and an old jail housing
the Abbeville County Museum. *215 Poplar St.,* ☎ *803/459–2696.*

The **Abbeville Opera House** faces the historic town square. Built in 1908,
it has been renovated to reflect the grandeur of the days when lavish
road shows and stellar entertainers came center stage. Current productions range from light, contemporary comedies to Broadway-style
musicals. *Town Sq., Abbeville,* ☎ *803/459–2157. Reservations taken
weekdays 10–5.*

Greenwood
About 14 miles away on SC 72 is **Greenwood.** Founded by Irish settlers in 1802, the city received its name from the gently rolling landscape and dense forests. Andrew Johnson, the 17th U.S. president,
operated a tailor shop at Courthouse Square before migrating to eastern Tennessee. The **George W. Park Seed Co.,** one of the nation's
largest seed supply houses, maintains colorful experimental gardens
and greenhouses here. The flower beds are especially vivid June 15
through July, and seeds and bulbs are for sale in the company's store.
The South Carolina Festival of Flowers—with a performing-artists
contest, a beauty pageant, private house and garden tours, and live entertainment—is held here annually at the end of June. *On SC 245, 7
mi north of town,* ☎ *803/941–4213 or 800/845–3369.* ☛ *Free.* ☼
Gardens daily; ☼ *Store Mon.–Sat. 9–6.*

Ninety Six
Drive southeast about 10 miles to the **Ninety Six National Historic Site,**
which commemorates two Revolutionary War battles. The visitor center museum has descriptive displays, and there are remnants of the old
village, a reconstructed French-and-Indian-War stockade, and Revo-
lutionary-era fortifications. The nearby town of Ninety Six, on an old
Indian trade route, is so named for being 96 miles from the Cherokee
village of Keowee in the Blue Ridge Mountains. *SC 248,* ☎ *803/543–
4068.* ☛ *Free.* ☼ *Daily 8–5.*

Shopping

Antiques and Flea Markets
Many of Columbia's antiques outlets are in the **Congaree Vista Shop-
ping District** around Huger and Gervais streets, between the State
House and the river. A number of shops and cafés are in the **Five
Points Shopping District,** which is around the intersection of Blossom
and Harden streets. Other antiques shops are across the river on Meet-
ing and State streets in West Columbia. The **Old Mill Antique Mall** (310
State St., W. Columbia, ☎ 803/796–4229) and **Thieves Market Antique
Flea Mall** (502 Gadsden St., Columbia, ☎ 803/254–4997) show off
the wares of dozens of antiques and collectibles dealers.

Arts and Crafts
Abbeville's Town Square is lined with attractive gift and specialty
shops in restored historic buildings dating from the late 1800s. **Historic Camden** also has gifts and crafts for sale. In Walterboro, the
South Carolina Artisans Center was recently opened. You can shop for

one-of-a-kind pieces of handcrafted jewelry, pottery, baskets, and other wares while watching top South Carolina artists and craftsfolk ply their crafts. *334 Wickman St.,* ☎ *803/549–0011.* ☛ *Free.* ☉ *Mon.–Sat. 10–8, Sun. 1–6.*

Farmer's Market

The **State Farmer's Market** in Columbia (Bluff Rd., ☎ 803/253–4041) is one of the 10 largest in the country. Seasonal fresh vegetables are sold each weekday, along with flowers, plants, seafood, herbs, and more.

Wineries

Free tours and wine-tastings are offered by **Cruse Vineyards & Winery** (Woods Rd., off SC 72, 4 mi north of Chester, ☎ 803/377–3944) and **Montmorenci Vineyards** (U.S. 78, 2.5 mi east of Aiken, ☎ 803/649–4870; tours by appointment).

Participant Sports

Canoeing

A haunting canoe trail leads into a remote swampy depression at **Woods Bay State Park** (from Sumter, take U.S. 378E to U.S. 301N, ☎ 803/659–4445), where rentals are available for $2 per hour or $10 for a full day. Self-guided canoe trails traverse an alluvial floodplain bordered by high bluffs at the **Congaree Swamp National Monument** (20 mi southeast of Columbia off SC 48, ☎ 803/776–4396). Canoe rentals are available in Columbia at **Adventure Carolina** (☎ 803/796–4505) and the **River Runner Outdoor Center** (☎ 803/771–0353).

Fishing

Lakes Marion and **Moultrie** attract serious anglers after bream, crappie, striped bass, catfish, and large- and small-mouth bass. Supplies, camps, guides, rentals, and accommodations abound. For information, contact Santee Cooper Counties Promotion Commission (Drawer 40, Santee, SC 29142, ☎ 803/854–2131 or, outside SC, 800/227–8510).

Golf

The many fine courses in the area include **Highland Park Country Club** (Aiken, ☎ 803/649–6029), **Sedgewood** (Columbia, ☎ 803/776–2177), and **White Pines Golf Club** (Camden, ☎ 803/432–7442).

Hiking

Congaree Swamp National Monument (*see* Canoeing, *above*) has 22 miles of trails for hikers and nature lovers and a ¼-mile boardwalk for visitors with disabilities. Guided nature walks leave Saturday at 1:30 PM. For information on trails in the **Francis Marion National Forest** and the **Sumter National Forest,** contact the National Forest Service (1835 Assembly St., Columbia 29201, ☎ 803/765–5222).

White-Water Adventures

Rafting, kayaking, and canoeing on the Saluda River near Columbia offer challenging Class-3 and Class-4 rapids. Guided river and swamp excursions are also offered. In the Upcountry, the Chattooga National Wild and Scenic River, on the border of South Carolina and Georgia, provides guided rafting, canoeing, and kayaking. Contact **Wildwater Ltd.** (☎ 800/451–9972) or **Nantahala Outdoor Center** (☎ 800/832–7238).

Spectator Sports

Baseball

The **Columbia Mets** (☎ 803/256–4110), a Class-A affiliate of the New York Mets, play from mid-April through August at Capital City Stadium.

Equestrian Events

In Aiken, polo matches are played at Whitney Field (☎ 803/648–7874) on Sunday afternoons September–November and March–July. Three weekends in late March and early April are set aside for the famed **Triple Crown** (☎ 803/641–1111)—thoroughbred trials of promising yearlings, a steeplechase, and harness races by young horses making their debut. Camden puts on two steeplechase events: the **Carolina Cup** in late March or early April and the **Colonial Cup** in November (☎ 803/432–6513).

Stock-Car Races

Darlington Raceway (SC 34, 2 mi west of Darlington, ☎ 803/393–4041) is the scene of NASCAR's TranSouth 500 (part of the Winston Cup Series) in late March and the exciting Mountain Dew Southern 500 on Labor Day weekend.

Dining

South Carolina Heartland fare ranges from regional specialties like barbecue and country ham with red-eye gravy to unself-conscious Continental cuisine. This is a great place to discover a Southern institution—one of the family-style "fish camps" serving lavish portions of fresh catfish and other catches from fish farms or nearby rivers and lakes. In Columbia, ethnic and specialty restaurants have appeared at a rapid clip in recent years. Costs throughout the region are usually pleasingly moderate. Dress is casual unless otherwise noted.

CATEGORY	COST*
$$$$	over $25
$$$	$15–$25
$$	$7–$15
$	under $7

per person for a three-course meal, excluding drinks, service, and 5% sales tax

Abbeville

$$ **Yoder's Dutch Kitchen.** In the heart of the Sun Belt, here's authentic Pennsylvania Dutch home cooking in an unassuming redbrick building with a mansard roof. There's a lunch buffet and evening smorgasbord with such choices as fried chicken, stuffed cabbage, Dutch meat loaf, sausage and kraut, breaded veal parmesan, and plenty of vegetables. Shoo-fly pie, Dutch bread, apple butter, homemade salad dressings, and other house specialties can be bought to go. ✕ U.S. 72, ☎ 803/459–5556. No reservations. No credit cards. No dinner Wed. Closed Sun.–Tues.

Aiken

$$$ **No. 10 Downing Street.** This stately Southern Colonial dates to 1837
★ and serves some of the best—and most diverse—food in town. The menu changes regularly: One month might focus on such Italian fare as *pollo al proscuitto* (chicken wrapped in proscuitto and fresh herbs with

fettucini Alfredo) and baked beef tenderloin with tomatoes, garlic, and oregano; another month may salute country French or regional cuisine. A delicious pâté with french bread is always among the appetizers. A bakery on the premises is open during all meals. ✗ *241 Laurens St.,* ☎ *803/642–9062. Reservations advised. D, DC, MC, V. Closed Sun. and Mon.*

Camden

$$$–$$$$ **1890 McLean's House.** On the first floor of the Victorian Greenleaf Inn, cane-back chairs, fox-hunting prints, elaborately tiled fire places, and hand-painted walls set the tone for an elegant meal. McLean's opened early in 1994 and has quickly become a success with six delicious steak specialties (from Diane to *au poivre*), plus such other options as walnut-crusted chicken with a spicy apricot sauce, and good ole' shrimp and grits. ✗ *1308 Broad St.,* ☎ *803/425–1806. Reservations advised. Jacket and tie. AE, D, MC, V. No lunch Sat. Closed Sun.*

$$$–$$$$ **Mill Pond Restaurant.** In a historic building overlooking a sprawling
★ mill pond, this is one of the state's finest eateries. The creative Low Country cuisine features such starters as grits with andouille sausage, roast peppers, and garlic toast; and marinated quail on mixed greens with Boursin cheese and fried onions. Follow this with blackened mahimahi with crawfish hollandaise or perhaps the mouthwatering crab cakes on shrimp tartar sauce. About a 10-minute drive south of Camden proper, dinner here is worth the drive. ✗ *84 Boykin Mill Rd., Rembert,* ☎ *803/424–0261. Reservations advised. Jacket and tie. MC, V. No lunch. Closed Sun.*

Columbia

$$–$$$ **McCrady's Restaurant.** McCrady's, in the lower level of the AT&T Building, has an extensive menu. It includes fresh seafood, steaks, and egg dishes, plus daily luncheon and dinner specials and nouvelle Southern dishes like speckled grits and tasso. ✗ *1201 Main St.,* ☎ *803/771–2410. Reservations advised. AE, D, DC, MC, V. Closed Sun.*

$$ **Motor Supply Co. Bistro.** Dine on cuisine from around the world at this restaurant in the heart of town. Fresh seafood and homemade desserts are among the many offerings; on Sunday there's a Thai menu. A happy hour is celebrated in the bar. ✗ *920 Gervais St.,* ☎ *803/256–6687. Reservations advised. AE, DC, MC, V.*

$–$$ **California Dreaming.** A splendid example of adaptive use, here's din-
★ ing in an airy, greenery-bedecked space that is the renovated old Union Train Station. Specialties include prime rib, barbecued baby-back ribs, Mexican dishes, and homemade pasta. There's a lounge with a disc jockey. ✗ *401 S. Main St.,* ☎ *803/254–6767. Reservations advised on weekends or for large parties. AE, MC, V.*

$–$$ **Maurice Gourmet Barbecue–Piggie Park.** One of the South's best-
★ known barbecue chefs, Maurice Bessinger has a fervent national following for his mustard sauce–based, pit-cooked ham barbecue. He also serves barbecued chicken, ribs, and baked beans, plus hash over rice, onion rings, hushpuppies, cole slaw, and home-baked desserts. ✗ *1600 Charleston Hwy.,* ☎ *803/796–0220. No reservations. D, MC, V.*

Lodging

In addition to the accommodations listed here, you might seek out chains and bed-and-breakfasts in the area. For a complete list of B&Bs, write to the South Carolina Division of Tourism (Box 71, Columbia, SC 29202, ☎ 803/734–0122) and ask for the pamphlet *Bed & Breakfast of South Carolina.*

CATEGORY	COST*
$$$$	over $100
$$$	$75–$100
$$	$40–$75
$	under $40

All prices are for a standard double room, excluding 7% tax

Abbeville

$$ **Belmont Inn.** Built just after the turn of the century, this restored Spanish-style structure is a popular overnight stop with Opera House visitors. Rooms, which have seen better days, are comfortably furnished rather than opulent. White spreads cover brass beds, and antique quilts decorate some walls. Theater-and-dining package plans are offered at the inn. ⊞ *Court Sq., 29620,* ☎ FAX *803/459–9625. 24 rooms. Restaurant, lounge, meeting rooms. AE, MC, V.*

Aiken

$$$ $$$$ **Willcox Inn.** Winston Churchill, Franklin D. Roosevelt, and the Astors have slept at this elegant inn, built in grand style in the early 1900s. The lobby is graced with massive stone fireplaces, rosewood pine woodwork, pegged oak floors, and Oriental rugs. The room decor reflects the inn's early days, with floral-print spreads and high four-poster beds. ⊞ *100 Colleton Ave., 29801,* ☎ *803/649–1377 or 800/368– 1047,* FAX *803/643–0971. 30 rooms, 6 suites. Dining room, bar, croquet. AE, DC, MC, V.*

$$ **Briar Patch.** You can learn plenty about both the Old and New South from the knowledgeable innkeepers of this terrific B&B, which was formerly tack rooms in Aiken's stable district. Choose either the frilly room with French Provincial furniture or the less dramatic one with pine antiques and a weathervane. Breakfast here is Continental. ⊞ *544 Magnolia La. SE, 29801,* ☎ *803/649–2010. 2 rooms with bath. Tennis courts. No credit cards.*

Camden

$$–$$$ **Greenleaf Inn.** Alice Boykin, whose name is to Camden what Carnegie's
★ name is to Pittsburgh, opened the Greenleaf in late 1993. The inn comprises three buildings: There are four rooms in the main inn, on the second floor above McLean's Restaurant, seven rooms in a nearby carriage house, and a guest cottage—the latter is particularly good for families. All rooms are done with classic Victorian furniture and wallpaper; they're spacious and have modern baths. You won't find a nicer or more economical lodging in the region. ⊞ *1308 Broad St., 29020,* ☎ *803/425–1806 or 800/437–5874,* FAX *803/425–5853. 8 rooms with bath, 3 suites, 1 cottage. Restaurant. AE, D, MC, V.*

$$–$$$ **Holiday Inn.** This well-maintained unit of the nationwide chain is three miles west of downtown Camden, in Lugoff. The restaurant is excellent. ⊞ *Box 96, U.S. 1/601S, Lugoff 29078,* ☎ *803/438–9441 or 800/465–4329,* FAX *803/438–9441. 120 rooms. Restaurant, lounge, pool, whirlpool baths. AE, D, DC, MC, V.*

Columbia

$$$ **Adam's Mark.** This upscale downtown hotel (formerly the Columbia Marriott) is conveniently located near state offices and the University of South Carolina. Public areas and guest rooms are contemporary in feeling. The Palm Terrace Restaurant is in a spectacular atrium with stunning views of decorative details; Veronique's provides an intimate, elegant setting for gourmet dining. ⊞ *1200 Hampton St., 29201,* ☎ *803/771–7000 or 800/228–9290,* FAX *803/254–2911. 288 rooms, 12*

suites. 2 restaurants, bar, indoor pool, sauna, health club, business ser-vices. AE, D, DC, MC, V.

$$$ **Claussen's Inn.** This welcome retreat from the downtown bustle is a converted bakery warehouse in the attractive Five Points neighborhood. The inn has an open, airy lobby with a Mexican tile floor; the rooms, some two-story, are arranged around the lobby. There are eight loft suites, with downstairs sitting rooms and spiral staircases leading to sleeping areas furnished with period reproductions and four-poster beds. 🖼 *2003 Greene St., 29205,* 🕾 *803/765–0440 or 800/622–3382,* 🖷 *803/799–7924. 21 rooms, 8 suites. Hot tub, meeting facilities. AE, MC, V.*

$$$ **Richland Street B&B.** Relax on the front porch or in the spacious com-
★ mon area of this no-smoking inn in the heart of Columbia's Historic District. Each antiques-furnished room has its own personality; the bridal suite includes a whirlpool tub. A Continental breakfast is compli-mentary. 🖼 *1425 Richland St., 29201,* 🕾 *803/779–7001. 7 rooms with bath, 1 suite. AE, MC, V.*

$$–$$$ **Embassy Suites Hotel Columbia.** In the spacious seven-story atrium lobby with skylights, fountains, pools, and live plants, overnight guests enjoy sumptuous breakfasts and an early evening manager's cocktail recep-tion—both complimentary. 🖼 *200 Stoneridge Dr., 29210,* 🕾 *803/252–8700 or 800/362–2779,* 🖷 *803/256–8749. 214 housekeeping suites. Indoor pool, health club, gift shop, billiards, dance club. AE, D, DC, MC, V.*

$–$$ **La Quinta Motor Inn.** At this three-story inn on a quiet street near the zoo, the rooms are spacious and well lit, with large working areas and oversize beds. 🖼 *1335 Garner La., 29210,* 🕾 *803/798–9590 or 800/531–5900,* 🖷 *803/731–5574. 120 rooms. Pool. AE, D, DC, MC, V.*

Greenwood

$$–$$$ **Inn on the Square.** This elegant inn was fashioned out of a warehouse in the heart of town. Though the rooms suffer from rather unre-markable views, they're bright and spacious with reproduction 18th-century antiques, four-poster beds, writing desks, and such thoughtful touches as turndown service and complimentary morning newspa-pers. The staff is congenial and attuned to the needs of business trav-elers and vacationers alike. 🖼 *104 Court Sq., 29648,* 🕾 *803/223–4488,* 🖷 *803/223–7067. 48 rooms. Restaurant, lounge, pool. AE, D, DC, MC, V.*

Pendleton

$$ **Liberty Hall Inn.** There's great food and lodging at this country inn in the heart of Historic Pendleton near Clemson University. The inn, which was built in the 1840s and restored in the 1980s, caters to busi-ness travelers and vacationers. Rooms are furnished in antiques and family heirlooms; a Continental breakfast comes with the room. 🖼 *621 S. Mechanic St., 29670,* 🕾 🖷 *803/646–7500 or 800/643–7944. 10 rooms with bath. Restaurant. AE, D, DC, MC, V.*

Sumter

$$ **Holiday Inn.** This well-maintained motor inn is 4 miles west of town, near Shaw Air Force Base. Simple, clean rooms are as you would ex-pect from this chain. 🖼 *2390 Broad St. ext., 29150,* 🕾 *803/469–9001 or 800/465–4329,* 🖷 *803/469–7001. 124 rooms. Restaurant, pool. AE, D, DC, MC, V.*

$$ Magnolia House. In Sumter's Historic District, this imposing four-columned Greek Revival structure is a nice alternative to the region's generic chain motels. Antiques, many of them French, furnish the rooms; there are also stained-glass windows, inlaid oak floors, and five fireplaces. A full breakfast is included in the rate. ⌧ *230 Church St., 29150,* ☎ *803/775–6694. 3 rooms with bath, 1 suite. AE, MC, V.*

The Arts

Concerts, Opera, and Dance

In Columbia, call the **South Carolina Philharmonic and Chamber Orchestra Association** (☎ 803/771–7937) for information about scheduled concerts of the Philharmonic, the Chamber Orchestra, and the Youth Orchestra. The **Columbia Music Festival Association** (☎ 803/771–6303) can inform callers about events of the **Choral Society,** the **Opera, Opera Guild, Dance Theatre, Brass Band, Caroliers, and Cabaret Company.**

Theater

Columbia's **Town Theatre** (1012 Sumter St., ☎ 803/799–2510), founded in 1919, stages six plays a year from September to late May, plus a special summer show. The **Workshop Theatre of South Carolina** (1136 Bull St., ☎ 803/799–4876) also puts on plays. The **Abbeville Opera House** (Town Square, ☎ 803/459–2157) stages high-caliber productions in an early 20th-century setting.

Nightlife

In Columbia, **Cracker Jacks** (1325 Longcreek Dr., ☎ 803/731–5692) features lively "beach" music for listening and dancing, and occasionally a lusty floor show. **Nitelites Dance Club** (*200 Stoneridge Dr.,* ☎ 803/252–8700) at the Embassy Suites Hotel boasts state-of-the-art lighting and presents a lavish free hors d'oeuvres buffet weekdays 5–7:30. Also try **Dance Factory** (2100 Bush River Rd., ☎ 803/731–0300) at the Sheraton Hotel & Convention Center and the Adams Mark's **Palm Terrace Lounge** (1200 Hampton St., ☎ 803/771–7000).

There's live entertainment at **Jockey's Lounge** in the Holiday Inn Express in Aiken (155 Colony Pkwy., ☎ 803/648–0999). **Plums Restaurant & Lounge** at the Holiday Inns in Lugoff (U.S. 1/601S, ☎ 803/438–9441) and Sumter (2390 Broad St. ext., ☎ 803/469–9001) provides pleasant evening unwinding with live entertainment. Another Camden option is **Paddock Restaurant & Pub** (514 Rutledge St., ☎ 803/432–3222).

Heartland Essentials

Arriving and Departing, Getting Around

BY BUS

Greyhound (☎ 800/231–2222) serves all of South Carolina.

BY CAR

I–77 leads into Columbia from the north. I–26, I–20, and U.S. 1 intersect at Columbia.

BY PLANE

Columbia Metro Airport (☎ 803/822–5000) is served by Air South, American Eagle, Com Air/Delta, and USAir.

Amtrak (☎ 800/872–7245) makes stops at Camden, Columbia, Denmark, Dillon, Florence, and Kingstree in the Heartland.

Guided Tours

Richland Country Historic Preservation Commission (☎ 803/252–1770) runs guided tours and rents out historic properties. In Sumter, the charismatic former Mayor **"Bubba" McElveen** (☎ 803/775–2851) gives walking, bus, and auto tours of the area. The **Aiken Chamber of Commerce** runs a 90-minute tour of the historic district and will customize tours to suit individual interests. Customized tours of Camden are also available through either the **Kershaw County Chamber of Commerce** or from **Greenleaf Tours** (contact Louise Burns, ☎ 803/432–1515).

Important Addresses and Numbers

EMERGENCIES
Dial **911** for police, fire, and ambulance assistance. Emergency room services are available at **Richland Memorial Hospital** (5 Richland Medical Park, Columbia, ☎ 803/765–7561).

PHARMACY
Taylor Street Pharmacy (1520 Taylor St. at Pickens in Columbia, ☎ 803/256–1611) is open 7 AM–9 PM weekdays, 9–9 weekends.

RADIO STATIONS
AM: WCOS 1400, country; WOMG 1320, oldies; WVOC 560, news/talk. **FM:** WHKZ 96.7, country; WLTR 91.3, classical; WMFX 102.3, classic rock; WUSC 90.5, alternative (jazz, blues, folk, reggae).

VISITOR INFORMATION
Greater Abbeville Chamber of Commerce (104 Pickens St., Abbeville 29620, ☎ 803/459–4600). **Greater Aiken Chamber of Commerce** (400 Laurens St. NW, Box 892, Aiken 29802, ☎ 803/641–1111). **Greater Columbia Metropolitan Convention and Visitors Bureau** (1200 Main St., Ninth Floor, Box 15, Columbia 29202, ☎ 803/254–0479 or 800/264–4884). **Kershaw County Chamber of Commerce** (724 S. Broad St., Box 605, Camden 29020, ☎ 803/432–2525). **Ninety Six Chamber of Commerce** (Box 8, Ninety Six 29666, ☎ 803/543–2900).

ELSEWHERE IN THE STATE

Those with more time may want to take an excursion into the **Upcountry,** the northwest corner of the state, long a favorite for family vacations. For information, contact: Discover Upcountry Carolina Association (Box 3116, Greenville 29602, ☎ 803/233–2690 or 800/849–4766). The abundant lakes, waterfalls, and several state parks (including **Caesar's Head, Keowee-Toxaway, Oconee, Table Rock,** and the **Chattooga National Wild** and **Scenic River**) provide all manner of recreational activities. Beautiful anytime, the 130-mile **Cherokee Foothills Scenic Highway** (SC 11), through the Blue Ridge Mountains, is especially delightful in spring and autumn. At **Devils Fork State Park** (161 Holcombe Circle, Salem 29676, ☎ 803/944–2639) on beautiful Lake Jocassee, visitors clamor to stay in the luxurious villas at one of the system's newest and most upscale facilities.

The comfortable communities of **Greenville, Spartanburg, Clemson, Pendleton,** and **Anderson** take justifiable pride in their educational institutions, museums, historic preservation, and cultural accomplishments.

Any one of them is worth a day's visit—particularly charming Pendleton, near Clemson University, which has a historic district, interesting architecture, and good restaurants.

Greenville County Museum of Art. Housed in an innovative modern building, the museum displays American art dating from the Colonial era. Exhibited are works by Paul Jenkins, Jamie Wyeth, Jasper Johns, and noted Southern artists along with North American sculpture. *420 College St., Greenville,* ☎ *803/271–7570.* ☛ *Free.* ☉ *Tues.–Sat. 10– 5, Sun. 1–5.*

Kings Mountain National Military Park. The "turning point" Revolutionary War battle on October 7, 1780, was fought on this site. Colonial Tories commanded by British Major Patrick Ferguson were soundly defeated by rag-tag patriot forces from the Southern Appalachians. Visitor Center exhibits, dioramas, and an orientation film describe the action. A paved self-guided trail leads through the battlefield. *20 mi NE of Gaffney off I–85 via a marked side road in North Carolina,* ☎ *803/936–7921.* ☛ *Free* ☉ *Daily 9–5, until 6 Memorial Day–Labor Day.*

INDEX

Before Catching Your Flight,
Catch Up With Your World.

Fueled by the global resources of CNN and available in major airports across America, CNN Airport Network provides a live source  of current domestic and international news,  sports, business, weather and lifestyle programming. Plus two daily Fodor's features for the facts you need: "Travel Fact," a useful and creative mix of travel trivia; and "What's Happening," a comprehensive round-up of upcoming events in major cities around the world.

With CNN Airport Network, you'll never be out of the loop.